Praise for *The China Mission*

"Thoroughly researched and compellingly written, [*The China Mission*] is at once a revealing study of character and leadership, a vivid reconstruction of a critical episode in the history of the early Cold War and an insightful meditation on the limits of American power even at its peak."   —*New York Times Book Review*

"A compelling portrait of a remarkable soldier and statesman, and an instructive lesson in the limits of American power, even at its zenith."   —*Economist*

"Deeply researched and written with verve, [*The China Mission*] ought to be read by any U.S. foreign-policy maker practicing diplomacy in Asia. . . . Mr. Kurtz-Phelan has performed a service in reviving this important episode with such aplomb, rigor and pace."   —*Wall Street Journal*

"[Marshall's China mission] has been brilliantly described in the detail it deserves by Daniel Kurtz-Phelan . . . who seems to have consulted all relevant primary and secondary sources. . . . Kurtz-Phelan is particularly good at using his various sources to bring Marshall's personality to life."

—Roderick MacFarquhar, *New York Review of Books*

"At once a character study of the charismatic and dedicated Marshall; a narrative account of the mission's miraculous early successes and prolonged, painful collapse; and a meditation on the impossibility of reconciling parties that are determined to remain enemies."   —*Foreign Affairs*

"*The China Mission* is a must-read for foreign-policy makers practising diplomacy in Asia."   — *Globe and Mail*

"The best character study of Marshall I've yet seen. He comes alive here as in nothing else that's been written about him. A major achievement."

—John Lewis Gaddis, author of *George F. Kennan* and professor of history, Yale University

"*The China Mission* has much to teach us about both the past and future of American leadership—and about what individual leadership means in the face of hard choices. I have rarely read such a vivid account of how diplomacy really works."

—Madeleine Albright, former secretary of state

"Was America's greatest statesman to blame for America's greatest diplomatic failure? In this wonderfully written book, Daniel Kurtz-Phelan sheds a bright light on a crucial but dimly understood chapter in U.S. foreign policy. His portrait of General George Marshall is a model of empathetic but clear-eyed biography and a memorable lesson in the limits of power."

—Evan Thomas, author of *Ike's Bluff* and coauthor of *The Wise Men*

"In gripping, crystalline detail, Kurtz-Phelan has given us a vital new chapter on American statecraft. The lessons from what he calls the 'unsettled world' of the early Cold War are urgently relevant today. *The China Mission* will be read for years to come as a window on the origins of American power—and the limits of its reach."

—Evan Osnos, *New Yorker* staff writer and author of *Age of Ambition*

"Kurtz-Phelan has written a marvelous narrative about General George Marshall's valiant effort to bring Chiang Kai-shek and Mao Zedong together at the end of WWII and head off a civil war and a Communist takeover of China. . . . But apart from the engrossing China saga, what makes this books so absorbing—and sometimes even touching—is that it draws the reader into the life of a truly great American, reminding us of a different time in America's odyssey when a sense of modesty, service to mankind, and duty to country were enthroned and esteemed."

—Orville Schell, Arthur Ross Director of the Center on U.S.-China Relations

"America has always sought to convert rather than understand China, whether to Christianity or capitalism. In this brilliant historical study, Daniel Kurtz-Phelan focuses on the pivotal moment of misunderstanding between these two very different countries. As a bonus, he provides a beautifully written portrait of George Marshall, a statesman of such integrity that he seems as far removed from Washington, D.C., today as would an ancient Roman."

—Fareed Zakaria, CNN host and author of *The Post-American World*

"An outstanding book on a very important subject: how to use American power judiciously and effectively in a rapidly changing world."

—Odd Arne Westad, S. T. Lee Professor of US-Asia Relations, Harvard University

"This deeply researched, gripping account is enhanced by the author's striking portrayals of [Mao Zedong and Chiang Kai-shek]. . . . [A] page-turning narrative of an important chapter in Cold War history."   —*Library Journal*, starred review

"A superb researcher, Kurtz-Phelan ably narrates an exasperating story featuring a genuinely peerless hero doing his best in a no-win situation."   —*Kirkus Reviews*

THE
CHINA
MISSION

GEORGE MARSHALL'S UNFINISHED WAR,

1945–1947

Daniel Kurtz-Phelan

W. W. NORTON & COMPANY

Independent Publishers Since 1923

New York · London

For information about permission to reproduce selections from this book, write to
Permissions, W. W. Norton & Company, Inc., 500 Fifth Avenue, New York, NY 10110

For information about special discounts for bulk purchases, please contact
W. W. Norton Special Sales at specialsales@wwnorton.com or 800-233-4830

Manufacturing by LSC Communications, Harrisonburg
Book design by Chris Welch
Production manager: Lauren Abbate

Library of Congress Cataloging-in-Publication Data

Names: Kurtz-Phelan, Daniel, author.
Title: The China mission : George Marshall's unfinished war, 1945/1947 / Daniel Kurtz-Phelan.
Other titles: George C. Marshall's unfinished war, 1945/1947
Description: First edition. | New York : W. W. Norton & Company, 2018. | Includes
bibliographical references and index.
Identifiers: LCCN 2017053909 | ISBN 9780393240955 (hardcover)
Subjects: LCSH: China—History—Civil War, 1945–1949. | Marshall, George C. (George Catlett),
1880–1959. | United States—Foreign relations—China. | China—Foreign relations—United States.
Classification: LCC DS777.54 .K866 2018 | DDC 951.04/2—dc23
LC record available at https://lccn.loc.gov/2017053909

ISBN 978-0-393-35686-1 pbk.

W. W. Norton & Company, Inc., 500 Fifth Avenue, New York, N.Y. 10110
www.wwnorton.com

W. W. Norton & Company Ltd., 15 Carlisle Street, London W1D 3BS

1 2 3 4 5 6 7 8 9 0

To Darin

"History will be kind to me for I intend to write it."

—WINSTON CHURCHILL

"So long as I do not give a damn about what they say in the future,
I probably will be able to do a fair job at the present time."

—GEORGE MARSHALL

CONTENTS

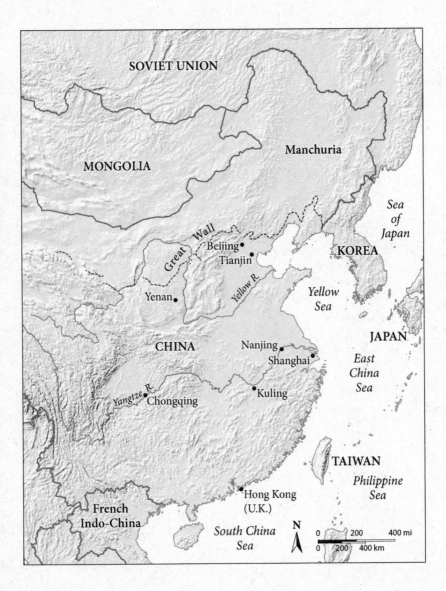

Oh! General Marshall,
We Communists Honor You

Soon, such a scene would become unthinkable. It was a cold morning in early March 1946, a rocky airstrip laid along a broad, barren valley in China's northwest, lined by mountains of tawny dust blown from the Gobi Desert. Six months earlier, one war, a world war, had ended. Six months later, a new war, a cold war, would be under way. Yet here stood General George C. Marshall and Chairman Mao Zedong, two of the great antagonists in the war to come, in intent conversation. Each wore the uniform of his army: the crisp khaki of a five-star general, the plain tunic of a revolutionary. On this morning, they spoke of friendship and peace.

Mao had pledged to give up armed revolution, to embrace old enemies, to join in building a democracy, in keeping the peace of a new and better world. "I can tell that an unprecedented era of progress awaits China," said Marshall, a man not given to grand pronouncements, as he prepared to board his plane. Mao was equally grand: "The entire people of our country should feel grateful and loudly shout, 'long live cooperation between China and the United States.'"

The afternoon before, searching for this airstrip, Marshall's pilot had gotten lost in a tangle of gullies where a wrong turn could end against the side of a mountain. The remoteness was not incidental. Mao's Communists had come to this "mountain fastness," as Marshall described it, to take refuge and rebuild after the Long March. Most came to know the place as the "cradle of revolution," but its name, Yenan, meant "long peace."

Marshall's arrival in Yenan was to have signaled that the Communists' time in the wilderness was over. When the plane landed, its pilot spotting the 1,000-year-old pagoda that marked a hill above town, a large crowd was waiting, 6,000 people by the count of Yenan's *Emancipation Daily*, summoned by Mao. The aircraft was itself a symbol of American might, a C-54 Skymaster sent under Lend-Lease to Winston Churchill and outfitted in the wood and leather of an aristocrat's club before being returned to the United States for use by one of its great heroes.

When Marshall had emerged from the plane and shaken hands with Mao, a cheer went up from the assembled cadres. A Communist honor guard fired a salute, then stood straight and tall, instructed to impress, as Marshall strode past in review. A band of five hundred (again by *Emancipation Daily*'s count) played a song written for the occasion: "Let us extol your great spirit! You have used your power to extinguish the fire of war sweeping the plain. Oh! General Marshall, let the red troops pay you their highest salute. We Communists honor you."

Over the course of that evening, Marshall had conferred with the top leaders of the Communist Party—Mao, the diplomat Zhou Enlai, the military chief Zhu De—about China's future as a democratic great power. (Mao "sits and masks his face completely," an aide wrote in his diary, but "Marshall told him frankly what was expected.") He had toasted their common future at a banquet. ("All were satisfied," the official press reported.) He had sat for two hours in a freezing auditorium and watched a Communist troupe perform songs about revolutionary heroics, beneath a proscenium hung with images of Lenin and Stalin that he did not fail to notice. He had toured the ruined town center in a jeep, a model of vehicle he had ordered built and shipped around the world a few years before. (Mao would ride in a sun-bleached van that had printed on the side, "Presented to the heroic defenders of China by the Chinese Hand Laundry, East 42nd street New York NY.") He had spent the night in an eight-room outpost of American soldiers and spies—the Dixie Mission, America's station behind rebel lines.

Despite an aversion to triumphalism, Marshall could not help but feel that this was something of a victory tour. He had been in China for two and a half months. By all appearances, he had done the impossible again. In World War II, he built the American military machine and led it to victory—"armies he called into being by his own genius," as Churchill put it. Then, when the war was over, Marshall was tapped for a last mission. President Truman needed him in China. It would be a short mission, a few months. This time, rather than win a war, his charge was to save the peace.

China was supposed to take its place as one of the Big Four powers that would together rebuild the postwar world. But the central government, led by Generalissimo Chiang Kai-shek and his Kuomintang, the Nationalists, had few of the attributes of a modern power, and only loose control over much of the country's territory. Here in the northwest, Mao's Communists had gained strength and followers, threatening a battle for the future of China. For the United States, that would have dire implications, whether or not the Communists had a chance of winning—and few, not even Stalin, thought they did. Truman's instruction to Marshall was to go to China, bring Chiang and Mao together in a single government, and avert a war. American power would be used to create "a strong, united, and democratic China."

In a matter of weeks, Marshall had achieved what even cynics were calling a miracle. Under his guiding hand, the Nationalists and Communists agreed to a cease-fire in a civil war that had raged on and off for two decades. They settled on the principles of a democratic government, listening as Marshall explained the Bill of Rights and read aloud from Benjamin Franklin's speech to the Constitutional Convention of 1787: "It therefore astonishes me, Sir, to find this system approaching so near perfection as it does." They signed off on a plan to merge their troops into one national army. Mao told his followers that they were entering "a new stage of peace and democracy."

And so on the airstrip in Yenan this cold morning, as he shook hands with Mao in the shadow of the magnificent C-54, Marshall could be forgiven for speaking in uncharacteristically grand terms. In Washington, they were saying he had saved China. In China, he was being called a "god of peace." As Marshall himself had reported to Truman, there was hope that "peace will really reign over China."

That same day, March 5, 1946, 7,000 miles away, Marshall's admirer Winston Churchill was also speaking of the future. His was a darker prophecy. In Fulton, Missouri, with Truman on the stage beside him, Churchill warned of an "iron curtain" falling between the West and the Communist world. And he was not the only one sounding such a warning. Senior American officials were decrying Stalin's treachery. The American army was announcing a ban on Communists in the officer corps. American newspapers were reporting on the theft of atomic secrets by Soviet spies. There were dark currents everywhere.

On the airstrip that morning, Marshall could see the way to a different future. There would be no Chinese civil war and no Communist China. Autocrats would become democrats. An enduring alliance between the United States and China would serve as a pillar of stability in Asia. China would help keep order and calm across the globe, Chiang and Mao a bridge between the Americans and Soviets. Marshall, the revered general, a man of war for almost fifty years, would end his career and go off into retirement with a valiant stroke for peace.

But history would flow from Churchill's words that day, not Marshall's. Over the next ten months of his "short" mission, Marshall's achievements would collapse. The agreements he brokered would fracture. Civil war would come after all. There would be talk of World War III, of American boys fighting Soviet boys on Chinese battlefields. A few years later, Mao and the Communists would conquer China. Soon enough, American boys would fight Chinese boys on Korean battlefields. Millions of Chinese would perish in the throes of revolution. Once Marshall's plane took off over the mountains that morning, Mao would not meet another high-level American representative until Richard Nixon's visit twenty-six years later.

In the United States, the question would be put crisply: Who lost China? In the angry debate, many Americans would give Marshall and his mission a bitter share of the blame. Ultimately, he would be remembered for leading the Allies to victory in World War II, for forging a new model of global leadership as secretary of state, for the effort—the Marshall Plan—that saved Europe and became shorthand for American power at its best. But others would remember him for this mission—some as the man who lost China, some as the man who kept his country from a more catastrophic fate there.

The scene that morning on the airstrip would become the high-water mark of hope—not just for China, but for a different kind of world, for a new order of peace after the worst war ever known. "The next war," Marshall had said in the final hours of the last one, "might destroy the world. It must not come." When hope broke apart, the scene that morning would also become the image of failure, of weakness, of betrayal.

Not long before, it would have seemed unthinkable that George Marshall could have gotten this far, face-to-face with these men, on this airstrip, on this mission. Not long after, it would seem unthinkable that he ever could have come here at all.

I

WINNING THE PEACE

CHAPTER 1

Peace Is Hell

J ust minutes before the phone rang, George Marshall pulled up to a stately brick house in Leesburg, Virginia, stepped onto the porch with his wife, Katherine, and stopped to reflect in a way he had not in years. The day before, November 26, 1945, he had marked the end of more than four decades in the United States Army. His tenure as army chief of staff, the capstone of that career, started the morning Hitler invaded Poland; a call with news of Wehrmacht divisions crossing the border woke him at 3 a.m. Six years later, when Emperor Hirohito surrendered over Japanese radio, Marshall was long since ready to pass leadership of the army to his protégé, General Dwight Eisenhower. On the last day of 1945, Marshall would turn 65.

For weeks, he had listened as the good and the great praised him as few Americans had ever been praised. The previous day, in a ceremony in the courtyard of the new Pentagon building, he received a special citation from President Harry Truman: "In a war unparalleled in magnitude and in horror, millions of Americans gave their country outstanding service. General of the Army George C. Marshall gave it victory. . . . To him, as much as to any individual, the United States owes its future." Earlier, Truman had paused during a press conference to call Marshall "the greatest military man this country ever produced— or any other country, for that matter." Henry Stimson, the secretary of war, told him, "I have seen a great many soldiers in my lifetime, and you, sir, are the finest soldier I have ever known." (In his diary, Stimson had referred to Marshall as "the strongest man there is in America . . . the one on whom the fate of the war depends.") In naming him Man of the Year, *Time* magazine pronounced that the American people "trust General Marshall more than they have trusted any military man since George Washington." Stalin said he would trust Marshall with his life.

At the Pentagon ceremony, when Truman pinned an oak-leaf cluster on Marshall's uniform, some in the audience noted a broad smile on the stoic face. It was a smile less of satisfaction with feats behind than of anticipation of quiet years to come. After Truman had agreed to Marshall's resignation, Katherine had seen an immediate change in her husband: "At breakfast he was carefree, the heavy lines between his eyes began to disappear, he laughed once more." One of his wartime code names was Atlas; with war over and retirement imminent, Katherine watched a burden lift from his shoulders. Marshall made no secret of his relief. "We are off again this morning," he wrote General John Pershing, his mentor, before leaving the capital, "and I soon hope to be able to clear my skirts pretty generally of Washington involvements." He could hardly be blamed. On the home front, few had endured a harder war, and no one had done more to win it.

On this bright late fall afternoon, Marshall could look across his lawn and instead of troubling over the world's freedom, contemplate his own. Katherine had found this house, forty miles up the Potomac from Washington, when the war's end was a distant hope. As soon as he saw it, Marshall recognized that it could be a true home after decades of wandering. Now he was here, with little to preoccupy him beyond his books, vegetable garden, and hunting trips. "My ambitions are clearly defined and very simple," he wrote a friend, "a little of home life for Mrs. Marshall and me . . . my limited activities, whatever they may be, of a strictly nongovernmental or political nature." They went inside, and Katherine went upstairs to rest.

It was then that the phone rang. Marshall had never been a man of unnecessary words. During the war, his efficiency of approach could be unnerving. "General Marshall speaking," he would say when answering the phone, and then expect the caller to go right to the point. When the point was made, the conversation was finished. Even by Marshall's standards, this call was short. Almost the only thing that could be heard from the Leesburg end of the exchange was Marshall's "Yes, Mr. President."

Later, Katherine came downstairs. At first Marshall said nothing. But the radio was on, and there was a news flash: "President Truman has appointed General of the Army George C. Marshall as his Special Ambassadorial Envoy to China." Marshall rushed to explain—he had not wanted to tell Katherine about the call until she had a chance to relax. Just the day before, he had celebrated the end of the longest-ever tenure of an army chief of staff, the nation hailing his already unsurpassed record of service. But the president had called, and he needed Marshall to take on a final mission.

A few hours earlier, President Truman had been dealt a shock of his own. He was scheduled to join his cabinet for lunch in the West Wing. For Truman, half a year into an accidental presidency, even a meal with his own administration could feel treacherous. When Roosevelt named him his running mate for the 1944 election, the senator from Missouri made an unlikely *vice* president. As president, he was thought by many—including some in his own cabinet—to be not just unlikely, but ludicrous.

"Son-of-a-bitch," Truman spat as he walked into lunch, a rolled-up yellow sheet of teletype in his hand. He passed the sheet around. It was a report of trouble he did not need, another challenge to his authority when they seemed to come from every direction.

For the past year, the United States' man in China had been a wealthy Oklahoman named Patrick Hurley. Earlier in the war, Hurley, a veteran of Herbert Hoover's cabinet, had been casting about for a role that would accord with his self-image. Marshall, hoping to get him out of the president's hair, thought to send him across the Pacific. There his exuberance might even do some good. The United States had made much of its alliance with Chiang Kai-shek's China. Japan's push into the Chinese mainland a decade earlier had in a sense marked the real beginning of World War II, and in the face of aggression and hardship, Chiang and his people presented a picture of brave resistance in the face of Axis brutality. Since Pearl Harbor, the United States had been proud to stand with them. It sent an American general to serve as Chiang's chief of staff and American planes over the Hump of the Himalayas to keep Chiang supplied.

But before long, there was a strong undercurrent of acrimony beneath the surface solidarity. Chiang thought Washington was not doing enough for him; Washington thought he was not doing enough for it. From the American perspective, a large part of the problem in the Chinese alliance was the parlous state of Chiang's domestic alliances— especially with the Chinese Communists. Until the Japanese invasion had forced them together, the Nationalists and the Communists had been a decade into their own struggle to the death; round after round of Nationalist extermination campaigns drove Mao's Communists into the 6,000-mile retreat of the Long March and ultimately their refuge in Yenan. With the arrival of a common enemy, however, they were supposed to fight together, in a united front backed by the United States and the Soviet Union. But to many Americans, Chiang still seemed more focused on weakening his old Communist enemies than on joining with them to defeat the Japanese. And what supplies and weapons were not stored away for internal battles to come were, the gossip went, siphoned off by corrupt generals and officials. Hurley was supposed to take care of all that.

He crossed the Hump all mustache and bluster. "I can handle these fellows," he said, "they're just like Mexicans and I can handle Mexicans." When he landed for his first visit to Yenan, he let loose a Choctaw war whoop. He became better known for his dirty mouth (he referred to Zhou Enlai as a "motherfucker" and wanted to tell Chiang a lewd joke) than his silver tongue ("I am opposed to being leaked on by the career men in the State Department"). Mao called him the Clown. Nationalist officials called him the Big Wind. And when the Japanese surrendered to end World War II, Chiang and Mao went back to frantic preparations for civil war, despite Hurley's repeated efforts to bring them together.

Truman's secretary of state, the South Carolinian James Byrnes, had walked gloating into the White House lunch. Waiting for the president, he told his fellow cabinet members that he had just persuaded Hurley, in Washington for a visit, to go back to China and keep trying. But when Truman entered the room, the sheet in his hand said otherwise. Hurley was resigning, according to a release that had come in over the wire—and not just resigning, but resigning in a paranoid public rage. In a statement, he contended that his difficulties in China stemmed not from any diplomatic missteps, nor from the insolubility of the conflict he was supposed to solve. Hurely instead blamed his problems on subterfuge by a "pro-Communist, pro-imperialist" faction in the American government. (He had railed against this faction before and had a number of diplomats working under him transferred out of China for their supposed allegiance to it.) "The professional foreign service men sided with the Chinese Communist armed party and the imperialist bloc of nations whose policy it was to keep China divided against herself," he charged. "A considerable section of our State Department is endeavoring to support Communism generally as well as specifically in China."

Hurley's eruption consumed discussion over lunch. It was disquieting in part because it coincided with other pieces of ominous news from across the Pacific. Truman mentioned a report on Soviet actions in Manchuria, the region of northeastern China that Stalin's Red Army had taken from the Japanese in the final days of the war—and where it was now dismantling factories, power plants, and railway lines and carrying the pieces back toward Siberia. Byrnes mentioned intelligence reporting on Soviet transfers of seized Japanese weapons to Mao's fighters.

But the immediate problem raised by Hurley's charges was political. They would dominate headlines. They would become a weapon for Truman's opponents. And when, over lunch, a promising solution to this political problem emerged, it came not from the secretary of state or the secretary of war; it came in a suggestion from Clinton Anderson, a New Mexico politico who was serving as secretary of agriculture. To preempt a damaging partisan flap, why not replace Hurley with a man of unquestioned nonpartisan credibility? It would be a triumph of political jujitsu, Anderson argued. Hurley's self-aggrandizing tantrum would be overshadowed by General of the Army George Catlett Marshall's selfless return to service—a political crisis remade into a bold diplomatic salvo. James Forrestal, the secretary of the navy, seconded Anderson's proposal.

Marshall, a White House aide would say, "in Mr. Truman's eyes could never do anything wrong." Other officials used words like "reverence" to describe Truman's feelings for the general. So Anderson's proposal had easy appeal for the embattled president. He acknowledged that Marshall had "earned a rest," with his retirement ceremony the day before and his departure from Washington that very morning. But there was no one in America like Marshall. No one had his stature. No one embodied American might the way he did. No one could solve Truman's immediate problem, the political problem, the way Marshall could. Perhaps, they reasoned over lunch, Truman could make it a short mission, a temporary appointment. Marshall would not have to take over as ambassador to China. He would have no formal position beyond special representative of the president. He could do what needed to be done and then come home, postponing his freedom only briefly. After lunch, Truman walked to the Red Room and placed a call to Leesburg.

Marshall would go, as Truman knew, as everyone knew. That was the kind of man he was.

The frequent comparisons to George Washington were not just hyperbole or platitude. As a boy, Marshall had been fixated on the first president; near Marshall's hometown in western Pennsylvania was a fort—Fort Necessity—that Washington had once tried, and failed, to defend. And there was much about Marshall as a man that seemed modeled on the first great American soldier-statesman. There was the same reserve; the proud and somewhat stiff, thoroughly military bearing; the manner both understated and imposing. There was the renown not so much for brilliance of insight as quality of judgment. There was also the temper, which flared in displays all the more fearsome for their rarity.

There was the same reluctance when it came to power—a cultivated impression, but acted on enough, in meaningful enough ways, that it could not be dismissed as posturing or false modesty. Marshall was suited to wielding power, but hesitant when it came to seeking it.

During World War II, there was broad agreement that the most glorious act of generalship, command of the D-Day invasion of Europe, should by all rights go to Marshall. He had built the Allied war machine, he should lead it to victory. "Ike," President Roosevelt said to Eisenhower, whom Marshall had picked out as a one-star and promoted above hundreds of officers, "you and I know who was Chief of Staff during the last years of the Civil War but practically no one else knows, although the names of the field generals . . . every schoolboy knows them. I hate to think that 50 years from now practically nobody will know who George Marshall was." Roosevelt thought that would change only if Marshall was allowed to step down as army chief of staff to lead the cross-channel invasion. But the president had come to rely too much on Marshall for his continual counsel, his command over the war effort, his grasp of global strategy and authority at the high table of alliance diplomacy. If Marshall went off to Europe, Roosevelt would lose all that. Marshall, for his part, did not so much as voice a preference, though it was not hard to sense what he wanted. He became "upset and shy" when pressed, Stimson recorded in his diary. "I had begged him not to sacrifice what I considered the interests of the country to the undue sensitiveness of his own conscience in seeming to seek a post." Marshall did not listen. Ultimately, Roosevelt concluded, "I feel I could not sleep at night with you out of the country." Eisenhower got the D-Day command instead, and with it the attendant glory.

Marshall was the sort of man who sent those around him into rap-tures. They spoke of his presence, "a striking and communicated force" felt as soon as he entered a room. It "compelled respect" and "spread a sense of authority and calm," yet still conveyed "abject humility." They marveled at his aura of command, above all self-command, and his capacity for decision, for decisiveness. "Don't fight the problem, decide it," he would tell them. "To say what makes greatness in a man is very difficult," Dean Acheson, the undersecretary of state, wrote Marshall. "But when one is close to it one knows."

To those who knew him well, Marshall's steel-country stoicism came with an overlay of southern charm. It was the product of lineage, on both sides, and education at the Virginia Military Institute. They saw warmth in the blue eyes that at first seemed piercingly cold. But even to those who knew him very well, he was almost always General, never George. Even Roosevelt would call him General to his face, George only behind his back. When the blithe president slipped, Marshall objected. "I distrust this first-name business," he said. "I have no feelings," he liked to say, "except those I reserve for Mrs. Marshall."

In the first years of World War II, this steely image had become famous—and for some, infamous. When Marshall took command of the army, the officer corps was populated by time-servers. He set about clearing the "dead wood" with meritocratic ruthlessness. "Those who stand up under punishment will be pushed ahead," he said. "Those who fail are out at the first sign of faltering." He was said to carry a little black book to keep track, but it was in fact just his exceptional memory; names captured by it, Eisenhower, Patton, Bradley, Ridgway, became known to the entire country. With the others, Marshall heard from wives that he had "ruined" their husbands. He could see the toll—"I had to relieve him, and I am afraid I broke his heart"—but the ruthlessness was essential. Defending it before Congress, seemingly every member irate over a favored officer felled in the killing spree, he argued, "You give a good leader very little and he will succeed. You give a mediocrity a great deal and he will fail."

"Modern warfare has little of drama and romance," Marshall had observed when he was younger. "It becomes more and more a proposition of horrible possibilities, with an extremely complicated approach in each instance." He obsessed over means, over the complicated approach, while fellow officers held forth on ends and left it for others to figure out the details. He hated it when someone agreed with a proposal *in principle*, or urged an objective while offering nothing about how to get there. If you had nothing to say about the means, how could you be sure you believed in an end? Success in reaching it hinged less on flashy stratagems or gutsy maneuvers than on more prosaic matters—the training of troops, the coordination of officers, the efficiency of supply lines.

If anything matched the importance of leadership for Marshall, it was this last element, logistics. He had risen through a career consumed with the mundane concerns of headquarters, his reputation made less by battlefield heroics than by bureaucratic foresight and finesse. He was such an ideal staff officer, such a "brilliant planner," that his D-Day disappointment was just the last in a string of failures to escape to the combat command he craved. In the first world war, stationed in France, he organized the great American offensives, an "appalling proposition"—getting 600,000 men and almost 3,000 heavy weapons from one front to another, on overcrowded bad roads with names he could not pronounce, keeping them supplied with ammunition and blankets, trucks fueled, horses and infantrymen fed and healthy, all on no sleep. In the second world war, leading the American Army, he spent much of his time worrying about aluminum and antifreeze and netting to protect airmen from malarial mosquitoes, all to be distributed over 59,000 miles of supply routes he had to protect from enemy attack. He started one early memo to Roosevelt with the unglamorous declaration, "The future effort of the Army is dependent upon shipping." Without boats to resupply them, it did not matter how gallant the men or skilled the commanders. The liberation of Europe was at one point stalled because Patton's tanks ran out of gas.

Others at first complained about this tedious fixation. "The destinies of two great empires seem to be tied up in some goddamn things called LSTs," Churchill barked, when told a strategy was unworkable because of a shortage of amphibious landing craft. But he came to see Marshall was right: without logistics, strategy was fantasy. When eventually Churchill called Marshall "the true 'organizer of victory,'" the formulation—the organizer—was meant not as faint praise. Marshall had taken a gentlemanly army of 200,000 and built it into a war machine of more than 8 million. He had produced 2.5 million jeeps and trucks, 88,000 tanks, 12.6 million rifles, 2 million machine guns, 129,000 combat planes. The single-paragraph citation that Marshall received at his retirement ceremony included the sentence: "It was he who first recognized that victory in a global war would depend on this Nation's capacity to ring the earth with far-flung supply lines."

And it was not just in this regard that men like the aristocratic Churchill—or the hyper-verbal, always-at-ease, to-the-manor-born Roosevelt—came to realize they had underestimated Marshall. In look and manner, he seemed the plain-spoken military man: the straight-backed six-foot frame; the rugged face (though with an incongruously weak chin); the precise speech and no-nonsense syntax; the briefs on production and transport amid lofty discussion of grand strategy and the future of empires. They could take this general's measure at a glance and know what they were getting.

Marshall surpassed every judgment in little time. Roosevelt observed that he had emerged as "the best man at the conference table." Churchill, not easily impressed, conceded that "he has a massive brain." (This even though Marshall exploded at Churchill in an argument, "Not one American soldier is going to die on that goddamned beach," prompting Roosevelt to speculate, "I think Winston is beginning not to like George Marshall very much.") Marshall had lived up to advice he once gave Eisenhower: "Persuade by accomplishment rather than eloquence."

The effects of such persuasion were public as well as private. One of Marshall's aides fretted near the end of World War II, "It will take history a long time to find out how much he has done and is doing because of his continuing modesty." In fact, the public celebration was far from modest. A reporter wrote that Marshall had "the memory of an unnatural genius, and the integrity of a Christian saint." In another unlikely formulation, he was a cross between Abraham Lincoln and Robert E. Lee. His final official report on the war spent twelve weeks on the *New York Times* bestseller list. Thomas Dewey, Roosevelt's Republican challenger in 1944, promised on the campaign trail that he would keep Marshall in place, despite rumors that Marshall himself would run for president in the next election. "The Democratic Party owes it to the people to draft General Marshall for President," one senator proclaimed. To such suggestions Marshall would reply, "I have never voted, my father was a Democrat, my mother a Republican, and I am an Episcopalian."

When the war was over, for the three months between V-J Day and his retirement, Marshall had taken on a new preoccupation. He worried that Americans were prone to being careless in peace and thus reckless in war. "The hour war is declared," as he saw it, "we take a boy out of high school and give him a couple thousand men." He had seen what happened when his country withdrew from the world in the 1920s and 1930s. It could not make the same complacent peacetime mistakes again, not with the new burdens that history, in the aftermath of this last war, had laid upon it. No longer could it rest secure behind two oceans and rely on nations far away to keep threats from its shores. The world had changed, and "we are now," Marshall said, "concerned with the peace of the entire world." He exhorted in his valedictory remarks, "We must not waste the victory."

Over the course of the war, his hair had gone from auburn to gray. His face had become lined, a look of determination set in place. The six years, Katherine wrote, "had taken a terrific toll."

Every day, he had read the casualty lists—"a constant stream, a steady stream, and I can't get away from them." He had compiled them in graphic reports for the White House, vividly designed in color, so the president could not get away from them either. Four hundred thousand Americans, many friends or the children of friends, had died under his charge. Katherine's son Allen, his stepson, had been shot by a sniper during an Allied campaign in Italy that Marshall had thought ill conceived; when he visited Allen's grave, was it clear he had done all he could to avert it? "I loathe war," Marshall said. "I have finished my military career, but I feel that I must do my best to have us avoid a tragic repetition of our past neglect, our past failures."

As chief of staff, Marshall insisted that his commanders rest before a new mission. But on November 28, the day after getting the president's call about China, he was in the Oval Office by 10:30 a.m. With Katherine the night before, he told Truman, there was "the devil to pay."

The relationship between these two men had grown from an unpromising beginning. As a senator, Truman made his name heading up the Special Committee to Investigate the National Defense Program—to investigate, in other words, impropriety and ineptitude in the mobilization Marshall was leading. Then, when Truman tried to enlist in the army, Marshall told him he was too old. Yet both had watched proud fathers fall on hard times. Both had wanted to go to West Point but found it out of reach. Both were seen as men of an earlier age, nineteenth-century men, in their own ways. By the time Vice President Truman learned of his sudden ascension to the presidency in April 1945—"Boys, if you ever pray for me, pray for me now"—the fact that Marshall would be at his side was a badly needed comfort. Truman had been granted just two one-on-one meetings with Roosevelt. He knew little of the inner workings of U.S. strategy—nothing of the secret weapon being built in New Mexico or the secret agreements struck at Yalta to bring Stalin into the war against Japan. Marshall was unsettled by the hold he seemed to have on the new president.

For Truman, just a few months after V-J Day, the burdens of peacetime seemed no less trying than those of wartime. He took to saying that Sherman had it wrong: "Peace is hell."

Now Truman's most pressing problems were those at home. Americans recalled the stagnation that followed World War I, and the Great Depression was a fresh memory—a nightmare that ended only with the military buildup a few years before. There was panic about the threat of mass unemployment, about inflation, about strikes by autoworkers, steelworkers, and packinghouse workers. There was a shortage of meat and a call to cut wheat consumption in half. It was, Truman said, a "time of great emergency." Amid all that, few Americans saw events abroad as their foremost concern; victory should entitle them to focus on their own problems for a while, and as one official put it, to "go to the movies and drink Coke." In a survey, only 7 percent said that securing the peace was the most important issue at hand, a fraction of those who picked jobs, reconversion of the economy, and labor unrest. (More than two-thirds also said they did not believe that Hitler was really dead.)

But whatever the worries of his voters, Truman, like Marshall, knew that much of the world was in ruins. It fell to the United States—with its homeland all but unscathed, more than one-third of global economic activity within its borders, two-thirds of all gold reserves in its hands—to help restore this world. "We have virtually been elected by the acclamation of the harassed and suffering people of the world to the leadership of the greatest and most beneficent movement in world history for the good of mankind," Marshall had told an audience in Kansas City the week before. And to make things more complicated, there was growing concern about what Stalin was after in this ruined world. The extension of the wartime alliance into the postwar era, Roosevelt's vision, seemed ever more fraught.

With the return of Marshall—Atlas—at least one of Truman's peacetime burdens could be shifted to other shoulders. In the headlines that morning, the news of Marshall's return had already done much of what it was meant to do. If it had not driven Hurley off stage entirely, it had at least taken the spotlight away from his wildest accusations. A "shrewd political counterstroke," one editorialist judged. A "stroke of genius," a judge applauded. Henry Luce, the powerful publisher of *Time* and *Life*, coiner and champion of "the American century," and China-born son of missionaries, wrote Marshall directly: "I do not need to tell you how glad I am that you have undertaken the mission to China. . . .

My basic conviction is that peace, with justice, can be achieved in the critical area of Northeast Asia if our country exercises sufficient intelligence and will."

Americans had long harbored grandiose ambitions of transforming China. For a century, capitalists, missionaries, teachers, and diplomats had gone with their visions and schemes, some nefarious, some noble, and treated China as "plastic" in the hands of "strong and capable Westerners," as Woodrow Wilson put it. Looking back over that history, Americans could tell a pleasing story of their role. While China was being devoured by imperialist powers that both inflamed and fed off internal strife, America had represented something better.

In part it was a matter of self-interest. The British, French, and Germans, and eventually the Japanese, were threatening to carve China into pieces. The United States had neither the inclination nor the wherewithal to get in on the imperialist scramble. So in 1899 and 1900, it issued the Open Door policy—a demand, wrapped in principle, that no foreign power violate what was left of China's sovereignty by claiming a slice of territory for itself. It was also a matter of sentiment. The United States would remake China in its own image, through ministry, through commerce, through education. "With God's help," said a U.S. senator, "we will lift Shanghai up and up, ever up, until it is just like Kansas City."

Yet to most Chinese, although Americans might be better than the worst aggressors, they were hardly innocents. Acts of supposed beneficence looked different from the other side of the Pacific. That vaunted Open Door policy, for example, was at bottom a covenant among thieves, as some would describe it, a way for the United States to reap the spoils of imperialism without incurring the costs, to its self-image or its global image. John Hay, drafting the policy as secretary of state, said as much: "The inherent weakness of our position is this: we do not want to rob China ourselves, and our public opinion will not permit us to interfere."

Washington made much of devoting its share of the Boxer Indemnity, a $300 million payment Western powers extracted from China's late-imperial government, to educational institutions in China; it got that share in the first place by joining a coalition of foreign armies to intervene against the Boxer Rebellion in 1900. Wilson preached universal rights and self-determination everywhere; his principles counted for little after World War I when he got to the negotiating table in Versailles and allowed Japan to take concessions in China—the moment of betrayal that sparked the May Fourth Movement and formed modern Chinese nationalism. "All fairness, all permanent peace, all President Wilson's fourteen-point declaration," a future founder of the Chinese Communist Party lamented, "have turned into hollow words not worth a cent." And whatever the gauzy hopes for the Chinese in China—the peasants of Pearl Buck's *The Good Earth*, which tens of millions of Americans consumed in the 1930s as a Pulitzer Prize–winning novel, Academy Award–winning film, and Broadway play—the Chinese in America were subject to atrocious institutionalized racism. U.S. exclusion laws banned Chinese immigration from 1882 until 1943, when the rhetoric of wartime solidarity finally made them unsupportable. The best that might be said was that Americans were the best of a bad lot—more "pure-minded" than the Europeans, a Chinese imperial official assessed, and thus perhaps more "exploitable."

What Marshall gently referred to during the war as "our difficulties in China" followed this pattern with woeful predictability. After Pearl Harbor, the *New York Times* rhapsodized about "our loyal ally China . . . from whose patient and untiring and infinitely resourceful people there will now return to us tenfold payment upon such aid as we have given." Such proclamations became cliché: indomitable China, spiritually kindred China, freedom-loving China, "with democratic traditions extending back two thousand years," according to *Time*. Its sister publication *Life* ran a piece called "How to Tell Japs from the Chinese"; the former, it advised, "never [have] rosy cheeks." The public consumed tales of the iron-willed Generalissimo Chiang Kai-shek and his beautiful wife, Madame Chiang Kai-shek, Bible-reading Christians both. Prominent Americans returned from brief visits—they got what one young official would call the "quick airport-warphanage-dugout-hospital-Madame-airport treatment," the shacks and beggars cleared along every route traveled—and said it was all true.

This proselytizing had its purpose. By not submitting, China was keeping hundreds of thousands of Japanese troops occupied with occupation. These were hundreds of thousands of troops that otherwise, as Marshall needed no reminding, might be killing Americans on islands in the Pacific or, as Roosevelt feared, joining the Nazis in a "giant pincer" that would give the Axis control of the entire Eurasian land mass. "The determination with which the Chinese nation under your great leadership has defended its freedom," Marshall wrote Chiang, "has been an inspiration to the American Army as well as to the American people." The United States had a vital interest in doing what it could to sustain Chinese resolve. With a virtual siege by Japan, American planes ferried ton after ton of supplies over the Hump, hundreds crashing into the Himalayas below. Dashing American pilots, the Flying Tigers, flew combat missions from Chinese airstrips. Hundreds of millions of dollars in military support flowed to Chiang's army under Lend-Lease.

This material aid was never enough, not in Chiang's eyes and not in Marshall's either. Yet U.S. resources were already overcommitted, in the sprawling multifront war Marshall had to manage. So it took other measures, more symbolic, to elevate an ally. The United States scrapped the exclusion laws. It gave up quasi-imperial privileges in China, and leaned on the British to do the same—aside from control of Hong Kong, which would be relinquished, Churchill said, over his dead body. China's "Century of Humiliation" had started with British victory in the First Opium War. Now, perhaps, it was over. "Today marks a new epoch in Chinese history," Chiang proclaimed. "Henceforth if we are weak, if we lack self-confidence, the fault will be ours."

Washington's hopeful vision for what would come after world war also gave China pride of place. "An unconquerable China will play its proper role in maintaining peace and prosperity not only in Eastern

Asia but in the whole world," Roosevelt told Chiang during the dark-est days of the Japanese invasion. It would join with the United States, Great Britain, and the Soviet Union—the Big Four, the four policemen—to forge a just and lasting settlement. Together they would guarantee, Roosevelt explained to Americans in one of his fireside chats, that "there will be no possibility of an aggressor nation arising to start another world war." For the moment, China's inclusion in this club of great powers might be aspirational; Arthur Vandenberg, a prominent member of the Senate Foreign Relations Committee, described it as a "three-power alliance (with China added as a pleasant gesture)." But Roosevelt was looking further into the future. Whatever the country's weakness today, he believed that "450,000,000 Chinese would some day become united and modernized and would be the most important factor in the whole East." Plus, in the event that Stalin could not be fully trusted despite talk of long-term cooperation, China would help balance Russia in Asia.

The rest of the Big Four never really accepted his logic, but Roosevelt fought for China's place. Churchill, baffled by this "great American illusion," quipped after a transatlantic trip, "If I can epitomize in one word the lesson I learned in the United States, it was 'China.'" The Sovi-ets, too, were dubious. British dismay was more than a little imperial, and racial. A strong China, one officer warned, "would jeopardize the white man's position immediately in the East and ultimately through-out the world." But there were other grounds for skepticism: how could China be regarded as a great power when it was more failed state than unified country?

Before long, the high-flown rhetoric took on a bitterly ironic tone in the United States and China as well. This bitterness was given crude, savage voice by the officer sent on Marshall's recommendation to assist Chiang with his war effort—"Vinegar Joe" Stilwell.

The Stilwell saga came to be a saga of mutual grievance. For Marshall, it was a headache almost from the start. Over two decades, despite their contrary temperaments, he had come to respect General Stilwell as one of the toughest fighting men in the army. He also knew that Stilwell loved China: he had served there, traveled its countryside, studied its language. But if Stilwell was a fierce fighter, he was an appalling diplomat. While he had love for China, he came to have only contempt for Chiang Kai-shek. The contempt was reciprocated. Stilwell and Chiang clashed over both claims of authority and questions of strategy. Chiang wanted to keep his best troops on the eastern front, saving many for later fights against the Communists, while pursuing the promise of almighty airpower peddled by the commander of the Flying Tigers, Claire Chennault, an approach Stilwell (and Marshall) found asinine. Stilwell wanted Chinese troops to head west to retake lost supply lines in Burma and build a road through the jungle. When the route was opened, at enormous cost in lives and treasure, Chiang named it the Stilwell Road; he meant it more as curse than honor.

Friction turned into hatred—hatred that the irascible Stilwell was unable to keep to himself. He described his job as "shoveling the manure pile." His expletives and invective were repeated by GIs and junior officials. His name for the Generalissimo, the Peanut, gained common usage. A less colorful but just as cutting stream of censure made its way back to Marshall and U.S. officialdom. Chiang, Stilwell reported, "had a ring around him, half-informed, and they gave him a distorted view of everything"; "he wanted to keep all his subordinates in the dark, because he didn't trust them"; "the Chinese soldier is excellent material, wasted and betrayed by stupid leadership." In his diary, Stilwell went further: "The cure for China's troubles is the elimination of Chiang Kai-shek."

Marshall chided Stilwell for his indiscretion and at one point wanted to summon him home. Roosevelt reprimanded him for treating "the undisputed leader of 400,000,000 people" as if he were "the Sultan of Morocco." But Marshall also understood that Stilwell was in a thankless position. He was answering to two masters, Chiang and his own army. He was getting scant support, what relatively little could be spared given demands everywhere else. "I read your profane message," Marshall replied to a complaint, "and I sympathize with your reaction."

Most consequentially, Marshall sided with Stilwell in a showdown with Chiang over control of military decision-making in China. Roosevelt eventually agreed to issue an ultimatum on Stilwell's behalf, in a sharp letter to Chiang backed by an implicit threat. When Stilwell had the letter in hand, he rushed to deliver it, with as insulting an air as he could manage. "The most severe humiliation I have ever had in my life," Chiang wrote in his diary. Stilwell was exultant. He sent his wife a lyric: "I know I've still to suffer / And run a weary race, / But, oh, the blessed pleasures! / I've wrecked the Peanut's face."

The confrontation backfired on Stilwell. Chiang insisted that he leave the country, and despite the ultimatum in the letter, Roosevelt conceded. But it also backfired on Chiang. Vinegar Joe was a character made for a newspaper interview, and his indiscretion meant that reporters covering his departure had rich material. His exit from the scene, in late October of 1944, let loose a flood of damning copy—"the bursting of a great illusion," CBS reported, "the long delayed washday for China's dirty linen."

If Marshall seemed uncharacteristically tolerant of bad behavior in this case, it owed in part to his recognition that, while Stilwell's poisonous tongue and poor discipline did not help, the real disconnect was more fundamental. Underlying all the rancor and recrimination, the feuds and insults, was strategic calculation on both sides. The United States had good reason to focus its resources on the war in Europe. Without Japan, Germany could still fight and maybe win. Without Germany, Japan was finished. So the United States would start with Europe, condemning China to low priority in its war effort. Chiang and his government also acted with reason. "China could not lose if the democracies won," one reporter pointed out, "nor could she win if the democracies lost." China had borne the initial terrible brunt of Japanese force and pinned down Japanese troops. Now, there seemed little point in risking everything on fights that always took second or third or fourth place for its allies—especially since for

Chiang, success against Japan would still leave the problem of the Communists.

Strategic disconnect set off spirals of disenchantment. Chiang concluded he was "a decorative object" in the Alliance. His requests to join the high councils of strategy—the Combined Chiefs of Staff and the Munitions Assignment Board—went nowhere, in part because of British opposition, in part because of apparent Chinese difficulty keeping secrets. At the great summits, Roosevelt, Churchill, and Stalin made decisions about China's future and did not even tell Chiang what they decided. "This meeting of the three leaders has already carved the seeds of the Third World War," he fumed after Yalta. "Roosevelt is still calling this a diplomatic victory—this is really laughable." When Chiang got his own war summit and sat side-by-side with Churchill and Roosevelt in Cairo, commitments to China collapsed almost immediately afterward, when the European front turned out to need more help—a stab of humiliation in what was to be a moment of glory. And while the Chinese got copious sympathy, what they really wanted was money and weapons. Their share of global Lend-Lease assistance to American allies was 1 percent of the total in some years, never more than 4 percent. Why, they asked, should they do more of what the Americans wanted? Chiang threatened collapse, demanded billion-dollar payments, hinted at capitulation.

If the Chinese looked at the Americans and saw high-handed inconstancy, the Americans looked at the Chinese and saw two-faced ingratitude. While their Lend-Lease share was small compared to the enormous shipments crossing the Atlantic, it was still hundreds of millions of dollars in matériel and supplies, flown death-defyingly across the Hump—the Skyway to Hell, pilots called it. There was another $500 million in financial support. Yet Chiang's war, as one diplomat put it, seemed to be "much sound and no fury."

Marshall was at times sympathetic to Chinese frustrations. The United States could offer relatively little and needed from Chiang a lot. "Because the Pacific is a secondary theater," he told colleagues, "we must depend on the Chinese to contain increasingly more Japanese

divisions than at present." But he was also frustrated. Chinese officials showed little understanding of his global concerns. They lectured
Washington about what it owed them, to which Marshall would react:
"I thought these were *American* planes, and *American* personnel, and
American materiel." They had little regard for the constraints of logistics. Every piece of equipment sent to China had to cross the Atlantic, round the Cape of Good Hope, and then pass over the Hump on a
flight that burned a gallon of fuel for every gallon delivered. (That was
why Marshall supported Stilwell's road: in a long war, it would be the
only way to supply China in large quantities.) "The whole problem of
maintaining China in the war," Marshall said, is "one of logistic difficulties which must be linked to our capabilities of overcoming them."

For many Americans stationed in China, not just Stilwell, familiarity brought more than just frustration. It bred contempt. There
was a story about Chinese soldiers eating a puppy kept by American
soldiers—a puppy, the Chinese noted, fed better than they were. There
were rumors of aid lining the pockets of generals and officials. GIs
took to calling their government Uncle Chump from over the Hump.
There was the sight of starving Chinese recruits, roped together to prevent flight, dropping dead after marches of less than a mile. Stilwell's
successor, General Albert Wedemeyer, had his own harsh observations.
"We Americans here are doing our utmost to help the Chinese, but it
is really difficult, for they know so little about modern warfare and in
addition seem to be honeycombed with corrupt officials," he reported
after arriving. "The Chinese are not fighting."

That, ultimately, was the most explosive issue—the extent to which
Chiang was leaving Japan to the Americans while he saved his fire for
the Communists. Riled by one report from the front, Marshall complained that the Chinese were "confining themselves to lip service
and letting someone else do the fighting." Many Americans, including Stilwell, figured a way around this: if Chiang would not fight as
much as or where the United States wanted him to, it should work
with Chinese armies that would—most pointedly, the Communists.
Enticed by this possibility, Mao and his comrades worked to convey

a spirited readiness to take up the charge. They said they would serve under American officers. They purveyed their own myth of heroic resistance, telling tales of guerrilla attacks behind Japanese lines— though far from scrutiny, they were making the same calculation that Chiang was, working for position after Japan's defeat and letting him and his allies pay the greater costs for now. To Chiang, the prospect of US-Communist cooperation was infuriating and unacceptable. Only under pressure did he finally allow the small American outpost, the Dixie Mission, in Yenan.

By the last phase of the war, accumulated disappointment had brought Chiang's fear to fruition: the China front truly had become a sideshow. American strategists initially wanted it as a base for attacking Japan. The island-hopping campaign in the Pacific and frustrations in China changed their plan. They had other angles of attack. Before his death, even Roosevelt had come to doubt his vision of China's role. He allowed that "three generations of education and training would be required before China could become a serious factor."

War's sudden end was not an unalloyed blessing. In an instant, complications of a wartime alliance became threats to a peacetime vision. Almost no one had thought Japan's surrender might come when it did until soon before. U.S. military planners operated on the assumption that there would be a year or more, rather than three months, between Germany's defeat and Japan's. Even once the power of atomic weapons started to become clear, Marshall expected the war to go until the end of 1945. Days before it collapsed, Mao was predicting that Japanese resistance would last well into 1946.

"If peace comes suddenly, it is reasonable to expect widespread confusion and disorder," Wedemeyer warned Marshall in the war's final weeks. In the wake of Japan's surrender on August 14, such confusion added new urgency to Washington's long-standing objectives—to bolster Chiang Kai-shek's government, to bring the Nationalists and the Communists together, and to see China stand up as one of the great powers of the postwar world. In the confusion, it fell to Marshall to find a way.

After leaving the Oval Office the morning of November 28, Marshall received a message from Chiang. "I am delighted with your appointment," it read. "I hope that you will come as soon as possible." Marshall replied that he would depart the following week. First he had to take care of some lingering business from the war.

CHAPTER 2

Horrid Dilemmas

A democracy in triumph can present a strange spectacle. The week after getting Truman's call, Marshall walked into the cavernous Senate Caucus Room to find the seats filled with onlookers and ten congressmen framed by columns in front— "Hollywood's idea of what Washington is like," the *New Republic* cracked. Days earlier he had been credited with giving the country victory. Now the people's representatives were preparing to set into him, a journalist noted, "as if he were being tried for losing the war rather than winning it."

This was the latest in a string of investigations into the Japanese attack on Pearl Harbor, and Marshall was expected to answer any and all questions the congressional committee had before starting his new mission. He had told Chiang Kai-shek that he would depart for China by December 7 (four years to the day after Pearl Harbor, as it happened). When the questions began, it quickly became clear he would not be leaving so soon. Why had he not done more to warn commanders in Hawaii? Where had he been that morning? Who had known what, and when? Marshall reminded his interrogators that a plane was waiting nearby to take him across the Pacific; the questions continued.

There was an ominous insinuation to many of these questions. Members of the committee were pushing a theory that the Roosevelt administration had let Pearl Harbor happen so that the United States would be forced into war. If that were true, the suffering and struggle of the last four years had been not a necessary sacrifice, but the fruit of conspiracy, of subversion by enemies within. (Patrick Hurley's resignation tirade had similarly fixated on subversion and prompted another congressional investigation, this one by the House Un-American Activities Committee, which was moving beyond its original Nazi-hunting purpose.) Marshall, the charge went, was an agent of this conspiracy.

In the face of grandstanding and insinuation, Marshall was straightforward and composed. He was a lackluster orator with a prepared text; speaking off the cuff, on a subject he knew, he could be entrancing. He earnestly and lucidly reconstructed his "thinking at the time" in response to questions about minute decisions four years earlier. "I prefer to rest on the evidence," he said after a sneering recitation of his alleged lapses. Only occasionally did his restraint falter and sarcasm come to the surface. "If we had failed," he grumbled, "I presume there would have been a full investigation as to why we went into Normandy." Afterward, he clipped a newspaper editorial for his files: "It was quite evidently General Marshall's conviction that if he answered fully, reasonably, patiently, that the committee would see Pearl Harbor as the national tragedy it was—a tragedy in which fallible men had made mistakes in judgment."

When Marshall left the room for the last time, the crowd applauded. He had answered questions for more than twenty-four hours over six days. December 7 had come and gone, his plane sitting on the tarmac.

"God bless democracy!" Marshall would say. "I approve of it highly but suffer from it extremely."

"We shall have to breed a race of supermen to endure the strains of American public life," the columnist Walter Lippmann mused while watching Marshall's interrogation. But Marshall was by now used to the strains; the story of his becoming the kind of man who could endure them centered on encounters like the one with the Pearl Harbor Committee. Over and over, not just during the war but before, he had faced doubters and detractors and persuaded them, as he would advise, by accomplishment rather than eloquence.

In his telling, it began with an overheard conversation. He had grown up a forgettable student and unremarkable boy in the same western Pennsylvania town where he was born in 1880. When he decided to follow his older brother, Stuart, to the Virginia Military Institute, he caught Stuart arguing against it: lanky George would disgrace the family name. (Their father made embarrassingly much of the fact that the name traced back, circuitously, to the early Supreme Court justice and secretary of state John Marshall.) His brother's slight stirred in Marshall what he called an "urgency to succeed"—a fervor that drove him forward, almost destroyed him, and then hardened into self-mastery.

At VMI, it was the fervor of a lone Yankee in the land of Jackson and Lee. Early on, weak with typhoid and forced to squat over an unsheathed bayonet, Marshall fainted and almost impaled himself. By the end, he was his class's "first captain." In his thirties, he again and again pushed himself to the point of breakdown, or past it, agitated by the slow progress of his military career. At 35 he was just a lieutenant, ready to give up on the army. "I do not feel it right to waste all my best years in the vain struggle against insurmountable obstacles," he confessed. He was known for edgy intensity, a quick temper, a heavy smoking habit. Twice he was hospitalized, exhausted and overrun, for "neurasthenia." Once he collapsed in the street.

Twenty-five years later, it seemed a different man who led his country in World War II. The restless drive had given way to assured determination, the nervous energy to Olympian calm. He would still curse, but now only for effect. His temper was still feared—"I've never seen a man who apparently develops a higher pressure of anger when he encounters some piece of stupidity," wrote Eisenhower—but now rarely seen. He had developed exquisite self-control, an aptitude for focusing on what was necessary, and a commitment to relaxing "completely." Even during the war, he napped on a lounge chair after lunch and went riding almost daily. (*That* is where he was the morning of Pearl Harbor.) In the hours before the D-Day landing, he went to bed at his usual time—he had already done what he could. "It was as though he lived outside of himself," said Katherine. Secretary of War Henry Stimson extolled him with a proverb: he who controls his spirit is better than he who takes a city.

Along with this transformation had come another trait central to Marshall's persona: a reputation for truth-telling, for almost insolent integrity in rooms of yes-men. His army career took off when he challenged the top American general in World War I, John "Black Jack" Pershing. Those watching thought this middling officer was finished. Instead Pershing made Marshall his aide and protégé. Before World War II, Marshall challenged Roosevelt in a meeting at the White House: "Mr. President, I am sorry, but I don't agree with that at all." Again those watching thought Marshall, not yet army chief of staff, was finished. Instead the president promoted him over several higher-ranking generals. Marshall accepted on the condition that he always be allowed to speak his mind. "You said 'yes' pleasantly," he added when Roosevelt assented, "but it may be unpleasant."

Marshall was characteristically blunt when, after meeting with Truman in the Oval Office, he reviewed a suggested "course of action" drafted by the State Department. The president had given him an objective, but he wanted to go to China with more than an objective. He wanted a strategy, a clear statement of what he was to do there and what he was to do it with. The State Department's policy paper, he told Truman's chief of staff, William Leahy, "appeared susceptible of serious misunderstanding." What was needed was clarity, something "saying what we mean so that the people at home and the people in China, and the Russians also, will clearly understand our intentions."

While Marshall answered the Pearl Harbor Committee's questions, administration officials started working out a more satisfactory plan. He stepped out of the Senate Caucus Room for hurried briefings between rounds of testimony and marked up drafts when he went home at night. But as he noted to a former colleague, "For the past week I have been all day, every day, before a congressional committee and during the few remaining hours I have been engrossed in preparations for my departure for China, which up to the present have of necessity been very superficial."

On Sunday, December 9, with the Pearl Harbor Committee off for the day, Marshall joined the discussions under way at the State Department. Secretary Byrnes was in his office, across an alley from the White House in the State, War, and Navy Building, along with two members of his team. John Carter Vincent, the head of the Department's Office of Far Eastern Affairs, had spent much of his career in China and come back to Washington with a reputation for unsparing analysis of events there. Dean Acheson, Byrnes's debonair and sharp-tongued deputy, was also known for sure and usually trenchant views. Less so Byrnes himself. A South Carolina politician, he was certain of one thing in particular: that he rather than Truman should have gotten the 1944 vice presidential nomination—and that he rather than Truman should by extension now be president. On other matters Byrnes was less resolute. It was said around Washington that he would lay out three hats in the morning so he could compromise on the one in the middle.

The men in Byrnes's office agreed on the basic objective for the mission. Marshall was to guarantee China's unity, secure Chiang Kai-shek's leadership, and at the same time encourage enough reform and compromise to undercut the force of revolution and avert a civil war. By doing so, he would take China off the table as both a source of US-Soviet tension and an easy target for Soviet subterfuge. Without a strong and unified China, Byrnes reminded Marshall, "we could expect Russia to ultimately take control of Manchuria and maintain a dominant influence in North China."

They also, however, knew that similar objectives had sent Stilwell to his ruin and Hurley into his rage. Marshall was taking over where those others had failed, and the circumstances had not gotten dramatically more promising, even with the Japanese defeated. As one U.S. officer stationed in China put it, "I am still trying to find where the war left off and the peace commenced."

Yet there was a reason they kept coming back to the objective: the alternatives were dreadful. Marshall had been hearing contrary warnings through his final months as army chief of staff. Total abandonment of Chiang could mean at best a weak and divided China and at worst a Communist victory, either of which would invite Soviet domination; total commitment could mean a long, costly, and potentially futile war. General Wedemeyer, commanding U.S. forces from postwar headquarters in Shanghai, had sent message after message sounding the alarm about doing too little. "If China were to become a puppet of the Soviet which is exactly what a Chinese Communist victory would mean," he wrote in a classified report, "then Soviet Russia would practically control the continents of Europe and Asia." The warnings about committing too much were just as vehement. John Carter Vincent had cautioned against "the establishment of a relationship with China which has some characteristics of a de facto protectorate with a semi-colonial Chinese Army under our direction." The implications of such a relationship, a diplomat stationed in China predicted, would be dire: "should Chiang attempt to liquidate the Communists, we should find ourselves entangled not only in a civil war in China but also drawn into conflict with the Soviet Union."

It was, as Walter Lippmann framed it in his widely read column, "a horrid dilemma—to become entangled by intervention in China's civil war, or to get out of China in such a way as to leave China hopelessly divided, and dangerously weak."

Yet there was also some cause for hope that, with a mix of support and cajoling from Washington, Chiang might succeed in building something like the postwar China Roosevelt had envisioned. Compared to his challengers, Mao included, Chiang had the most resources, the most modern military, the most territory, and explicit recognition as the legitimate leader of China by all of the world's powers, including the Soviet Union. A Sino-Soviet Treaty signed with Washington's prodding on the last day of World War II exchanged Stalin's support of Chiang for Russian economic advantages and a dominant role in Manchuria (concessions that Roosevelt and Churchill had, without Chiang's consent, mostly already made to Stalin at Yalta anyway).

The challenge was to achieve the right mix of support and cajoling, and to use it to persuade the Communists that their best option, their only option, was taking part in a government led by a longtime nemesis. It was a matter of leverage, of sending Marshall to China with, as Byrnes put it, "sufficient weapons . . . to induce the Central Government and the Communistic Government to get together." To this end, Marshall had asked former aides in the War Department to rework the State Department's draft policy, before the State Department reworked the War Department's reworking—a negotiation in line edits.

What most preoccupied Marshall, however, was a question not answered by any of these drafts. They could lay out what was expected of the two sides, but what would the United States do if it failed to persuade them, particularly if the Communists cooperated and Chiang did not? Byrnes conceded that Washington might in that case have to withhold support from Chiang's government. But no one aside from Marshall wanted to spend much time contemplating failure. A man of his caliber, Vincent suggested, would find a way forward once there.

In the wake of Japan's surrender, the most pressing question for American policymakers had been just how much to help Chiang as he tried to take control of his country. At first they moved quickly. Washington's Order Number One to its forces in the region was supposed to make his supremacy clear: except in Manchuria, where the Soviet occupiers were in charge, the Japanese were to hand over their weapons to Chiang's troops alone, even when Nationalist forces were months away and the Communists were nearby. To facilitate this handover, the United States moved hundreds of thousands of Chiang's troops from China's interior toward the coast—"the largest troop movement by air in the world's history," according to General Wedemeyer. Military assistance also continued to flow. And by the fall of 1945, more than 50,000 U.S. Marines had started landing, welcomed as "angeles of peace," as one sign had it, to help evacuate the Japanese and guard key points in northern China: railway lines, ports, coal mines, and cities that otherwise might have fallen into Communist hands.

After a few months, this support started to run up against the limits of what the United States said it was willing to do. Washington insisted that any advantage given to Chiang in his fight with Mao was "incidental"; the main purpose was to facilitate the repatriation of 3 million Japanese soldiers and civilians and the recovery of 9,000 American prisoners. This was the explicit charge given to the Marines, as well as to teams of agents—Team Eagle, Team Cardinal, Team Magpie, Team Duck—dropped behind Japanese lines on behalf of the Office of Strategic Services, or OSS, the wartime U.S. intelligence operation. U.S. personnel would help Chiang take China back from the Japanese, but they were not to back him in "fratricidal warfare" against the Communists.

To those out in the field, this injunction hinged on a distinction without a difference. As Secretary of the Navy James Forrestal asked, "How do you draw the line between internal security and internal war?" Wedemeyer complained insistently about the "conflicting orders" he was to execute. "Under the present circumstances," he wrote, "it is impossible to avoid involvement in fratricidal warfare or political strife, yet I am admonished by my directive to do so." American ships and planes were helping American-armed troops take territory that the Communists claimed. Marines were protecting supply lines and resources, and even allowing the Japanese to continue as de facto occupiers until government troops could arrive. Whatever the stated goal, Wedemeyer pointed out, "we are making an important contribution to preclude successful operations by Communist forces."

What was more, the fight against the Communists was proving more challenging than many had expected. In briefing Marshall a few months earlier, Wedemeyer advised that it would take only moderate U.S. help for Chiang to defeat Mao's forces. (Wedemeyer still wanted more American troops to land in China, but Marshall, who had to consider other needs in the region, told him that Japan and Korea were more urgent priorities.) Encouraged by the upbeat assessments, the new secretary of war, Robert Patterson, had recently boasted that the

Communists were so negligible a force that U.S. Marines could walk from one side of China to the other without encountering any trouble.

The war with Japan, however, had turned out to be a major boon to the Communists' prospects. With the central government bearing the brunt of Tokyo's firepower, Mao had taken the opportunity to infiltrate guerrillas and organize peasants behind Japanese lines as Chiang fought for China's survival. The Communists started the war with fewer than 100,000 soldiers and scant territory beyond the desolate landscape surrounding the revolutionary headquarters in Yenan. By the end, they had a million troops and more than a million party members, controlling territory that was home to nearly 100 million people, almost a quarter of China's population. "China's destiny is not Chiang's but theirs," a young American diplomat had written of the Communists, contradicting the assurance of his superiors.

When the Soviet Red Army swept into Manchuria in the final days of the war, Mao saw a chance to build on his progress. He ordered hundreds of thousands of regular and irregular Chinese Communist fighters into the region as the Soviet invasion began. They did not always get the kind of welcome they expected from their revolutionary brethren. But a combination of the occupiers' enabling indifference and quiet help meant that within a few months of Japanese defeat, the Communists had managed to establish a strong presence in a large swath of China's northeast. "Without Soviet assistance," the State Department assessed, "it is difficult to see how the Chinese Communists could have become so securely entrenched in Manchuria as they appear to be today."

Chiang invoked this assistance, a violation of the deal he had struck with Stalin, as an argument for further U.S. support, whatever the injunction against "fratricidal warfare." He wrote Truman about "Soviet Russia's connivance with Chinese Communists." He reminded Wedemeyer again and again that the Soviets "collaborate with the Chinese Communists in making Japanese arms and equipment available and in placing definite obstacles in the way of Chinese Central Government troops when attempts are made to move them by sea and/or air to Manchuria."

Wedemeyer was sympathetic, but he needed further guidance from his government before he could do anything. Should he offer more help, or was it time to start withdrawing the more than 100,000 U.S. troops in China?

By the time of Marshall's selection, Wedemeyer had been presenting versions of this question for weeks, hoping that the stark choice—fully commit or go home—would force Washington's hand. The State Department wanted to equivocate, postponing any more troop movements until Marshall could arrive and persuade the two sides to make progress in peace talks. But to Marshall's military advisers, this position was another of "the vague, indecisive, delaying tactics which have characterized U.S. policy toward China since the Japanese capitulation." Marshall himself worried that it would give the Communists reason to stall once he arrived, maneuvering to "block all progress in negotiations as far as they can, as the delay is to their advantage."

So a new order again split the difference, giving Wedemeyer some leeway, but not as much as he wanted. He could immediately transport another 200,000 of Chiang's troops north, then be ready to transport more without yet committing to it. Once in China, Marshall could perhaps use the uncertainty about further troop movements to his own advantage.

But Wedemeyer's estimate of what might be needed was growing, his view of the situation becoming darker. No longer was he saying, as he had at a press conference in August, "I do not anticipate any difficulty with the Communists." In fact, the challenge was great, and overcoming it would mean assuming great risks. "If the unification of China and Manchuria under Chinese National Forces is to be a United States policy," he advised, "involvement in fratricidal warfare and possibly in war with the Soviet Union must be accepted." War with the Soviets might be the price America had to pay for the China it wanted.

Something else happened in the days after Japan's surrender. The OSS agents dropped behind Japanese lines in China were not just looking out for American prisoners. They were also taking stock of Communist positions. One of them, a brash former missionary who spoke Chinese well and detested the CCP, happened on a Communist troop detachment in eastern China. When he refused to give up his gun, an argument started, and before long, he was dead. The Communists cut his throat from ear to ear and mutilated his face with bayonets.

Mao was apologetic. It was all, he explained afterward to Wedemeyer, a "very unfortunate" misunderstanding. Members of the agent's party reported that his behavior had been provocative. But U.S. officials also recognized that the agent was intruding on important geography for the Communists; the killing might have been meant to send a message. Wedemeyer told Mao that it would have "a very disturbing effect" in the United States. "The Chinese Communists are doing their utmost," Wedemeyer related to Washington, "to involve United States forces in military operations that definitely can be construed as offensive in nature. They hope . . . to influence public opinion in the States."

For now, however, few Americans took much notice of John Birch's death.

Two days after the meeting at the State Department, Marshall returned to the White House, this time with Secretary Byrnes, to go over the plan with Truman and his chief of staff, Leahy. American power, wielded by Marshall, would bring the two sides together in a truce. Chiang would reform his government, Mao would give up his independent army, and China would be unified. And this new China would be rewarded with considerable American assistance, economic and otherwise—an incentive for both Chiang and Mao, since all Chinese would benefit from such support.

Truman had no reason to object. He had been hearing for months, from a variety of sources, that this basic course offered the best hope of realizing American objectives in China. "As I see it, there is only one way to get off the horns of the dilemma," an emissary wrote him after a visit. "That is to aid the Chinese Government to take immediate economic and political measures which can produce political unity before our troops leave China." John Carter Vincent, a skeptic of Chiang, would argue that "a reduction in the influence of the Communists might be more readily achieved if the Government 'took them in' (in more sense than one) on a minority basis rather than try to shoot them all." Wedemeyer, a champion of Chiang, advised that the government would "not be able to stabilize the situation in North China for several months perhaps years unless a satisfactory settlement with the Chinese Communists is accomplished," followed by "economic, political and social reforms through honest, competent civilian officials." And Henry Luce, perhaps Chiang's greatest American advocate, had recently endorsed "the policy of Byrnes, Truman, and Marshall," while warning, in black tie at the Council on Foreign Relations in New York, that Chiang's government must "produce a solution for the current social ills."

Whether a stable unity government could be other than democratic had been a matter of debate. Marshall accepted the State Department's formulation of a "strong, peaceful, united and democratic China" over the War Department's "strong, peaceful, united and effective." (Wedemeyer argued that China "is not yet capable of implementing, nor is she psychologically prepared for, democratic procedures in government.") Yet the fact that Chiang's regime required fundamental change was not in dispute: only fundamental change would allow it to survive.

Nor was the goal of a united China. Around Asia, countries were splitting in two: Korea along the 38th parallel between American and Soviet occupation zones, Vietnam along the 16th parallel between north and south. China was different. Just six months earlier, in San Francisco, the United Nations Charter had delivered on Roosevelt's promise of anointing China a great power. A divided China would make that status meaningless. It would be easily dominated by the Soviet Union and sow tension among other governments. "A divided

China will obviously further the forces of insecurity, invite foreign intervention, and may eventually bring about conditions which will plunge the world into a third world war," a State Department analysis concluded.

So Plan A was clear enough. Marshall remained uneasy, however, when it came to Plan B. He pressed Truman on the scenario others had wanted to brush aside: what if this course failed, and what if that failure was, in whole or in part, Chiang Kai-shek's fault? The president gave a different answer than his secretary of state had given two days earlier. In the "unfortunate eventuality" of such intransigence, as Marshall recorded it, "this Government would have to swallow its pride and much of its policy." Otherwise, the consequences would be "tragic"—"a divided China," "a probable Russian reassumption of power in Manchuria," "the defeat or loss of the major purpose of our war in the Pacific." Even if Chiang did little of what Marshall demanded, the United States would have to do most of what he wanted.

Underneath the wishful thinking and the optimistic evasions, Marshall's key source of leverage over Chiang looked like a bluff.

When Marshall went back to the White House for a final conversation with Truman, he wanted to go over this point one last time. It was not part of his directive, it would be written nowhere official, so he repeated his understanding of the instruction: "in the event that I was unable to secure the necessary action by the Generalissimo, which I thought reasonable and desirable, it would still be necessary for the U.S. government, through me, to continue to back the National Government of the Republic of China—through the Generalissimo within the terms of the announced policy of the U.S. government." Truman told Marshall that he had it right. Withdrawing all support from Chiang was out of the question, even if he resisted Marshall's efforts.

Marshall's interrogation by the Pearl Harbor Committee had ended the day before, on Friday, December 13. The following morning he would start a five-day airplane journey across the Pacific. Truman reiterated his faith in Marshall and then gave him the final version of his directive, the policy that had been worked out through edits, negotiations, and rewrites in the two and a half weeks since his selection. It described the scope of his authority, the means at his disposal, and the stakes of his mission. "The fact that I have asked you to go to China," Truman's note read, "is the clearest evidence of my very real concern with regard to the situation there."

There was also a version of the directive that would be released to the public—abridged, but, for Marshall at least, hardly an afterthought. He had worried that he would find himself on "the horns of a dilemma," caught between his own desire for as much public clarity as possible and the government's usual aversion to any public clarity at all. He had worked through drafts with Byrnes and with his own aides. "U.S. support," the public statement stressed, "will not extend to U.S. military intervention to influence the course of any Chinese internal strife." Yet some key details were left out. It said nothing of either the further transport of Chiang's troops or of Marshall's authority to transfer even more, or not, depending, as the private version specified, on whether doing so would "prejudice the objectives of the military truce and the political negotiations." The statement also said little about just how involved in those negotiations Marshall would be.

Instead, it sought to persuade Americans that their country's involvement was worthwhile. "Events of this century," it read, "would indicate that a breach of a peace anywhere in the world threatens the peace of the entire world." The country could no longer act as if affairs across oceans were not its concern. And Marshall's private directive from the president was even starker. Whatever the apparent costs, "they will be infinitesimal by comparison to a recurrence of global warfare in which the new and terrible weapons that exist would certainly be employed." If Marshall did not succeed, the consequences would be dire, possibly even nuclear.

With these two versions of the directive in hand, Marshall said good-bye to Truman and went next door to the State Department with Dean Acheson. Acheson had joined the meeting in place of Byrnes, who had left for a summit meeting in Moscow—an effort to salvage the faltering spirit of Allied cooperation amid growing geopolitical tension. Officials hoped the summit would, among other things, help Marshall right the situation in China.

No one in Washington officialdom doubted that there was, as Chiang had written to Truman, connivance between Stalin and Mao. How much, and what exactly it meant, were murkier questions—in part because the answers frequently changed, leaving even Mao confused and dismayed. American policymakers had long worried that Stalin "would make full use of and support the Chinese Communists." Yet he had gone out of his way to reassure them that his basic goals in China and theirs did not have to clash. The U.S. ambassador to Moscow, Averell Harriman, sensed Stalin's frustration with Mao and wariness about investing too much in a far-fetched Chinese revolution. Another American diplomat in Moscow, an up-and-coming Soviet specialist named George Kennan, would point out Stalin's "use of words which mean all things to all people." But Mao himself had been spooked by the Sino-Soviet Treaty with Chiang. When Stalin followed it by insisting, soon after Japan's surrender, that Mao restrain his forces and engage in face-to-face talks with Chiang, Mao had no choice but to comply, taking his first-ever airplane flight for the encounter.

In Moscow, Byrnes thought he could secure more Soviet cooperation and less connivance. He was more optimistic than many of his colleagues; Henry Stimson had contended that "no permanently safe international relations can be established between two such fundamentally different national systems." Yet even skeptics saw the need to try, including in China. Stalin might be unlikely to cut the Communists off completely, but the difference between limited and lavish backing could be decisive. As an assistant secretary of war had remarked recently after returning from China, if the Soviets "decide to give active support to the Chinese Communists, then we are in a real mess."

With Byrnes on his way to Moscow, Marshall finalized the logistics of the mission with Acheson. The success of even the best strategy would depend on the unglamorous details of implementation, and Marshall was intent on getting those details right. Over the course of the war he had come to have high regard for the aristocratic Acheson; Acheson had come to worship Marshall, and would now make sure to provide whatever he said he needed. He would have a three-man staff to take with him. He would have a special expense account, in order to operate without the meddling of the State Department. He would have a "rear echelon," his man in Washington, who could quickly and discreetly take care of what needed taking care of without worrying about bureaucracy and go straight to Truman, Byrnes, or Acheson with any message or request.

Marshall also wanted one other assurance: that no one in Washington would try to work around him. If his mission was to have any chance of success, he needed full authority to carry out his orders from the president, to use the leverage he had without being undermined by other officials with other priorities or views; otherwise, the Chinese would assume, as they often had during the war, that they could always try other channels if they did not like what Marshall was telling them. Acheson agreed to draft a letter for signature by the president directing the rest of the government to do nothing on China without permission from Marshall.

In the meantime, Marshall would say nothing about what he planned to do and insisted that no one else say anything either. Any stray comment, he worried, "might by some chance, because of the unusual complexity of the problem in China, prejudice my freedom of action in reaching conclusions on the ground." He would need that freedom of action once the mission began.

The next morning, a small crowd gathered on the tarmac at National Airport, across the Potomac from the White House, to see Marshall off. The propellers on his C-54 were turning, photographers' bulbs flashing, as he arrived in uniform, khaki coat belted and peaked general's cap on.

The newspapers had hailed him and his mission in lofty terms—"the most difficult diplomatic mission anywhere in the world," a commentator proclaimed. "Upon General Marshall, who did so much to win the war," said the *Washington Post*, "there devolves a responsibility for winning the peace." He will be armed "as few U.S. diplomats have been armed for years," said *Time*. He was carrying the great hopes Americans had for China; in a survey, 86 percent of respondents predicted a future of Sino-American cooperation. With his mere selection, the *New York Times* editorialized, "The situation in China has taken a turn for the better."

For Katherine, none of this softened the "bitter blow" of the departure, and she had trouble hiding her anger. "I give a sickly smile when people say how the country loves and admires my husband," she wrote to a former aide. "This sounds bitter. Well, I am bitter. The President should never have asked this of him and in such a way that he could not refuse."

Marshall himself expressed no such bitterness. But those close to him could see that the only thing driving him was a sense of duty. "I know it is a great honor," a friend wrote, "but—nuts—you've got enough honors." Others worried he had been handed an impossible mission that would threaten the historical reputation he deserved. It was, one quipped, "the simple, rapid, one-man task of unifying 400 million-odd people who have practiced disunity for a thousand years and coaxing into being an efficient and honest government where none has ever existed." During the war, China had come to be seen as a "graveyard for American officials."

The most infamous of them was not there on the tarmac that day. In fact, Marshall had not spoken to Joe Stilwell since getting Truman's call. Quietly, however, he had sent an aide to visit Stilwell in his spartan quarters at a nearby base. Vinegar Joe had a grim analysis for his former chief: the Chinese respect power, he said, and Marshall was going with little.

Marshall waved to the well-wishers and posed for the photographers. He told Katherine he would be gone just a few months. He shook hands with a somber Chinese ambassador and a grinning Eisenhower. He climbed the stairs, turned and raised his right hand, and then boarded the C-54.

John Carter Vincent watched it take off, his son beside him. "Son, there goes the bravest man in the world," Vincent said. "He's going to try to unify China."

CHAPTER 3

Marshall Is Too Big

For much of the winter, thick fog covered China's wartime capital of Chongqing. The inland city lay at the confluence of two rivers, the Yangtze and the Jialing, and fog rose from their banks, suffusing the streets with darkness and damp. During the war this was a blessing, since Japanese pilots had a hard time bombing what they could not see. But for Americans posted there, it became a source of both incessant complaint and irresistible metaphor. Trying to navigate local intrigues was "like walking in the fog." Foreign machinations had "so many threads that in the Chongqing fog now you see it now you don't."

The day of Marshall's arrival, December 22, was seasonally bleak. It had rained through the night, and black clouds lingered over the mountains. At an airfield outside the city, groups of Americans, Nationalists, and Communists stood in the mud, waiting for the plane to appear. The Americans had been in a state of high anticipation for days. "Everybody scurrying around doing not much of anything, but under the impression of great accomplishment, and all scared to death over the impending arrival of the great man himself," recorded a young diplomat named John Melby. "No one knows what he is going to do, what his instructions, or how long he will be here."

Marshall had left almost a week before on his island-hopping journey across the Pacific: Washington to San Francisco, San Francisco to Honolulu, Honolulu to Kwajalein atoll, Kwajalein to Guam, Guam to

Manila, Manila to the Chinese coast. In the Philippines, he stopped to revisit the country where he had done his first tour more than forty years earlier. When the plane passed low over his old post, he thought back to that rugged and innocent time—an officer new to the army, an army new to the ways of global power and distant imperial occupation.

It was on long flights, aides said, that you got to know the general. The standard C-54 was a simple transport plane, so they gushed when they boarded this one, outfitted for Churchill: bedroom in the tail, deep leather chairs, wood paneling—"the plushest of all plush jobs," one wrote home. Marshall had recruited three aides for the mission: Henry Byroade, a fast-rising officer who had been in China during the war; Richard Wing, a Cantonese-American orderly and cook; and James Shepley, a reporter on leave from *Time* who was, in a peer's judgment, "never at a loss for any answer to anything." For Marshall, it was not a familiar team. He was going, Katherine lamented, "without anyone to be close to him—whom he had known and depended on."

They had spent the journey plotting his first moves. Shepley and Byroade observed that Mao would not give up control of his insurgent armies until the Communists had a secure place in a transformed government. Chiang, however, would not share real political power until Mao had given up his armies. They sketched out a rough plan to get around this impasse. First Marshall would press the two sides to agree to a cease-fire and interim government, with Mao, Shepley suggested, taking on the role of Chiang's deputy. Then Mao would surrender his forces "to bona fide control of the Central Government . . . not too much to expect from the Communists if Chiang gives them a voice in a coalition government." From there, American money and advisers would back a long-term effort to secure a stable peace, build a true democratic government, and reconstruct a war-ruined China. The odds of this working might not be especially high, they acknowledged, but it was the best they could do.

Marshall's first stop in China had been Shanghai. A Nationalist honor guard saluted him as he landed. Flag-waving crowds lined the ten-mile route to the Cathay Hotel, the lush Art Deco bastion that housed the postwar U.S. headquarters. American and Chinese officers toasted him with cocktails. But once the toasts were over, he met with Wedemeyer, the polished, handsome, and ambitious commander of U.S. troops, and Walter Robertson, the senior American diplomat in China. They related the same grim message that had dominated their recent reports to Washington—the two sides were implacably hostile, the Communists were intent on power, Stalin was backing Mao, Chiang's government was alienating the people, his commanders were inept. As ever, the problem was what else could be done. Contemplating the alternatives led back to the same basic formula: bolstering Chiang's government while promoting a settlement and pressing for reform.

The next day, Marshall continued inland to Nanjing, where Chiang himself was waiting. Before the Japanese onslaught drove his government to its redoubt in Chongqing, Nanjing had been the capital of Chiang's Republican China; soon it would be again. Chiang had overhauled it on the model of Paris and Washington to be "a source of energy for the whole nation" and "a role model for the whole world." There, he would look like the leader of a great power, a head of state to be approached with respect, not the equal of a "bandit" like Mao. When Chiang found the Nanjing airfield unpresentable the morning of Marshall's arrival, he was furious.

After flouting protocol to greet him on the runway, Chiang took Marshall to his house in the city, with Madame Chiang Kai-shek, in fur, sitting between them in the back of the car. They talked until almost midnight, Wedemeyer listening and Madame Chiang translating.

"I should make him realize," Chiang had written in his diary that morning, "that the U.S. and China share the same stake." He focused on the Soviets, hoping to persuade Marshall that "we cannot emulate Eastern Europe or Yugoslavia and set up coalition government under the guise of 'fake' democracy." Marshall wanted to reassure Chiang that he bore no grudge over the Stilwell affair. But he also wanted to convey the importance of American public opinion—for American policy and, by extension, for Chiang's own prospects. Americans were "warmly disposed" toward Chiang's government. They hoped to see him succeed. But whether that lasted, Marshall warned, hinged "almost entirely upon the United States public appreciation of the reasonableness and determination on the part of both sides to reach satisfactory settlement." Chiang said he appreciated the candor; he would do all he could, "in spite of the past," pursuing a political solution as long as the Communists proved willing to give up their armies. Marshall added that while he would listen objectively to all sides, he would share his personal views with Chiang alone.

"I sensed that he made an excellent impression," Wedemeyer wrote of Marshall afterward, in a letter to Patrick Hurley. Marshall's "deference" had been "remarkable." Chiang registered Marshall's respect for his leadership ("he will advise only me") and apparent wariness of Communist aims and "deceptive propaganda." Chiang summarized in his diary: "The more deferential we are to the Communist Party, the more advantageous it is to us, and the easier to materialize Truman's aims." It was the conclusion Marshall had wanted him to reach.

But here in Chongqing such commitments would be put to the test. As Marshall's plane approached, the mood at the airfield was far from joyous. Government agents tried to chase away the Communists, stopping only after American officials stepped in, a trivial yet telling reflection of broader hostilities. Still, many hoped "that Marshall will fix everything," as John Melby put it. Newspapers were reporting an instantaneous lull in fighting. Both sides had released optimistic statements of welcome.

When he stepped off the plane into the mud and the gray, Marshall said little. A band played the Chinese and American national anthems. He greeted T. V. Soong, Chiang's Harvard-educated brother-in-law, and Zhou Enlai, the Communist representative in Chongqing, and then drove off toward the city.

Melby wondered: "Is Marshall more than a great soldier and a fine man?"

Although few people remarked on it at the time, Marshall had lived in China before. For three years in the 1920s, he served in the Fifteenth

Infantry Regiment in Tianjin, a coastal city southeast of Beijing. The Fifteenth was one of the most coveted assignments in the army. "In China one can live like a prince-of-the-blood on the pay of a second lieutenant," reported the *Infantry Journal*. Marshall's first wife, Lily, had relished the posting: "Everyone over there lives in the most unbelievable luxury. Beautiful houses—wonderful food—& tremendously gay & interesting." (A Virginia beauty with a faulty heart, Lily died shortly after their China sojourn.) There was a country club, a tennis club, a polo field, an ice rink, a dancing pavilion, and a lively cocktail bar, all with a pleasing air of late-imperial glamor. There was also, as Marshall noted with concern, an abundance of "cheap liquor and cheaper women—Chinese, Japanese, Russian, Korean." The Fifteenth was said to have record rates of venereal disease.

The draw for Marshall, however, was the prospect of "interesting events." China had been in a state of almost continuous upheaval for decades. Since the Qing Dynasty's defeat in the First Opium War in 1842, foreign powers had grabbed territory and wealth, extracted imperial privileges, and otherwise done whatever they could to curtail China's sovereignty. Internal uprisings—the heavenly kingdom of the Taipings, the secret societies of the Boxers—compounded the instability. And the end of the Qing in 1912 had brought not a new order, not the triumph of Sun Yat-sen's republican vision, but new chaos, with warlords and regional armies vying for dominance. Foreign powers fed on the disorder and deepened it, a vicious cycle that seemed likely to consume China.

The Fifteenth was hardly unimplicated in this record of humiliation. Americans might not have liked to see it that way. Surely, they thought, we are not like the imperial powers, whose troops guard concessions they claim as their own. But to many Chinese, the 1,000 men in Marshall's regiment, on Chinese soil to protect American interests, were as much an occupying army as the British or French.

"We are in the midst of a Chinese civil war," the 43-year-old Marshall wrote home after arriving in Tianjin, and he thought himself "very lucky" to be there to see it. With guns sounding in the distance, he had his troops guarding rail lines and clearing blockades. ("Can do" was the regiment's motto.) He observed warlord armies marching by and tried to trace the webs of alliance and betrayal. He learned that the effectiveness of Chinese forces depended "on leadership and ability to secure pay for troops," and that "a Chinese soldier will go farther on a dough ball than an American soldier on a full ration." He also registered the human toll of civil war. One Christmas morning, he watched refugees crawl down the road like "animals hunted to exhaustion."

He studied the language and ordered other officers to do the same, so they could carry out their work "without provoking the fatal first shot." Before long, he related proudly, he knew 2,500 characters and could "grunt and whine intelligible Chinese," whether to "discuss treaty rights" or to decipher "the wranglings and squabbles of the coolies and rickshaw men." He wrote a friend, "I am getting to be quite a Chinaman now."

Yet the more Marshall saw, the more he realized how much he did not understand. In China, he wrote his mentor, General Pershing, "you can rarely judge by surface or apparent conditions. The real scheming is entirely beneath the surface." Amid chaos, "no one ventures to predict just what is to happen. Chinese methods are too devious for foreign penetration."

But one development was clear: nationalism was on the rise, with ominous implications for foreign privilege. To Marshall, the question was whether "a strong man combining the qualities of statesman, politician, and military chief" could harness a nationalist vision to real power. As he was finishing his tour, a force in southern China, the Kuomintang, looked increasingly capable of doing so. Its armies were making their way north, taking territory, co-opting and crushing warlords, occupying cities—including, just before Marshall returned home, the cosmopolitan metropolis of Shanghai. Their leader was a 39-year-old military commander named Chiang Kai-shek.

Chiang had a powerful sense of his own destiny. "Profound change first of all depends on one or two persons who manage deeply, delicately, and silently, then their successors join in and God responds to their call," he copied in his diary while still in his mid-thirties. "Can you believe that I regard myself as one of those one or two persons?"

He had, like Marshall, a ferocious will, impelled by brutal self-criticism. He compiled lists of his flaws: he was "conceited," "stubborn," "jealous," "arrogant," "extravagant," "stingy," "lascivious," "ruthless," "tyrannical." To overcome those flaws, he demanded "meticulous self-control." Every morning, he stood on his verandah, arms crossed, and contemplated his goals for the day. He, like Marshall, "loved to make decisions." And he had a temper that, like Marshall, he struggled to suppress.

Born to a merchant family south of Shanghai, Chiang grew up steeped in the duty and discipline of Confucianism; his given name, Kai-shek, meant "upright stone." He also grew up feeling his country's humiliation as his own. Ashamed of weakness, he fixated on power and how to win it. He studied military strategy in Japan, whose new-found superiority in such matters was both a model and a disgrace for proud Chinese. There, "utter depression" drove him to "riotous living," and he developed a taste for high-end prostitutes, resulting in an infection that left him sterile. (He already had a son with his first wife, to whom his parents had married him at 14.) Soon, however, that dissolution gave way to single-minded devotion to a cause greater than himself. He started eating simply, and drinking boiled water instead of alcohol. "From this day on," he pledged, "I will rise out of bed at six o'clock. I will remind myself of this humiliation and continue to do so until the national humiliation is wiped away completely." His cause was the renewal of Chinese greatness, and his leader in this cause was Sun Yat-sen.

Chiang had obvious value to Sun, the leader of China's republican movement. Sun's vision of a Chinese republic, founded on the Three People's Principles of democracy, nationalism, and "people's livelihood," had helped topple the Qing, but in the turmoil that followed, warriors proved to have the advantage over visionaries. When Sun's Nationalist party, the Kuomintang, won elections, a militarist rival dissolved parliament. Discovered as a willful young officer, Chiang rose quickly, becoming commandant of the party's military academy, Whampoa. And after Sun died in 1925, Chiang was well positioned to take charge and set about unifying China himself—not by the appeal of Nationalist principles, but by the force of Nationalist arms.

While Western governments fretted about their ascent, the Nationalists had looked to other patrons—the Soviets. Sun had dispatched Chiang to Moscow, bearing letters for Lenin and Trotsky, to discuss strategy and cultivate support. The Kremlin complied, sending money and advisers. This patronage had come with a condition—accepting members of the newly formed Chinese Communist Party into Nationalist ranks—but it was one Sun thought reasonable. A young party member named Mao Zedong took over the Peasant Movement Training Institute, while another, Zhou Enlai, became Chiang's deputy for political affairs. (Also on staff was a young Vietnamese nationalist who would become known as Ho Chi Minh.) Soviet advisers even worried that Chiang, who had sent his son to their country to study at the University of the Toilers of the East, was showing excessive favoritism to Communists at Whampoa; they feared it might backfire.

In fact, Chiang had doubts about this united front, and over time they grew. His three months in Moscow had left him wary of the Soviets. "I treat them with sincerity but they reciprocate with deceit," he wrote in his diary. They, in turn, came to find him too proud, too sensitive to slights against him and his nation; one Soviet official described him as "a peculiar person with peculiar characteristics, most prominent of those being his lust for glory and power and craving to be the hero of China." He began to fear the Kremlin would turn on him, and he was right to worry. "Chiang Kai-shek," Stalin said, would be "squeezed out like a lemon and then flung away." So after seizing Shanghai in April 1927, a key victory in his push north, Chiang enlisted a criminal syndicate called the Green Gang and purged his erstwhile Communist allies. Thousands were killed; Zhou, his Whampoa deputy, barely escaped, with an $80,000 bounty on his head.

"The Japanese are a disease of the skin, the Communists are a disease of the heart," Chiang took to saying. (Ernest Hemingway commented after visiting, "Personally, I have known no disease of the heart which has ever been cured by such a violent means.") Yet in the wake of the purge and military campaign, there was reason to think that this disease of the heart could be eradicated before long. The Communists were stuck in minor enclaves or on the run; Generalissimo Chiang was settling into his new capital in Nanjing, taking his place at the head of a new Chinese republic.

Over the next ten years, he achieved things no leader had for decades. He brought much of China under one government. He put in place pieces of a modern state: common currency, updated laws, expanded education. There were problems, to be sure. Unity rested on deals with opportunistic warlords and regional leaders, and was held together with corruption, cajoling, and violence. Control required playing faction against faction, maintaining constant suspicion, and frequently privileging loyalty over effectiveness. Supposed commitments to measures such as land reform—the foremost demand of the rural masses— were blocked by reactionary supporters. But whatever the unstable and unsavory alliances, whatever Chiang's autocratic tendencies, the achievements were real. "After a long waiting and desperate search," admitted a former opponent, "we, to our great joy, have at long last found our Leader."

Chiang had also found a partner in his cause. After years of infatuation, he persuaded Soong Mei-ling, a sister of Sun Yat-sen's widow, to become his third wife. Soon famous to the world as Madame Chiang, Mei-ling was unlike other women he knew: educated, opinionated, physically beautiful, intellectually fierce—and, like Sun, Christian. To win her hand, Chiang promised to convert, and Methodism became another element in his idiosyncratic worldview. In his imperfect Mandarin (it was not his native dialect), he told followers that only by embracing "the traditional virtues and the traditional spirits . . . will we be able to revive the highest culture of our nation, to restore our nation's very special standing in this world." Yet he also read the bible daily and wrote in his diary about "bear[ing] the cross along with Jesus." And for many Americans, Chiang did become a messianic figure. "The Chinese have understood that the signs portended vast upheaval and out of the anguish would come the man to lead them," Henry Luce proclaimed. "He has come."

Then, in 1937, came Japan's assault. In certain ways, war enhanced Chiang's stature, and thanks to adept diplomacy, his nation's. Foreign powers went from treating China as a virtual colony to recognizing it as a unitary state that stretched almost as far as it had in its imperial heyday, to include Manchuria, Tibet, and Xinjiang in the far west (Outer Mongolia was given up in exchange for Stalin's support). Chiang, his champions could claim, had made China great again.

But mostly war meant ruin—for the people, landscape, and economy, and for Chiang's national endeavor. It was not just the brutality of Japan's Three Alls policy: kill all, burn all, loot all. It was not just the lethality: some 15 million dead, along with perhaps 80 million displaced. War halted nation-building, and then shattered much of what Chiang had built. The demands of conflict strained government finances, triggering high inflation and crushing taxes. Warlords withdrew their support, and Chiang, one dispatch reported, began "trusting no one but himself." There were new opportunities for elite corruption—aid to be siphoned, black markets to be cornered—and new causes for popular resentment, as peasants sent their sons and crops to the army while officials and landlords sacrificed little. Millions died in a "man-made famine," the rich feasting as the poor starved. Half a million drowned, and millions were left homeless, when Chiang blasted the Yellow River dikes, flooding an area larger than Switzerland to slow a Japanese advance—an act so shocking that even enemies had a hard time believing he had done it. By the end, industry and agriculture were decimated, cholera, plague, and malaria rampant, and the people, an American official assessed, "seething with unrest."

With the war over, his 60th birthday a year away, Chiang reflected. "Fifty years of national humiliation, as well as the indignities and insults I have endured, are being washed away," he wrote. Yet "while old wrongs have passed into history, we are in danger of being engulfed by new ones."

The question now was whether Marshall's arrival would lessen that danger or heighten it.

Some of Chiang's closest advisers thought the latter. "Marshall is too big," warned Chen Li-fu, leader of the Nationalists' uncompromising conservative wing. "He will force a solution." Chen feared that failure might be unacceptable to such a towering figure.

But Chiang himself was mostly heartened. He reasoned that Truman would not have called on Marshall if the United States did not consider China important. After a Chinese envoy was promptly invited to Moscow for talks, Chiang concluded that Stalin must think the same. Truman's public directive was also reassuring: "not in line with the Communist Party's wishes, and therefore beneficial to my state."

Most heartening of all, a secret report had come from the Chinese embassy in Washington. The confidential deliberations in the White House had not been as confidential as Marshall thought. Someone leaked a key detail to Chiang's ambassador, a detail omitted from not just the public directive, but the private one as well. A message went to the Generalissimo: "When Marshall asked the President what to do if the Chinese Communists do not knuckle under or if our government is not willing to accept the Communists' conditions for being included in the government, the President answered, support your excellency." Marshall's bluff was already exposed.

Chongqing had been swollen, battered, and transfigured by war. Long considered a backwater, "an utterly feudal place full of opium and gambling," its rocky hills and steep river banks were now crowded with Chinese from all walks of life: peasants and workers with nothing, high officials with briefcases and Buicks, industrialists who had floated whole factories down the Yangtze to keep them from the Japanese. "It was as if a county seat of Kentucky mountaineers had suddenly been called to play host to all the most feverishly dynamic New Yorkers,

Texans, and Californians," an American reporter explained. The city's population, a few hundred thousand before, had quadrupled.

Unable to penetrate mountainous Szechuan by land, Japan had sent punishment by air, and Chongqing's suffering became famous. "Fathers, mothers watched their children burnt alive," Madame Chiang wrote an American friend, "children saw their parents struggling to fight across the flames only to disappear in the ruins of falling beams and pillars." So, too, the wartime capital's fortitude in the face of suffering. Chongqing, declared the U.S. Army's *Pocket Guide to China*, "is the most bombed out city in the world. Yet the people go on." Its inhabitants would crowd into shelters when an air raid started, then wash their clothes in bomb craters when it stopped. "They are unbeatable," arriving Americans were told.

Before long, however, most newcomers started complaining. "The prevailing Chinese attitude toward Americans in Chongqing is hatred; the prevailing American attitude toward Chinese is bitter hatred," said a U.S. intelligence report. In part the complaints were about the scheming and suspicion, the "rather medieval court intrigue." But even more, they were about the stench and noise, the cold winters and hot summers, the chaos and cultural friction—or as a general quipped, the "yells, bells, and smells."

John Melby had come after the war, fresh from a diplomatic posting in Moscow and charged with keeping tabs on Soviet activity in China. Letters to his mistress—Lillian Hellman, a prominent left-wing writer for Broadway and Hollywood, almost ten years his elder and also married—were litanies of woe: "a dreary expanse of mud and bedraggled Chinamen"; "you feel that never again can you get warm or dried out"; the available liquor was "a local gin which I simply cannot get down." A navy doctor warned new arrivals they would get "a postgraduate course in respiratory troubles" thanks to the fumes of burning coal and raw sewage that infused the fog. "Really the most foul sanitary place I've ever seen," an officer wrote in his diary. "No wonder they die by the millions." The Americans griped about rats, peddlers, and power outages, and the squeals of pigs slaughtered in the streets. They mocked mistranslations ("Sing Sing High Class Tailor—Ladies May Have Fits Upstairs") and spouted expatriate clichés ("Time means nothing"). Soldiers tore around in jeeps, spraying filth.

On the afternoon of his arrival, Marshall was driven through streets of deep brown mud, past bamboo shacks on stilts along the rivers and newer buildings painted black against Japanese bombers, and up a hill to a gray stone bungalow that was an odd hybrid of Western and Chinese styles. With the incongruous name of Happiness Gardens and the uncommon luxury of a semi-reliable water heater (T. V. Soong had lived there before), the house was to serve as mission headquarters. There were bedrooms for Marshall and his staff upstairs, the river visible below when the fog cleared. On the first floor, there was a living room where he could work by a fireplace and a curving bay window that overlooked the teeming city outside.

Marshall was met with an immediate barrage of invitations, appeals, warnings, suggestions, and supplications. The point of not becoming the official ambassador was to avoid such a crush. But official or not, Marshall was, one American remarked, China's white hope. Moreover, both press speculation and official chatter were rife with rumors that this mission was a prelude to some bigger job, maybe secretary of state. It was no surprise that half of Chongqing seemed to want to see or sway him.

"You arrive here just in time to save China from falling a prey to the civil wars," one correspondent wrote. "We are mad with joy when hear of your arrival," fawned another. A group of "sincere Christians" invoked Roosevelt's Four Freedoms to condemn Chiang's "terror." Others denounced Mao's "treachery" and said they preferred death to Communist rule. Marshall heard from postal workers, mill workers, engineers, farmers, soldiers, and a group of self-described "poorly educated Chinese women." His former "number one boy" from Tianjin wrote to request the cigarette concession at an American base; his former cook wanted the "privilege of collecting garbage" there, so he could sell it as scrap. An English-speaking man, knowing Marshall was a voracious reader, asked for his discarded novels, since "I am a big reader too . . . and long for new ones." One woman asked if she could borrow his airplane to visit her parents.

Messages also flooded in from across the Pacific. Senators wanted favors for constituents. Chinese-Americans wanted help locating relatives. Mothers wanted updates on soldier sons. A man from White Plains, New York, wanted the creation of "a great Christian republic in China." There were offers of honorary degrees and board seats, reminders of birthday messages and payments on the Oldsmobile Marshall was buying for retirement, requests for interviews and autographs. Churchill asked for a signed picture, "which I should cherish with the happy memories of our association during these last strenuous but glorious years." A former colleague sent a four-leaf clover.

The American diplomats and officers stationed in Chongqing, meanwhile, were anxious to see what Marshall would do now that he was here. They had been pulling the relevant files on Chinese politics, economics, and military affairs for his background, but most knew little about the mission beyond what was in public statements. The uncertainty was especially nerve-racking given how poisonous the official scene was, thanks to years of Hurley's accusations and Stilwell's barbs, not to mention the constant coming and going of operatives from various American intelligence outfits—in the words of one diplomat, "a pungent collection of thugs, post-debutantes, millionaires, professors, corporation lawyers, professional military, and misfits, all operating under high tension and in whispers." When Melby got to Chongqing shortly before Marshall, he was struck immediately by the "gestapo atmosphere," relating to Hellman, "Every officer here has taken me aside and given me advice on what I can say to whom and who should be trusted and who spies for whom." The result was not just personal unpleasantness, but also diplomatic paralysis. "Everything seems bitched up," he concluded. "There just ain't no policy any more. Just fiddling."

Although only 32, with a wry smile and receding hairline, Melby was cynical by nature, skeptical of both Soviet promises—he had spent the war in Moscow assuming he was always trailed or bugged—and his own country's self-serving myths. On top of that, he was lovelorn. "I wish to Christ I had never heard of China or any place else except where you are," he wrote Hellman.

Yet even Melby found cause for optimism in the selection of Marshall—"a natural for it, not something drawn from a hat." Ivan Yeaton, an army colonel whose time heading the Dixie Mission in Yenan had fanned his anti-Communism, also took comfort: "I feel that a national hero such as he would never be sent here at this time just to be destroyed."

To start, Marshall wanted to listen, to absorb as many facts and perspectives as he could. He recognized his mission was just the latest chapter in a long, intricate record of collaboration, betrayal, bloodshed, and negotiation between the Nationalists and Communists, including most recently the six weeks Mao had spent in Chongqing at Stalin's behest. The military situation was also complex, notwithstanding the upbeat headlines in American newspapers. ("All Fighting Ceases in China's Civil War" the *Washington Post* splashed across eight columns as Marshall was en route.) With U.S. help, the Nationalists had established a commanding presence in major cities and started making their way to southern Manchuria in preparation for Soviet withdrawal. Yet the Communists had a strong base in the north, centered in Yenan, a growing presence in Manchuria (thanks to intermittently active Soviet help), and a guerrilla network that posed a threat to railway and supply lines across much of China. Generals from both armies were maneuvering for position, while officials plotted to gain advantage in the coming negotiation. To further complicate matters, millions of defeated Japanese had yet to be shipped home, the ostensible primary function of American troops in China.

Both sides had been applauding Truman's statement. "We are gratified," said an official newspaper, "that the wishes of the National Government are exactly what is expected by the United States." Chiang asserted that if only Washington had said all this before, "the Communists would not have been so rambunctious." Communist spokesmen hailed progress in U.S. policy. But both sides were emphasizing the elements of the policy that best served them, overinterpreting particular points to their own benefit. The government praised Truman's condemnation of autonomous armies, the Communists his condemnation of one-party government. Melby summed it up with characteristic sarcasm: "All official attitudes here today rejoice in the great wisdom and understanding about China which has come from the lips of the great man from Missouri."

On Marshall's first full day in Chongqing, December 23, Zhou Enlai arrived in the afternoon for a meeting. Zhou had spent the war as Yenan's emissary to both the Nationalist government and, more consequentially, the community of foreign diplomats, reporters, and military officers stationed in the capital.

The Communists' praise of Truman's statement—and Marshall's arrival—was not just propaganda. "The U.S. has already decided not to intervene directly in the Chinese civil war," the CCP concluded from the statement. "Instead it is supporting China's peaceful unification." The CCP's strategy, accordingly, was to "make use of Truman's statement" for its own advantage. Party officials started insisting they had no problem with American troops and no interest in "Russian-style Communism in China." Party members were told to improve their relationships with Americans. When six downed U.S. airmen were handed over from CCP custody to U.S. officials in Tianjin, the consul reported, "Communist attitude recently changed to friendliness toward the U.S.A." Mao instructed Zhou to demonstrate flexibility in his dealings with the new envoy. "If Marshall uses the opportunity, the Communists will throw themselves in the lap of the U.S.," a dispatch from the Dixie Mission predicted.

Zhou was well suited to this diplomatic offensive, and he turned his charisma on Marshall as soon as they sat down that afternoon. Zhou talked about Lincoln's spirit of freedom and Washington's spirit of independence. He cited the power of the American model of government, the achievements of American agriculture, and the importance of American commerce. He stressed his party's interest in peace and democracy, in terms that struck Marshall as more hopeful and less qualified than those of Nationalist spokesmen. He emphasized that demobilization of Communist armies depended on democratization of the government but did not contest Chiang's leadership. He criticized Wedemeyer's continuing transport of government troops, arguing that it violated Truman's dictate against fratricidal warfare, but did not make a scene when Marshall reiterated the United States' commitment to helping Chiang's armies enter Manchuria. At the end, they toasted: Marshall to "generous understanding," Zhou to "lasting freedom." The meeting, Zhou said afterward, had been delightful.

Marshall revealed little in these first days. He spent hour after hour receiving visitors and listening—to anyone, he said, "who has a genuine interest in the settlement of China's problems." High-minded liberals came to tell him about their efforts to chart a course between the government and the Communists; "we have called, America has answered," said the University of Wisconsin–educated leader of one of the "third parties." T. V. Soong, currently Chiang's premier, came to ask if Marshall needed help with anything, and Marshall responded with a string of questions: "Where do you get coal?" "Where does your rice come from?" "What is behind your currency?" "Very roughly what do you need in freight cars?" And what, he wondered, were the similarities and differences between Soviet methods in Asia and in Europe? Others came to deliver messages in secret—dissident government figures, women afraid of reprisals from one group or another. "I have read a good deal and have listened," Marshall said, "but I have got to listen more."

On his second full day, December 24, Marshall agreed to meet with reporters at the American embassy. Still he revealed nothing. It would be "foolish" to try to answer any real questions, he pointed out, since "it will be some time before I can hope to get a fair picture of China." Reporters came away with so little that they resorted to including in their stories the number of rain-slicked steps he had climbed to the embassy—118—after declining to be carried in a sedan chair. They got little more when they tracked down people who had been to see him at his house. He had "expressed no opinion," they were told. With so little in the way of facts, and so great an appetite for information about the great man and what he was doing, the papers took to printing rumors, many false: Marshall will have a cease-fire by Christmas; he has "a special fancy for flowers."

Marshall's silence drove Chongqing officialdom, Chinese and American, to the brink of panic. "Marshall has this entire country in a stew by the simple expedient of not saying anything or reacting when he is asked a question," Melby wrote. "He just sits and listens impassively, breaking his silence only occasionally to ask a question." When an interlocutor tried to provoke some response, he would politely refuse to take the bait.

Some people noticed that Marshall, though now a diplomat, continued to wear the uniform of a general. That must be meant to convey something, they thought, though as with his words and countenance, no one was sure exactly what.

It was Chongqing's first Christmas since the war, and the exuberant holiday social calendar seemed like a boon for the cause of peace. Enemies and friends crowded into the same liquor-soaked affairs. "Women Communists were dancing with Kuomintang Ministers," a correspondent wrote, and "Russians and Americans were pledging boundless friendship over glasses of Chongqing gin fizz." Marshall made his first public appearance at a Christmas Eve party thrown by an American general. Officers of various militaries and diplomats of various embassies sipped eggnog and watched him have a fifteen-minute conversation with the Soviet ambassador before moving on to the Zhous. Marshall appeared "to handle the Communists well," Melby observed.

On Christmas Day, it was Chiang's turn to host. The setting was sumptuous—thick rugs, delicate vases—and the Chiangs always made for a striking pair: the Generalissimo, head closely shaved and face still except for quick dark eyes, distinguished in a belted tunic buttoned to the neck; his wife elegant in her fitted Chinese dress and spiky heels. Guests were fascinated to see Marshall and Chiang together, both straight-backed and stoic, Marshall a head taller and a few years older. But the real star of the party, as of most parties she attended, was the 47-year-old Mei-ling. "He puts on a good show," an American officer said, but "it's a second-rate show without her."

By now Madame Chiang was an icon for Americans, noble or sinister according to taste. In the press, she was China's Martha Washington, an Almond-Eyed Cleopatra. In the U.S. Congress, she was China's Joan of Arc, its Florence Nightingale. Her U.S. military code names included both Zeus and Snow White.

Western men fixated on her looks—more "*Vogue* cover than the avenging angel of 422,000,000 people," judged a reporter—and in particular on her legs. At Cairo, where she was the lone woman in the high councils of war, they elicited "a suppressed neigh" from the younger officers, the British military chief recorded in his diary. Even the hard-charging journalist Martha Gellhorn, traveling in wartime China on her honeymoon with Ernest Hemingway, noted the "lovely legs," reflecting, "She is so delightful to look at . . . that you forget you are talking to the second ruler of China." Indeed, Madame Chiang had learned how to take the Orientalist fantasies projected onto her and use them to her own ends. Though she expressed dismay when told she had "sex appeal," she could, Gellhorn wrote, "charm the birds off the trees, and she knows exactly what appeals to each kind of bird." Even Stilwell was susceptible. "You have a man's job ahead of you," Madame Chiang told him, "but you are a man—and shall I add—what a man!" He reciprocated with what was for him high praise: that given her forceful personality, she should be minister of war.

Like her husband, Madame Chiang had a backstory uniquely of her time. Charlie Soong, her Chinese-born father, studied theology at Vanderbilt University and returned home to save souls. But after experiencing the condescension of white missionaries, he redirected his energies: first toward getting rich, then toward the work of Sun Yat-sen. His money funded Sun's party. His enthusiasm for the Gettysburg Address—government of the people, by the people, for the people— inspired Sun's Three People's Principles. His eldest daughter became Sun's wife. Eventually, his youngest daughter married Sun's successor.

Before that, Mei-ling had gotten her education in America. She went first to New Jersey and Georgia, and then to Wellesley College in Massachusetts, to be near her brother T. V. at Harvard. Even with her "Scarlett O'Hara accent," she became popular and admired on campus. She excelled in philosophy and English literature, winning the class of 1917's top academic prize. She grew to be vivacious, ambitious, and self-assuredly intelligent, with "a first-class masculine brain," it was said, and "an almost terrifying charm and poise."

When she returned to China and struggled to figure out what to do with all of this, partnership with the Generalissimo helped provide an answer. "Our wedding," Chiang wrote her, "is a symbol of the reconstruction of Chinese society." He credited her with half his achievements. In danger, he summoned a line from the Book of Jeremiah: The Lord shall make a woman protect a man. He called her "da," a shortened version of what she called him—darling.

With the coming of war, her purpose became clearer. If she had a split identity, as so many claimed—"Madame's body was born in China, but her mind was born in America"—she would make it a weapon. She would fan the illusions Americans held about China and about themselves. She would give them the heroes they wanted. And she would do it all in her "flawless, tumbling, forthright *American*," as Clare Boothe Luce, a Republican congresswoman and the wife of Henry Luce, described her speech. When Madame Chiang toured the United States to rally support, 17,000 people came to Madison Square Garden, 30,000 to the Hollywood Bowl—among them Rita Hayworth, Shirley Temple, and Ingrid Bergman. She reminded businessmen about the size of China's market. When Roosevelt pledged to send China more aid "as soon as the Lord will let us," she replied with a smile, in front of 172 reporters, "The Lord helps those who help themselves." She was the second-ever woman to address both houses of Congress. "We welcome you as a daughter is welcomed by her foster-mother," said a legislator. After rapturous applause, a bill to abolish the exclusion laws was introduced. Newspapers deemed her "the world's most powerful woman."

The adulation brought a backlash. There were stories about her nasty behavior at the White House, the president calling her "a prima donna" and the first lady, seeing her treatment of the staff, cracking, "She can talk beautifully about democracy, but she does not know how to live democracy." There were stories about the Soong family's greed and corruption, their untold riches flown out of China. (Intelligence reports affirmed that certain family members, especially Mei-ling's brother-in-law H. H. Kung, were doing well off war; a State Department official claimed that T. V. Soong was "the greatest crook in the world.") There was gossip about strife and infidelity in the heroic marriage, so pervasive that it appeared in official reports: she hit Chiang with a vase; he impregnated a mistress.

By the time Marshall arrived in Chongqing, he was familiar with all of this—the attacks, the acclaim, and the reasons for both. He had met Madame Chiang in Washington and in Cairo. Although he recognized her allure, he was not especially taken in by it. More than her allure, he recognized her value. During the war, her influence over Chiang had more often than not been to the good. Now, Marshall hoped she would have the same effect in peacetime. Already it was clear that Chiang wanted her, and often only her, by his side whenever he and Marshall met: to interpret, to intercede when she saw her husband taking the wrong approach, to smooth the rough edges of his proud stubbornness.

When the Christmas party was over, Marshall crossed the river with the Chiangs to spend the evening at their country house. Chiang felt at ease among the tall pines and mist-covered hills, his face occasionally even relaxing into what Roosevelt had called a "delightful smile." Chiang was gratified to see that Marshall continued to treat him with respect—"massage his ego" was Wedemeyer's advice on handling Chiang—and the conversation centered on a welcome topic, the Soviet Union. The more they talked about the Soviets, the better. Chiang needed Americans to see Mao's menace and Stalin's machinations as a single threat that the U.S. and Chinese governments had to face down together. When Marshall asked about the extent to which Moscow was behind Yenan's activities and the nature of its ambitions in Manchuria, Chiang took it as a very good sign—and an encouraging ending to Marshall's first days in China, which had gone about as well as he could have realistically hoped. There was a discordant note: Marshall still seemed insufficiently skeptical of Stalin. But going forward, Chiang thought he could make Marshall see.

When Marshall sat down a few days later to draft a classified message to the president, he too was more hopeful than he had been for a while. He took the time to write the report himself and directed his rear echelon, his man in Washington, to deliver it to the Oval Office by hand. Otherwise, he explained in justifying this inconvenience, they risked the "possibility of a leak which might greatly embarrass if not hazard the success of my mission." Other than Truman, Byrnes, and Acheson, no one was supposed to see his dispatches.

In this first one, Marshall reviewed for the president his long days of listening—to Nationalists and Communists and "third party" liberals, to diplomats and students and missionaries and journalists. He related that Chiang "had little to say regarding Communists and much to say regarding Russians." But he "has been most friendly and I have endeavored to avoid posture of cracking the whip." As for the rest, "all agree to leadership of Generalissimo and to high-sounding principles or desires for a more democratic government, a coalition government, and reorganized and completely nationalized army." The details of how these objectives would be reached were another matter, Marshall conceded, but the parties "appear to be struggling to a more realistic point of view." He was getting ready, he told the president, to begin the real work of his mission.

That same day, an auspicious message arrived from Moscow. Marshall had radioed Secretary of State Byrnes for news of the summit there, particularly anything that would indicate "Soviet intent in Man-churia and regarding Chinese Communists." Byrnes replied that it had not been an easy conference overall, but not because of China. Once he previewed Marshall's approach, including the option of threaten-ing to withhold aid from Chiang, and explained that there was no rea-son to fear the U.S. troops in north China, he heard little complaint. Stalin belittled Chinese Communist strength ("All Chinese are boast-ers," he would say) and offered no objection when reminded of his past dismissals of their revolutionary seriousness ("The Chinese Commu-nists are not real Communists. They are 'margarine' Communists"). The Soviets, Byrnes concluded, "will not intentionally do anything to destroy our efforts for a unified China." They would withdraw the Red Army from Manchuria by February—after plundering its resources and securing the quasi-imperial privilege the Kremlin wanted—and other-wise stay out of China's problems.

Stalin, Marshall was informed, was likely to follow his recommen-dations on the assumption that if anyone could find a solution to the whole mess, he could. Stalin had observed that Marshall was turning out to be both a soldier and a statesman.

CHAPTER 4

The Committee of Three

At 4 o'clock in the morning on the first day of 1946, a 33-year-old colonel named John Hart Caughey was awakened by military police in Shanghai and ordered to get to Chongqing as fast as he could. Caughey was already unsure what to make of this new year. He was in an army that was no longer fighting but would not send him home. He was in a country where a war had ended but peace had not yet arrived. A few hours earlier, just after midnight, the flow of traffic had reversed. Drivers, bicyclists, and rickshaw pullers across China were ordered to switch from the left side of the road to the right, since a surge in American-made vehicles operating under British-inspired traffic rules had caused accidents to spike. The switch promised improved safety, maybe someday a fruitful partnership between American car manufacturers and Chinese car buyers, but on this day it meant confusion.

By 6 o'clock that evening, Caughey was in Chongqing, reporting to General Marshall himself. Marshall had been there for ten days and still revealed little. "He just sits and listens," a diplomat said, giving people "the creeps." At his 65th birthday dinner the evening before—Chiang invited 150 guests but told his staff not to make it too lavish, knowing the honoree's austerity—Marshall's toast was so subdued that some Nationalist officials took offense.

But Marshall was getting ready to act, and he needed a team. He had brought the three aides—knowing Jim Shepley, ambitious Hank Byroade, and cook and orderly Richard Wing. But he was accustomed to having the entire War Department behind him, and becoming aware of the full complexity of the task before him now. So he began enlisting others. Hart Caughey would become his executive officer; a quietly efficient standout on Wedemeyer's staff who was from Marshall's part of southwestern Pennsylvania, the clean-cut, square-jawed Caughey had been an Eagle Scout, a star at West Point, and a good enough baseball player that the New York Giants had tried him out at first base. The diplomats at the embassy, including John Melby, would draft analyses for Marshall. Dismayed to find that the Cantonese-American interpreter assigned to him could barely understand Zhou Enlai's Mandarin, Marshall tracked down a Chinese-born American intelligence officer named John Soong who was about to return to Chicago to complete a doctorate; Soong's return was delayed indefinitely, and his new wife and infant son were told to join him in Chongqing. Happiness Gardens started to buzz as Marshall prepared his moves.

Over the previous days, Caughey had mused about Marshall's prospects. He wrote long letters to his wife, Betty, in South Carolina, full of worry about "the seeds of the next war." On his flight, as the plane dropped through thick clouds above Chongqing, he anticipated seeing "a lonely man this evening, one who is shadow boxing in the midst of Chinese pressures."

Then Caughey met him. "I've never seen or been in the presence of a man like Gen. Marshall," he gushed. "Calm, persuasive, and infectious." He was "spell-binding," left leg crossed over right as he issued instructions and inquiries and then stared straight on, foot fidgeting but hands still, awaiting a response. "You sit there," Caughey wrote Betty, "so very much aware of his background and the things he has done for this country of ours," yet he was "modest" and "completely without vanity." There were rumors that Marshall was exhausted, maybe sick, fanned by the infrequency of his public appearances and his impassivity in meetings. On the contrary, Caughey concluded, Marshall was, in his quiet way, a "ball of fire."

To see Marshall close-up as he started into action was at once magnificent and terrifying. "You are only conscious of his dominating influence," at risk of becoming so awed, Caughey related, as to "lose the trend of his thought, which, I might add, is a most dangerous thing in his presence." Aides felt his mind at work, the intensity of its focus, and Marshall had, by his own description, a wicked memory. It was said he could skim a memo and recite its contents days later; during the war, he looked at nine newspapers a day. As he synthesized facts, speedily brought all elements of a problem together, he could be impatient when others struggled to keep up. "You can only make one mistake and boop," Melby observed. "In a few cases I think he has been a little unnecessarily inhuman about it. This ain't war still or yet." An officer who briefed him on military affairs compared the experience to "holding a lesson in flying for a bald eagle."

Never go to him with a problem, veterans warned, without having a proposed solution. You would be met with a silence that shook you more than the cruelest tirade. Caughey caught on quickly: "He does not like to be asked too many questions and the thing he dislikes most is to have someone *not* do something." Early in World War II, Marshall said as much to Eisenhower: "I must have assistants who will solve their own problems and tell me later what they have done."

He demanded directness, in interaction and in composition. He despised obsequiousness and the indefinite pronoun. Aides watched him slash through their drafts, changing "sentences to clauses, clauses to phrases, and phrases to words," one recounted, "the greatest course in English composition I ever was exposed to." Caughey would work into the night and take his effort to Marshall in the morning: "The General will pick up the paper, say nothing, but look at me over the top of his glasses in a piercing contemplating way and then pick up his pen—or mine if his is out of ink which it usually is. He will put new periods in, switch words, alter sentences, add thoughts and delete thoughts—all with lightning speed. The result is masterly to say the least. With the barest and only most essential changes he converts a clumsy effort into a finished product with almost biblical perfection."

He nagged the younger men about their smoking: he had quit, and they could too.

Those who could hack it grew to love "playing varsity ball for GCM," as one said. There was no better way, an already nostalgic wartime aide counseled a successor, "to learn at firsthand that nothing can beat the combination of intelligence, integrity, and appreciation." This last quality was what those who persisted came to recognize. For all the ruthless expectation and bluntness, Marshall was not a tyrant. "Formidable yes—that explains him to a 'T' but he is not formidable to a fault," Caughey told his wife. "With it he is kind, sympathetic and considerate but damn he is a stern man—strong in thought, principle, and purpose."

Caughey's preconceptions also proved off in another way. He did not, as he anticipated on the way to Chongqing, find Marshall mired in despair about the challenge. In fact, "it looked as though things were not only well under control but that they showed promise for the future," Caughey wrote a few days later. "General Marshall reflected that promise in his attitude and in his demeanor." The promise lay in the plan taking shape to sit down with one representative from each side and hash out an agreement. If there was cause for hope, it would be found in this Committee of Three.

Marshall had been listening, but that did not mean he had been passive. His questions, his looks, were meant to convey something. He was hearing principles and platitudes and goals. He wanted means, details, a way of getting there—that is what the repeated questions were getting at. Now, with both the Nationalists and Communists assenting to a three-sided discussion on stopping the fighting, means and details would become everything.

Chiang Kai-shek named Chang Chun, another Confucian-turned-Christian and a seasoned Nationalist official, to represent the government on Marshall's Committee of Three. Years earlier, Chang had been in charge of the Shanghai arsenal around the time of the massacre of Communists there. Despite that history, he was known as a dealmaker, and respected by opponents. He had been foreign minister, head of the National Military Council, and governor of Szechuan province, and also a chief negotiator with the Japanese.

As for his Communist counterpart, there was never a doubt that it would be Zhou Enlai. In his youth, Zhou had been an actor, with delicate mannerisms that suited him well for female roles. It was a profitable training in what turned out to be his most potent qualities: a graceful bearing, a talent for indirection, the deliberate and magnetic presence of a performer onstage. He learned to advocate, dissemble, and evade with a disarming air of directness and candor. At times even Chiang, betrayed before, insisted Zhou could be trusted.

He had charisma and knew how to wield it. Martha Gellhorn half-joked that she would follow him anywhere. (Hemingway, meanwhile, found him slippery.) He had warm eyes, thick and expressive eyebrows, slicked-back hair, impeccable clothing—when the occasion was right, a well-cut suit and black fedora.

He came from what he described, in a session of "self-criticism," as "a run-down feudal aristocratic family." Amid lush rice paddies north of Nanjing, his parents gave him a name that meant "advent of grace," and expected greatness. As a young man, he had lived in France. "Paris is beautiful," he wrote on a postcard, "and so are the women!" He had joined leftist discussion groups at cafes near the Sorbonne and read Marx in English translation. He met young Chinese radicals, including future comrades Deng Xiaoping and Zhu De. By the time Zhou left Europe and returned to China, he was a Communist.

At the time, the Nationalists and Communists were attempting their first united front, and when Zhou was assigned to work for Chiang Kai-shek at the Whampoa military academy, they struck a mutually satisfactory arrangement. Chiang focused on military affairs, Zhou on political. Only gradually did Chiang realize what Zhou was doing with this division of labor: turning cadets into Communists. Foreshadowing bloodier purges, the recruits were expelled and Zhou briefly put under house arrest. During this crackdown he met another rising party member, a specialist in peasant affairs named Mao Zedong.

They were very different men. When Zhou talked about his child-hood, he told stories of a loving mother. When Mao talked about his, he spoke of a savage father. Over the following years, they dealt with one another warily, shifting between collaboration and rivalry as each moved up, or down, the Communist hierarchy. But in time, the terms of the relationship started to clarify. For all his assets, Zhou did not, he realized, have what it took to win a struggle for supremacy, not against Mao's guile and cruelty and sheer will to dominance. Zhou knew how to defer graciously to authority; Mao could never but rage against it. After the heroic hardships of the Long March and the first years of ref-uge in Yenan, Zhou conceded: "The direction and leadership of Mao Zedong is the direction of the Chinese Communist Party!" The revolu-tion would be Mao's, its doctrine Mao Zedong Thought, his homespun improvement on Marxism-Leninism. "We are all Chairman Mao's good little children," toddlers recited.

Chairman Mao still needed Zhou, however, and Zhou stepped into his role with typical élan. "Mao's housekeeper," some sniped. Others were less damning: "Mao Zedong told Zhou all his thoughts and inten-tions, while Zhou Enlai translated them into action in the light of the actual conditions outside." Mao's insight had been to recognize, con-trary to Marxist orthodoxy, the power of the rural masses, and espe-cially of their hatred of elites. "A revolution is not a dinner party," he said in an assessment of rural conditions, "but an act of violence." But once hatred was unleashed, it took Zhou's tactical savvy and political acumen to channel it—means to Mao's ends. At times that meant urg-ing patience or compromise, at times restraining violence or cleaning up after it. Yet Zhou also learned to push only as far as Mao would tol-erate, at which point Zhou became extravagant in his deference. When he sensed Mao was going to criticize him, Zhou criticized himself. When Mao spoke, Zhou took notes on a pad held up in front of him so all would see.

Throughout, Zhou remained a man of many personas: urbane cos-mopolitan, Mandarin scholar-official, single-minded revolutionary. On the Long March, he had his bodyguard carry an inkwell from

France. When a Communist agent cracked under torture, he sent five assassins to kill every member of the man's extended family. Change-ability was a quality Mao found particularly useful in Zhou, and never more so than when, early in World War II, the Communists needed a representative in Chiang's capital. The politics and diplomacy, the plotting and public relations, the meetings and dinner parties—Zhou was made for the Chongqing scene.

Once there, he cultivated diplomats, officers, and journalists. Reporters in need of copy relished his potent and articulate analysis, which no matter how misleading still contrasted favorably with the also misleading banalities of officious government spokesmen. Even when you knew he was lying, it was said, you could not help liking him. Officers gave him the code name Mainbocher, after a French-American line of haute couture; Mao was Moby, after the white whale.

Over dinner, Zhou talked about books, world events, Paris, drop-ping French phrases into his tentative English conversation. He was a good dancer and drinker. Liquor brought out a flirtatious streak, but he never seemed to get drunk. Americans slapped him on the back and called him Joe. When he wanted to flatter them, he told them they were beginning to truly understand China.

He had a staff of young Communists whose idealism was appeal-ing even to skeptics. "They are vigorous," recorded John Fairbank, a Harvard professor serving in U.S. intelligence, "because they are a selected group of believers and workers for a social cause." Zhou taught the young believers to use their ardor for strategic purpose. When one asked why he, a revolutionary, wore Western suits, Zhou replied, "It is not the clothes that matter, little Zhu. If we dress like soldiers, we'll smell of gunpowder." When another blew up in a meeting, he chided, "Don't be impatient and don't hurt our friends' feelings."

The Communists, as much as the Nationalists, saw opportunity in wartime relations with the Americans. Shrewd diplomacy might suc-ceed in curbing support for the government and diverting some to Yenan. "Expose the darkness within the Chinese ruling circle to win their sympathy towards the CCP," a directive said.

To that end, Zhou traded avidly in nasty Chongqing gossip. Mao dispensed advice on handling Chiang to Americans: "You must not give way to his threats and bullying." The Communists vowed that, treated as partners, they would be "more cooperative than the Kuomintang." They claimed eagerness to fight, even as their armies shrank from combat and let Chiang's absorb Japan's fury. "If you land on the shores of China," said Mao, "we will be there to meet you, and to place ourselves under your command." They proposed that Mao and Zhou visit Roosevelt in the White House, though the offer never made it past the embassy. They also enthusiastically welcomed the idea of an American presence in Yenan—what became, once U.S. pressure swayed a resistant Chiang in the second-to-last year of the war, the Dixie Mission.

The party issued guidance before the Americans arrived: "The KMT tries to talk them into doing things every day, they want this and that. We don't raise the question at first and achieve instead their respect, and they will raise the question with us." When the first contingent of soldiers, diplomats, and spies landed, the remote Communist base made for an exhilarating change from overcrowded, overly formal Chongqing. Mao sat talking with them for hours—like a crafty merchant, Soviets observed, who knows what buyers want to hear—and fox-trotted alongside them at Saturday night dances. They played basketball and helped devise a local version of Monopoly, Shanghai standing in for Atlantic City. The situation is excellent, young cadres would say, projecting assurance and hope—qualities that seemed exhausted in Chongqing. The Communists, reported a Dixie Mission diplomat named John Stewart Service, "are a unified group of vigorous, mature and practical men, unselfishly devoted to high principles, and having great ability and strong qualities of leadership. This impression—and I suggest, their record—places them above any other contemporary group in China."

The Communists worked to turn cautious esteem into concrete support. Marshall, as army chief of staff, had signed off on Dixie with the hope that it would yield useful intelligence and assistance rescuing pilots who had crashed behind Japanese lines. But once in Yenan, some members of the mission pursued a broader mandate. The Office of Strategic Services shipped in thousands of pounds of radio gear to help the CCP communicate with its scattered troops. Intelligence agents offered lessons in spycraft, demonstrating how to use single-shot pistols as young Communists watched rapt. One OSS plan would have equipped and trained 25,000 guerrillas with special instruction in explosives.

Once, on a flight, the officer heading the Dixie Mission asked Zhou whether the Communists viewed the Soviet Union or the United States as a better model of democracy. Zhou answered that the Soviet Union was the greatest democracy in the world. But, he added reassuringly, Soviet democracy was a long way off in China. American democracy would be just fine in the meantime.

Washington had been asking versions of the officer's question for years. Were the Chinese Communists true radicals or just "agrarian reformers"? Soviet stooges or headstrong nationalists? For the Communists, uncertainty allowed them to tell their story as they wanted it told. In 1936, they had invited a young American reporter named Edgar Snow to visit Yenan. His book about the experience, *Red Star Over China*, was both a bestseller—Roosevelt got a copy—and a dazzling exercise in mythmaking. Snow described a movement "fired by the belief that a better world can be made," its philosophy more "rural equalitarianism than anything Marx would have found acceptable as a model child of his own."

The line became a common one, and not just in the Kremlin, with its skepticism of Yenan's "cave Marxists" and peasant armies. Other reporters followed in Snow's tracks, met ruddy-cheeked volunteers and spotted Mao tending his own garden, and returned to tell of "a cross between enlightened democrats and latter-day saints." A Marine officer came, confirmed the accounts of "Eagle Scout Behavior," and repurposed a Communist slogan as the battle cry of the Marine Raiders—work together, *gung ho!* Mao mused to visitors that the party might drop "Communist" from its name, since "the most conservative American businessman can find nothing in our program to take exception to." John Service concluded, "The Communist political program is simple democracy . . . much more American than Russian in form and spirit." In Washington, even avowed haters of Communism dismissed the Chinese strain as "so-called" Communism.

The Nationalists protested that the Communists were selling "a bill of goods," and with cause. Chiang had tried to keep American officials away from Yenan as long as possible out of fear of such "sinister intentions." In a way, he had succeeded too well. In Chongqing, hundreds of Americans had years to see through the heroic rendering of him and his government, admiration turning to disgust. Much less so with Mao and his movement in Yenan; even the Dixie Mission was just an eight-room outpost, constructed in the war's final year. Communist myth could easily look better from afar than Nationalist reality up close.

Yet many who doubted the myth still grasped something else: the Communists' strength could not be wished away. "Not that I like Communists," a navy lieutenant wrote after his tour in Dixie, "but whatever they are they'll have to be reckoned with." American diplomats, some more taken in by propaganda than others, had been saying the same; several, including John Service, were sent home by Patrick Hurley for telling it like they saw it with unwelcome insistence. (Several months after leaving, Service was caught up, and cleared, in an espionage investigation when some of his China reports were found in the office of a left-wing magazine called *Amerasia*.) Mao reinforced the assessment every chance he got. "Chiang could not whip us during the civil war when we were a hundred times weaker," he blustered. "What chance has he now?"

American military intelligence reached a similar conclusion. "The Chinese Communists are the best led and most vigorous of present-day organizations in China," a War Department study determined after hundreds of pages of analysis. It had an arresting opening as well: "The Chinese Communists *are* Communists." It pointedly left no room for ambiguity: they were part of a Moscow-directed international movement that had carved a Soviet sphere of influence out of eastern Europe and would try to do the same in China. "The past records of Soviet Russian-Chinese relations give little support to the contention of those who maintain that Soviet Russia has no intention to dominate China," the study elaborated. It was submitted to military leaders shortly before Marshall left the army.

Two months after Hiroshima's decimation and before Marshall's arrival in China, George Orwell published an essay that took stock of the new world. In "You and the Atomic Bomb," he looked toward a "peace that is no peace," with "two or three monstrous super-states each possessed of a weapon by which millions of people can be wiped out in a few seconds, dividing the world between them." He imagined a country "at once *unconquerable* and in a permanent state of 'cold war' with its neighbors."

This notion of a Cold War was new, but Orwell was hardly the only one struggling to make sense of postwar reality. Roosevelt had envisioned the Allies of the war going on to keep the peace, but doubts crept in even before his death. By the fall of 1945, American policymakers were well into a factious discussion about who Stalin was, what he was after, and what should be done about it. Would too much accommodation amount to appeasement, feeding his ambitions for domination? Would too little needlessly squander Allied comity, sowing tension that could lead back to war?

Marshall had first encountered Stalin at a meeting of the World War II Allies. In discussions of strategy, the Soviet dictator was straightforward and pragmatic. But after a collective toast to the bravery of Soviet troops, he quipped in chilling response: "We do not praise our soldiers for being brave—they dare not be otherwise."

When Truman decided to dispatch Marshall to China, Secretary of Commerce Henry Wallace thought "the President's attitude" would mean "World War Number 3." Wallace was a prominent cabinet member—vice president until Truman replaced him on the 1944 ticket—but had begun criticizing the administration for, as he saw it, antagonizing Moscow. He judged Marshall "very strongly anti-Russian." Others agreed, including Harry Dexter White, a senior Treasury official (and sometime Soviet intelligence asset), who thought Marshall would push a hard line. But hard-liners did not count Marshall in their camp either. They worried he was insufficiently animated by the Communist threat and placed too much stock in Soviet reliability during the war, when the Kremlin carried out commitments, he would note, to the precise day.

Marshall had received a string of warnings about Soviet intentions in China. Wedemeyer wrote that Stalin had "created conditions favorable for 'peaceful' and 'surreptitious' penetration of communistic ideologies." The embassy in Moscow reported that the Soviets considered the CCP "an effective machine to build upon and expand their influence in a somewhat similar manner to the methods they have used in central and Eastern Europe."

Yet viewed from Yenan, the relationship was hardly that straightforward. Mao, as much as Chiang, was dismayed by the inconstancy and imperiousness of his backers. "Soviet policy cannot be understood," Communist leaders had recently declared in frustration.

They had been saying much the same ever since Moscow's Communist International, the Comintern, helped found the party two decades earlier. The Kremlin treated its new comrades, one complained, "as serfs." Its dictates betrayed cluelessness about Chinese realities and, worse, disregard for Chinese outcomes when Soviet interests were at stake. (An early example not easily forgotten: Soviet insistence that the Communists be a "bloc within" the Kuomintang, leaving them exposed to Chiang's purge.) As Mao saw it, strict adherence to the Kremlin's "babble" would on more than one occasion have meant his death.

During the war, Soviet survival outweighed revolutionary solidarity, and in the Kremlin's judgment, the Nationalists, not the Communists, had the power to hold off Japan. When Chiang fell into the hands of a CCP ally, Stalin forbade his execution; Mao was enraged but compliant. When Yenan requested Soviet weapons, Moscow instead sent tens of thousands of guns, airplanes, and tanks, along with advisers and pilots, to Chongqing; Mao, the Soviets grumbled, was conserving strength for later rather than fighting now. Even when it came to revolutionary solidarity, Stalin was skeptical. The CCP, he scoffed, was not only questionably Communist, but also "obviously too weak to become the leader of the anti-aggression struggle." Mao, whose rise to party supremacy had come without much Soviet support, returned the sentiment: "We are certainly not fighting for an emancipated China in order to turn the country over to Moscow!"

But for all the discord and divergent interests, Mao needed Stalin, and knew it. He struck a balance: a posture of respectful allegiance, a policy of self-reliance. His Communists would stay loyal but look out for themselves. "We should listen to the Soviets, but we should not listen to them completely," CCP leaders said. Mao personally controlled a radio link to the Kremlin, transmitter and codes hand-delivered from Moscow. To keep it secret, he referred to Stalin as the "voice from the remote place."

Mao did not just need Stalin's help. He also believed in Stalin's revolution, even when Stalin did not believe in his. "Our party and every member of the Chinese Communist Party are Stalin's pupils," Mao said just before the end of World War II; he was ready to fight to carry the revolution forward. The Soviets, however, had other ideas. Without even the simple courtesy of a comradely warning, on the day of Japan's surrender Stalin inked the Sino-Soviet Treaty, pledging to support Chiang's government. He fired off orders to Mao: it was time to negotiate, not to fight. A civil war was certain to be destructive and, for the Communists, unlikely to be successful. It would also be an unwelcome irritant in Moscow's interactions with Washington. And Moscow's interests came first.

Mao was furious. But a master of tactical agility, he quickly set a new course. "Neither the Soviet Union nor the United States favors a civil war in China," a directive instructed. "The party therefore has to make concessions." Its rallying cry became "peace, democracy, and unity." Its avowed path to revolution became political—"the way of France, which means a government led by the capitalist class in which the proletarian class participates." The Soviets had decreed it a time of peace, and so the CCP deemed itself the party of peace. "We want to bore our way in and give Chiang Kai-shek's face a good washing," Mao said, "but we don't want to cut off his head."

To comrades, he rushed to justify his reversal, and Stalin's betrayal. In a contorted analysis, he reasoned that China fell in America's sphere of influence: the most Moscow could do was to preserve space for the CCP's survival. He pointed out that overt Soviet support for Yenan would spur increased American support for Chongqing. "Third world war should be avoided," he explained. Still, in late August, when he boarded his first airplane for six weeks of Moscow-mandated negotiations in Chongqing, he looked, some thought, like a man traveling to his own execution.

Soviet support continued, but with limits. Communist infiltration into Manchuria could proceed, a Kremlin envoy told Yenan, but cadres should travel on back roads and avoid major cities. They could take caches of Japanese arms—but sometimes after a staged firefight, so Moscow could claim the weapons were seized by force. "We must not make this public," a CCP directive emphasized. "We must avoid causing the Red Army diplomatic embarrassment." The Soviets also blocked American ships from depositing Nationalist troops at Manchuria's main port, to the Communists' considerable benefit, and stood by as Communists blocked landings elsewhere.

The CCP took advantage of the opportunity to build a secure presence in Manchuria, a source of leverage with Chiang. The Soviets might demand peace, but it could be peace through strength. "The greater the current victory," Mao said, "the sooner peace will come."

In the weeks before Marshall's arrival, however, Mao was reminded once again how suddenly Moscow could take away what it had given. Stalin was in talks with the Nationalists, and when expedient, he did not hesitate to undercut the Communists. He recalled Soviet representatives from Yenan, so they could not be blamed for CCP behavior. In Manchuria, Soviet officers threatened to use tanks to expel CCP troops from a city where they were not wanted and refused to hand over Japanese weapons to some who had arrived unarmed. An American reporter noted that the Chinese Communists seemed "puzzled and disappointed by Soviet policy." One angrily pointed to his hammer-and-sickle tattoo—how could comrades treat one another this way? In late November, the Soviets stood by as Chiang's troops drove the Communists out of an important gateway to Manchuria, at the point where the Great Wall meets the sea. American advisers were there to help.

After ten days in China, Marshall voiced an opinion. He had listened, solicited ideas, and pressed for details. He had considered those details and distilled common elements from contrary positions. Out of those elements, he had fashioned a plan—the Committee of Three, a roadmap for negotiations, an agenda for keeping peace. When he voiced his opinion, it was to make the case for this plan.

First he made his case to the Nationalists. They had struck him as resistant, but hearing him out, they started to bend. Then he made it to Zhou, who was quickly amenable. The next day, the government issued a public call for Marshall to lead peace talks. The day after that, the Communists said they would take part.

"The prospects of domestic peace in China grow daily fairer," said a radio announcement. Even naysayers were encouraged. "Practically everyone now admits that there is little or no hope for unity," the caustic John Melby had observed weeks earlier. "Unity means suicide for whichever side compromises the most." Now he was expressing cautious optimism about "a sort of truce which will permit the solution over the years to be worked out politically rather [than] militarily."

What had changed, of course, was Marshall. The Communists were persuaded by his reassurance that Committee of Three decisions would be unanimous—a sign he was serious about compromise, not conspiring against them. The Nationalists were won over by his understanding of their security needs. "He holds that the Communist army should be mixed with our army," Chiang wrote in his diary. "If that's truthful, then he can be trusted to join the three-person conference and take charge."

In assuming "the role of referee in China's civil war," as a correspondent put it, Marshall was aware of the long, sorry record of peacemaking and long, bitter history between the two sides. "I was here when the present situation got under way," he would say of his earlier China sojourn. They had effectively been at war for the better part of the previous two decades. The first attempt at unity, in the 1920s, had ended with Communist subterfuge and Nationalist crackdown. Their united front against the Japanese had collapsed into fratricidal battles, including an infamous clash known as the New Fourth Army Incident. Recent negotiations had deadlocked over questions of local governance. "The Communist Party is perfidious, base, and worse than beasts," Chiang fumed afterward. Mao called him "a gangster," "a turtle's egg," "China's Fascist Chieftain." Communists sang, "Chiang Kai-shek has a stubborn heart."

All sides, however, had imperatives pointing toward a negotiated solution, at least for the time being. Chiang needed to neutralize Moscow, placate Washington, and persuade a war-weary populace that he was no enemy of peace. Stalin had explicitly warned that a full-fledged assault on the Communists, especially in Manchuria, would provoke a strong Soviet reaction. Even with American help, facing a Communist army with full Soviet backing would be "bleak," Chiang thought, perhaps worse than facing Japan. With a military solution unlikely—"we cannot use military measures to solve the Communist problem in the postwar era," he told his generals—he had to at least attempt a political one. "We are striving sincerely to reach an equitable and reasonable arrangement," he assured Truman. On New Year's Eve, he gave a radio broadcast hailing unity and cooperation.

The Communists, for their part, needed to placate Moscow and do whatever possible to neutralize Washington, while projecting the same public image of nonaggression. ("The people are fed up with war," Zhou noted.) Stalin told them to consider Marshall's mission a US-Soviet effort to avert civil war—a war, he warned repeatedly, they were too weak to win. Better to negotiate a coalition government and build influence by political means.

Disappointing as such restraint might be, it held a silver lining for Yenan. If Moscow and Washington were together "looking for a peaceful way out," as Zhou put it, a renewed diplomatic offensive—this time conveying readiness to make peace with Chiang rather than war with Japan—would have an effect on the Americans. By demonstrating an interest in compromise, in joining a democratic government on fair terms, the CCP could limit the risk of a major U.S. intervention, Zhou assessed, while winning "the sympathy of international public opinion and of domestic centrist forces." It was even possible, many in Yenan granted, that the path of negotiation would succeed. Mao had spoken of a phase of "new democracy" that would precede full-fledged Communism. "This is a big chance," he had said, "and one not anticipated in Marxist writings." In a coalition government, the CCP would be positioned to expand its base and "raise the Chinese people's consciousness." In a long-term political fight, party leaders thought their prospects good.

Yet for Mao, diplomacy was ultimately a continuation of war by other means, part of a "two-sided policy of unity and struggle." He saw the value of negotiation, but the Communists could not let themselves be tricked by Chiang into giving up weapons or territory until their political place was assured. They must remain ready to fight. "Every single rifle and bullet of the people's armed forces must be preserved," Mao directed. If peace talks failed, they would at least give the Communists valuable time to prepare for war. "The strategy of peace is our spear," Zhou explained, "and strengthened resistance is our shield."

At the start of Marshall's mission, the logic of Yenan's approach was reinforced by the proclamations from Washington and Moscow. Communist spokesmen started praising U.S. policy. Cadres were told to focus their energies on pressing for reform, not overthrowing Chiang. "Ideas of friendship," Mao told Zhou as Marshall approached, are "worthwhile to consider."

A few weeks later, the joint communiqué from the Moscow summit pledged support for a "unified and democratic China" and the speedy withdrawal of foreign troops—"the most hopeful document that has been presented to the world since Germany and Japan signed the instruments of their surrender," proclaimed the *New York Times*. Stalin followed it with a message to Yenan reminding them of the need for cooperation. (Although Chiang was livid that decisions about China were yet again made without him, "an unforgettable insult to the Chinese people," even for him the upshot was clear.) Mao had asked the Soviets to join the mediation—it was an old stratagem, using barbarian to check barbarian—but Stalin declined. He would leave it to the Americans.

The Americans, of course, had their own reasons for advocating a negotiated solution. Chiang could not win a civil war—they were sure of that. The CCP might not be able to win either, but in a warring, divided China, the Nationalist government's position would likely erode over time, even with substantial U.S. assistance. Ivan Yeaton, the staunch anti-Communist heading up the Dixie Mission, submitted an analysis ahead of Marshall's arrival: "The Generalissimo's military strength if not constantly revitalized will slowly crumble when forced into a long drawn-out civil war of attrition while the Communists' deep-rooted political strength in their stabilized bases will best develop and spread under military and civil suppression together."

Yeaton shared the view of other military observers: Chiang must attempt a deal. Claire Chennault, dashing commander of the Flying Tigers and a Chiang favorite, advocated US-sponsored "political reconstruction at Chongqing, followed by true unification between Chongqing and Yenan." The War Department's intelligence report ("The Chinese Communists *are* Communists") concluded that "unity between the Chinese political parties is the key to a solution of China's problems." At worst, the thinking went, a negotiation would give Chiang time to strengthen his own government and initiate badly needed reforms—a valuable delay even if war came. At best, with American help, it might bring the Communists into government and contain them there.

Yeaton thought it could be done. "Both parties," he advised, "have presently greatly overplayed their hands, both are exhausted, both want to save face and both greatly desire peace. All of which leads up to the fact that the time is ripe to bring them together." He urged withholding all assistance until they complied. "We held the cards before but were bluffed out. We still hold the hand, we should play them adroitly this time."

On January 6, a day before the Committee of Three was set to convene, American troops around the world rose up in protest against their own government. From Paris and London to Manila and Shanghai, enlisted men massed by the thousands and heckled officers, shouted profanities at generals, and waved signs for the cameras—SERVICE YES, BUT SERFDOM NEVER. They did not particularly care about America's global responsibilities. The war was over, and they wanted to go home.

Marshall had long worried about such an eruption. "In a widespread emotional crisis of the American people," he said in his final weeks as chief of staff, "demobilization has become, in effect, disintegration not only of the armed forces but apparently of all conception of world responsibility and what it demands of us." Truman, fretting about the "old isolation fever," was using every ship available to bring the boys home. Fifteen thousand a day were turning in their uniforms, and he was still savaged for not doing it fast enough. Americans had never supported a large peacetime military. As Marshall left for China, the president reiterated the need to withdraw troops "as soon as possible." He had been reminding Chiang as well.

"The invasion of a foreign shore, generally is a pretty grim experience," an orientation pamphlet had explained to U.S. personnel arriving in China. "However no group has ever been so welcome!" To the extent that was ever true, it did not last long. Boisterous greeting and attentive hospitality—one mayor offered marines an "inventory of White Russian girls"—gave way to what felt disconcertingly like occupation for residents and troops alike.

The *Pocket Guide to China* urged GIs "to show the Chinese ... that we respect them as human beings." But as a *Life* correspondent put it, "discipline dissolved like starch in rain," and locals suffered most from the dissolution. "If I were Chinese," Hart Caughey said, "I'd politely but firmly ask all the U.S. forces to get the hell out as soon as possible." Americans mocked the "chinks" and "slopies" they were supposed to be advising. Pedestrians lived in mortal terror of careening American jeeps. When Marshall arrived, an editor of the War Department daily, *Stars & Stripes*, sent a personal report on the American presence. Troops looked upon the Chinese with "disgust, contempt, and despair," it related, and "have little hope that China may become a strong, unified nation or a worthwhile ally."

That second point was especially troubling. While most American servicemen were luxuriating in triumphant homecoming, those in China found themselves patrolling railways and guarding ports for purposes few understood and fewer believed in. When the *Stars & Stripes* editor asked a senior Marine officer what his mission was, the officer answered, "It beats me. I'm told what to do and I do it." One GI commented to a reporter, "If anybody had meddled in our civil war we'd shot the hell out of him. That's what the Chinese ought to do to us."

The furor at home was equally intense. Mothers accused Truman of sacrificing their children for political gain. Citizens wrote their representatives in Congress: "Why should my son's life, and those of thousands of other American boys, be placed in jeopardy, in order to force any particular form of government, down the throats of the Chinese people?" One day in early January, the White House received 2,000 postcards: "Our troops must leave China at once!" The AFL and CIO labor unions sponsored a "mass meeting" to denounce "American intervention." Truman bristled at the attacks. "Chiang Kai-shek supported us wholeheartedly in the war and I am inclined to be patient with the situation in China," he replied to a critic. "Generalissimo Stalin says the so-called Chinese Communists are nothing but bandits and he has nothing whatsoever to do with them." Whatever the president said, the reaction persisted.

In Chongqing, Marshall also felt the pressure. Transporting additional Nationalist armies required delaying the return of the more than 100,000 troops still in China; upon getting the order, Wedemeyer had immediately canceled two homeward-bound ships. Parents wrote Marshall to beg for their sons' release from service. (In the case of an older couple who had one son killed and a second wounded in the war, he was persuaded to find their third son and send him home.) He got updates on the rough treatment of Eisenhower, his successor as chief of staff, who had been cornered and berated by dozens of army wives. "You got out at the right time," a friend wrote. Yet Marshall knew from years of waging war in a democracy that, even on his new mission, such sentiments could not be ignored or wished away. Without public support, no military effort could be sustained for long.

The height of strategy, says an aphorism in Sun Tzu's *The Art of War*, is "defeating the enemy without ever fighting." It was widely known that Mao was a disciple of Sun's ancient text. But Marshall had also studied it; there was a well-thumbed translation on his bookshelf back in Leesburg. He, too, was thinking about how to win without fighting.

By Monday morning, January 7, Happiness Gardens had taken on the feel of a full-fledged headquarters. Marshall's newly expanded staff was crowded into bedrooms on the second floor. Downstairs, maps of troop positions and railway lines were pinned on a board, a meeting table set in front of the fireplace. At 10 a.m., when Zhou Enlai and Chang Chun came up the front stairs for the first session of the Committee of Three, Marshall and his team were prepared for what they hoped would be a significant step toward a sustained peace—and a successful mission. Above the peaked roof, under a gray sky, an American flag waved gently in the wind.

Marshall's house was considered neutral ground. Top Nationalist officials lived nearby in mansions along Sun Yat-sen Avenue; the day before, they had convened with Chiang to determine strategy for the talks. Communist headquarters was farther away, down a crowded alleyway toward the confluence of the rivers. Mao had told Zhou to be friendly; a directive on diplomacy enjoined, "We must be punctual, and we must keep any promises we make." Zhou hardly needed the guidance. "For the sake of our revolution, we can play the role of concubine, even of a prostitute, if need be," he once said. And he was quickly coming to respect Marshall of his own accord. "Marshall is plain, does not exaggerate things, considers issues calmly, doesn't jump to conclusions," Zhou reported. "He is a rather plain capitalist." For the Communists, it was marked praise.

Marshall had a clear vision for the Committee of Three. He understood that there were formidable obstacles standing in the way of progress toward a long-term solution. The Nationalists demanded an end to Communist armies, the Communists an end to Nationalist one-party rule, and whether either could be achieved on mutually acceptable terms, and in a mutually reassuring sequence, was an open question. An agreement to stop the fighting might provide the time, space, and good faith necessary to find an answer.

As soon as Zhou and Chang sat down at the table, Marshall started driving toward an agreement. He had claimed to have no interest in the exact terms of a deal, only in the fact of a deal getting done. Yet minutes into this first meeting, he produced his own draft order for a cessation of hostilities. He had decided it was the only way to make progress. If they started with a blank page, they would get nowhere. So he would make proposals and let the others react. He would control the negotiating text, and the notes taken by his aides, in English, would serve as the transcript of record. Otherwise, the two sides might end up in protracted arguments about what exactly had been said.

Marshall read his draft order aloud. The headline was the easy part: "all hostilities will cease." He went line-by-line through the rest, glasses perched on his nose, turning to Zhou and Chang as each was translated: "Will you accept that?" When expedient, Marshall skipped over a contentious issue; at other times, he fixed on details. "What does 'these' mean?" he asked when presented with a reviled indefinite pronoun. When he thought a point was mischaracterized or misunderstood, he interrupted to set the record straight. He was relying on his new interpreter, John Soong, rather than trying out his old army Chinese, but Zhou knew enough English to follow the translation, and he did carefully. Not necessary, he would correct, "I said mandatory." Not strategy, tactics. Not in *a* month, in *this* month.

It went on like this for three hours. Before letting Zhou and Chang leave the house, Marshall indicated the reporters outside. Premature announcements or dueling leaks would be fatal. He urged them to keep any messages to the press upbeat and vague.

"Things are going quite well," Chang said. "Things are going very well," Zhou said.

When the Committee reconvened the next morning, the atmosphere was good. Concord on basic points seemed to have generated rapport, as Marshall intended. He invited photographers to capture the three of them at work. When he sensed a looming disagreement, he called a break. "Now, Gentlemen, it is a little after 11 o'clock and I have given you no tea, so I presume that I have offended Chinese custom," he said. "Also to follow an American custom, when you reach a certain stage of a baseball game, which is the 7th inning, all business ceases and everybody stretches their legs." Soong sometimes swapped in a Chinese joke or reference for an American one, so that Marshall would see Zhou and Chang smiling without in fact knowing what they were smiling at. In any case, the seventh-inning stretch worked. By the time the three of them sat back down, Zhou and Chang were ready to work it out.

Anyone who had witnessed Marshall in action at a conference table over the previous four years would not have been surprised by his deft orchestration. World War II had provided an extended training in fractious diplomacy, with bitter disagreements, personal hatreds, and violent tantrums even among the Allies. "As a negotiator he was without peer," General Wedemeyer marveled of his performance at a wartime meeting. For the aides now seeing Marshall the diplomat for the first time, it was, Caughey wrote, "a pleasure to watch him operate. Completely open, completely firm and resolute. No punches were pulled and finally the opposition pulled none, which is rare—if not unprecedented—and the major points were ironed out through sheer sweat." John Melby thought of Marshall as the "guiding spirit" of the Committee of Three.

By this second day, January 8, the press was ready to declare victory. "The promise of peace in China," went the stories, "looked brighter than at any time for years." In reality, however, the Committee was getting to the hard part. That fighting should stop was not in dispute; what each side should be obligated or allowed to do after fighting stopped was another matter. As differences came to the surface, Zhou and Chang started to argue over word order, preposition choice, definitions. They quibbled over the meaning of "communications" in the process of working out a guarantee, essential to the Nationalists, that railways, roads, and telegraph lines would not be sabotaged or blocked. Even Marshall, typically a zealot for precision, was driven to ask, "Are hostilities going to depend on the word 'the' here?"

Ultimately, the discord came down to one issue: where Nationalist troop movements would be permitted after a cease-fire went into effect. Most troops would have to stay in place, to avoid clashes, but both sides accepted that the government should be allowed to continue moving armies in certain areas in order to reestablish rightful control. The question was, which areas? Zhou conceded on Manchuria, in keeping with Stalin's promises to Chiang. But in two provinces bordering Manchuria, Rehe and Chahar, the Communists were intent on holding ground against further Nationalist incursions. "By raising this point, it would only make the realization of cessation of hostilities impossible," Zhou protested when the prospect of troop movements in the provinces was mentioned. He questioned Nationalist good faith—if the goal was to bring the two armies together as one, what did it matter who controlled the territory now? Chang, however, wanted explicit recognition that Nationalist troops would be able to enter.

As the third day of the Committee of Three got under way, it seemed at risk of coming apart. The rancor quickly rose, and Marshall cut in: "Gentlemen, it appears to me that there is a complete disagreement with no prospect immediately before us of reaching any acceptable compromise." Everything else was settled. It would be a "tragedy to have this conference fail at the last moment." Tragedy or not, neither side gave ground. Marshall ended the session early, certain it would only get worse.

At 10 o'clock that evening, Marshall went to see Chiang. He had thought about laying out his argument in a note. But then he thought better: the only way to persuade Chiang to compromise would be face-to-face.

The Nationalists' hard line on Rehe and Chahar had come on Chiang's orders. In fact, in the days ahead of the Committee of Three's launch, Nationalist armies had been battling to take control of the territory before talks began. The CCP had reason to hold out. The two provinces included important junctions, at Chifeng and Tolun, and offered a route into Manchuria from its base area around Yenan. "We must completely control them," the Communists had resolved.

Marshall had some grasp of the territory's significance, and he respectfully acknowledged Chiang's concern. But the trade-off was worth it, he argued; Chiang gained far more than he lost from the Committee of Three's agreement. Zhou had consented to a Nationalist takeover of Manchuria, and he had also agreed to start talks on bringing Communist armies under the government's control. These were major gains, as Chiang recognized. What was more, Marshall noted, the Nationalists did not have to cede the two provinces; they just had to postpone a settlement, to be worked out in the coming weeks and months. And finally, Chiang should have an interest in announcing a cessation of hostilities quickly. The next day, he was going to be presiding over the start of a multiparty conference on China's political future. Opening with a declaration of peace would send a powerful positive message—while opening with a tacit acknowledgment of the Committee of Three's failure would send a powerful grim one, to both Chinese and American audiences. Politically, that would make it extremely difficult for Washington to provide Chiang the extent of aid he needed.

When Marshall left at midnight, Chiang had given in. They would issue an order to stop fighting without mentioning the two provinces.

At 8:30 the next morning, January 10, the Committee of Three was back together. Zhou and Chang had gotten calls after midnight telling them to come early. Marshall recited the order clause by clause, with the others assenting—"yes, sir"—and Marshall then ratifying each as official: "It is so ordered." For the signing, Marshall invited the photographers back in. He staged the scene like a theater director, arranging it carefully to present the image he wanted. He prepared his fellow members of the Committee of Three like a team captain: "There is no 'I' in this, it is all 'we.'" As each signed the order—Marshall in uniform, Chang in a dark suit with a white pocket square, Zhou in a tailored black tunic—the other two stood behind and observed approvingly. Marshall paused to reflect on the promise of the Committee of Three's success: "I think it may be looked upon in general as a very important foundation stone in achieving an effective unity for China, which of course means a great deal to the future peace of the world."

Over the coming days, American military planes would take off from airstrips across China. They flew low over ravaged landscapes, above far-flung armies that had been at war for many years. When the pilots released their loads, not bombs but leaflets fell to the ground below—hundreds of thousands of sheets of paper printed with news of peace.

CHAPTER 5

Unity Out of Chaos

The Committee of Three had finished its work just in time. Hardly an hour later, Chiang Kai-shek rose before Chinese political leaders of all stripes and announced that fighting would stop. In the room there was a roar of applause. Reporters hailed a "long stride in a new march toward peace and greatness." Some registered it as "an important gain—both politically and militarily—on the part of the Nationalists," while in Yenan *Emancipation Daily* pronounced "the beginning of a phase of peaceful development, peaceful reform, and peaceful reconstruction." An American commentator declared victory: "General Marshall's mission is complete."

Marshall knew better. "I hope it will prove historic," he said to Zhou and Chang. Yet all they had really achieved, he reminded them, was "a pause for deliberation"—a window of opportunity for working out more fundamental solutions. In the meantime, if peace was going to keep, Marshall had to find some means of keeping it.

In fact, he had quietly put plans into motion days before the Committee of Three first convened. Since January 1, his staff had been drawing up blueprints. Officers had been scouring military posts for spare trucks and radios and holding secret late-night conferences. When, on January 10, shortly after the Committee of Three came to agreement, Marshall turned to his aide Hank Byroade and told him to have a peacekeeping operation started the following afternoon, the pieces were in place. The next day, Byroade was in room 308 of a Beijing hotel launching a new body called the Executive Headquarters. What the Committee of Three had managed in the living room of Happiness Gardens, three-man Executive Headquarters "truce teams" would attempt in disputed territory across China. It was Marshall's way of turning principles on paper into facts on the ground.

There was a three-day lag between the signing of the order and the start of the truce. Although Marshall worried that both sides would use any delay to maneuver for final advantage, Zhou and Chang jointly overruled his objection, on the grounds that they needed time to get the news to commanders. The immediate result of the Committee of Three's success was thus more violence, as Marshall feared, with armies scrambling to claim or entrench positions up to the last moment. Even once the cease-fire started on January 14, Zhou and Chang repeatedly complained of violations, charges that, when relayed to the other, elicited identical excuses of poor communications and self-defense. Byroade suspected both sides were exaggerating for purposes of pre-emptive propaganda, to deflect blame if the cease-fire failed. But it now fell to the Executive Headquarters, working out of Beijing, to resolve such disputes and stop transgressions.

"You have my full confidence," Marshall told Byroade. "You are free to call on me direct and personally for any assistance whatsoever." Marshall wanted Byroade's operation up and running quickly, since for the cease-fire to work, "there must be an impartial source of direction and authority on the ground." He offered his C-54 to ferry personnel and summoned one hundred colonels, "ages 42 to 58, physically fit," to staff the Executive Headquarters. He had Byroade, just 32 and not a decade out of West Point, promoted to Brigadier General to bolster his authority. Within days, truce teams were on their way into the field to enforce peace, armed with a basic set of rules ("One force holding a city—other will withdraw one day's march," "two forces in a city—both will withdraw one day's march") and uniform kit (truck, axe, compass, sketching set, six rolls of toilet paper).

The peacekeeping effort replicated the principle of the Committee of Three. The Executive Headquarters had three senior commissioners, an American, a Nationalist, and a Communist. (When Walter Robertson, the senior diplomat in China and Marshall's pick for the American slot, had said he wanted to go home, Marshall replied, "I want to go home too.") Each truce team consisted of three officers, American, Nationalist, and Communist, and made decisions by consensus. According to instructions, the American role was "solely for the purpose of assisting the Chinese members in implementing the Cessation of Hostilities order." (Marshall had inserted "solely" to allay suspicion of other agendas.) But as in Chongqing, the American served as "chairman" and controlled the record. Disputes, the idea went, would be assessed, argued over, and adjudicated in the field rather than escalating to higher levels or reverting to violent means. The first destination for a truce team: Rehe and Chahar, the two provinces that had brought the Committee of Three to the brink of failure a few days earlier.

Something like peace seemed to take hold. At first, the Executive Headquarters reported merely "an inclination among American military observers to agree that there is less fighting." Before long, however, there was grand talk of "a courageous experiment to substitute negotiation for warfare as an instrument of national policy."

But Marshall knew this peace was only a pause. The question now was how it would be used—whether, as he hoped, the "good faith that will be built up" would reveal solutions to insoluble problems. The gathering of political leaders under way, the Political Consultative Conference, was taking on one of those problems. But the "hardest problem of all" and "great fundamental requirement for a peaceful China," in his mind, was bringing Communist troops into Nationalist armies. Marshall had planned to leave this task to the Chinese. A few days after the cease-fire went into effect, however, Chiang proposed that Marshall join a new Committee of Three, officially the Military Subcommittee of the Committee of Three, to address military integration. Zhou readily seconded the suggestion: "This will make us come to agreement."

In China less than a month, Marshall was more entangled than he had ever intended. "Conducting war," he would say, "is a relatively simple profession, because one understands clearly the objectives to be attained. To make peace seems to me to be a more complicated matter."

The next time the original Committee of Three came together, it was for dinner and a movie. Zhou and Chang shared a ride to Happiness Gardens and chatted as they ate—like "old Jeff Davis and Seward, attending a dinner together with a special British delegate during the Civil War," as Hart Caughey put it. The movie that evening was *True Victory*, a documentary about the American invasion of Germany. "You know, now that I'm away from that, I find it unreal," Marshall remarked when images of concentration camps appeared on-screen. "Hard to believe that it ever happened." Zhou and Chang were transfixed.

With the cease-fire on, the machinery of peace in place, life took on a kind of normalcy. At the table, over Chinese dishes he had come to relish, Marshall told stories about hunting trips, about his time in the Philippines, about military history, about World War II. "I'm almost convinced he knows more about everything than anybody," Caughey raved to his wife. "He can pull out of his head more ideas and facts than you can shake a stick at—all without the slightest effort and all in the most interesting sort of a way."

Marshall also had a striking ability to detach. "You ought to see the way he relaxes when the pressure is off," Caughey wrote. "That is very uncommon among people who fight with their minds. Usually those kind of people wear their minds out, if they have a mind." Marshall had learned that lesson years before and, more recently, discovered an added imperative: when he looked worn out, the public assumed a mission was going poorly. In Chongqing, he napped briefly nearly every afternoon. He took sightseeing walks with Caughey. His demand for books—"he reads cheap fiction endlessly," Melby scoffed to Lillian Hellman—put a strain on staffers charged with keeping him supplied. His rear echelon in Washington sent a steady stream of movies. Sometimes they were along the lines of *The Atom Strikes*, a documentary about devastation in Hiroshima and Nagasaki; more often *Tarzan and the Leopard Woman* or *Home Sweet Homicide*. Either way, Marshall concentrated as intently in a screening as in a negotiation. In the middle, to the amusement of guests, he broke for ice cream.

Through it all, Marshall wrote a friend, "I long for personal freedom and my own home and simple pleasures. My shooting trips were all arranged for this winter with horseback rides on the lonely Pinehurst trails and a month in Florida at a luxurious cottage that had been placed at my disposal. But, here I am."

The Chiangs were solicitous hosts. When he met with the Generalissimo—the only interlocutor too important to come to Happiness Gardens—Marshall would often arrive early, to strategize with Madame Chiang, and stay late, for cocktails or dinner. Madame Chiang perfected her technique for making his preferred Old Fashioned—Wedemeyer gave her a crystal cocktail shaker—and corrected American staff when their attempts fell short. She cultivated his aides, sending their children back in the United States birthday presents. (It reflected long-standing Chinese practice: a century earlier, an imperial diplomat advised showering "barbarians" with gifts.) She urged him to make use of their country estates: "Go out and get some color into your cheeks." At one, a leafy complex spread over hills across the river, the thick canopy an effective defense against bombers, Marshall was given a cottage with superb feng shui and studded walls that impeded eavesdropping.

The Chiangs were hardly the only ones eager to host him. Invitations came from generals, warlords, journalists, and foreign representatives. Over dinner and vodka at the Soviet embassy, Marshall and Ambassador A. A. Petrov talked amiably of past cooperation between their countries and the need for democracy and unity in China. (Petrov had no idea what his government was actually up to; his directions from Stalin were to not interfere, and he begged off meetings with the Communists whenever possible.)

Aides partook of a similarly ecumenical social scene. Nationalist circles were most congenial, full of English speakers in Western suits. But booze was most abundant at Russian parties—local beer, Argentine gin, Ukrainian brandy. Communist gatherings meant repeated toasts of *baijiu*, a potent grain alcohol. Americans continued to wonder at the fraternizing between enemies. At one party, "right-wing KMT who had always thought of the Communists as something from a nightmare suddenly met and some found they were related, others had gone to school together." At another, Communist officers jocularly pinned down a Nationalist official and forced liquor on him.

Still, intrigue was never far from the surface. Chongqing remained "a city of rumors," a playground for merchants of information and disinformation, for agents and double agents. Marshall was warned of a "lack of secrecy in all discussions," and officials were on the lookout for frauds, worrying that, say, a Communist contact was actually a Nationalist stooge. Servants used false names, some for Americans' ease (Wong was popular), some for murkier reasons. "We have to assume all our Chinese employees report to someone else," Melby cautioned. Jeeps left on the street sometimes disappeared. So did a bundle of Marshall's clothes, allegedly taken by a "houseboy." When Americans toasted with *baijiu* at CCP parties, they did not know that, beneath them, secret tunnels ran to the river, used to spirit agents in and out. Zhou himself was as adept at espionage as diplomacy. With long experience creating covert cells, he had planted scores of moles in the upper ranks of the Nationalist government and military. At one point, he had even gotten hold of Chiang's codebook.

Marshall also knew this game well. As army chief of staff, he had been among the few Americans aware of the complete penetration of German and Japanese communications during the war. After a few weeks in Chongqing, he realized he needed to step up intelligence efforts there as well. He asked Eisenhower for military surveillance of key locations, including Yenan and Beijing. He requested more, and more immediate, global intelligence, including "Top Secret code reports" on "world matters as they affect China, Manchuria in particular." A cryptographer was sent and quickly cracked Nationalist codes, providing access to high-level messages. The Communists proved more challenging.

Marshall was as focused on protecting his own communications as he was on penetrating those of others. The cryptographer brought a SIGABA cipher machine, and its encrypted messages went through War Department channels to Marshall's personal representative in Washington, who delivered hard copies to the president and secretary of state. Marshall appended frequent reminders to destroy after reading. "The security of this must be guarded with every precaution," he prodded. "There must be no slip." The State Department was infamously indiscreet, and even the White House was as secure, said Dean Acheson, "as a sieve"; at a certain point, Truman's chief of staff, William Leahy, was denied access to Marshall's messages.

Marshall drilled discretion into aides—no gossip, no chatter, nothing of the "tactlessness" and "outrageous talking" that were, in his eyes, Stilwell's great sin. When an underling sent a dispatch to the State Department without clearing it, Marshall delivered a reprimand. "I am carefully refraining from giving Washington such details to avoid destructive leaks in the press," he snapped. "Your channel is to me direct and probably for my eyes only." When a State Department spokesman issued an unwisely expansive statement, Marshall sent a note demanding that nothing at all be said about China without his explicit approval. He even decreed that no updates on his mission appear in intelligence reports, given the "frequent leaks and the disastrous effect they might have here on the delicate business in which I am engaged." He began holding off-the-record sessions for a few trusted reporters, mostly to check rumors; anyone who broke the ground rules was never invited back.

"He tells nobody nothing as to what goes on in his mind," said Melby, after Marshall had been in China for weeks, and it remained "baffling" to many. But after watching closely, Melby was starting to see the point: "Marshall seems to have them all bluffed."

"Now the ancient battle of words can get started on the political questions. This one can go on forever."

It was Melby's line, but also Washington's rough plan. Truman had directed Marshall "to persuade the Chinese Government to call a national conference of representatives of the major political elements to bring about the unification of China." There was already agreement about this Political Consultative Conference in principle, but only after Marshall's arrival was a date for it set. On January 10, after announcing the truce before PCC representatives, Chiang went on to speak of freedom of speech, assembly, and the press, of ratifying political parties and releasing political prisoners. "If we remember those few essentials, our country will be on the road to democratic reconstruction," he proclaimed. Zhou followed with a pledge to "acknowledge Chiang's leadership." And with that, the thirty-eight members of the PCC were off, "going full blast using all the epithets in everyone's vocabulary," in Melby's description, to shape the coming Chinese democracy.

The discourse thrilled Washington, even if China was by most measures more failing state than rising democratic power. A century of internal rebellion, imperial aggression, and social breakdown had brought heightened landlord exploitation and warlord domination in much of the country. Japanese invasion had left behind starvation and disease, driven inflation into triple digits, and destroyed more than 90 percent of the railways. Perhaps one-fifth of the population could read. Three-quarters worked in the fields. Life expectancy for males was under 40.

Then there was the question of whether Chiang and his party were plausible champions, capable of leading China out of devastation and onto that "road of democratic reconstruction." The familiarity of much of the Nationalist elite made it easy for Westerners to assume they were. Missionaries regarded the Bible-quoting Chiangs and concluded, "We can thank God that these two and other Christians in the Chinese Government cast in their lot with the free nations and have so turned the scales for democracy and Christian liberty." *Life* reasoned that Chiang, given his martial ways, must be more of an Old Testament Christian.

Other Americans took their faith from figures like T. V. Soong. Chiang's chief economic policymaker, sometime premier and foreign minister, and brother-in-law, Soong had not just a degree from Harvard, but also a background in New York banking, and three American-educated daughters, Laurette, Mary-Jane, and Katherine. ("Foreigner," some Nationalists spat.) With slick hair, horn-rimmed glasses, tailored suits, and an imperious strut, he was called China's J. P. Morgan. "I have never associated with a group of foreigners whose speech and thought seemed so much like those of a similar group at home," a prominent New York lawyer, Paul Cravath, said after a visit. When Teddy White, a young *Time* reporter, organized a Harvard Club of China, he joked that half the government could join.

As ever, ample cause for disenchantment lay just below the surface. Chiang's power rested on a balance of factions, some made up of Western-trained liberals or high-minded Confucians, many of a different cast. The brothers Chen Li-fu and Chen Kuo-fu, namesakes of the conservative CC Clique, were said to have a "a monopoly of one of the Generalissimo's ears" and to promote "a kind of Chinese fascism." Nationalist "blue shirts" modeled themselves on Mussolini's Blackshirts. The secret police was run by a man known as "the Himmler of China," gold-toothed Tai Li, whom Chiang would reportedly "receive at any time, any place." Wedemeyer decried Tai's brutality, and Melby charged, hyperbolically, that Tai's "Chinese Gestapo behaves in a way and with methods that would make the Nazis look like schoolboys." Such figures pervaded Chiang's party, and the party controlled the government and military.

More prosaic shortcomings were also damning. Chiang's ranks, Wedemeyer lamented, included "literally thousands of incompetents who are parasites living off an impoverished country." Quotidian corruption, "squeeze," was a staple of life, but Nationalist officials presented flagrant examples. The head of Chiang's military council, a U.S. embassy report detailed, had one son who was a major opium producer, another who ran a network of brothels, and a third who operated gambling halls. (A fourth was in school in the United States.) Stories of Soong family chicanery were legion. In rural areas, Chiang's power depended on landowners, some of whom were prone to such practices as seizing crops, animals, or daughters when rent went unpaid. "One is faced with the hard fact of a central government which is a coalition of landlords and militarists with tremendous vested interests in the status quo," said an embassy analysis.

The Nationalists were once "the flaming revolutionaries of the Orient," Melby reflected. "Now they are sleek, polished, well-fed, worldly, cynical, reactionary." It was, in his view, "the saddest and most depressing thing in Chongqing."

Chiang could see it too. He condemned his party as "weak and rotten," obsessed with "ease and pleasure," regarded with "hatred and repugnance." He attributed Communist success to "the inefficiency and corruption of our government machine." He warned of the implications: "If we do not weed the present body of corruption, bribery, perfunctoriness, and ignorance, and establish instead a clean and efficient administration, the day will soon come when the revolution will be started against us."

That warning was in 1936. Chiang could see the decay but not reverse it. If his power rested on a balance, he upset it at his own risk. "The most astute politician of the twentieth century," Stilwell called him, in something like a compliment. "He must be or he wouldn't be alive." Chiang sidelined effective generals or governors who grew too strong, and protected venal or incompetent ones. He made deals with warlords. He tolerated conspicuous corruption, though few observers thought him personally corrupt—his love of power, one said, did not extend to its trappings. He ignored abuses by supportive landlords, despite recognizing the need for land reform as "the most fundamental problem of China." He prized loyalty, trusted few, stayed always suspicious. Before World War II, an envoy from Nazi Germany had registered Chiang's interest in "how our party leadership succeeds to maintain such strict discipline among its followers and takes harsh measures against dissidents or opponents."

Wedemeyer, a defender, wrote an assessment before Marshall's arrival. Although he judged Chiang's commitment to unity and democratization "sincere," his finding was bleak: "Considering his background, training and experience as warlord, politician and his oriental philosophy, his approach to problems presented would probably be inefficient, incomprehensible and unethical by American standards." Anyway, Wedemeyer added, "The task is beyond the capabilities of one man."

A political solution, the hope went, would help correct or offset those shortcomings. During the war, some American officials—not just Stilwell—had wanted to "pull the plug and let the whole Chinese government go down the drain." But the United States was not then in the habit of engineering the overthrow of difficult partners. So the challenge was to make Chiang the figure Washington thought he must be in order to survive. To that end, democracy might be tonic; some healthy political competition might check his and his party's worst tendencies. After all, Chiang himself had blamed Nationalist failure for Communist success. Bringing the CCP into a coalition and then "moving ahead with American support in the job of rehabilitation and reconstruction," reasoned the State Department's John Carter Vincent, would "cut the ground from under the Communists, even though they were in the Government."

Vincent and others thought Chiang could prevail in a long-term political contest. "If the Nationalist Party showed as much zeal for bringing good government to China as it was showing for eliminating opposition," Vincent argued, "there would be no question that it could 'out-compete' the Communists in gaining the support of the Chinese people." But when Melby talked to CCP contacts, he was struck by their assurance. "The Communists of course prefer political war to military since they are quite confident they can win that in time, and I think rightly so," he wrote.

In Melby's view, other American diplomats were struggling to face reality: "So far they only admit who loses, but do not commit themselves as to who wins."

Marshall was hardly immune to the great American faith in the curative power of his country's form of government and persuasive power of his country's example. He sometimes preached in meetings about "the fundamental requirements of democracy"—"free speech and free-dom of peaceable assembly and a governmental structure that per-mits a genuine will of the people to be given effect." He held forth on the value of a political opposition and unruly press, "the most pow-erful thing in the world." He not only quoted Benjamin Franklin's speeches—his demand for reading material had turned up a volume printed for American troops—he also had them translated into Chi-nese for distribution. He reflected on the power of nationalism and self-determination, "the awakening of backward and colonial peoples."

As political negotiations got under way, Marshall did not see much he could do to help. He confessed he was "completely confused by the debates" in the Political Consultative Conference. Still, he had been pestering aides for facts and background and political analysis, map-ping the lay of an unfamiliar land. "Marshall needs help that he did not need before," Melby grumbled, which meant "a hell of a lot of scrounging around in odd corners for information and too many Chi-nese meals which my still aching guts can ill afford."

On January 22, the day the PCC was set to unveil an agreement, Marshall went to see Chiang. The talks, it turned out, were stuck, and Chiang wanted help bringing the Communists around. After nearly two weeks of holding back, Marshall was prepared for much more. Anticipating an impasse, watching from afar and seeing rhapsodic speechmaking but few real proposals, he had been working on his own. He handed Chiang a draft bill of rights, a procedure for devising a con-stitution, and a plan for an interim coalition government—a rough design for Chinese democracy.

"Even the Communists would never dare to make this proposal," Chiang raged in his diary that night. "He is too tolerant of the Com-munists, and very ignorant of my state affairs."

The following afternoon, pale sunshine had cleared the fog, and Marshall returned to hear Chiang's response. The Communists, Chiang argued, would take advantage of any opening. But to Marshall, fears of Communist malevolence only strengthened the case for mov-ing quickly toward democratic unity—especially since the United

States, he noted pointedly, could not keep 100,000 troops in China forever.

As for the bill of rights, it was "a dose of American medicine." Marshall thought Chiang found the line amusing. In fact, Chiang was fuming. The "tragedy of the Stilwell era," he feared, was happening all over again.

Chiang nonetheless took some of Marshall's democratic ideas, repackaged them to conceal their origin, and introduced them into the ongoing PCC debates. He implored Marshall to keep this secret, and Marshall understood why—"to preserve 'face.'" When informing Truman, the message stamped EYES ONLY, Marshall nagged yet again, "Please destroy the record of this radio, for a leak in the press would be disastrous to my mission." (Truman evidently did not comply.)

"I interfered with a meat ax," Marshall would joke in private. The interference seemed warranted, however, because so much else depended on political unification. "You may state, in connection with the Chinese desire for credits, technical assistance in the economic field, and military assistance," Truman had instructed, "that a China disunited and torn by civil strife could not be considered realistically as a proper place for American assistance along the lines enumerated." Marshall had expedited some aid since coming—railroad supplies, transport ships, ammunition—but the promise of a large-scale package was held in reserve as an incentive for both sides to cooperate. Even Mao had told his comrades that China needed a "huge amount of capital" and that the United States was the only country that could provide it.

For Chiang there was also the promise of long-term military support. In the five months since Japan's surrender, U.S. aid had continued flowing to his armies under the auspices of unfulfilled Lend-Lease commitments—more than half a billion dollars' worth, on top of the benefits of American troops guarding ports and mines and railways. But Lend-Lease could not continue indefinitely (China already had a special extension). Nor could a large-scale troop presence. Marshall wanted to start laying the groundwork for sustainable military assistance sooner rather than later.

In the midst of political negotiations, he made a quick visit to Shanghai to sketch out the future U.S. military role with Wedemeyer. The bulk of American troops were likely to go home in the spring. But Marshall was considering holding some Marines back to keep peace in trouble spots. He would also need officers to staff the Executive Headquarters, pilots and engineers to build China's air force, and several hundred personnel for a new Military Advisory Group.

Shanghai offered a change in atmosphere after Marshall's month in the interior. While Americans in Chongqing complained about the weather and smells and court politics, life in Shanghai was good for officers, enlisted men, and diplomats alike. The highbrow had Stravinsky at the Lyceum or the "Moonlight Sonata" at La Ballet Russe; the high-living, every strain of debauchery and vice. "One part is slick with too much money, elegance, and callousness," Melby wrote. "Another side is sordid with horrible slums, starvation, corruption, opium, and more streetwalkers than I have ever seen anywhere." Or in Hart Caughey's words: "Shanghai is treacherously Westernized and it is wicked."

One Sunday afternoon in late January, Caughey was panicked. He had been preparing for the arrival of a distinguished visitor on January 28. But it was January 27, and a call had come through: Averell Harriman, U.S. ambassador to the Soviet Union, had landed at the airfield outside Chongqing, and no one was there to meet him. Caughey needed to intercept Harriman and get him to Chiang's country estate. He jumped in a jeep and raced along roads slick with mud.

Chiang had chosen the setting with an agenda in mind. A few days from now, Harriman would be in the Oval Office resigning his post and giving valedictory counsel to the president. If Marshall was not doing enough to educate Washington on Communist perfidy, perhaps, with the right cultivation, Harriman would.

A banker-turned-statesman with the inborn assurance of a first-born heir, Harriman brought an intimate view of Soviet foreign rela-

tions. He had been at Roosevelt's side at Yalta the year before, extracting
the Soviet promise to attack Japan's troops in Manchuria. He had been
in the wings for negotiations over the Sino-Soviet Treaty, stepping in
to back up the Chinese when Kremlin demands became excessive. He
had spent hours face-to-face with Stalin. In a farewell meeting, when
the topic of the CCP came up, Stalin remarked that it was "stupid" to
think China was ready for "Sovietization." If the Nationalists moved
toward democracy, everything would be fine.

Harriman had heard such assurances for years. Lately he had become
more skeptical, influenced by his deputy, George Kennan. "USSR seeks
predominant influence in China," Kennan had written a few weeks earlier in a memo Harriman sent along to Chongqing. Whatever the talk
of democracy and cooperation, Moscow would be satisfied only with
"influence eventually amounting to effective control."

Chiang arranged a welcome banquet at his country house, but first
saw Harriman and Marshall over tea. Marshall's recent political intervention had triggered a torrent of bitterness. "Both his thoughts and
ideology are influenced by the Russians," Chiang seethed in his diary.
"Marshall's proposals to cease political and military conflicts are ten
times more dangerous and absurd than those of the Communists."
So now, with Harriman, Chiang was pleased when discussion turned
quickly to Soviet ambitions in China. It was a chance to remind the
Americans that Moscow and Yenan should be treated as a single—and
shared—threat. Harriman seemed to share his doubts about Communist cooperation.

But when they entered the dining room, late for dinner, Chiang
appeared tense. Eighteen guests were waiting, a fire burning, cherry
blossoms on the table and calligraphed scrolls on the walls. He worried
he had said too much, perhaps overplayed his hand. More important,
he was increasingly concerned about Manchuria, and Harriman had
not entirely consoled him.

On the same day that the United States dropped an atomic bomb
on Nagasaki, eleven Soviet armies had, as Stalin promised at Yalta,
surprised the Japanese during a rainstorm and swept into China's

northeast. Ever since, the withdrawal of 300,000 Soviet troops from Manchuria had been repeatedly pledged and repeatedly postponed. At first, the delays came at Chiang's request: he wanted more time to get troops in position to take over. A week before Harriman's arrival, Moscow announced another delay—this one without consulting Chiang. The stated reason was weather. But it came in the context of mounting protest, Chinese and American, over the Red Army's seizure of "war booty" in Manchuria. The message was clear: if Chiang challenged the Kremlin, there would be consequences.

For all the geopolitical intricacy, Soviet conduct in Manchuria was, at bottom, old-fashioned pillage and plunder. Had world revolution been the priority, the Soviets would have ceded Japanese-built industrial infrastructure to the CCP, in service of China's own revolution. Instead, they took everything they could. Factories, power plants, and railways were dismantled, lashed onto trucks and tanks, and carted into Siberia. Even Chinese Communists were appalled—by the greed, by the inability to distinguish between Japanese foes and Chinese friends, by the "capacity to drink." Stalin was unapologetic: a conquering army was due its "trophies."

The predation hinted at the true Soviet objectives in Manchuria. What Stalin wanted above all was domination, the commanding position Tsarist Russia had before the humiliation of the Russo-Japanese War. Domination meant economic privileges and a warm-water port, but also, most important, security. Despite victory in World War II, Stalin was still "trembling inside," as those around him could see. He was afraid of Manchuria becoming a launching pad for an invasion of Russia's vast, vulnerable east. He was afraid of it becoming a "showcase for the economic and political influence of another great power." And he was afraid of it becoming a bastion of American military might—which, he informed Nationalist envoys, he could never accept.

That was where the Communists came in. Stalin told them bluntly that they could not win a war for control of China. But he did not need them to win. He needed them to survive. As long as they remained a threat, on the ground in Manchuria or in the chambers of a coalition government, they gave him leverage over the Nationalists—a blade he could hold to Chiang's neck. His warnings to Chongqing were pointed: he would not tolerate an attempt to eradicate the CCP in Manchuria. But so were his warnings to Yenan: when he deemed cooperation with Chiang advantageous, they must cooperate. He would not let the CCP be destroyed, but nor would he let it provoke American intervention.

Chiang had a sense of Stalin's approach. He had been playing his own double game, also attempting to use barbarian to check barbarian. He wanted to secure as much U.S. support as possible without spooking Moscow, and to placate Moscow without angering Washington. To that end, he had offered Stalin a lot: control of Manchurian railways, rights to Manchurian ports, broad commercial advantages. After Marshall's arrival in Chongqing, Chiang had even sent his son to Moscow with additional promises: he would not "liquidate" the Communists, the Soviets would get their "dominant position," American troops would never be allowed in Manchuria. But recently, Chiang's hopes of simultaneously securing Moscow's support and Washington's friendship had started to recede. The Kremlin's price was turning out to be far higher than he was willing or able to pay. The Red Army's continued presence in Manchuria sent an ominous signal of the consequences.

When Marshall, Harriman, and Chiang met again the following night, Manchuria figured prominently. Harriman had a strong and personal interest. Thirty years earlier, his magnate father had tried, and failed, to acquire the South Manchuria Railroad from the Russian government. (A distant cousin of George Kennan, also a Soviet specialist and also named George Kennan, had written a monograph on the episode called *E. H. Harriman's Far Eastern Plans*.) Harriman was primed to hear Chiang's description of Soviet conduct in Manchuria and come away indignant. It was "a case of vandalism and theft," he said, a threat to "the whole policy of the Open Door." America could not "acquiesce."

Before they parted at midnight, Chiang gave Harriman a message for Truman. He hoped Marshall would stay in China for some time, even once an agreement was struck. It might all come apart otherwise.

"He thought there was a chance of success," Harriman recorded, "if General Marshall remained." Afterward, Marshall added a cautionary message of his own: progress so far was extremely fragile.

Harriman left the next morning, eager to reach Washington and raise the alarm on the Soviets in Manchuria. On the way, he stopped in Shanghai and saw Wedemeyer. After their conversation, Wedemeyer decided he had better reread *Das Kapital.*

But in Yenan that same day, the Communists were choosing a different path. As political talks approached a conclusion, eased along by Marshall's democratic designs, Zhou had gone to confer with his comrades. After greeting a smiling Mao on the rocky Yenan airstrip, he outlined the PCC proposals. The five top Communist leaders—Mao, Zhou, Zhu De, Liu Shaoqi, and Ren Bishi—came to a quick decision: accept them all. Peace was truly possible, Mao said. Others wondered which of them should join Chiang's government. Zhou thought he might make a good minister of agriculture and forestry.

After landing back in Chongqing late on January 30, Zhou was in Marshall's living room first thing the next morning to deliver the news. "The door toward democracy is now pushed open," he said. "The conditions necessary to the introduction of socialism do not exist." The Communists would follow "the American path"—"U.S.-styled democracy and science," "free enterprise," "agricultural reform," "industrialization," "the development of individuality." They were "prepared to cooperate with the United States in matters both of a local and national character"—a signal, some of Marshall's aides thought, that the CCP was choosing Washington over Moscow. Zhou also shared an anecdote. Mao, when asked if he was going to visit the Soviet Union, had laughed and replied he would rather visit the United States, where he could "learn a lot of things useful to China."

Before leaving, Zhou handed Marshall a letter. "I greatly appreciate your fair and just attitude in the course of negotiating and implementing the truce agreement," it read. "On behalf of the Central Committee of the Chinese Communist Party, I wish to extend you our deepest thanks." It was signed by Mao.

Later that day, the PCC finalized the agreements. "All meaningless political strife can from now on be thoroughly eliminated," Chiang proclaimed at the close of three weeks of debate. "Our important problem today is how to safeguard unity and how to establish a democratic system." The PCC resolutions were full of venerable democratic principles and hopeful democratic plans—"a charter for the development of a democratic nation," the press said. All parties would be legalized, all armies nationalized. In May, a National Assembly would ratify a constitution enshrining basic rights. Until then, Chiang's government would be run by a State Council, half the seats controlled by Nationalists, half split among other groups, while local governments remained as they were until elections. Some analysts thought the Communists had "achieved big political gains," as the *New York Times'* Tillman Durdin wrote. But in Marshall's view, a key outcome was to the Nationalists' advantage: recognition of the "national leadership of President Chiang Kai-shek."

The political agreement was promptly hailed as a second great step toward peace, with Marshall again due a share of the credit—though just how large a share was known only to him and Chiang. Students cheered at the mention of Marshall's name, calling him "a true and great friend of the Chinese." An Executive Headquarters spokesman announced that "there is no longer any doubt that both parties want peace and will do everything within their power to attain it." Walter Lippmann published a laudatory column: "It would have been only too easy to drift, and to be pushed and pulled, into a horrible mess. . . . It is not, I think, too soon to say that we have prevented it."

Even Chiang allowed himself some optimism. He detected a drastic change in Zhou's attitude and genuine support for cooperation. And Marshall, Chiang wrote in his diary, was starting to see the Communists for what they were. He added a few days later, "Marshall and I are bonding." In public, Chiang said he might retire once the government was reorganized and armies combined: "I shall have finished my responsibility." Americans called him China's George Washington.

Chiang might have been even more heartened had he seen the orders issued by Yenan. A directive on "the current situation and its tasks" went to party members across China: "The Chinese revolution has now shifted from a phase of armed struggle to one of peaceful mass and parliamentary struggle." A series of dictates followed: "domestic issues should be settled politically"; "the party will no longer issue direct orders to the army." Failure to adapt to the "peaceful new democratic stage" was classified as a revolutionary sin: closed-doorism. Yenan stressed that Marshall "not only represents the United States, in fact, he is the representative [of the international community] to carry out the agreement of the Moscow Conference."

Communist officials ordered cadres to brush up on their politics, since "all of the party's activities must be suited to this new stage." They were to cooperate with Chiang and other relatively moderate Nationalists to "isolate" hard-line factions, such as the CC Clique. They were to advocate popular reforms, at which "our party should be relatively more skilled than the KMT." Mao himself sent instructions to his commanders in Manchuria, emphasizing that "a policy of civil war" would mean "failure."

In Yenan, Mao gave his first interview in months. "China has stepped into a stage of democracy," he offered buoyantly to an Associated Press reporter. "Marshall has made an indelible contribution." Liu Shaoqi tracked down a Dixie Mission officer and spent two hours expounding on the Communists' commitment to peace. "The main task is drafting the constitution through which a parliamentary and cabinet system of government akin to that of the United States and Great Britain will be adopted," he explained. The CCP started making plans to close its revolutionary headquarters and set up shop in a major city, though Mao hoped it would not be anywhere too hot.

Seeing all of this unfold, Marshall radioed Washington. He needed a message in Harriman's hands urgently: the cautionary note he had wanted conveyed to the president was no longer necessary. Things were going well. Marshall was aware that, as Melby put it to him, "so far it is only words, words, words." But, Marshall wrote, "I do not now see any heavy storm clouds on the horizon."

February 2 was Chinese New Year, the Year of the Rooster (signifying exorcism of evil spirits) giving way to the Year of the Dog (signifying coming good fortune). There was jubilation in Chongqing, sounded out by firecrackers and gongs. The skies were clearing after days of rain. A note arrived for Marshall from Truman: "It looks as if the Chinese program is working out exactly as planned. Thanks to you."

Meanwhile, Katherine had been saying a "daily prayer": that her husband would manage to "bring some sort of unity out of chaos and come home."

On February 11, hopes still running high, there was a burst of outrage in Chongqing. One year after Roosevelt, Churchill, and Stalin signed the Yalta Agreement, the text of it was released. As many had suspected but those few in the know denied, it included—along with understandings on Germany, Eastern Europe, and the United Nations—a secret protocol on Asia.

When struck, the secret deal had seemed straightforward. After Germany's defeat, Stalin would be able to do what he wanted, when he wanted, in Manchuria. Better, Washington figured, to persuade him to invade in time to help against Japan, and with attendant promises to support Chiang, rather than let him wait until it was no longer militarily useful or carve off a Soviet-backed People's Republic of Manchuria. In exchange, Stalin wanted "preeminent interests" and a naval base in Manchuria, along with independence for Outer Mongolia (which had been part of imperial China). It was a small price to pay, the Americans reasoned. Marshall, at Yalta but not centrally involved, had given his military assessment that a timely Soviet attack would have significant value, measurable in American lives. The secrecy also seemed straightforward. The attack was unlikely to stay a surprise if the Chinese government, or the U.S. Congress, knew in advance. Stalin did not tell Mao either.

As Chiang came to realize what Yalta gave away, he despaired: "American diplomacy has no center, no policy, no morals." But he also saw the logic. Although ceding Outer Mongolia was a "maximum sacrifice" and Soviet influence in Manchuria "an ache in the joints," the concessions might allay a greater threat from the Communist "disease of the heart."

Yet what looked like a sensible trade-off in the heat of battle could look like an indefensible sellout in the light of victory. That was especially true as it became clear that Yalta had not sated Soviet appetites: demands for economic concessions and "war booty" continued. When the secret deal became public, angry Chinese took to the streets.

In Chongqing, 10,000 students marched for full restoration of sovereignty in Manchuria, shouting "Down with imperialism!" as they passed the Soviet embassy. They held signs: "The USSR = Germany + Japan," "Stalin = Hitler + Hirohito." Mobs split off and ransacked the offices of two newspapers, one published by the CCP, the other by a liberal party, the Democratic League, sending staffers to the hospital. It soon emerged that Nationalist toughs had spearheaded the violence, with Chen Li-fu operating somewhere behind the scenes.

Marshall went into unusual detail when updating Truman. "I feel that it not only involves me in matters beyond my mission but is perhaps more dangerous to world accord than any other present issue," he explained. "It is clear to me that the survival of much of what has been accomplished this past month will depend to an important degree on an early disposition of the festering situation in Manchuria." But if escalating tensions were a threat to the success of his mission, the success of his mission would be the best way to address the tensions. "China must proceed with her projected unification at the fastest possible pace," he wrote, "so as to eliminate her present vulnerability to Soviet undercover attack, which exists so long as there remains a separate Communist Government and a separate Communist Army in China."

So it was with added urgency that Marshall turned to his next task. He had secured a cease-fire. With his quiet help, the PCC had laid a path to democracy. Now it was up to his new Committee of Three to make two enemy armies one.

Marshall's fellow members arrived at Happiness Gardens before lunch on February 11—perhaps inauspiciously, the day the Yalta text became public. But the sun was out, plum trees were blooming, and Marshall was feeling confident about what he had seen as the hardest problem of all. "Things today," he said while preparing, "give some indication that the Nationalization of the Army—integration and demobilization—will not be too difficult." Zhou was joined by a new Nationalist representative, General Chang Chih-chung, instead of Chang Chun, and they knew each other well. Both taught at the Whampoa military academy in the 1920s, and General Chang had recently been Chiang's envoy to Yenan. He had an aptitude for both intrigue and conciliation, and a fondness for corny quips. Marshall, he said, was like a matchmaker in a marriage.

All three understood the importance of their task. "Political power comes from the barrel of a gun," Mao had observed after the bloody end of the first Communist-Nationalist united front. This time, the Communists would give up their guns only once political power was secure. "Our armies are the only guarantee of our continued existence in our liberated areas until the Government is reorganized," said a CCP spokesman. Chiang also knew where power came from. "If I control the army, I will have the power to control the country," he had realized years before. Persuading the Communists to give up their armies was like trying "to negotiate with the tiger for his skin," he told Marshall. But in Marshall's view, as Melby recorded it, "unless this one works the rest is pure illusion."

As usual, Marshall had the wheels already turning. A general named Alvan Gillem was on his way from the United States to help design a national army. Other officers came from Shanghai for support. Wedemeyer plotted out a reduction in troop numbers, for a smaller, higher-quality force that would be superior to the "cancerous sore" of Chiang's current military. Both sides, the idea went, would demobilize large portions of their armies, then Mao's units would be folded into Chiang's—made, in Byroade's words, "digestible." American intelligence estimated that Chiang had about three million troops, Mao almost one million.

Distrust was hardly the only obstacle. What Marshall envisioned was fundamentally new for both sides: the military as an institution of democracy rather than an instrument of party control. "You are accepting the proposition of westernizing your armies according to our democratic system," he told Zhou and Chang. He hoped to do this, he said, "with as little variance to Chinese methods and traditions as possible." But however it was handled, the change was a revolution in its own right.

Even with existential stakes, the atmosphere was warm. Over lunch that first day, there was frivolous chatter about how Americans eat rice and the prevalence of syphilis among dissolute Tibetan monks. Chang took to calling Marshall the Professor—"the Professor has full control of his students"—and threw a party after the Committee had wrapped up one evening. Zhou brought Madame Mao, said to be in town for dental work; a band played American songs.

Still, sessions were slow going. The table would be covered in thick reports and planning documents, stacks of Chiang's British-import letterhead for notes, Dixon pencils and sharpeners—it was a "war of papers," Marshall said approvingly. Despite his efforts at efficiency, they would start with an extended "exchange of compliments" and end with an "exchange of platitudes." Discussion of a sentence could take an hour. Translation was often contested; when it dragged, Marshall would write letters. Amid the "long and extremely delicate negotiations regarding the unification of the army," he told a friend, "I would like to boil this business all down to the simple proposition of negotiations with Katherine over where we plant the shrubs and flowers, shall it be cabbages or cauliflower, who gets the car this morning, and what are we doing this evening." A couple hours in, they would break for hot towels, sweet cakes, and tea. Chang would emit a "raucous belch," and talks would continue.

Only weeks earlier, Marshall had intended to stay out of these talks. Now he was moving them along with a sometimes heavy hand. He pushed for concrete proposals, since "a discussion without a definite paper is endless and usually arrives nowhere." He had his staff develop plans, figuring that "the quickest way was to let the Americans try to take a crack at it by themselves." (Some recommendations he ran by Chang privately first, both to check on Nationalist interests and to urge flexibility.) The Professor could be didactic: "That is the way every democracy works." He held forth on American military thought and reflected on his past success bringing leery Allied militaries under one command, his "education in this sort of business."

Day by laborious day, a plan came together. A week in, on a pleasant afternoon, they seemed to be nearing their goal. "You as umpire would be temporarily out of a job," Chang joked. "I will welcome it," Marshall replied. There was remaining disagreement on two questions: how quickly the process would move, and how thoroughly the armies would combine. Marshall had strong views on both. Integration must be fast and "fusion" total. There could not be intact Communist units that were part of a national military by insignia alone; it would be too easy to split off again. Zhou was resistant. "We must fully realize that the armies in China have been hostile to each other for 18 whole years," he protested. That evening, Marshall asked to see him alone.

Over two months, Marshall and Zhou had come to respect one another. In manner they were different: Marshall impassive, his lined face stoic, Zhou with "quick, deft gestures," in a diplomat's words, and a "personality full of mobility." But both had presence, precise minds, and powerful recall. Like Marshall, Zhou had his staff working sixteen-hour days, reviewing translations, writing memos, reading American newspapers—"if there is anything new, tell," he instructed. "He could run General Motors," Marshall's aides said.

Marshall told Zhou he had an idea. He knew any delay was dangerous. Military integration could not wait or go halfway. It needed to move quickly and be complete, or the choreography of his mission would falter, democratic reform stall, and peace come apart. To avert that outcome, Marshall wanted to set up an American-run "elementary school" for Communist troops.

The premise behind it was that a major obstacle to integration was the "serious loss of face" that might result from throwing "unorganized swarms of Communist soldiers" into Nationalist units that had modern training and weapons. Marshall had in mind a three-month basic training where the Communists would learn how to be part of a twentieth-century army—how regiments and divisions work, how to care for weapons, how to parade in "a presentable manner." As one American officer put it, "There will be no National Government units in the area to sneer at the Communists' first efforts to organize a modernized force." Marshall hoped the training would quash excuses for delay, speeding the end of autonomous Communist armies by months. And as he emphasized privately, it was essential "to expedite the integration to enable China to present a solid front to the Russian infiltration."

Marshall made the case to Zhou—for demobilization, for integration, for the elementary school—and asked him to convince other Communist leaders. Marshall had pressured Chiang to give ground on political reform; now the CCP had to give ground on military unification. The next morning, Zhou flew to Yenan on an American plane.

"Nobody thought this could be done," Marshall said when the Committee of Three reconvened two days later. Zhou had returned with assent in hand. Within eighteen months, armies at war for eighteen years would be a unified force, with five Nationalists for every Communist—or, rather, five *former* Nationalists for every *former* Communist, for it would be a truly integrated national army, answerable not to a leader or party, but to a democratic government. In Manchuria, the ratio was even more lopsided: there would be fifteen divisions, fourteen of them made up of former Nationalists, a steep reduction in

Communist strength. Chiang understood that the package was advantageous for him. "Since agreement on reorganizing the armies has been
reached, the harm will not be too bad," he wrote in his diary. "Even if
the Russians favor the Communists, they cannot inflict harm on me."

They had only to work out final details—how to draw military zones,
how to structure commands. Then, to Marshall's displeasure and dis-
belief, they got stuck on one: how to title the agreement. Chang rejected
the inclusion of "nationalization," arguing that it implied the illegiti-
macy of current Nationalist forces; Zhou demanded it, on party orders.
Suddenly they were deadlocked again.

The dispute, however petty, reflected deeper unease. Although Zhou
had gotten his comrades to sign off on the plan, Mao had been under-
scoring the dangers. "We want unification, but we do not want to be
eliminated," he said. "How we should go about it should be decided
according to the concrete circumstances of the time. This is the difference between our way and the way of the French Communists," who
had disarmed too carelessly, too soon.

In Nationalist circles, there was pressure from the right. Marshall
recognized that "the conservatives political and military are naturally
rather bitter against me," as he wrote Truman, and that Chiang "is in
an extremely difficult position struggling with the ultraconservative
and determined wing of each group, many if not most of whom will
lose position and income all or in part by the changes proposed." There
were signs that hard-liners were striking back: the Manchuria riots,
protests against the Executive Headquarters in Beijing, attacks on PCC
representatives in Chongqing.

Marshall decided to fire a shot across the hard-liners' bow, in hopes
of deterring outright sabotage. On February 23, he gathered local newspaper editors for a blunt meeting. "Now I have been sent on a diplomatic mission, but I am not at all a diplomat," he began. He warned of
what would happen if Nationalist opponents of unification succeeded
in thwarting him. "When you terminate my mission, you terminate a
great many other things," he said. "If you are not already aware, please
understand that there is a very large group in the United States who

are opposed to practically anything outside of the United States and all they need is a good argument to force the Government's hands." He asked the editors to help make those risks understood.

It took two more days, but Marshall ultimately devised an unwieldy but acceptable title for the military agreement: "Basis for Military Reorganization and for the Integration of the Communist Forces Into the Nationalist Army." On February 25 at 4 p.m., Chang arrived in his dress uniform, Zhou in a blue suit and with a fresh haircut. Marshall had given each a personalized leather briefcase as a token of thanks.

There was one last argument to be had before they proceeded. Marshall did not want to put his name on the agreement—he thought it was not his place. But the others insisted, and he conceded. "So if we are going to be hung," he sighed, "I will hang with you." Sixty reporters, Chinese and foreign, watched as the Committee of Three signed, Zhou and Chang with the same calligraphy brush, Marshall with a fountain pen he had taken from his pocket.

"The signatures this afternoon put an end to the long struggle between the Government and the Communists," said Chang. "We will completely change the picture which has been dominating in China for the last 18 years," said Zhou. They credited Marshall. Chang reeled off epithets: midwife of unification, leading strategist of the world, ambassador of peace.

Marshall added only a few words. "This agreement, I think, represents the great hope of China," he said as camera shutters clicked. "I can only trust that its pages will not be soiled by a small group of irreconcilables who for a separate purpose would defeat the Chinese people in their overwhelming desire for peace and prosperity." Amid the celebration, it was a deliberately discordant message, meant to put "on notice" anyone who might want to upset progress.

CHAPTER 6

First Lord of the Warlords

few days later, the Committee of Three boarded Marshall's C-54, took off into a morning sky of rolling dark clouds, and flew north. It was the start of a journey across the ground where high-level accord would have to take root. "At the top they drink toasts to one another," went a local saying, "but here we plunge the white sword in and drag the red sword out."

The first stop was the Executive Headquarters in Beijing.* From Hank Byroade in a hotel room, it had grown into a sprawling operation, as Marshall envisioned, officers spread over three floors in the Rockefeller-built Peking Union Medical College: Communists on one, Nationalists on another, Americans in between. Nearby, the Forbidden City and Tiananmen Square, heart of the imperial capital, were starting to recover from years of Japanese occupation; Chiang Kai-shek's portrait now hung from the Gate of Heavenly Peace.

The Committee was greeted by Walter Robertson, the American Executive Headquarters commissioner. A well-mannered Virginian, conservative in politics and scrupulously professional in conduct, Robertson led a briefing on the work of truce teams in the field. Then, in a

---

*At the time, the city was called Beiping ("northern peace") rather than Beijing ("northern capital"), since Chiang had chosen Nanjing ("southern capital") as the seat of his government.

wood-paneled auditorium, Marshall addressed the American, Nation-alist, and Communist officers carrying out his experiment. "It is not so very difficult to reach a general agreement on a policy gathered around a table at Chongqing," he told them. "The real test is in carrying that policy into successful execution, which the little teams of three men from this headquarters have succeeded in doing." Their effort was "unique in the world's history."

Marshall knew any success so far had not come easily. To work, the Executive Headquarters had to "swing a heavy stick," as an aide said, and Marshall himself was the heaviest stick available. "My time was largely consumed last week in furthering special actions to suppress fighting in isolated regions," he had written Truman as the effort got up and running.

He received a daily "trusum," a truce summary that registered infractions, charges, and countercharges by both sides. He pressed his counterparts in Chongqing to keep commanders in line. He brokered a propaganda truce to end sniping in the newspapers. He weighed in on how much cash and radio gear each truce team should carry. He directed the Americans to provide their Chinese partners with jackets, socks, and mittens when setting out for wintry battlefields—they will "be your friends for life."

Everything from basic facts to destinations of truce teams was a matter for dispute. "Both sides," Byroade recorded, "are especially eager to get teams to the areas where they are outnumbered and have reason to fear the other side." Each promoted its own tales of griev-ance, sometimes much embellished, while denying more incriminating anecdotes. Early on, the contested provinces of Rehe and Chahar—the sticking point in the first Committee of Three—had proved especially problematic. A Communist team member had turned recalcitrant, being generally evasive and occasionally vanishing. Then there had been a Nationalist troop movement that prompted Marshall to warn Chiang against "establishing unfortunate precedents and disrupt-ing the armistice." It took days of attention, from both Beijing and Chongqing, before an uneasy stasis set in.

Most Americans found the Communists to be the more troublesome partners. In Beijing, they frequently stalled, pleading a lack of personnel or the need to "study a matter further." Some chalked this up to malice, some to incompetence. "This can probably be attributed to the guerrilla nature of their past operations," Byroade surmised. In the field, there was, an American officer reported, "a degree of cooperation and cold consideration of facts and evidence presented, from the National member, but only one-sided consideration from the Communist."

The Nationalists, however, proved difficult on one important question: whether the Executive Headquarters had authority over Manchuria. The Committee of Three agreement had not made it clear, but Marshall was surprised when he learned that Chiang wanted to keep truce teams away for the time being. It meant that, when the Red Army withdrew from Manchuria, truce teams might be absent where they were needed most.

Still, Marshall considered the Executive Headquarters "the most important instrument we have in China," and he had been adding to its functions. The number of truce teams quickly jumped from six to seventeen, then doubled again, so that one was always on hand to rush out and thwart a bellicose commander's "pleasant dreams of conquest." A special unit was charged with overseeing restoration of railways. There were still nearly half a million Japanese in north and central China, and the Executive Headquarters was supposed to get them home. And now it had another responsibility, implementation of the military agreement. The task was immense: reducing total divisions by 80 percent, stripping generals of control over civilian affairs, instituting democratic checks. "The prosperity of China is directly dependent upon your execution of this new mission," Marshall told the officers in Beijing.

So was the success of his own mission. This infrastructure of peace was key to the endgame. With agreements on a cease-fire, democratic unity, and military integration now signed, Marshall had started putting that endgame into motion. He radioed the State Department to say it was time for an assistance package and notified Chiang and Zhou that he would soon go to Washington to ensure that the new China got its due. He would return, but then leave China for good by late summer. Even that, he pointed out, would be "a great deal longer than I anticipated."

Everywhere the Committee of Three went, Marshall was received as a conquering hero. Smiling families thronged his car. Bands struggled spiritedly through the "Star-Spangled Banner." School groups clapped in unison. A governor presented a painting of the Taoist god of war and pronounced Marshall "god of war of the world." Crowds waved homemade signs: "Most Fairly Friend of China," "Terror of the Evildoers," "First Lord of the Warlords."

With Marshall, Zhou, and Chang conversing in its leather armchairs, the three Executive Headquarters commissioners along for the ride, the C-54 crisscrossed the North China Plain, a heartland stretching from the Yangtze in the south to the Great Wall in the north, bleak in winter and sun-scorched in summer. General Gillem, also accompanying Marshall, had a stateside analogy for most locales: west Texas, the Dust Bowl, the Chicago of China. They went from commander to commander, trouble spot to trouble spot, the spirit of the Committee of Three meant to stir a generalized spirit of cooperation. "The situation," Marshall was saying by their tenth stop, "is most encouraging." They did so much toasting, *ganbei*, that the trip was referred to as "the *ganbei* circuit."

Marshall gave each truce team a pep talk. He lauded their "great personal sacrifices" and "high spirit for the good of the Chinese people." He appealed to them to let go of historic antagonisms: "The rights and wrongs of the past 18 years will be debated for 18 years to come. We have something now that demands that we look entirely in the future." He talked about baseball. "Everybody disagrees with the umpire," he said. "But the game can't go on without him."

Truce teams were operating in remote, rugged places—Americans said that going from urban to rural China was like going a thousand years back in time—and Marshall could see it was "a rough and thankless business." Food supplies were uncertain, clean water scarce, illness frequent, support minimal. (Marshall chided Byroade, now head of operations, for not taking good enough care of men in the field.) Communications back to headquarters were fitful at best; even getting messages from Chongqing to Beijing could be a struggle. Each team carried a letter: "From evaluation of reports carefully considered by this Headquarters, it appears that the forces of your command are carrying on offensive action. You are specifically directed to cease action and movements." But there were intransigent and hostile commanders on both sides, along with warlords, bandits, and puppet armies of indeterminate loyalty. "When I went into the lines," an American colonel recounted, "I looked down the Nationalist rifle barrels, and when I came back, I looked at the Communist rifle barrels."

Marshall took an almost paternal pride in the work of the trios—"an amazing task," he glowed, "a great service for China and for American prestige." He noted to Washington that each American "with communications almost nonexistent will have to dominate a region larger than Pennsylvania and bring factions who have been at war for 18 years to a peaceful understanding." One officer stoutly assured him, "The biggest problem we have got here is how to break down the feeling of distrust that has existed in the past between the Communists and the Nationalists. And, General, we can do it."

Traversing North China, the Committee of Three became well acquainted with the difficulties. (Zhou had suggested continuing into Manchuria, but Marshall demurred, worrying it would give Moscow "a new opportunity for conjecture and possible propaganda lines.") There were commanders who had heard nothing from their leaders in months and knew little of the agreements struck in Chongqing. There were florid accounts of blockades and sabotage. "The team meets, holds its temper, and talks amicably, but is unable to take action," one American officer said.

The Committee attacked each problem directly. Marshall lectured inflamed local commanders about "the much larger issues at stake." Zhou and Chang reprimanded unruly underlings. They invariably departed with promises of harmony ringing in their ears. "If reiteration after reiteration of intention to cooperate in every way means any-thing," Marshall concluded, "I think we are on the way to immediate clearing up of conditions through North China."

Four days into the journey, after a turbulent flight over desolate ter-rain, there was a stop so contentious that even the Committee of Three lost its cool. The CCP member of the truce team deployed there had gone missing for twelve days; his partners were paralyzed under the consensus-based rules of operation, while Communist forces toppled telegraph lines, ripped up track, and kept the city under virtual siege. Chang said he needed "4 glasses of water to quell my temper." He and Zhou argued heatedly. Marshall, however, kept pressing. They skipped dinner. They stayed overnight. And in the morning, after more dis-cussion, they settled on a solution. "Marshall made best speech of the trip!" Gillem wrote in his diary. "Outlined plan and told them they had better perform—or else!"

That afternoon, the C-54 took off for Yenan, cradle of revolution.

In Yenan, the Communists were ready. They had been preparing, intent on making the right impression. The band had been rehearsing, the honor guard drilling. A work team had built a bridge across the icy Yen River for easy travel between party headquarters and the Dixie Mission. A women's group had stitched a five-star flag.

The Americans posted to Yenan were equally intent on a successful visit, and they knew what Marshall wanted. "He likes things to click," said Ivan Yeaton, the Dixie Mission's commanding officer, "and nobody can make a Chinaman go fast on his own." He urged the Communists to create a "war room," with maps on the walls, so Marshall would take them seriously. The Americans even helped build it.

"Things locally have reached an all-time high, due of course to the masterful manner in which General Marshall has handled the situa-tion to date," Yeaton had reported. The Communists drew a distinction between American imperialists and American progressives; Marshall, many believed, was a progressive. Zhou compared him to Stilwell.

Yeaton mentioned one particularly good sign of local spirits: the Chairman was showing up at dances again. For most of the winter, Mao had been withdrawn, said to be sick. It was what a rival had once mocked as a "diplomatic illness." In trying times, his strength depleted and the way forward unclear, Mao would retreat into isolation. From watchful convalescence, he could let a situation clarify before making his next moves. While Zhou was navigating the tricky currents in Chongqing, Mao was lying in bed, cold towels on his forehead.

In his twenties, Mao had made a list of his flaws: he was vain, emotional, arrogant, and quick to blame others. Worst of all, he was weak-willed, and this he resolved to overcome. He scrawled notes in the margins of a book of German philosophy: "Why should you obey God rather than yourself? You are God." He pondered what it meant to be a great man: "His force is like that of a powerful wind arising from a deep gorge, like the irresistible sexual desire for one's lover, a force that will not stop, that cannot be stopped. All obstacles dissolve before him." In his first publication, "A Study of Physical Education," he declared, "The will is the antecedent of a man's career." He swam in freezing rivers and climbed mountains. He studied biographies—Napoleon, Montesquieu, Rousseau. He admired Theodore Roosevelt and wrote of George Washington, "We need great people like these."

Born in a village in Hunan in 1893, Mao was 17 before he heard of America, 19 before he saw a map of the world. But from an early age, he knew humiliation and anger. He clashed violently with his on-the-make father. He seethed at the smugness of well-to-do classmates. He loved books and study but hated school and its authorities. By the time he could connect his own humiliation to country and class, he was also coming to understand the force of his rage, and the rage of those he sought to lead. He called forth all "who were formerly despised and kicked into the gutter by the gentry, who had no social standing, and who were completely deprived of the right to speak." One of his first organizational efforts was an Avenge the Shame Society.

When it came to power, Mao was ruthless. If nothing eclipsed the will of a great man, nothing would constrain him. But at first many comrades were skeptical. Although he was present at the creation of the CCP, in 1921, it took him many years to build his position. Only with the Long March a decade and a half later—a 6,000-mile flight from Chiang's "extermination campaigns," which nearly 100,000 Communists started and fewer than 10,000 finished—did he emerge as the party's clear leader.

From there, he solidified his power, honing his shrewdness, revolutionary vision, and apparatus of control. A new disciplinary code specified all manner of counterrevolutionary sins, many punishable by death. An ambitious sadist named Kang Sheng, trained in cruelty by Stalin's greatest practitioner, became his head of security and led an inquisition, a "rectification campaign," to eliminate dissent. Rivals confessed transgressions, under torture when torture was necessary. "Leniency has a limit," Kang told already brutalized victims.

Now, in Yenan, Mao had not just power, but supremacy. He laid down doctrine, writing essays and poems on coarse yellow grasspaper and storing them in Standard Oil drums. (The Rockefellers had sunk wells nearby three decades earlier.) He cultivated earthy charisma, unbuckling his pants in public to search for lice, like a peasant. With acolytes, he held forth, bestowing the idiosyncratic insights of an autodidact and the enigmatic slogans of a visionary. With young female idealists, he took full advantage. One was a Bohemian actress known for playing Nora in a Shanghai production of Ibsen's *A Doll's House*. Kang Sheng had brought her into the party and introduced her to Mao, who renamed her Jiang Qing and made her his fourth wife. Once Madame Mao, she raged against the "shameless hussies" and "dance-hall bitches" he continued to consort with. Throughout, Mao held up the Communists as champions of women's liberation.

It was hardly his only instance of philosophical flexibility. Tactical agility was central to his approach. "Dogma is less useful than excrement," he said. "We see that dog excrement can fertilize the fields and man's can feed the dog. And dogmas?" (Among the less conceptual examples of flexibility: while denouncing Nationalist corruption, the CCP traded profitably in "special product," its codename for opium.) Mao quoted an old maxim: seek truth from facts. It meant responding to circumstances pragmatically without forsaking ultimate goals—or going, as he did, from bloodthirsty revolutionary to advocate of peace and back again, sincere, in his way, at every step.

Late in the afternoon of March 4, the preparations in place, Mao waited on Yenan's airstrip. That morning, *Emancipation Daily* had set out the party line on Marshall: "His effort has achieved glorious success. The Chinese people will cooperate with him, because his endeavor is in accordance with the fundamental interests of the Chinese people and world peace." As in all things, Mao insisted on discipline in diplomacy, with messages and postures uniform across the party. "Diplomatic attitudes should be cautious and open," an earlier directive had instructed. "Hospitality should be simple but warm."

Marshall's C-54 was approaching over the forbidding landscape of intersecting ravines, its pilot searching for Yenan's pagoda, eager to land before dark. In the cabin, Gillem looked out the window and reflected that it was bad country for a parachute drop. "It's easy to see why the capital is out here," he wrote in his diary as the pilot searched. "Words inadequate to describe how isolated this eroded impassible area." They began to see terraced fields planted on otherwise barren hilltops and arched doorways cut into slopes, entrances to caves where residents lived. When the pilot at last spotted the destination, the drop into the valley was abrupt.

Mao stood on the rocky airstrip, winged by American and Communist officers, crowds massed behind him, band and honor guard ready. Marshall came down the plane's ladder alone, hat and leather gloves on, double-breasted tan coat buttoned to its fur collar against the cold. He and Mao shook hands for the first time.

Many Americans met Mao and came away perplexed. No longer the "gaunt, rather Lincolnesque figure" journalists encountered after the Long March, he was getting pudgy and losing his hair. His voice was soft and handshake weak. Where was the charisma, the command?

Some met him and understood. The Mao of Edgar Snow's *Red Star*

Over China was a figure of myth, the *ubermensch* Mao willed himself to be: "a man with an unusual memory and extraordinary powers of concentration," "a deep student of philosophy and history," "a military and political strategist of considerable genius." He was even "quite free from symptoms of megalomania," Snow waxed. There were others less taken yet still capable of seeing what Snow called the "force of destiny" in Mao. The marine who co-opted *gung ho* spoke of his "uncanny faculty of piercing through the heart of a problem." A diplomat first struck by the fact that Mao was "plump" went on to perceive his "incandescence" and "immense, smooth calm and sureness."

After reviewing the guard with Zhou and Chang, Mao and military chief Zhu De a step behind, Marshall climbed into a Dixie Mission jeep. Standing in the front, he greeted crowds that lined dirt streets decorated as if for a holiday. A banner welcomed the members of the Committee of Three, but there were only two flags flying above it: the Stars and Stripes and the Hammer and Sickle.

The buildings were mud and brick with white-washed walls. Most cadres lived in the hillside caves. So did many leaders, including Mao for a time. (Dignitaries had two-room rather than one-room caves, lit by kerosene lanterns rather than cotton wicks soaked in bean oil.) Even inside it was cold. Heat came from charcoal braziers—there was little wood anywhere nearby.

Marshall kept his coat on and his hands in his pockets when he entered CCP headquarters. He lowered himself onto a small couch, alongside Gillem and Robertson, before a table crowded with tea and snacks, beneath pictures of Communist luminaries. Mao sat in a chair, gripping the armrests, and looked at his guests as if across a distance. But he was gracious. He thanked Marshall for his efforts and pledged to adhere to the three agreements, under the guidance of the United States and the leadership of Chiang Kai-shek. Marshall was gracious in turn. He wanted to convey the importance of Mao's role in building a peacefully unified China, and of a peacefully unified China's role in the world.

Marshall praised Zhou, blamed friction on "irreconcilable elements," and agreed that it was important to get truce teams to Manchuria soon. He stressed he was there not to meddle, but as a friend. He noted that American troops could not stay in China for long, and that American assistance would be possible on the scale needed only if China was stable. He appealed for differences to be set aside, common good embraced. As long as he was in China, he said, he would do all he could to help.

As Marshall spoke, his host's face revealed little. But at dinner afterward, Mao toasted Marshall's "selfless dedication to the firm establishment of a peaceful, democratic, and unified China," as Marshall, coat still on, lifted a teacup. Over a simple meal, seated side-by-side on battered wooden chairs, they spoke of China's peaceful future. (A Communist who had attended the University of Michigan interpreted.) Afterward, they went to a larger hall for folk dances and skits.

Marshall spent the night on a straw mattress at the Dixie Mission. For all the controversy it had generated, the mission itself was nothing more than a low-slung stone building of eight small rooms, a covered timber porch in front. Luxurious by local standards—there was a generator and a movie projector, and the Maos sometimes came for screenings—for Americans it still had a romantically spartan air. At night, the howls of wolves echoed among the hills, and lights bobbed up the slopes, as locals returned to their caves. The next morning, there was strong coffee, eggs, and pancakes; the Americans had fashioned a griddle from the wreckage of a downed fighter plane.

By 10 a.m., Marshall was back at the airstrip, the dignitaries and crowds back to see him off. In the shadow of the C-54, he said goodbye to a smiling Madame Mao. He posed for a photograph with Mao, Zhou, and Zhu De. He and Mao had a parting conversation, positive and hopeful and vague. Mao, cap askew, face relaxed, said his party would work hard to sustain peace. They shook hands, and Marshall looked back over the crowd and barren hills and boarded his plane.

"We completely agree with General Marshall's view of China's future," *Emancipation Daily* summed up afterward. Marshall thought the visit had done what it needed to do. He was unsatisfied, however, on one count. A famously assured judge of men, he conceded that Mao remained a mystery.

"A shadow has fallen upon the scenes so lately lighted by the Allied victory," Winston Churchill said a few hours later, Truman onstage with him in Fulton, Missouri. "Nobody knows what Soviet Russia and its Communist international organization intends to do in the immediate future, or what are the limits, if any, to their expansive and proselytizing tendencies."

While hosting Marshall, the Communists had been tracking Churchill's visit to the United States. Churchill said little about Asia; his "iron curtain" was falling across Europe. But to them, the message seemed clear enough: the world was splitting in two.

In Yenan the next day, Mao received other visitors, a pair of doctors sent by Stalin to look after his health—physical and political, an American officer quipped. With Marshall gone, Mao invited the doctors into his bedroom to chat. The symbolism was intended: the Americans got the public fanfare, the Soviets access to the inner chamber.

In Washington, Truman, back from Missouri, received a note from Marshall, a muted but triumphant account of his journey. "I had a long talk with Mao Zedong at Yenan and I was frank to an extreme," he wrote. "He showed no resentment and gave me every assurance of cooperation." Marshall said he was ready to come to Washington, to secure support for the "strong, united, and democratic China" he had been sent to help build.

Truman replied promptly. He suggested Marshall rush if possible. Churchill hoped to see him before heading home.

"If things continue going as favorably as they are going now," said Truman, "I believe we can have all our forces out of China before the year is out." For him, it was very good news. He had again and again reminded Marshall, Chiang, and pleading spouses and parents of his "anxiety to get American armed forces out of China just as soon as they are no longer essential to implement our policy."

In the weeks after Japan's surrender, some 60,000 troops in the China combat theater as part of the global war effort were joined by more than 50,000 additional Marines. Their mission started to creep almost immediately. Rather than disarming Japanese troops—which Chiang wanted to keep armed and in place to block Communists, disease of the skin being preferable to disease of the heart—most Americans found themselves holding a port, bridge, or stretch of track in aid of the Nationalists. Policymakers in Washington repeated: no support of fratricidal warfare. Officers in China repeated back: how are we supposed to help Chiang without supporting fratricidal warfare? Or as one marine cracked, "Colonel, who are we neutral against?"

In Marshall's view, the troop presence was big enough to get Americans in trouble but too small to do much else over the long run. He had seen occupation before, in the Philippines. Enlisted men, a "rough, tough, hard-drinking" crowd, would get restless, rowdy, and destructive. Anti-American resentment would mount. Chinese students were already shouting in the streets, "Why don't you go home?"

It would also be hard to avoid fighting. Since the killing of the brash OSS agent John Birch, there had been numerous worrying encounters with Communists. "Never fire the first shot," Mao ordered. But that did not mean ceding ground. The idea, as Zhou put it, was to force "retreat in the face of difficulty." After several confrontations in which Americans stood down to avoid breaking the fratricidal-warfare injunction, Wedemeyer complained that the Communists were "doing their utmost to intimidate me and to cause precipitous offensive action on my part." He was trying to keep his troops from being provoked.

But to Marshall's mind, the key factor was the Soviets. The Red Army still had hundreds of thousands of troops in Manchuria; no one was certain when, or if, they would leave. While Marshall admitted to uncertainty about just how much help the Kremlin was giving the CCP, he knew it was far from all-out support. A sharp increase would mortally threaten Chiang, even with additional help from Washington. It was a matter of geography: the long Siberian border made it easy for the Soviets to arm, guide, and give refuge to their Chinese comrades.

"We must clear our hands out here as quickly as possible in order to avoid the inevitable Russian recriminations," Marshall wrote Truman. In part, he hoped to reassure Stalin, who was seized with fear of a major American presence in Manchuria or north China. But more than reassure, Marshall hoped to shame. Wedemeyer laid out the logic to Eisenhower: "General Marshall feels that the inactivation of the China Theater at an early date will greatly strengthen the Generalissimo's pressure for the removal of Russian Forces from Manchuria. I concur in this idea." With Americans leaving and the Soviet Union still occupying, "the more clearly she becomes a deliberate treaty violator in the eyes of the world," Marshall reasoned.

He wanted quick action on a sustainable long-term presence. But sustainable did not mean trivial. He had, soon after arriving, pushed to continue sending ammunition for the Nationalists' US-supplied weapons. A US-backed air force would have hundreds of fighters, bombers, and transport planes. American officers would serve as "middle men" in the military unification process. And the new Military Advisory Group would give training and advice.

Some American officials found the advisory group a bridge too far. Others wanted the mission to continue creeping, stretching the definition of "advisory." There were proposals for a 4,000-man operation, with officers accompanying Chiang's troops into the field, and for additional navy forces (raising suspicions among army men, who worried about an inter-service takeover almost as much as a Communist one).

Chiang pushed for an expansive American mission. He offered commercial advantages as a sweetener and mentioned pointedly that, if Washington was not interested in a serious military relationship, he had other offers. Wedemeyer worried that Chiang "aimed to create conditions that render our military assistance against the Chinese Communists, and possibly the Soviet Communists, mandatory or inevitable." Such suspicions were exacerbated by Chiang's meddling in personnel decisions, in an attempt, Wedemeyer groused to Marshall, to secure "the services of an American who will practically sell out his heritage." There was also a dispute about African American troops; Chiang had allowed them into China only on the condition that they stay far west, out of sight.

With Marshall's prodding, Truman authorized the Military Advisory Group's creation at the end of February. He capped its size at 1,000. As important as what it would do was what it would not do. The Joint Chiefs of Staff were explicit: "This participation in training would not under any circumstances extend to U.S. personnel accompanying Chinese troops in any combat operations."

After seven days and 3,600 miles, Marshall landed back in Chongqing on a sodden afternoon and soon came down with a heavy cold. Still, he was feeling good about the Committee of Three's journey. He also received a radio message from Washington. His aide Jim Shepley had recently gone home and sent back some words from Truman: "His praise of your achievements was glowing. He indicates a strong desire to leave China to you and is interested largely in determining what if any further support he can give you."

Congress, however, was not feeling quite as giving. Marshall had promised Chiang "liberal American assistance" to secure unity and help rebuild. "I get the impression many of the things you have in mind may be a little harder to get than we supposed," Shepley cautioned. "Your scheduled return is extremely well advised."

First Marshall needed to settle one lingering issue. There was still disagreement on whether truce teams would enter Manchuria, even as tensions over the region grew. Already dismayed by ongoing Soviet occupation and economic demands, Marshall was also hearing from Washington that "all you have accomplished may be undone by a serious depreciation of Sino-Soviet and U.S.-Soviet relations over Manchuria." Secretary of State Byrnes had recently taken it up with Moscow, invoking the Open Door and decrying "discrimination" against American economic interests.

Chiang, meanwhile, was giving up on Soviet support entirely. The

Kremlin's price had been rising, and finally it was too high. His people were incensed. It was time for a tougher line. Marshall had advised him to stall on negotiations with Moscow until he had made progress with Yenan—unity being the best defense against Soviet mischief. But on March 6, as Marshall returned to Chongqing, Chiang's government made its first formal protest against Soviet troops in Manchuria.

Ready to depart, sick with a cold, Marshall was exasperated. He pressed Zhou about Manchuria and got only evasions: it was a matter of foreign affairs, no business of the CCP's. "General M. looked badly this evening. First time I noticed it in him," Caughey recorded. "He is a very angry man," Melby thought, "and Chinese time is beginning to run very short in his mind." Marshall hardly needed the reminder he got from a leader of the Democratic League: "If no peaceful solution is found for the Northeastern situation. . . . even the foundation of peace in China you have laid will be shaken."

On March 9, Marshall visited Chiang in the country. A sumptuous dinner was waiting: whole fish, roast beef and mashed potatoes, English custard, and Taiwanese fruit in gold lacquer bowls. The wine, which Madame Chiang poured generously, was the best Caughey had ever tasted, like "liquid black walnuts."

After the Generalissimo said his evening prayer, he and Marshall talked. Chiang liked what he had heard of Marshall's trip north with the Committee of Three. "His impression of Mao Zedong is that he is a deceptive person," Chiang recorded. "I think he judges people very well." Chiang took the opportunity—one rarely missed, as Marshall had noticed since their first conversation nearly three months earlier—to highlight Yenan's ties to Moscow. In a war between China and the Soviet Union, Chiang repeated, Mao would surely fight on Stalin's side.

But Marshall was more focused on truce teams, which he thought essential to keeping Manchuria from destroying all progress. Each time he had pressed the point, Chiang balked. The stated rationale was that the Soviets would demand a role; the real fear was that truce teams would impede him from taking control of Manchuria. If the Communists wanted the teams, Chiang figured they could not be good.

Scrambling to allay Chiang's unease, Marshall wrote a directive by hand, forbidding the truce teams from hampering the "reestablishment of sovereignty" by the Nationalists. A secret instruction to the American team captains would address the risk of Soviet interference: "acquiesce with casual politeness," then "carry the ball without discussion." Marshall asked Chiang to consider it.

Chiang was also worried about mounting resistance from the "irreconcilables" in his ranks. Since March 1, the Nationalists' Central Executive Committee had been in session, under heavy secrecy, charged with party ratification of the PCC political resolutions. Many Committee members had good reason to fear the course charted by Marshall's agreements. Military unification threatened "power, prestige, money, and squeeze," in Melby's words, prompting rumors of a "revolt of the generals"; democratic reform meant "one of the greatest purges in the history of the country." Conservative advisers warned Chiang of a "revolution" in the party, and his power depended on these anxious factions. He also had his own misgivings about democracy. "Most of the people are irresolute, uneducated, and inexperienced," he said, and likely to be fooled.

Marshall sensed "the heat of a political struggle" within the Nationalists' central committee—"a Committee which *rules* China and whose officials and subordinates down the line hold their position of power and personal income by virtue of the Committee's rule, now due to be abdicated to a coalition government." He thought Chiang was making an effort to bring irreconcilables into line; Chiang had even asked Marshall to stay for part of the meeting, in case it developed "precariously."

But reaction was surfacing not just in Nationalist ranks, as those paying close attention saw. A well-sourced embassy staffer flagged "considerable change in the attitude of the Chinese Communists," including frequent use of "fascist," a staple of Kremlin invective. Melby, the resident Communist watcher, found them "an increasingly worried gang" and "quite prepared to take to the caves and ditches again if necessary." When Zhou complained of "provocations" by Nationalist hard-liners, Marshall—not entirely disagreeing—asked for forbearance, urging him to refrain from matching every taunt. But Melby wondered if both sides were simply saving "the dirty work" for Marshall's absence: "He says he is coming back, but they may be gambling that something will happen and he won't."

"If your subordinates can't do it for you, you haven't organized them properly," Marshall had told Eisenhower in the thick of world war, ordering him to take a vacation. Now, in Chongqing, Marshall knew there were unsettled problems. But on March 10, the day after dinner at the Chiangs', he instructed General Gillem to take over while he reported to Washington.

Gillem had both impressive military acumen and an agreeable temperament. In the war, he had commanded an army corps that made it closer to Berlin than any other American force. On the Committee of Three's tour, he had been earnest and attentive at Marshall's side. "I could have been here for months without getting the knowledge gained in this week's trip," he wrote in his diary.

Marshall hoped to fly the next day. First, he was intent on finalizing agreement on truce teams in Manchuria. Chiang had accepted Marshall's proposal, with conditions, but then Zhou had raised his own issues with it. Still, Marshall's fellow Committee of Three members wanted to send him off "with an easy mind." Finally, as evening approached, there was a breakthrough. The terms were clear. Marshall could leave. His machinery of peace could be put in place in Manchuria, keeping it from becoming the flashpoint of the next war.

As Marshall drove to the airfield, correspondents rushed off their dispatches: Marshall's truce teams would go to Manchuria after all. It was fitting punctuation to the glowing coverage of the Committee of Three negotiations and North China tour. "He gave me far more hope for the future than anyone else I have seen here," wrote a young journalist named John Hersey, born to missionary parents in Tianjin and bound soon for Japan to report on Hiroshima for the *New Yorker*. "Even when he was making random small talk, he revealed such a lively, pellucid memory and such scrupulous editing of all but the significant details that, had he said nothing about China, I would still be hopeful about the results of his mission."

On the flight home, Marshall noted in a memo that one of the last barriers had fallen: "I succeeded in getting an agreement for the entry of field teams from Executive Headquarters into Manchuria." And more good news from Manchuria had come as he was preparing to leave: the Soviets were withdrawing. A Red Army commander in Mukden, Manchuria's largest city, informed the Nationalists that his troops would be gone before the week was out.

The C-54 was loaded with gifts—rugs, vases, trinkets—and warm clothes, since Marshall presumed he would not be in China another winter. He also carried a letter from the Generalissimo, for delivery to the Oval Office. Marshall and Chiang had talked at length before Marshall left, plotting future cooperation between their countries. Chiang had one request: that the United States not put conditions on its assistance, at least not explicitly, since conditions would only help the Communists. Otherwise, said Chiang, American policy was correct. "What General Marshall has been able to accomplish during the short period that he has been here, I feel certain, fulfills your expectations," the letter to Truman read. Chiang asked that Marshall return soon and stay three more years, "for the seed that he has sown needs his presence to bring it to germination."

Marshall and Madame Chiang had bantered in front of a reporter. "They want to keep me in China and maybe bury me in China," he said. "And what better place to be buried than in China?" she replied.

A few days before his flight, Marshall sent a note to Shepley in Washington: "I received your message regarding the Secretary of State business. I am beginning to think that would be my only way to escape from this burden."

II

SEEK TRUTH FROM FACTS

CHAPTER 7

If the World Wants Peace

"A tall man with a weathered homely face, in which there was the visible touch of greatness, stepped briskly down the ramp of the plane," opened *Time*'s account of the hero's return. Katherine was waiting on the tarmac with Eisenhower and Acheson. Marshall kissed her, and they drove off. His mission so far, *Time* rhapsodized, had been an exercise in "the power, prestige, and principles of U.S. democracy." He made his third appearance on the magazine's cover. "Democracy," said a caption, "is an exportable commodity."

Marshall had kept his return quiet as long as possible, to stave off a deluge of demands and give himself some time with Katherine. Fifty-eight hours of flight had worsened his cold; talking over the engine's din had left him hoarse. Yet appeals flooded in—dinner invitations, speaking requests, a summons from the Pearl Harbor Committee for a last round of interrogation. A "Draft Marshall" movement entreated him to run for president: "We now need him more than ever."

Acclaim had come from all quarters. The cease-fire, the democratic reform, the military unification—they said he had done the impossible. "Really a stupendous accomplishment, and I doubt seriously whether any other person in the world could have done as much in so short a time," Wedemeyer reported to Eisenhower. Henry Luce conveyed "how grateful we all are for what you have been able to do in China." Carsun Chang, of the Democratic League, wrote, "It is miraculous how much you have accomplished in so short a time." Chiang told the restive Nationalist ranks, "Ever since his arrival in China three months ago, he has worked indefatigably and sincerely as a friend to help us attain peaceful national unification." A journalist made much of a supposed rethinking of the unsuitable Chinese name Marshall had been given: *Ma-shieh-erh*, "resting horse."

On the way home, Marshall had made two brief stops. In Tokyo, it was for lunch with General Douglas MacArthur, Pacific commander in the war and now proconsul of the Japanese occupation. While MacArthur's fighting abilities were renowned, Marshall had long been wary of the bluster, narcissism, and politicking that came with them. (Roosevelt thought that MacArthur was one of the two most dangerous men in America.) But he hoped to borrow some officers from MacArthur's occupation, and to send Chinese troops to Japan in return, as a boon to national pride.

In Hollywood, it was dinner with the director Frank Capra, who was getting ready to shoot a movie called *It's a Wonderful Life*. A few years earlier, Marshall had enlisted Capra to produce *Why We Fight*, an Oscar-winning documentary series on the war. Now he wanted Capra's help on a series for release in China: short films that, "using the highest Hollywood professional standards," would teach the masses how democracy worked.

On March 15, the day after landing in Washington, Marshall saw Secretary Byrnes at the State Department, and they then crossed the alleyway to the White House. From Chongqing, Marshall had made it a personal priority to keep Truman informed, even if the response was often nothing more than: "I know very little about Chinese politics. The one thing I am interested in is to see a strong China with a Democratic Form of Government friendly to us." Marshall had seen how quickly officials fell into disfavor when Truman felt disregarded. Byrnes, for example, had announced the outcome of the Moscow summit without any notice and been on shaky ground with the president since.

So when Marshall spoke to Truman, the substance was familiar.

What Marshall had seen over the past three months had reinforced his mission's logic. To have even a chance of militarily defeating the Communists outright, he assessed, the Nationalists would need "full-scale American intervention," likely including combat troops. Even then, the probability of increased Soviet support for the CCP would make success, against a force with outside assistance and easy crossborder refuge, far from certain. If Moscow reacted more aggressively, the Generalissimo would be in serious trouble. Either way, continued chaos would make a divided China "easy prey" for Stalin. So unity remained the best hope—for aiding Chiang, for averting war, and for countering Soviet expansionism, in Manchuria and beyond.

The next day, Marshall spoke to the public. He needed the American people to understand how much peace in China was worth to them, so the Chinese would see how much they stood to benefit from keeping it.

"If we are to have peace, if the world wants peace," Marshall, brow furrowed, told a room of journalists, "China's present effort must succeed, and its success will depend in a large measure on action of other nations." He hailed the past months' "political and economic advances which were centuries coming to western democracies." And he stressed that the United States had a "vital interest in a stable government in China, and I am using the word 'vital' in its accurate sense."

Marshall was proud of the American role so far. "We were able to resolve almost every difficulty," he said, "once we got the people together." He was particularly gratified by "the most important instrument we have in China," the Executive Headquarters and its truce teams. He acknowledged that there had been some disagreement about their presence in Manchuria. But on that score he had reassuring news: "They should be on their way there now."

One important factor got too little attention in Marshall's account: Marshall himself. "Marshall's presence is what is holding China together," Caughey had observed a few days earlier. The paean Wede-

meyer sent to Eisenhower included a similar caution: "The permanence of his accomplishment, however, is in my mind contingent
upon his physical presence."

When Marshall spoke to the press, the truce teams were not, it
turned out, on their way to Manchuria. He had taken off late in the
afternoon with agreement all but inked, teams ready to go. That evening, Zhou reconsidered the directive, insisted the teams needed more
authority, and refused to sign. Gillem, a genial man but new to diplomacy, lost his temper.

"He is definitely not a Marshall," another officer said of Marshall's
stand-in. Gillem hardly needed reminding. He had been in China just
over a month, starry-eyed at Marshall's side. ("Well she is worth seeing," he wrote in his diary after encountering Madame Chiang. "I hope
I am not to act against her too often.") When Marshall's C-54 took off,
Gillem watched from the airstrip and wished he were on it. Announcing his new role, the press had trouble getting his name right.

A story went around. "What's this Kuomintang thing?" Gillem
was said to have asked a few weeks after arriving. Whether or not the
account was true, Gillem conceded that the political intricacies were
beyond him. He spent the day after Marshall left reading every memorandum he could. "Gentlemen, this reminds me of a poker game," he
told the Committee of Three. "We have lost the first hand," but "maybe
everything will be all right." He slept poorly.

As Gillem struggled, Manchuria was in bewildering flux. The Soviets were leaving, that much was clear, taking their "war booty" with
them—pieces of industrial infrastructure, as well as pieces of furniture and jewelry. They refused to coordinate with Chongqing as they
withdrew, and Communists were taking over freshly evacuated ground
before Nationalists could get there. "Too rapid Soviet withdrawal" was
the new complaint. "The Russians are pretty cute starting to pull out
now," Melby wrote, "because with the awful confusion that is breaking
and that will become worse all they have to do is say, 'Well? You asked
for it.'" Both sides seemed to be maneuvering troops for position. In
some places they were starting to shoot.

Still, withdrawal was withdrawal, and many, in Washington and Chongqing, had feared it might never come. As it proceeded, Chiang even related a "softening" in the Kremlin's attitude, with promises to stick to the Sino-Soviet Treaty and support Nationalist control over Manchuria. The Soviets alerted Chiang that the last Red Army troops would cross into Siberia by the end of April. He credited American resolve.

Gillem, meanwhile, kept at it. "Further delay may be fatal," Marshall wrote back when informed of the discord over truce teams in Manchuria. "Force the issue."

Gillem tried shame. "Now we have for seven days, one week since General Marshall left, attempted to resolve this problem without success," he deplored. "I ask you to please reach an agreement this morning." He tried sympathy, reminding Zhou and Chang of his heavy responsibilities. He tried prestige: "The Army had 7 and a half million men and one more thing—the atomic bomb. Now the man who directed this terrific Army through the war was General Marshall."

Eventually, Gillem started to get somewhere. Zhou had been quibbling and stalling. He claimed he could do little without permission from Yenan—"my responsibility is too great"—and was having trouble making contact. Gillem put him on an airplane and dispatched it north. When it returned with Zhou no longer on it, Gillem sent Caughey to drag him back. Zhou seemed bitter about criticism he was getting from his comrades. But Caughey invoked Marshall, and Zhou said he was touched by such concern from so far away. Finally Caughey sent word: "I have Zhou." Back in Chongqing, they signed an agreement directing truce teams to enter Manchuria and visit every "point of conflict or close contact between the Government and Communist troops." It had been two weeks since Marshall left. Gillem radioed the news to Washington with less triumph than relief.

Marshall got news from Chiang as well. He had closed the proceedings of the Nationalists' Central Executive Committee declaring, "United States policy is in accord with our national policy." The hardliners, he wrote Marshall, had been tamed. "You need not worry about the anxieties I expressed to you before you left Chongqing."

Still, with Marshall gone, it was clear the situation was not quite as settled as many had hoped.

In Washington, Marshall was as busy as he had ever been, including during the war. He worked long days out of an office in the Pentagon. "General Marshall frequently treats the War Department as if he were still Chief of Staff," an officer cracked.

American generosity would be essential to the survival of the "strong, united, and democratic China" that, against long odds, was coming into existence—but Marshall quickly realized that America was not in a generous mood. He had already warned the Nationalists of "a return to the old isolationism," to underscore how sharply public opinion could turn against support. Over the past three months, that pressure had gotten stronger, amid inflation, labor unrest, shortages of consumer goods, and Americans' widespread desire to let the rest of the world handle its own problems for a while.

Marshall knew that was not an option, not "if the world wants peace." A memo from his staff, noting with condescension "the inability of the Chinese to carry out even the things they agree to in good faith," had emphasized: "Without American assistance and 'know how' there is no chance." The Chinese government would be "almost certainly foredoomed to collapse."

The scale of need was enormous. The $500 million in financial assistance under discussion was, according to T. V. Soong, a fraction of what was necessary.* The task of restoring communications would alone require a million timber railroad ties, 100,000 telegraph poles, and 1,000 tons each of iron and copper wire. Marshall, after freezing talks on all but urgent requests at the start of his mission, had asked Washington to quietly prepare an aid package as negotiations progressed. But he had returned to find withering skepticism of China's

---

* Equivalent to roughly $6 billion in real dollars today, and roughly $40 billion today measured as a percentage of GDP.

ability to use it effectively. A congressionally mandated oversight body, the National Advisory Council, set strict conditions, worrying that "a loan of the public's money would be wasted." T. V. Soong complained of American paternalism.

Marshall campaigned assiduously for China's cause. He saw cabinet secretaries, economists, members of Congress, sometimes multiple representatives of the same agency in a day. He pushed for financial assistance, a massive transfer of surplus equipment, and hundreds of millions of dollars in humanitarian aid, through the United Nations' effort, to relieve what he described as "famine conditions." He advocated for "as favorable terms as possible." He even tried to get Chiang his own C-54. To the skeptical National Advisory Council, Marshall highlighted the already "substantial advances toward peace and unity."

The aid was a good investment for the United States, he argued. It would not just keep China afloat; it would promote farsighted reform, the best defense against threats internal and external and the key to turning China into the kind of ally Washington wanted rather than the kind of client it had. To that end, a slew of advisers would come along with support. One would counsel Chiang on finances, at his request. A team of agronomists would examine farming and land issues. And at Marshall's insistence, a communications adviser would help Chiang understand how his words and deeds were received across the Pacific. The *Time* reporter chosen for the job, John Beal, did not know China, but he knew Washington, and that was what mattered. "Your mission," he was told, "will be to keep the Chinese out of trouble with the United States."

Marshall pressed the State Department to send its best diplomats, as many as it could, not just for the embassy, but for outposts around China, including several cities in Manchuria. He recruited officers for the Executive Headquarters and his "elementary school" for Communists. He pushed for congressional approval of the Military Advisory Group and prompt announcement of the China combat theater's deactivation. He was hearing from Wedemeyer that the Marine presence—already down by 20,000—was "really an irritant and inasmuch as we do not have sufficient strength to cope with a serious Russian effort, it is better to remove the irritant"; the navy also wanted to "reduce the scale of its commitments in China as rapidly as possible." At the same time, Marshall wanted to be sure that enough troops remained to hold critical points until the Nationalists could take over. As Soviet withdrawal from Manchuria continued, he directed Wedemeyer to transport two more of Chiang's armies north.

"My most difficult problem," Marshall had said during the war, is that "the man on the ground, or the commander in each area, clearly sees his own problems but can know little of what is happening elsewhere." He called it "localitis": each theater commander complained about his paltry share of overall resources, while Marshall, as the commander of a global campaign, had to weigh "the priority of this theater against that one" and "meet the demands without available means." Now he was on the other side of the table, as he was well aware—"no localitis involved," he insisted in the course of an appeal. But as he pleaded for help in China, needs were rising everywhere: Great Britain, continental Europe, the German and Japanese occupations.

And far from expanding American means in the face of expanding global demands, Congress was zealously curtailing them. Truman pushed back. On April 6, as Marshall made China's case, the president flew to Chicago to speak to an Army Day crowd at Soldier Field. After World War I, Woodrow Wilson had called for peace without victory; now Truman warned of victory without peace. "Victorious nations cannot, on the surrender of a vicious and dangerous enemy, turn their backs and go home," he exhorted. "Nobody should play politics with the national safety."

As a rallying cry, it failed. "Rebuffs mark Truman's first year," read headlines afterward. The "Truman policy" was excoriated on the floor of Congress: he would have America "police the world," he would "expend its dwindling resources to bring to other countries a degree of prosperity we have not attained at home." His call to extend the draft was voted down, the continuing troop presence in Asia denounced. "The quarrel in China," Senator Mike Mansfield, a former professor of

Asian history, had written him, "is a problem for China to solve." The administration was charged with selling out American interests for abstract international causes and surrendering sovereignty to shadowy international bodies. When whiskey distilleries struggled to get enough grain to meet demand, relief shipments to starving foreigners were blamed.

In pressing for aid to China, Marshall battled these currents, day after day. He turned down invitations and skipped social events, including his goddaughter's baptism, which had already been delayed for his sake. His time, he wrote a friend, was "so overcrowded with Chinese affairs that I literally had none left for anything or anyone not immediately concerned with them." That included Churchill, who had hoped to see Marshall before returning to England. Marshall sent a note of regret.

In the weeks since Churchill had given it, the Iron Curtain speech had been causing a furor everywhere. It "gave people the feeling that World War III was approaching," said Chiang. "Churchill now takes his stand among the war-mongers," railed Stalin. American newspapers printed arguments and counterarguments, alongside cheerful ads for new cars and dandruff treatments and golf clubs.

The furor made for a different Washington than the one Marshall had left three months before. There were public predictions of war with Russia and backroom whispers about "appeasement." Members of Congress threatened to out supposed high-ranking State Department "pinkos" on the floor of the House. J. Edgar Hoover, director of the Federal Bureau of Investigation, had started warning of spies in the U.S. government. A poll registered 7 percent approval of Soviet conduct; the percentage of Americans who thought Moscow could be trusted had fallen from 55 percent to 35 percent in a year.

Another recent speech drew less immediate public reaction than Churchill's, but had even bigger repercussions. On February 9, Stalin had spoken before an audience in Moscow. When the State Department asked the U.S. embassy there for an analysis, the diplomat George Kennan saw an opportunity to capture in one document what he had been telling superiors for months. He dictated a telegram while lying in bed and sent it to Washington.

A strength of Kennan's "long telegram," as it became known, was that it was not in fact all that long. There had been a slew of protracted exegeses of Soviet behavior. Kennan crystallized the challenge into a paper easily read in a sitting. "We have here," it declared, "a political force committed fanatically to the belief that with U.S. there can be no permanent *modus vivendi*." It depicted a Stalin fueled by a volatile mixture of fear, suspicion, and delusion. Kennan recommended a strategy in response: "We must formulate and put forward for other nations a much more positive and constructive picture of the sort of world we would like to see." But most readers focused on his description of the Soviet adversary: "A police regime par excellence, reared in the dim half world of Tsarist police intrigue," "impervious to logic of reason" but "highly sensitive to logic of force."

The telegram reached the State Department on February 22. Harriman, Kennan's former boss, gave it to Secretary of the Navy James Forrestal. Forrestal read it and promptly had it mimeographed. Before long it was being passed around official circles in Washington. Amid disputes over Europe and the Middle East, broken promises and exposés of espionage, and the start of a quarrelsome session of the United Nations Security Council, Kennan offered a key to interpreting an unsettling new world.

Before Marshall had left Chongqing, his aides had given him a translation of Stalin's speech. They had also alerted him to mounting attacks on him in the international Communist press. "Over the hard whiskey glasses," went one, "he will tell anyone who is willing to listen that the United States must fight the Soviet Union within two years, and the plains of Manchuria are ideal for this noble purpose." Surely, it reasoned, the Soviet Union could not be expected just to stand by.

The longer Marshall was away, the more seemed to go wrong.

Truce teams were supposed to be guaranteeing peace in Manchuria. But those that did reach their destinations were "completely immobilized" by disagreements over what they should do once there, both Nationalists and Communists resorting to delaying tactics when convenient. Marshall told Gillem to make a more serious show of force, leading the Committee of Three itself to Manchuria, but that too was delayed by procedural disputes.

The Nationalists were supposed to be moving forward on democratic reform. But they were instead walking back political agreements struck in January, despite Chiang's upbeat assurance to Marshall. Condemning the PCC resolutions as a "form of national suicide," the "diehard" elements Marshall feared had in fact, in the course of the Central Executive Committee proceedings, forced several "revisions"—revisions that would keep basic control in Nationalist hands. American intelligence reported "a new political impasse," thanks to "continued opposition to the program by right-wing elements of the Kuomintang, who may fear loss of power and influence with termination of one-party rule and the reorganization of the armies."

The Communists were supposed to be moving forward on military unification. But Zhou had stalled on the first step: submitting a list of which units would demobilize and which would join a unified army. He sent Gillem a litany of excuses—Nationalist hassles, he grumbled, "have rather upset my original working schedule"—and promised to deliver the list soon. Instead came a series of public complaints: the Nationalists were delaying democracy, violating the bill of rights (Marshall's "dose of American medicine"), disregarding press freedom, attacking Communist units, pouring troops into Manchuria, blocking truce teams. It was a plot to "instigate civil war," Zhou said, and by transporting additional armies the United States was abetting it; how could the Communists relinquish their forces in such circumstances? In fact, Yenan had already sent Zhou an instruction: "Without simultaneous resolution of reciprocal deals on political affairs, military affairs, and territory, we must absolutely not give up any positions."

The inventory of problems went on. Chinese members of truce teams were flouting orders and issuing transparently spurious charges. The Executive Headquarters was floundering, earning a new nickname: the Temple of One Thousand Sleeping Colonels. Communists were disrupting the reconstruction of railway lines, claiming that prior understandings no longer applied, since Nationalist troops were traveling by train. Chiang expressed second thoughts about Marshall's "elementary school" for Communists. Yenan seemed to be having second thoughts as well: the Americans were scrambling for a mid-April start, until Zhou said the Communists could not send troops to the school for months.

There were mysterious plane crashes. An American aircraft carrying Tai Li, the gold-toothed chief of the Generalissimo's secret police, slammed into a mountain near Sun Yat-sen's mausoleum outside of Nanjing. The weather was bad, and Tai himself had overruled the pilot's recommendation against flying, but his demise begged for conspiracy. Some pointed to the Communists, some the Americans, some the spirit of Sun; some thought Tai had staged his own death. Then another American plane, this one carrying a CCP delegation, got lost and went down in the forbidding terrain around Yenan. Among those killed were close friends of Zhou—he suspected sabotage—and the 13-year-old daughter of the Communists' representative at the Executive Headquarters.

To the Americans it seemed clear: the unraveling had begun with Marshall's departure; only Marshall's return could reverse it. "I think Marshall can fix it," Caughey wrote a few weeks into his boss's absence, "but he has got to be here to do it." His prestige could get both sides in a room. His persuasiveness could get them to strike agreements. Without him, suspicions spiraled, and moves for advantage went unchecked. Arrangements came apart even faster than he had put them together. "It is appalling how bad things have gotten," Melby wrote. "All parties now admit that things are a mess, but that when the General gets back he will straighten them out." The embassy cabled drily: "all groups have expressed a desire for the early return of General Marshall."

The appeals became more and more exigent, until finally they were desperate. On April 6, Walter Robertson implored from Executive Headquarters: "It is my carefully considered opinion that the situation is so serious and is deteriorating so rapidly that your immediate return to China is necessary to prevent your mission being dangerously jeopardized." Madame Chiang wrote out a petition by hand. "I feel that I should tell you frankly that your presence is vital," it read. "I hate to say 'I told you so,' but even the short time you have been absent proves what I have repeatedly said to you—that China needs you! And so hurry back to us, and bring Mrs. Marshall."

Marshall hurried, but only after getting what he had come to Washington for. "It has been a hard battle," he reported, "considering the political reactions or fears here, the past financial difficulties in dealing with the Chinese government, etc." But he concluded with satisfaction, "I think I have sold China." He had managed to secure, in his assessment, an aid package with generous terms and solid backing. He had not taken a single day off.

The day before flying, Marshall went to the White House. He planned to finish his mission over the summer, by early fall at the latest, and he wanted to ensure an official American ambassador would be in place to secure progress—perhaps, he thought, General Wedemeyer. Wedemeyer had experience in China, a sharp military mind, and enough command to keep hold of all lines of policy. "I will serve in any capacity gladly and as effectively as I can, for I owe much to you, to the Army and to my country," Wedemeyer had replied when Marshall floated the idea.

Truman was more focused on filling a bigger role—secretary of state. Since December, there had been speculation, in Washington and

Chongqing, that Marshall's mission to China was a prelude to another position. The rumors had gotten to the point that, the day Marshall landed back in Washington, Truman felt the need to give a press conference rebutting them. "A big lie," he said. But in reality, he had been fuming over Secretary Byrnes's performance for months, especially when it came to relations with the Kremlin. "I'm tired [of] babying the Soviets," Truman scrawled in a note after the Moscow summit. By then, he had already mentioned the possibility of secretary of state to Marshall, and he raised it again, via Shepley, in early March; Marshall was considering it seriously enough that he talked it over in confidence with some aides.

Wedemeyer, for one, was vehement: Marshall must take Truman's offer, but his service to the country should not end there. "When the time comes for the nomination of a Presidential candidate, you should accept the same," Wedemeyer argued. He made a rousing case: "You are still young and vigorous mentally and I do hope that conditions will be created whereby your talents will be exploited. General, I am not a damn flatterer when I state sincerely that we need <u>now</u> a man of your character to serve as a bulwark in defending the principles of democracy as well as decency in human relationships."

First, Marshall had to return to China and finish his mission. This time, he would bring Katherine along, as Madame Chiang had urged. ("She says George needs me," Katherine told a friend.) They were set to start the journey back on April 12, a month and a day after Marshall had left Chongqing.

Just before their flight, an urgent message came from the American embassy in China. The situation was deteriorating rapidly. Political democratization and military demobilization had both stalled, amid a flurry of fresh reservations and mutual recrimination. The Communists were issuing anti-Chiang screeds and ranting about his "lust for battle and slaughter." The Generalissimo was giving fiery anti-Communist speeches and interviews. The embassy made a hurried recommendation: wait on announcing the aid Marshall had secured until his return, so as not to "seriously weaken his hand in reversing the present trend and bringing parties back to path on which he had set them."

Marshall assented. He would hold off on an announcement until he could see the situation for himself. When reporters intercepted him and Katherine in Honolulu on their way to Chongqing, he had only one thing to say: "We don't know how long we'll be in China."

CHAPTER 8

Balance of Mistrusts

In the spring of 1914, First Lieutenant George C. Marshall, 33 years old and fresh off his second hospital stay for nervous exhaustion, crossed the battlefields of Manchuria on horseback. He had been given leave from his post in the Philippines and told to rest. Instead, he took his wife, Lily, and headed north, for an on-the-ground study of what he called "the most stupendous and ghastly struggle of modern times."

A decade earlier, the Russo-Japanese War had raged across southern Manchuria. Its end, a crippling humiliation for Tsarist Russia, marked two turning points: the first modern defeat of a Western power by an Asian one, and the first American foray into a new kind of global activism, with Theodore Roosevelt orchestrating the peace conference. First Lieutenant Marshall was more interested in the battles themselves. Guided by solicitous Japanese officers, he rode trenches, surveyed terrain, and searched out signs of destruction. Afterward, he gathered his overwrought descriptions into a personal account titled "Forgotten Scenes of Heroism": not just the "hopeless struggles of the ignorant Siberian peasant" and "grim determination of the Japanese warrior," but also the "Chinese farmer and his picturesque villages" and the "missionary and his thankless task." Marshall proudly recorded that according to his hosts, he had seen more than any foreign officer before.

Manchuria had long been an object of intense outside interest—

thanks to its geography, its resources, and its history as a staging ground for incursions into the rest of China. After a Manchu invasion broke south through the Great Wall, unseated the Ming Dynasty, and replaced it with the Qing in 1644, settlers had flowed north into Manchuria, drawn by its abundant fertile land and, later, stocks of timber, coal, and iron. In the early twentieth century, as the Qing Dynasty weakened and then fell, the same attributes drew in other powers, with their own clashing ambitions.

After its victory over Russia, Japan built up control year by year, until in 1931 it launched a full-scale takeover and created the puppet state of Manchukuo, over the world's feeble protest. While the Chinese shouted for the return of "Chinese Manchuria," the Japanese set about pioneering it, said the propaganda, as the Americans had California. They built mines, factories, steel mills, power plants, and railroads. Soon Manchuria was producing as much coal and more electricity than the entire rest of China. "The Ruhr of the Far East" some called it, after Germany's industrial heartland, though Manchuria was much bigger, twice the size of France. Others called it "the cockpit of Asia," the place where wars began. And with reason: whoever controlled Manchuria controlled one of the region's great industrial and agricultural centers, with a rich resource base, warm-water ports, and a commanding position over the North China Plain.

In 1914, after his leave, First Lieutenant Marshall made a recommendation to his army superiors: that they send other officers on the Manchurian tour he mapped out. He even specified the best time of year: late April or early May, when "there is little or no rain and a minimum of the frequent and trying dust and wind storms."

In late April of 1946, Marshall was once again preoccupied with the battlefields of Manchuria.

With Katherine along, the trip west across the Pacific was slower than the trip east a month earlier. In Tokyo, the Marshalls dined with the MacArthurs as cases of canned spring water were loaded onto the

C-54, for the sake of Katherine's health in Chongqing. In Beijing, Marshall checked on his faltering Executive Headquarters while Katherine toured the Forbidden City. As they continued inland, she peered down at villages built of mud and fields that seemed to cover every inch of ground. It was like nothing she had ever seen.

When they landed at the airfield outside of Chongqing, in the middle of the afternoon on April 18, Madame Chiang and Madame Zhou were waiting to welcome Katherine. But it was 100 degrees, with 90 percent humidity, and Katherine was struck mostly by the heat, dust, and smells. The one consolation was that they would not be there long. Chiang's capital was in the process of moving back to Nanjing.

Like his arrival four months earlier, Marshall's return brought a surge of expectation. "Everyone says that there is only one thing and one man that can save the situation," wrote the *New Yorker*'s John Hersey. Chang Chi-chung sent a note: "With your wisdom and sagacity, I am sure this task"—peaceful unification—"can be accomplished under your guidance." Zhou expressed confidence "that Marshall will take any necessary steps in the fair and just spirit he has used in dealing with the problems of China in the past." At Happiness Gardens, Caughey waited with a combination of shame and hope—shame that so much had come undone, hope that Marshall would put it back together. "He will be disgusted I did not do more," Caughey fretted, anticipating long days and sleepless nights ahead. Yet he believed Marshall could "pull the situation out of the fire." Melby added merely: "About time."

At the airfield, reporters clamored for a statement. "It is about like it was when I arrived before," Marshall said. "I will have to study the situation first."

It was not in fact like when he arrived before. This time, not much study was needed to realize that the situation was, as he soon put it, "completely out of hand." Even as he and Katherine were leaving the airfield, tens of thousands of CCP troops waged an all-out assault on Changchun, the capital of occupied Manchuria, firing artillery at a ragged Nationalist force. Later that afternoon, the city fell. An American officer there when the conquerors entered described them as "young, well disciplined, battle experienced, with excellent morale and well indoctrinated with Communist principles." Many carried automatic weapons with Japanese markings.

From the airfield, the Marshalls went to see Chiang. Over the previous weeks, he had gotten frequent updates from Washington. At first pleased by Marshall's exertions—the financial assistance would be a major boost—he soon started to find the terms of American support galling. And then came word that assistance would be delayed, to give Marshall time to assess what had gone wrong. Chiang lamented in his diary that the Communists were making "every effort to ruin Marshall's arrangement to get loans." Truman's December policy statement had conditioned maximal American assistance on Chinese unity, and Zhou had been pointedly citing that condition as Marshall lobbied in Washington: how could Chiang get aid when he was thwarting unification? ("America needs China to be peaceful and stable before it makes any big loans," Zhou had reminded Yenan. "This is the crux of the contradiction between America and Chiang.")

As Marshall registered the extent of the past month's deterioration, he was dismayed—though not because he thought his staff had done too little, as Caughey feared. The Nationalists had lost a chance to lock in a good deal and secure it with hard-won American support. Before, the Communists had been in a weak position and willing to negotiate; now, given developments in Manchuria, they could make stiffer demands. It was, Marshall said, a "tragedy."

He let loose his frustration in a meeting with one of Chiang's generals, Yu Ta-wei. Yu had a Harvard doctorate in mathematical logic, German training in ballistics, and a love of Greek literature. Stilwell had considered him one of the few figures, on either side, who could be fully trusted, and Marshall judged him forthright enough to give Chiang a relatively unvarnished version of the truth.

In the living room of Happiness Gardens, Marshall erupted. "I do not know who the Generalissimo's advisors are but whoever they may be, they are very poor ones," he said. "Instead of constructive action they got the Government into trouble." The list of offenses and lost chances was long. There were Chiang's bellicose speeches while Marshall labored in Washington. "They murdered my effort," he fumed. "The Generalissimo accused the Communists of sabotaging the loan but it was what he said that ruined it." There was the stalling on truce teams. "The Kuomintang had a good chance to have peace in Manchuria but it did not utilize this chance," Marshall said. "The Government has gotten into a bad spot and I have to figure a way out." There were other recent infractions that inflamed tensions for no apparent gain—such as Nationalist fighters buzzing Yenan, the original American markings on Lend-Lease planes still visible.

"A great part of these difficulties could have been avoided by the National Government but now the whole situation is reversed," Marshall continued. He stressed to Yu that "no one has offered any alternative except a great war and you can not support a great war." Nor, Marshall added, would the United States.

While Nationalists were getting blasts of Marshall's frustration, Zhou, to his distress, was getting nothing at all. Marshall seemed to be avoiding him. Marshall's anger at the CCP's seizure of Changchun, a clear violation of the cease-fire, was evident. But Zhou also drew other, more extreme conclusions. "Marshall probably intends to let Chiang fight, and appears not eager to see me," he wrote Mao; the Communists, accordingly, should be ready for battle. To Americans, Zhou seemed worried and depressed.

Katherine was miserable as well. She found Chongqing dreadful, the crowds so overwhelming that she hardly went out; when she did, she would stare straight ahead to avoid eye contact as faces pressed against the car window. The foggy wet cold of winter had given way to thick wet heat. (Stilwell composed a lyric about springtime in Chongqing: "Not to speak of the slush, or the muck and the mush / That covers the streets and alleys. / Or the reek of the swill, as it seeps down the hill,—/ Or the odor of pig in the valleys.") Katherine wrote home bitterly: "I walk to the bathroom & watch the Chinese out the window & I have one desire—To have the entire administration & their *wives* sent out here to stay and let me bid them a farewell of 'How nice you are going to China with your husband.' "

Some aides had wondered as Marshall returned from Washington: Would he regret having gone? "I have forced so many compromises on both sides," he had acknowledged beforehand, "that I am in the awkward position of being obligated by pressure from both sides to stay on and maintain a balance between the mistrusts of the two parties." Once back, he quickly recognized that this balance had collapsed entirely, and his return had come too late to stop a recurrence of fighting. He was more slowly coming to see just how deep the breakdown went, deep enough to suggest that not even his presence could have averted it—which raised the question of whether there was anything he could do to reverse it now.

Signs of breakdown were visible on all fronts. The political process had collapsed into public recrimination, and preparations for the National Assembly—the constitutional convention for the new China, supposed to open on May 5—were frozen. The Communists refused to submit military demobilization plans, and Chiang was blocking the "elementary school" meant to speed integration. Both sides were escalating in Manchuria as the Soviet presence receded north. They seemed to be making aggressive moves for advantage before Marshall could get them back to the negotiating table—"taking the most extreme position possible," as Melby put it, "in order to have plenty of leeway for compromising when he puts the screws to them." At least that was the optimistic take.

But calculations were changing. The international landscape was shifting, tension between Washington and Moscow growing, politics everywhere unsettled. There were new considerations and new opportunities. To both sides, the path of negotiation was looking less promising, but also less essential—since the prospect of outside support was looking better every day.

In Chongqing, Chiang had seen his hopes of neutralizing Moscow fade and recalcitrance in his party mount. If there was little chance, as he had come to believe, of real Soviet help in establishing control of Manchuria, he had lost a key piece of his argument with the Nationalist "diehards" who maintained that negotiation was foolish. Decrying the democratic promises of the Political Consultative Council as a "coup against our party," they had successfully maneuvered, in the March Central Executive Committee meeting, to ensure that control of government would stay in Nationalist hands. But Chiang thought a flip side of Soviet hostility would be American solidarity. His ambassador in Washington was keeping him apprised of the anti-Soviet frenzy there. Before, postwar comity had left him little choice but to attempt some degree of cooperation. Now geopolitical friction should give him an opening, a play for unstinting U.S. support. "I should wait for the evolution of the international situation and then make policy," Chiang wrote in his diary after reading Churchill's Iron Curtain speech.

In Yenan, the Communists were doing their own rethinking. Mao, fully in command after his winter in retreat, had expressed increasingly sharp misgivings about his side's commitments. He was warning that mediation was a ploy, "a long cord" to catch "a big fish." He sent Zhou a message: "All that has happened lately proves that Chiang's anti-Soviet, anti-CCP, and anti-democratic nature will not change." Zhou was to backtrack and stall. In late March, when he flew to Yenan with the ostensible purpose of selling his colleagues on Gillem's Manchuria truce-team directive, CCP leaders instead gathered to plot strategy. Communist "diehards," as opposed to negotiation as those on the other side, invoked Nationalist "revisions" to the political agreements to bolster their case. "Chiang Kai-shek and the Nationalists will not put down their swords because of our substantial concessions," two hard-line commanders argued. After five days of discussions, CCP leaders resolved, "We can neither participate in the National Assembly nor join the government."

A year earlier, at the Seventh Party Congress in Yenan, Mao had told the Communist ranks that they were entering an era of global concord. "The Chinese people feel that the American people, who before were thought of as living in a distant place, now have become a close neighbor," proclaimed his tract "On Coalition Government." A year later, he was expounding on a rising "counterrevolutionary tide" and a fascist plot to kindle World War III. Like Chiang, Mao saw opportunity in the ferment. Before, global dynamics had constrained his ability to fight. Now global tensions held out the promise of true revolutionary solidarity and support. Warning of Washington's imperial designs in China, the Kremlin had stopped demanding cooperation and started chiding Chinese comrades for being "too courteous to the Americans." Moscow had instructed its representatives to expand contacts with the Communists. An American military assessment summarized, "the Soviet government is giving increasing aid to the CCP in the form of advice and leadership, coordination of troop movements and supply of captured enemy materiel."

Moscow's shift was not simply a matter of revolutionary solidarity. It was a way of punishing Chiang. He had proved less supine than hoped, more resistant than expected to a Soviet sphere of influence; a bolstered CCP would be the price he paid for insolence. It could also help check the Americans. The U.S. agenda in China no longer appeared as benign as it had a few months earlier, when the Moscow summit anointed Marshall de facto representative of the international community. The Kremlin now worried that his early success presaged more expansive American aims. And if Chiang could not be trusted to keep American influence at an acceptably nonthreatening level—Stalin's threshold for feeling threatened was not very high—a more aggressive CCP could help guarantee Soviet interests.

Mao had started making bold ideological declarations: "The democratic forces of the people of the world are more powerful than the world reactionary forces." But to Stalin, the Communists were still more means than end.

Months before his Long Telegram was passed around Washington, George Kennan had written another, less-noticed telegram on the Soviet Union's objective in China—in his analysis, "maximum power with minimum responsibility." He charted out the Kremlin's likely approach: "She would prefer to work through an inwardly strong and nominally independent national Chinese Government sufficiently reliable and subservient to constitute an effective channel of influence. If this cannot be achieved, she is quite prepared to work . . . through local forces which will not hesitate, where necessary, to challenge central authority." When it came to challenging authority, Mao was not known to hesitate.

On his second morning back, Marshall sat down for breakfast at Happiness Gardens. It was already clear that, unlike in December, he could not afford days of listening. With aides across the table, he launched into a comprehensive analysis of what had happened. He knew he needed to move fast, with "strong blows" that would "crack the major points one at a time." By the end of breakfast, Caughey was newly confident they would find a way forward. "It may not be too good," he recognized, "but it will be better than anyone else could do with the same set of circumstances before him." Whatever happened, he thought, "there will never be any recriminations against General Marshall because he is not a defeatist."

The typically buoyant Caughey had been hit with waves of foreboding in recent days. "I have never before been in on the ground floor of a war in the making," he wrote his wife. Each side swore not to want it, but neither would stand down, and he found himself understanding why. "The strangest things happen every day to make you think one is right and then to make you think the other is," he wrote. Or, he allowed, "Maybe everybody is wrong."

Marshall came down closer to this latter view. His approach over the winter had depended on precise choreography, a virtuous cycle of commitments and concessions overcoming suspicion and building toward unity. Step by step, the Nationalists would give up political supremacy as, step by step, the Communists gave up their armies. But a vicious cycle of doubt and distrust, of moves and countermoves, had taken hold instead. Both sides stalled on their commitments, justifying equivocation as a reaction to bad faith. Even Marshall's machinery of peace, meant to preempt such excuses, proved vulnerable. The Committee of Three was paralyzed, Zhou claiming he lacked authority to make key decisions, Chiang dispatching Chang Chi-chung to the far western region of Xinjiang and assigning a succession of less capable replacements. The Executive Headquarters had become a forum for debates that went nowhere. (That was no accident: the Nationalists had seeded their staff with secret-police agents and the Communists had seeded theirs with underground organizers, all more focused on espionage and incitement than compromise and negotiation.) In the field, members of truce teams outright refused to cooperate when it served their side not to. In one case, an American was shot at by Communists who did not like where he was looking.

Marshall searched for some way back onto the path of negotiation. But what he heard in response was not encouraging. Each side said negotiation had been rendered impossible by the other's treachery.

On their first weekend back, Marshall and Katherine drove out to the Chiangs' country house. On the surface it was a picture of amity, two couples on a getaway from the city. For the Generalissimo, however, it was a chance to prosecute a case. He was struck by Marshall's anger, particularly at Nationalist hard-liners who, in Marshall's view, had sabotaged their side's best opportunity and given ammunition to CCP hard-liners in the process. "It was as if all blame should fall on us if compromise cannot be reached," Chiang wrote in his diary. He tried to persuade Marshall that the time for negotiation was over, explaining that the Communists were doing the Kremlin's bidding. They had no intention of following through on their commitments, and they never had. In Chiang's view, Marshall's prior efforts and apparent successes rested on a misguided faith in Communist sincerity.

On Monday, Marshall finally saw Zhou, who was also bent on blame. He argued that the Nationalists had shown themselves unwilling to share power and bore responsibility for fighting in Manchuria. Conditions on the ground had changed, Zhou said, and the old agreements had to change as well. The terms of military unification—especially the

14-to-1 ratio of Nationalist to Communist troops in Manchuria—were no longer acceptable.

It was a startling new posture for the usually courtly Zhou. Marshall thought "radicals and militarists" in the Communist ranks must have gotten the upper hand. Among CCP leaders, however, even Zhou was pushing a harder line. He had backed the attack on Changchun, flagrantly disregarding the January cease-fire he had done so much to secure. Upon Marshall's return he had advocated driving talks to an impasse. It took Mao, of all people, to remind Zhou to "maintain friendly relations with Marshall."

As more and more of Chongqing relocated to Chiang's new capital, Marshall scrambled for some move that would stop fighting from spreading across Manchuria and beyond, some formula that would get the faltering political and military agreements back on track. He ferried proposals back and forth, fruitlessly. He insisted to each side that it stood to lose from full-scale war in Manchuria. Neither seemed to agree.

Marshall realized he would be in China for some time to come. Harvard was due to award him an honorary degree later in the spring, but he wrote the university's president to say he would not be back for the June ceremony. Maybe next year.

On April 29, Marshall summoned Zhou to Happiness Gardens one last time. Bags were packed, much of the staff already gone. Marshall's message was uncharacteristic, an admission of despair. "I do not see anything more I can do in the way of mediation and I think it best this be understood," he said. "I've exhausted my resources." Zhou replied with another litany of accusations. He charged that Chiang was just as bad as the hard-liners in his ranks—"a difficult man to convince," willing to compromise only when he had no other option. Marshall repeated himself: he did not know what else he could do.

Chongqing was reverting to the city it had been. Officers and officials flew east, diplomats and journalists following. Industrialists and traders returned to the coast. Refugees filed back to villages. Machines, vehicles, and furniture were hauled down steep banks and loaded onto barges for the trip downriver. "It is a strange, sad, lost feeling to watch a city die," observed Melby. On the morning of April 30, Marshall took off for Nanjing.

Over the first three days of May, the last remaining Red Army regiments crossed from Manchuria into Siberia. The Soviet invasion was over. In Chiang's government and in Marshall's, some had feared it would go on indefinitely.

But the Soviets were proving they could cause as much trouble leaving as staying. Nationalist and Communist troops rushed to take freshly evacuated ground. "Minor civil war in Manchuria probably cannot be averted," Gillem conceded. Perhaps, he offered optimistically, it would not spread.

For all sides, there was cause to contest the territory. Manchuria lay at the heart of Nationalist prestige, Communist strategy, Soviet ambition, and American dread. For Chiang, it would complete his restoration of Chinese greatness. For Mao, controlling even a swath would guarantee his party's survival. There were Communists across three of Manchuria's borders—with Mongolia, Korea, and the Soviet Union—who could be counted on for supplies and sanctuary. But it was Moscow's intentions that most aroused Washington's fears. If Stalin succeeded in harnessing Manchuria's resources, it would mean, a military analysis predicted, "continued expansion of Soviet power in Asia southward through China and towards Indochina, Malaysia, and India." With Manchuria lost, countries would topple one by one into the Kremlin's camp.

Yet American certainty about the dangers of Soviet dominance did not mean confidence in the prospects of Nationalist control, particularly if Moscow and Yenan sought to thwart it. Chiang, Wedemeyer told Marshall, "is completely unprepared for occupation of Manchuria against Communist opposition." The hazards were formidable: long supply lines, logistical complexities, unfamiliar territory, unhelpful neighbors. And the closer Chiang came to succeeding, the more sharply the Kremlin would respond—Moscow had long warned it would not stand by if the Communists in Manchuria were threatened with destruction. Wedemeyer had advised Chiang to shore up his presence in north China before going any further. Marshall had advised him to do everything possible to negotiate the takeover.

Chiang knew the risks. He recognized that an all-out battle for Manchuria might end badly—in the event of expanded Soviet support, he thought the Communists would likely win—and that the prudent move would be to consolidate control before pushing north. But as the Red Army left, his reservations fell away. Besides, he was not sure he could afford restraint. Without Manchuria, he noted in his diary, "how can we say we are a unified country?" An aide laid out the rationale: "Militarily, it is dangerous to go into Manchuria. . . . Politically, we have no choice."

Chiang counted on the United States' help. Hundreds of thousands of his troops, many American-trained and -armed, had already been transported up to and in some cases into Manchuria by the American military. Thousands more were on their way. Marshall had resisted Communist demands that such assistance cease altogether. To Zhou's claim that it was "turning the truce agreement into a piece of sheer waste paper," Marshall pointed out that Chiang had a right to move troops, under agreements with both the Communists and the Soviets. Nothing prohibited the Americans from helping.

The Soviets were less forthright. But it was clear that, as Chiang resolved to take what was his, they had resolved to play spoiler, despite assurances to the contrary. Throughout the winter, CCP cadres flocking into Manchuria had been under strict instructions: do nothing aggressive that might disrupt the Kremlin's broader agenda. (When Chinese comrades overstepped their bounds, the Soviets threatened them with force.) But Stalin's approach had changed. He now worried that complete Nationalist control would open the way to American dominance. As the Red Army left, his message to the CCP was a sharp change from winter: "fight without restraint." Nationalist commanders were told little about specific withdrawal plans; Communist commanders often knew just where to be, and when. Sometimes Soviet trains even helped them get there. And while the Soviets carried away all the "war booty" they could, they left tens of thousands of seized Japanese weapons, from rifles and machine guns to artillery and tanks.

The Kremlin-CCP collusion in Manchuria was no secret to the Americans. They had been watching since the war, when two OSS detachments, Team Flamingo and Team Cardinal, had parachuted into Manchuria ahead of the Soviet invasion. More recently, the postwar successor to the OSS, the Strategic Services Unit, had been building a presence, and Marshall had pushed to send diplomats, "to give us the advantage of lookouts." He had already seen persuasive evidence of Soviet weapons handovers, and the reports coming from Executive Headquarters were clear: there was extensive cooperation, aimed, Byroade assessed, at "the establishment of a Manchuria virtually dominated by Russia." (He added, "I state the above knowing the full import of such statements.") In an earlier discussion with Zhou, Marshall had pressed for an honest accounting of the relationship. Aides detected his growing anger in the face of decreasingly plausible denials. "Now he is not so sure they are not playing the Russian game," Melby noted.

American intelligence had concluded by the beginning of May: "Due to their initially favorable strategic position the Communists gained an early political and military advantage in the race for control of Manchuria." The Communists knew it. After months of restraint—staying away from large cities, focusing on political work, establishing "facts on the ground" without being too conspicuous—they were, reporters said, "cocky." Some 300,000 of their troops had made their way in, picking up conveniently abandoned Japanese arms and demonstrating "high morale and fairly capable leadership," according to American officers. Mao had sent a proven commander, Lin Biao, an insomniac and hypochondriac who was anxious in his personal habits but calm and tenacious in battle. "Everything is decided by victory or defeat on the battlefield," Mao told Lin.

Yet for all his bravado, Mao did not actually foresee a fight to the death. He still saw a fight back to the negotiating table. Despite their anti-American fulmination, the Communists had not given up on Marshall's mediation: they were sure he would soon compel Chiang to compromise, and they had only to stay strong until then. They had grabbed what they could and dug in, waiting for Marshall's cease-fire. "Chiang has no choice other than to do what the Americans want," Zhou argued; the desire for expansive American aid, conditioned on stability, would leave him little choice. The Nationalists could not afford a break with Washington.

So for now, the Communists would make their stand. They chose to do so at Siping, a Manchurian railway depot south of Changchun that they had occupied early in the Soviet withdrawal. The anticipated Nationalist counterattack came quickly. Day by day the exchanges grew bigger, with entrenched positions and masses of troops. It was starting to look like real war. And it was unfolding on the Manchurian terrain Marshall had crossed on horseback thirty-two years before.

Chiang's new capital was rich with dark symbolism. After the First Opium War, in 1842, the Treaty of Nanjing marked the start of China's Century of Humiliation. Ninety-five years later, the Rape of Nanjing marked the apex of Japan's savagery, with hundreds of thousands of the city's residents killed, many by imaginatively sadistic methods— castrated and hanged, half-buried and consumed by dogs. The tally of rapes ran into the thousands, maybe tens of thousands. W. H. Auden wrote a sonnet that ended:

> And maps can really point to places
> Where life is evil now:
> Nanjing; Dachau.

That dark past was to be part of a story of resurrection. It was in Nanjing that China's Century of Humiliation started; it was in Nanjing that Chiang would bring it to a definitive end. It was in Nanjing that weakness had allowed China to be brutalized; it was in Nanjing that

Chiang would make it strong again. "The greatest shame of my life," he had said when fleeing ahead of Japanese conquest. A new China would rise out of shame, built on the ruins of the old.

First, though, came a more mundane task: moving a government and its appendages 750 miles and getting it up and running in a city scarred by years of war. Nanjing still bore marks of its past majesty. It was ringed by twenty-two miles of Ming dynasty wall, built of dark gray brick with crenellated battlements on top. It had a stately government complex and wide asphalt boulevards like those of Washington and Paris—vestiges of the first time Chiang made it his capital, in 1928. Mimicking a Ming emperor's tomb, Sun Yat-sen's mausoleum sat on the slope of Purple Mountain, to the east. The mountain and the Yangtze River, arcing from west to north, were said to guard the city "like a coiling dragon and a crouching tiger."

At the moment, however, Nanjing was in chaos. As Marshall's C-54 approached over green rice paddies striped with canals, the airfield was so overcrowded that planes had trouble landing. Many of the city's 700,000 residents lived not along the modern boulevards, but huddled into narrow old alleyways that snaked off them, refugees sleeping alongside water buffaloes. Even American diplomats struggled to find accommodation and had to settle for "barracks existence," as Melby put it—dirty, crowded, unruly, with unreliable electricity and a shortage of pillows. The new U.S. embassy had two vehicles: a broken-down Ford and a Cadillac missing a transmission. Inflation made it hard to buy anything new. "Basic foodstuffs sell at prohibitive prices," Marshall alerted Washington, pleading for more support for staff. "Rents for suitable quarters are beyond capacity to pay."

The Communists had trouble getting to Nanjing at all. The Nationalists had offered to help move Zhou and his team, then failed to follow through as rancor grew. Marshall protested: how could he restart negotiations if there were no Communists in town? That may have been the point; he gave up protesting and lent his own plane for the job.

But Zhou arrived in Nanjing no less strident than before. "Being too eager to see your mission crowned with an early success," he entreated Marshall, "I hope that you would not mind, if I venture to remind you that you still have other resources at your hand which would add immense weight to your talk with the Government." Why not stop transporting troops? Why not cut off equipment and ammunition? Zhou also continued to deny that the CCP was in league with the Kremlin. "The Chinese Communists favor Lincoln's idea of government of the people, by the people, for the people," he told an American reporter. Yet in Manchuria, his side would not stand down: the Nationalists had "abandoned" it to the Japanese in World War II, so why did they deserve to hold it now?

In the face of hostilities, Marshall could do frustratingly little, even as he worried that fighting in Manchuria would spread through China and beyond. He proffered formulas for a cease-fire: the CCP handing over Changchun in exchange for political talks; both sides stepping back and granting control to Americans; empowering the Committee of Three to oversee troop movements; guaranteeing Nationalist "authority" along with Communist "rights." None got purchase. Nor did truce teams help. Marshall thought Chiang's shortsighted refusal to permit them in Manchuria earlier, for fear they would hold the Nationalists back, both provocative and exceptionally unwise. Now the Communists seemed equally opposed. Both sides had ambitions that truce teams could only hinder. Mao was holding out for better terms, Chiang for complete submission.

For Chiang, Marshall's doggedness was a source of growing outrage. This moment, his return to Nanjing, was supposed to signify a new beginning, an end to his and his country's shame. Instead, he found Marshall's pressure to be an unexpected tribulation. In his diary, Chiang wrote of being humiliated by Marshall: "Nothing is more shameful and unbearable than this."

Chiang believed the Communists would fold if confronted with enough force. "The Americans should help us prepare for war, if they really want to stop the Russians' ambition of expansion," he insisted. But Marshall was "afraid and helpless," Chiang complained, "terrified at the thought of the breakdown or suspension of the negotiation," perhaps even poisoned by the Communists. He "cannot let go of the old ways—appeasement and compromise." The same kind of retreat, Chiang noted, had brought about World War II.

He asked rhetorically: "Is the United States quitting on the whole Asia problem? Or do they want to actively participate and lead?" Whatever Marshall's failings, Chiang thought he still had a good idea of the answer: ultimately, America would have no choice but to support him in his war.

On May 5, Chiang celebrated the official return of his capital to Nanjing. With a clear blue sky above, he climbed the steps to Sun Yat-sen's mausoleum, bowed three times, then stood straight for a 101-gun salute. Afterward, there was a party at his house just outside the city walls, at the base of Purple Mountain, watched over benevolently by Sun. When the Marshalls arrived, guests spilled from a large wood-floored living room onto a bright terrace, its railing carved with images of the phoenix. Locating the capital in Beijing, Chiang explained to Americans, would have recalled an autocratic past. Nanjing evoked "revolution and people's government."

May 5 was supposed to have marked another milestone as well: the opening of the National Assembly—a major step on the road to democratic unity, or so it was hoped. Days earlier, the opening had been postponed, neither side agreeing to basic terms. A new date had not been set.

After the party, the Marshalls stayed for dinner, and then Marshall and Chiang talked until 10:30. The Generalissimo was feeling confident. Marshall, he thought, was coming to see that "the Communists are hard to deal with" and that "I cannot be pressured into doing anything."

To Chiang's satisfaction, Marshall seemed to have given up for now on pushing a solution in Manchuria. The hope that had accompanied his return to China two and a half weeks earlier—that his very presence would have a restorative effect—had proved illusory. There were bigger forces at work. Americans may have assumed that it was Marshall's departure in early March that started the breakdown. Events on the ground in Manchuria indicated that the Soviets' departure, also starting in early March, had been an even bigger factor.

The next day, Marshall wrote Truman for the first time since returning. "I have delayed in sending this report in the hope that I would have reached an agreement on Manchuria ere this," began the unusually detailed note. Marshall ran through the reasons he had not. The Nationalists had backed away from political agreement and refused to allow truce teams; the Communists had taken Changchun and broken the January cease-fire with their conduct in Manchuria, and they were now "jubilant" over their success, well armed with Japanese weapons and "in a very strong strategical position." The Nationalists, meanwhile, were dominated by overconfident hard-liners who "urge a policy of force which they are not capable of carrying out even with our logistical support and presence of Marines." Marshall opposed transporting additional Nationalist armies to Manchuria, since it would amount "to supporting under the existing circumstances a civil war." (Also, ships were needed for what he considered an even more critical function: to deliver food to starving populations elsewhere in China.) Yet he would not at the moment cut off ammunition or resupply support to Chiang, since it would be "most unfair for our government to leave, as it were, his troops now in Manchuria completely in the lurch." Nor would he give up on negotiations, for fear of the consequences: "the only alternative to a compromise arrangement is, in my opinion, utter chaos in North China to which the fighting will inevitably spread."

"At this moment I submit no recommendations," Marshall concluded. "I am going ahead in the hope that I can resolve the difficulties without troubling you and while I am taking many diplomatic liberties I am trying to do so in a manner that will keep the skirts of the U.S. Government clear and leave charges of errors of judgment to my account."

CHAPTER 9

Fighting While Talking

Marshall was a different man with Katherine around. His mood was brighter. He made jokes at meals, eliciting a teasing "Oh, George" from across the table. "A wife is a very necessary part of the balance of life in a man," he had counseled an unmarried former aide a few months earlier. "His judgment and efficiency will always lack otherwise." Current aides were struck more by other qualities. "The affection between those two people is very lovely to watch," said Melby, hardly a sap. "Every time he looks at her his eyes soften." Katherine's presence, Marshall wrote a friend, "makes my moments here of possible relaxation very pleasant." In the two years between the death of his first wife and meeting Katherine, also widowed, when he was 48 and she 46, Marshall had not known what do with those moments.

In Nanjing, Katherine started to get her bearings. Other than the food ("all fungus and entrails"), her main complaint was how hard her husband worked, keeping on with "the patience of Job." As in Washington, Marshall continued to find himself as busy as he had been during the war. But Katherine was becoming a presence in her own right, one much appreciated by aides. She "tempers the General's formidability," said Caughey, who deemed her "my favorite General's wife."

They lived in one of the best houses in the city, #5 Ning Hai Road. It was on a placid strip of large gated homes—outer walls painted yellow, the color of power—that had belonged to foreign ambassadors and top Nationalist officials before the war. Imported London plane trees lined the street and shaded #5's tile roof, which curved upward in the Chinese style, the character for "longevity" carved into its trim.

Marshall found the house luxurious. There were rooms for aides and visitors, space on the second floor for screening evening movies, a suite for him and Katherine, with a sun porch, where she could sit and look out, and one of Nanjing's few working air conditioners. The previous occupant had been Nazi Germany's ambassador to the wartime puppet government. The former ambassador was said to be in a detention camp nearby, but his possessions remained: rugs, appliances, a library of German books, and a croquet set the American staff put to use in heated matches on the back lawn, which covered a spacious bomb shelter, also courtesy of the Germans.

In the nice spring weather, Marshall conducted business on the back terrace, sometimes with an Old Fashioned in hand. (Under Madame Chiang's tutelage, his cook, Richard Wing, had become expert at mixing them.) Katherine hosted lawn parties, with live music, spiked punch, and "the best looking girls available," according to Caughey— "Russians, Germans, German Jewesses, Chinese and of course the local American element."

Even with Chiang's improvements, Nanjing was a provincial place compared to Shanghai or Beijing. Within the city wall, among the boulevards and electric lines, farmers still cultivated fields. Bullfrogs could be heard at night and birds at dawn. Damage from the war was prevalent, along with plenty of problems of the postwar: unrepatriated Japanese roaming the city, a shortage of cars and housing, inflation that left many consumer goods out of reach even in dollars.

Still, most Americans thought the new capital a step up from tumultuous Chongqing. The social scene took on some of the glamor of a prewar China posting. At the choice night spot, they ordered martinis and watched Jimmy Wong's trio. The embassy organized an excursion to a production of *Tosca*. A new Officers' Club had a pool, a bar, and a house band. Arriving American women were cautioned by an orientation brochure, "It is quite easy to become engaged for every night of the week if one is not careful." A social commentator explained that the Marshalls were "probably the most sought after guests for any big diplomatic party." But Zhou was also a "catch," thanks to "one of the most easy and affable party manners." Even now, he and Chen Li-fu, Chiang's hard-line adviser, could be seen slapping one another on the back at evening gatherings. Americans were baffled. Everywhere else, the two sides seemed intent on killing each other, and in many places already were. Here they drank together. Zhou had a term for it: fighting while talking.

Eight hundred miles north, the two armies were fighting the biggest battle in China since the early days of the Japanese invasion. The Communists, in a departure from their usual mobile and guerrilla strategies, had dug in at Siping. "Do not fear blood or sacrifice," said signs on their gun emplacements. Waves of Nationalist troops were coming from the south to reinforce a brutal siege.

Both sides considered Siping vital. It lay on the route between Manchuria's two major cities, Mukden and Changchun, the former in Nationalist hands, the latter in Communist. A railway ran through the middle of town.

Chiang aimed to "defeat the Communists' main force in one blow." He sent his best American-trained troops. Mule carts hauled American-supplied weapons to the front.

Mao told his commander, Lin Biao, to hold Siping at all costs. He intended for it to be his "Battle of Madrid," the place where the Communists made their heroic stand. No matter what it took, they would overcome an elite Nationalist army, protect their hold on Changchun and northern Manchuria, and then return to negotiations in a position to wrench real concessions from Chiang, having crushed his will to fight.

As Mao had once written in an essay that played off Clausewitz: "Politics is war without bloodshed, while war is politics with bloodshed."

May 8 was Victory in Europe Day, the first anniversary of German surrender. Yet Caughey, still consumed with foreboding, took it as another
opportunity to brood. "The year after V-E Day the world is faced with
a situation in China that may make it necessary for another V Day," he
wrote in his diary.

The next morning, Marshall stood in the sunshine at Nanjing's
dirt airfield, waiting to greet the hero of V-E Day. When Dwight Eisenhower, now army chief of staff, stepped off his transport plane, they
shook hands warmly. Marshall's feeling toward Eisenhower, another
officer had remarked, was "that of a father to a son."

The amiable Ike and austere Marshall made for an unlikely pair.
Marshall had plucked Eisenhower from an obscure post after Pearl
Harbor and, for his first task, ordered him to craft a strategy to defeat
Japan. (Among its recommendations: "influence Russia to enter the
war.") Impressed, Marshall soon promoted him over 350 more senior
officers to a major field command, then stood back to let him lead
D-Day. On one of the rare occasions when Marshall questioned a decision he made, Eisenhower was so disturbed that he skipped breakfast
and lunch.

From the airfield, Eisenhower and Marshall went to see Chiang,
who made the case for a more aggressive stance in Manchuria. Only
afterward did they get to the visit's real purpose. A few weeks earlier, Eisenhower had been summoned to the presidential yacht and
asked to carry a secret message to China. Truman wanted a definitive
answer to a question he had raised before: whether Marshall would
accept an appointment as secretary of state. The query could not be
made through normal channels, because Byrnes was not supposed to
know. (By this point, Truman had such disdain for Byrnes that he had
pushed a change in the order of presidential succession, to make secretary of state fifth rather than third in line.) Marshall, Truman said,
would give him "a wonderful ace in the hole."

When Eisenhower conveyed the offer, Marshall quipped that he
would even reenlist in the army if it gave him a way out of his present

struggle. But Truman's desired timeline, with a July 1 transition, was unrealistic. Marshall could not in good conscience leave China until at least September. In order for him and Eisenhower to communicate about timing by radio, Marshall wrote out a code on a scrap of paper. COURIER would refer to the president, AGENT to Byrnes, AGREEMENT to confirmation. For secretary of state, he chose PINEHURST, his cabin in the sandhills of North Carolina, a place he associated with escape. Eisenhower put the scrap in his pocket and kept it there when he left Nanjing the next day.

Marshall now had his own exit strategy. The problem was that, with breakdown unchecked, other plays in his endgame were stalled. The wartime combat theater had officially ended on May 1, and the Military Advisory Group was starting to operate from Nanjing's Metropolitan Hotel. The number of American troops in China had fallen below 40,000—leaving them like a Peking duck, said one marine, able to eat but not to move. But further withdrawal was on hold. Additional reductions, timed wrong, could send an unhelpful signal as Marshall tried to resume negotiations. And Chiang was directing so many troops to Manchuria that he did not have manpower to take over from Marines guarding key points in north China—particularly railway lines crucial for Nationalist transport. (Marshall had a good idea of their importance, since one of his tasks in the 1920s had been to protect them from bandits.)

Some pieces of the aid package were moving forward. Marshall pushed for funds for railroad equipment and a good deal for Chiang's government on surplus American property left in the Pacific—25 percent of cost and more than $300 million in credits, which he hoped would help contain inflation and stabilize prices. "The Chinese problem," he pointed out in making the case for a generous offer on ships, "is very much our problem strategically and diplomatically." But the centerpiece of what Marshall had secured in Washington, the more than $500 million in financial aid, was still not announced.

The appointment of a new ambassador was also postponed. Wedemeyer had gone to Washington for a sinus operation and was there recovering. He was told to stay for now, out of concern that any announcement would be interpreted as signaling Marshall's imminent departure.

Instead, Marshall recruited a new member of his own team. Anticipating questions to come, he wanted someone to start work on a careful official account of the mission and thought the local *New York Times* correspondent, Tillman Durdin, suited to the task. Durdin, an introspective Texan with years of experience in China, had written when Marshall first arrived: "He will be tackling a situation unsurpassed for complications and filled with pitfalls for the unwary. He will be dealing with problems the handling of which may well determine whether there must be another world war." Marshall sent a request to Arthur H. Sulzberger, the *Times'* publisher: "Would you be agreeable to loaning him to me on a leave status at full pay?" Sulzberger consented, and in mid-May Durdin joined Marshall's staff, his paychecks still coming from the newspaper.

Shortly after, a message arrived from Eisenhower, now back in Washington. "I sent you a letter on the Pinehurst proposition," Eisenhower's note read. "Courier was more than pleased to have my report."

As Marshall thought about his future, Mao was initiating a new step on the way to his revolution. A directive went to Communist cadres: they were to adopt a more aggressive approach to land reform in areas they controlled. Until now, the tactically agile Mao had focused on reducing rural rent and debt. (While rural China was technically not "feudal," the term often used to describe it, most farmers spent their lives struggling to get by, cruelly beholden to landlords, lenders, and tax collectors.) His new approach was more radical: take land from those who have it and give it to those who do not.

The draw of Communism in China was not always philosophically precise. One American traveler came across a sign on a shop near Beijing: "After true Marxism is realized, this store will make great profits."

Many years before, however, Mao had fixed on his revolution's central force. In his blandly titled *Report on an Investigation of the Peasant*

Movement in Hunan, he spun a vision: "Several hundred million peasants in China's central, southern, and northern provinces will rise like a fierce wind or tempest, a force so swift and violent that no power, however great, will be able to suppress it. They will break through all the trammels that bind them and rush forward along the road to liberation. They will sweep all the imperialists, warlords, corrupt officials, local tyrants, and evil gentry into their graves."

There was a military logic to Mao's new approach, as well as an ideological one. Land redistribution would give the dispossessed something to lose and thus to defend. They would become soldiers fighting for their own. "The battle for China," declared Mao, "is a battle for the hearts and minds of the peasants." Hearts could be moved by hatred, and minds could be moved by fear. Newly radicalized peasants needed little reminding that the return of the Nationalists would mean the return of an old order and elite. And landlord retribution could be harsh, from beheading and dismemberment to immolation.

Chiang's takeover of areas formerly occupied by the Japanese had already provided distressing reminders of Nationalist misrule. Newly arrived officials seized land and houses, appropriated factories, and extorted bribes. "Officials down to the soldiers are using the resources of the country as their personal property," a Nationalist investigation found. Chiang railed against the exploitation and extravagance, but often to little effect. In many places he made it worse, by sending those he was certain he could trust to administer areas they hardly knew. Loyal southerners were given control of north China and then Manchuria. (Chiang was especially suspicious of Manchurian elites and made little attempt to co-opt them.) These representatives arrived, Wedemeyer lamented, as "conquerors" rather than "deliverers."

For American observers, the takeover was just one more cause for dismay with Nationalist governance. There were frequent scandals over corruption and profiteering that Chiang seemed unable to do anything about. High Nationalist officials were rumored to be cornering the rice market amid widespread hunger. An intelligence report relayed alarm over the implications: "The Chinese Communists are said to be gaining popular support in all areas as a result of the National Government's failure to provide either an attractive political and economic program, or even efficient local administration."

Marshall knew that the Nationalists had in the past managed real achievements, military and political. Now he wondered what power had done to them.

But in Manchuria they began to succeed. On the night of May 18, the Nationalist assault overcame the Communist stand at Siping. A six-week barrage by tank, airplane, artillery, and machine gun had battered and finally broken Lin Biao's defenses.

Chiang's confidence surged. Battlefield victory convinced the Nationalists that a "strategy of force is correct," said an embassy report. Days earlier, Stalin had invited Chiang to Moscow for talks. Although Marshall thought they might yield something constructive, Chiang turned the invitation down. He did not need to bargain for Stalin's help. He had the Communists where he wanted them.

Yet Lin Biao's forces, while defeated, had not been destroyed. By the time Nationalist troops marched into Siping on the morning of May 19, most of the Communists were hours into a northward retreat. They had slipped out of the city unnoticed as soon as defeat seemed inevitable.

While he retreated, Lin thought of Napoleon in Russia. Certain of success, Napoleon had been tempted deeper and deeper in, winning battle after battle until he was in too deep. Marshall was starting to worry that Chiang, like Napoleon, was overconfident to the point of peril.

When Marshall got angry, his eyes smoldered and the corners of his mouth turned down into something almost like a smile. He no longer raged as he had when young. He deployed his anger as a tool, only when useful. "You have to save your ammunition for the big fights and avoid a constant drain of little ones," he once advised his stepson. Still, the effect could be fearsome. "I don't believe I would like that man against me if he made up his mind," said Melby. As May progressed, fighting in Manchuria spread, and the situation in the rest of China grew tense, Marshall had ample opportunity to put anger to use.

As the battle for Siping entered its final hours, Marshall sat down for lunch on the sunny terrace of #5 Ning Hai Road. He was joined by Caughey, Till Durdin, and John Beal, the *Time* reporter enlisted to help Chiang manage his stateside image. Beal had spent his first few weeks in China politely reminding Nationalist officials how their words and actions came across on the other side of the Pacific. He was just beginning to understand Chiang's missteps—keeping truce teams out of Manchuria, issuing bellicose statements as an assistance package was being finalized, rejecting deals in moments of assurance and then coming back too late for the same terms. Marshall blamed the influence of the hard-liners, especially the CC Clique. They were sabotaging his mission, out of fear—unreasonable fear, in his view—of constitutional government. They had little idea, he told Beal on the terrace, how "close they are to an abyss."

Marshall took on a harder edge with Zhou as well. No longer willing to simply hear out litanies of CCP complaints, Marshall had litanies of his own. The Communists were disabling communications, blocking progress at the Executive Headquarters, paralyzing truce teams in the field, even endangering the lives of their American members. He also conveyed heightened awareness of the outside help the Communists were getting in Manchuria. While uncertain whether the orders were coming directly from the Kremlin, he understood what was happening on the ground. It prompted an alert from Zhou to Yenan: Marshall knew about "Soviet support." Chiang commented approvingly in his diary, "Marshall has gained a better knowledge of the mentality of the Communists."

For the time being, Marshall saw slim chance of success in another round of direct mediation. He was hesitant to insert himself into what seemed almost certain to be another stalemate. He ventured suggestions about what a settlement might look like, but otherwise focused his energy on preventing fighting from escalating from Manchuria into the rest of China. To that end, he struggled to get truce teams working again, with minimal results. "There have been so many violations I could not count them," sighed an American Executive Headquarters official. Ultimately, Marshall found he could do little beyond "scattering enough Americans around to see, so I can keep the ship trim." He warned that China was "trembling on the verge of a serious break which would inevitably involve a general civil war."

A reporter said he did not envy Marshall's position. "It never was enviable," Marshall snapped back.

Facing a complete break, Marshall would not give up entirely. "The General still has his fire and enthusiasm," said Caughey. Yet overpowering distrust meant that appeals to understanding no longer got traction with either party; both viewed Marshall as complicit in the other side's machinations. The vicious cycles of self-fulfilling suspicion continued, as "each side consulted its own fears and then estimated the other man's intentions," as Marshall put it, viewing every potential threat as "a 'will do' rather than a 'may do.'"

On May 20, for the first time since coming to China five months earlier, Marshall released a statement to the press—a "propaganda blast" directed at both sides. After standard diplomatic language of concern, it got to the point: "This reckless propaganda of hate and suspicion seriously aggravates the present serious situation and can lead to results that would be disastrous for the people of China." Marshall knew the message was likely to be denounced as inappropriate meddling in Chinese affairs, and Nanjing was buzzing within hours of its release. "But something had to be done," he explained to Truman, "and I appeared to be the only person who would do it."

And then, after days of holding back from full involvement, after his plaintive private pronouncements and angry public admonition, Marshall saw a way forward begin to clear. Chiang's forces were pursuing the Communists from Siping north toward Changchun, seventy-five miles deeper into Manchuria. Ever since the Communists had seized it in April, a flagrant violation of Marshall-brokered agreements on the day Marshall returned from Washington, Chiang had been adamant: he would not seriously talk peace until he got Changchun back. Now, defeated in Siping and retreating northward, the Communists were willing to make a deal. Marshall thought he could persuade them to relinquish Changchun to an Executive Headquarters team, and eventually to the Nationalists, while talks on broader issues resumed.

On May 22, Marshall went to see Chiang. With a dinner party waiting, Chiang stepped away for a short conversation. He had already heard Marshall's case for restraint in Manchuria—a case based less on the value of Nationalist magnanimity than on the risk of Nationalist overextension. "We are confronted," Marshall stressed, "with a definite and serious weakness in the Government's military position and a strategic military advantage of the Communist forces." The better course would be to stop and consolidate strength in southern Manchuria, and Marshall's arrangement would let Chiang pause without giving up Changchun.

Chiang judged it reasonable. He told Marshall he was willing to interrupt his offensive and discuss Communist political and military complaints in exchange for progress on other stalled fronts, especially military demobilization.

But Chiang had a concern: he had not heard from his generals on the ground in Manchuria in three days. He worried that, fired with bravado after victory at Siping, they might charge forward and attack Changchun. And Chiang did not dispute Marshall's assessment that an attack "would fatally terminate all hope of an agreement." Chiang proposed that he personally intervene, flying to Manchuria to prevent his troops from doing anything rash. Marshall approved, and offered his plane for the journey, both for safety and for the comfort of Madame Chiang, who though sick would go along. He urged them to leave as soon as possible, before the Nationalist offensive got much farther.

Later that night, back on Ning Hai Road, Marshall sat down to draft a report to the president. For the first time since his return from Washington, he allowed himself a measure of optimism. There might be grounds for compromise, he explained, if only events on the ground did not spin further out of control first: "I am working against time, otherwise I'd be quite hopeful."

The next morning, Chiang boarded Marshall's C-54 for the four-hour flight to southern Manchuria. He told Marshall he would be back within four days, maybe sooner. He would send word by courier once he landed and intercepted his armies.

Zhou visited Ning Hai Road that evening. He was suspicious of Chiang's purpose in going to Manchuria: was the goal really to rein in zealous generals, or to evade pressure while they continued to fight? Marshall pointed out that he had lent his own plane for the trip. He would not have done so for any purpose other than stopping the fighting.

A story about the Marshalls had been going around Nanjing. Katherine was unhappy, the story went, and had fled to Shanghai following a recent marital spat. A furious Marshall had personally traveled the 185 miles to retrieve her, and she still refused to come back. "Mrs. Marshall, though over sixty, demands her diversions," the gossips explained by way of background.

When the story reached Marshall, he took it with wry good humor; Katherine did, too, except for the part about "her diversions." In reality, she and Madame Chiang, fast becoming friends, had gone to Shanghai for a couple days away. Marshall had joined them for an evening and stayed the night in Katherine's opulent seventy-foot-long hotel room. Marshall figured that "some of the die-hard government political boys" had twisted the Shanghai trip into a petty line of attack.

However frivolous, the episode signified something darker. Marshall detected a mounting effort "to weaken my influence and clear the way for a war of extermination." There had been no shortage of attacks on American policy in recent months. Now they were becoming more personal. In conversations around Nanjing, senior Nationalist officials said openly that Marshall was out to help the Communists.

Perhaps more ominously, the same charge was being whispered in

Washington. Jim Shepley, now back in his civilian job at *Time*, sent Marshall a warning on May 23, the day Chiang flew north. There was "a serious undercover rumor campaign in Washington to effect that you have been working with the Chinese Communists against Chiang and that this is the reason for present state of affairs." Shepley knew members of Congress were involved, and suspected Chinese embassy officials, all intent on peddling the message that Marshall had "sold out to the Communists." There had also been leaks about the still-unannounced $500 million in assistance, which Marshall was said to be using as a "club" against the Nationalists.

It was no longer just hard-liners in Chiang's government plotting to thwart Marshall. Hard-liners in his own government were, too.

A group of prominent figures, including Henry and Clare Boothe Luce and Republican congressman Walter Judd, a former missionary in China, released a manifesto denouncing Yalta. Judd took to the floor of Congress to demand protection of the Open Door principle in China, proclaiming, "We cannot keep silent longer." An editorial in Luce's *Life* magazine, which had 13 million readers, called for a show of "U.S. might" in China (while wrongly asserting that Mao had visited Stalin in Moscow). Arthur Vandenberg, a prominent Republican member of the Senate Foreign Relations Committee, declared: "We can no longer compromise principles themselves. That becomes 'appeasement' and appeasement only multiplies the hazard from which it seeks to escape."

Wedemeyer was still back in the United States, recovering from surgery and awaiting his ambassadorial appointment. He kept Marshall abreast of the chatter. "There have been rumblings and rumors around Washington to the effect that you have been taken in by the Chinese Communists," Wedemeyer wrote. "I have been striving to obtain something tangible and pin down persons responsible." He said he wanted to confront them directly, in defense of Marshall's efforts to "minimize or remove the employment of force in the resolution of problems."

But Wedemeyer was savvy and ambitious. He could tell which way the wind was blowing. In letters to Marshall, he deplored the "lack of moral courage" in American political life, the abundance of opportunists eager to say "I told you so" about past events but with "nothing affirmative" to offer now. To others, he spoke out of the other side of his mouth. He told Luce's reporters that Marshall himself was responsible for American weakness. "If we do not support Chiang Kai-shek, firmly and categorically," he wrote Averell Harriman, "the Communists will take over and we will witness the substitution of one totalitarian power, Japan, for another (USSR) in the Far East."

One detail of Marshall's efforts sparked particular outrage in Washington. Information about the planned "elementary school" for Communists was leaked to the press, soon after Chiang finally gave approval for it to go forward. Washington grandstanding promptly turned an initiative to speed the end of Communist armies into a pro-Communist ruse. "We are about to train anti-American forces that might fight us in the future," inveighed a member of the Senate Foreign Relations Committee. On the floor of the House, there was a call for rooting out "the State Department official who is responsible for this sort of foreign policy," which was said to "emanate from Moscow."

To Marshall, all the invective missed the point. As he registered the charges of critics—many of whom had been preaching the need for compromise, unity, and reform just a few months earlier—he did not contest their desired ends in China. Like them, he wanted to check Communism. The problem was that most critics had little understanding of the means. And when Marshall contemplated means, when he appraised the prospects of an attack and intensified American involvement, his first question was whether it would work, whether it would bring desired ends closer or only create new, potentially greater problems. As he said to Chiang, "It is a matter of weighing the symbolic gesture against the actual power." But in a Washington increasingly shaped by the anxiety and acrimony of US-Soviet tension, the symbolic gesture tended to carry more weight.

According to the rumors, Marshall was ignoring ties between the Chinese and Soviet Communists, out of either naiveté or some secret pro-Kremlin proclivity. In fact, while the precise nature of the relationship between Moscow and Yenan was confounding even for those directly involved, Marshall was well aware of cooperation, especially in Manchuria, and had no doubt about CCP loyalties. He had never bought the notion that the Communists were mere "agrarian democrats"—after all, Zhou himself bristled at the characterization. Earlier in May, an analysis had come from the Dixie Mission: "Direct positive proof based upon personal observation together with much circumstantial evidence definitely establishes the fact that the Soviet Union is guiding the destinies of one of its strongest allies, the Chinese Communist Party, as it has in the past and will in the future." Other intelligence reporting offered the mortars, machine guns, tanks, and rifles in Communist hands as "irrefutable deductive proof" that the "plentifully supplied" Communists had been plentifully supplied by Soviet patrons.

Above all, Marshall's judgment was a military man's military judgment: an all-out offensive would not succeed. "The destruction of the Communist military forces in Manchuria," he had told Chiang, "I do not think is within the power of the government." In Washington, and in Nanjing, many heard about Communists with Japanese rifles and mismatched uniforms up against American-trained troops with American weapons, and assumed certain Nationalist victory. But Marshall considered what would happen if Chiang pushed north in Manchuria. His lines would stretch dangerously thin. Roads would be easily attacked, railroads sabotaged. The Communists would pick off Nationalist troops at vulnerable points. Logistics would break down. And eventually, if Chiang got far enough, the Soviets would respond with enhanced support for the CCP. Given the geography—long borders with Communist refuge on the other side—greater Soviet support would prove disastrous for Chiang, no matter how much help he got from the Americans. During his "encirclement" campaigns in the 1930s, a million Nationalist troops had failed to annihilate barely a quarter as many Communist "bandits."

Doubts about the state of the Nationalist army, and Chiang's leadership of it, reinforced skepticism. Officers and units vied for position and supplies when they should have been cooperating against a common enemy. Profiteers sold off American arms, which often ended up in CCP hands. A Communist needled Melby, "It is all right for the United States to arm the Kuomintang because as fast as they get it we take it away from them." Commanders were afraid to give Chiang bad news—showing an "utterly unscrupulous disregard of truth," as Stilwell earlier bemoaned, that fed overconfidence.

Then there were political factors, the importance of which was not lost on Marshall. As he had learned in his own long war, a leader had to be sure his society and economy would sustain his strategic choices. He had to have his people behind him.

"We all want peace," a Nationalist general had recently said. "The reason is simple. If the Government did not advocate peace but wanted to fight, it would not have the support of the people." The people had lived through many years of war, and they were now living amid widespread destruction and displacement. Chiang's government was spending nearly 70 percent of its budget on the army—an "exorbitant" burden, Marshall said, that with inflation already raging would bring "financial chaos." (It was also the inverse of how Chiang had once described the formula for success: "70 percent political and 30 percent military.") In Marshall's view, given the longing for peace in China, Chiang had to show he was doing everything possible to achieve it.

The Communists were highly attuned to such impressions. Negotiation could be a "means of educating the people," in Zhou's words, an opportunity to demonstrate interest in compromise and avoid taking blame for strife. On May 23, with Chiang headed to Manchuria in Marshall's plane, Mao was making public calls for a peaceful solution.

The next morning, the residents of #5 Ning Hai Road woke to another pleasant spring day with hope renewed. A cease-fire and return to negotiation seemed within reach. The Executive Headquarters was reporting improved attitudes in the field, perhaps thanks to Marshall's forceful public statement a few days earlier. Marshall was waiting to get word from Chiang that the Nationalist offensive in Manchuria had been stopped.

Then press reports started coming in. Nationalist armies had seized Changchun. There was every indication they were pressing on.

It was time for Marshall to dial up his anger. At 5:00 that afternoon, John Beal brought the Nationalists' Minister of Information to the back terrace. Having still heard nothing from Chiang, Marshall set into a tirade. The takeover of Changchun wrecked the chance for a good agreement. It ruined his credibility. It marked the latest in a string of Nationalist blunders. Watching the "harangue," Beal had no doubt that Marshall's ire was meant to be conveyed to others.

But in Manchuria, Chiang did not at the moment particularly care. He had landed the day before to find his troops already entering Changchun. He thought about halting and consolidating control over what he had (as first Wedemeyer and then Marshall urged); Chen Li-fu told a reporter that with Changchun in Nationalist hands, "there will be a truce." But after lunch with his commanders, Chiang changed his mind: his armies would keep going. He had let too many chances go by and would not make the same mistake again. The fall of Changchun was a sign of "the protection of God." As for Marshall's anger, Chiang returned the sentiment. He wrote in his diary that night: "Marshall shows no regard for the benefits of my state, nor does he care how best his state's policy can be implemented. What he solely cares about is his personal success."

Zhou returned to Ning Hai Road the next morning, May 25. Marshall expected an eruption. A day and a half earlier, he had been touting an agreement and pointing to the loan of his plane as proof of Chiang's peaceful intent. Now American-equipped divisions were driving north from Changchun, the offensive apparently directed by Chiang himself. But Zhou turned out to be far less exercised than Marshall had thought. Aside from a matter-of-fact mention of what the Communists would do if the offensive continued—attack long Nationalist lines stretching south from the Manchurian front, the risk Marshall had mentioned to Chiang already—Zhou was conciliatory. The Communists wanted a cease-fire, and he was ready to deal.

The day before, as soon as he got news of the Nationalist takeover of Changchun, Zhou had requested permission from Mao to approach Marshall with a new peace offer, and Mao had approved. The best hope of stopping Chiang's offensive in its tracks was to get Marshall to do it for them. Mao even instructed Communist members of truce teams to be nicer to their American colleagues—a change the Americans immediately noticed.

Marshall grasped the dynamic at work. Each side overplayed its hand when momentum seemed to be in its favor and then came back to negotiate when the momentum had shifted, at which point the other side was no longer interested. He wearily reminded Zhou that the Communists had been intransigent after taking Changchun in April. Now that the tables had turned, they were anxious for an agreement, and the Generalissimo was equally disinclined to relinquish momentum. He would exploit what he thought was a strong position to the hilt.

Marshall pronounced the odds of any agreement "rather gloomy." But he did not, he told Zhou, "quit in the middle of a fight."

Chiang was gone three days before a message from him reached Marshall in Nanjing. It was as Marshall expected—a stated desire for peace, but with harsh terms, including a rejection of the basic principle of simultaneous movement on political and military tracks. Marshall wrote back to recommend the immediate deployment of truce teams in Manchuria, but Chiang had already decided against it. "It is best if the mediation Executive Headquarters does not come to the Northeast and gain freedom of movement, so that the Communist bandits will not gain another chance at recovery under [its] protection," he wrote in his diary. He had the Communists where he wanted them; Marshall's peacekeepers would only thwart him from taking all he could.

Chiang had promised to return in Marshall's plane within four days, but the deadline came and went. Communication between him and Marshall was halting—thanks in part to stalling, in part to messages getting misplaced or, in one case, mistranslated. With attempts at persuasion succeeding neither at bringing a cease-fire nor forcing Chiang's return, Marshall resorted to a sharper line. "The continued advances of the Government troops in Manchuria in the absence of any action by you to terminate the fighting other than the terms you dictated," he wrote, "are making my services as possible mediator extremely difficult and may soon make them virtually impossible." When that message elicited no response, he sent another: "A point is being reached where the integrity of my position is open to serious question." Marshall understood how it looked: Chiang in Manchuria, in Marshall's own C-54, commanding an offensive that he had assured Marshall he would stop. It was both humiliating and discrediting.

On May 30, with Chiang gone a week and the most recent message to him unanswered, Marshall sat down with aides to take stock. He had been mulling options. He could take another plane and fly to Manchuria to personally intervene. He could give up and go home, which some aides thought he might be considering seriously. When the meeting ended, Marshall did not say what he would do. But it was Memorial Day, and he was scheduled to address a group of officers gathered in Nanjing's foreign cemetery. Among the graves of American soldiers killed in China in the last war, Marshall spoke of the consequences of another—above all for "the patient and starving women and children who more than any others are sacrificed to the inevitable brutalities of such a conflict." He concluded, "It is for Americans on this Memorial Day to recognize their plain duty to fulfill the obligations of the peace so dearly won by the sacrifices of our war dead."

It was June 3 when Chiang finally started his return to Nanjing. That morning, Zhou came to see Marshall. They stood, Zhou had declared, "at a turning point in history." Marshall said he could talk all day, and for the next six hours they ranged over the events of the past six months. Insisting he was addressing Marshall as a friend, Zhou said that everything that had transpired left only one viable conclusion: Chiang was intent on "total war," and the United States was encouraging it, thanks to its "double policy," with a "bright side" of mediation and a "gloomy side" of militarism. Marshall represented the "bright side," in Zhou's formulation, but the "gloomy side" had come to dominate.

Marshall took issue with the dichotomy, no matter that it was meant to flatter him. He alone was responsible for U.S. policy, and while both sides were now attacking him, he stood by it. To criticism of assistance to the Nationalists, he reminded Zhou that Chiang was an American ally who was leading a government that the Communists had pledged to join. To demands that U.S. troops leave China, Marshall noted that a major source of delay was the CCP's obvious intent to take "aggressive action" to fill any vacuum. To charges of militarism, he pointed out that the United States had in fact demobilized more quickly than it should have. And to suspicions of an imperial agenda, Marshall invoked history. America had never claimed territory in China, and it never would. If anything, it had been "foolishly idealistic."

At 6:00 that evening, shortly after Zhou left Ning Hai Road, Chiang finally landed at Nanjing's airfield in Marshall's plane. His trip had lasted eleven days, a week longer than promised, and brought diametrically different results than Marshall had hoped. "The boss man is beginning to get the idea he is getting pushed around, made a tool of; and he doesn't like it a good goddamn," Melby observed. "In short, he is about as angry a gringo as I have ever seen."

But perhaps Marshall's anger no longer mattered. The whispers in Washington had been picked up around Nanjing, and Chiang, Melby reasoned, was almost certainly getting "assurances of support from other U.S. circles." Their promises could render Marshall's displeasure a secondary concern.

"My endurance has worked," Chiang wrote in his diary. "God will definitely not let down a man as painstaking as me."

Both Chiang and Marshall were on edge when they met the next morning. Marshall arrived ready to do what was necessary to "force a truce," as Caughey put it, and found Chiang anxious and impatient, drumming his fingers on the arm of his chair. It was one of the tics Americans looked for as evidence of agitation: he would cross his legs and trace circles with his right foot, or run his hands over his closely shaved head. But Marshall did not need to press the point. Chiang was ready to declare a unilateral cease-fire. It would be a chance, he said, for the Communists to prove their good faith.

Chiang had made his decision a few days earlier, but waited to see how far his armies could get first. He recognized the prudence of not pressing too far north into Manchuria. He would give himself a chance to consolidate control, avoid overexposing his flanks to the Communist forces still present in much of north China and poised to take advantage of any vulnerability, and avoid provoking Moscow. (The Soviets had warned Chiang's officials that an attack on Harbin, the next major city north of Changchun, would elicit a response.) Nationalist victories had put him in a position of strength, which would allow him to drive a hard bargain in a negotiation.

Marshall, however, thought that the Nationalists were "pressing their temporary advantage to the limit"—temporary being the key word. Contrary to the initial triumphalism following Nationalist victories at Siping and Changchun, American analysis concluded that neither was a "crushing blow." At Siping, "the actual number killed and wounded was light." And Changchun had been a "voluntary" Communist retreat, Lin Biao ceding the city and sparing his forces for fights to come.

The Communists, in other words, were hardly on the verge of defeat. But Yenan was nonetheless eager for a cease-fire. "We want [Marshall] to succeed, not to fail," Zhou said, in order to give Communist forces in Manchuria time to regroup.

There was some haggling over the length of the cease-fire. Chiang offered a week, Marshall got him to extend it to ten days, Zhou demanded a full month. They settled on fifteen days. And this time, Chiang had a very particular vision of a cease-fire. An order would come not from the Committee of Three, nor as a joint announcement with Mao. Chiang would issue it alone, as a favor he was bestowing. So when, on June 5, the day after their meeting, Marshall sent a draft order, Chiang rejected it.

Intent on getting it right, Chiang sat down to craft his own order. He wrote through the afternoon and evening, took a break at 9 p.m. to make an appearance at a reception, then went back to writing until midnight. He slept for two hours, woke to write for two more hours until 4:00, then slept for two more hours before waking at 6:00. After his morning prayer, he was ready to present the text to Marshall.

Marshall arrived at 8:00. All fighting was to cease, Chiang informed him, by noon of the following day. Chiang also had a letter for Marshall. "The painful experience I have encountered during the past five months compels me to be more precise and definite in dealing with the Communists," it explained. In exchange for calling off all attacks by his armies, he wanted an assurance that the Communists would proceed with demobilization and cooperate in the repair and restoration of railways. He also stressed that "the sacred responsibility of restoring the sovereign rights of Manchuria to the Government should not be delayed." If the Communists interfered, he would not hesitate to strike back.

The cease-fire would last until noon on June 22. It would be, Chiang said, his "final effort at doing business with the Communists."

CHAPTER 10

Umpire on a Battlefield

Marshall agreed: the cease-fire might be his last chance. It gave him fifteen days to restore the political and military commitments of winter and find solutions to problems that had plagued negotiations for months—or in Caughey's words, fifteen days "for working out China's destiny." Melby had a more jaundiced take. Both sides needed "a little breather in which to lick their wounds," and would bend "just enough to get Marshall out of the country."

Chiang announced the cease-fire at noon on June 6, after sharing the text of his order with Marshall. The purpose, it specified, was "to give the Communist Party an opportunity to demonstrate in good faith their intention to carry out the agreements they had previously signed." If they chose not to use that opportunity, Chiang would resort to other means.

Zhou rushed to release a more soaring statement of his own, hailing "the persistence of the Chinese Communist Party, the aspiration of the Chinese people, and the efforts exerted by General Marshall." He stressed to reporters that "no opportunity for the realization of peace should be skipped over" and then, at dusk, came to Marshall with a question: what could be done to create an "amicable atmosphere" in the next fifteen days? Zhou planned to fly to Yenan the next morning to speak to Mao.

Marshall was ready with a list of demands. The Communists had to help restore communications—the railways, roads, and telegraph lines essential to both economic recovery and governmental control. They had to end repressive measures in their territory, as the Nationalists had to in theirs. They had to commit to a specific timetable for military demobilization and integration. Marshall also shared Chiang's letter on what would be required to turn the fifteen-day cease-fire into a sustained peace—pointing out Chiang's mention of the Nationalists' "sacred responsibility" in Manchuria. He urged Zhou to return from Yenan with proper authority to negotiate and a clear sense of how much the Communists could do to meet that demand. The only alternative, Marshall said, was "a world tragedy." To avert it, they had to move fast.

The next day, Zhou took off for Yenan in Marshall's C-54, carrying a box of candy that Marshall had asked him to give Madame Mao. At noon, the cease-fire began. In Manchuria, half a million troops, Nationalist and Communist, stopped in their tracks after almost three months of heavy fighting.

War was inevitable. That was the conclusion most CCP leaders had reached by the time Zhou arrived in Yenan on June 7: "Marshall's efforts to mediate the Chinese civil conflict have had no effect in stopping the Chinese reactionary forces. On the contrary, enjoying American support, the Chinese reactionary factions are even more active and unscrupulous." Three months before, the Communist masses had hailed Marshall's "great spirit," Mao had toasted his "selfless dedication." Now they were questioning not only his ability to restrain the Nationalists, but also his desire to even try. After all, Chiang had spent eleven days in Manchuria directing attacks from Marshall's own plane—a sign of winking support, many assumed, whatever Marshall's protestations to the contrary. Bitter and emboldened, Mao resolved not to be fooled again.

But as they assessed their options, CCP leaders realized that although they had lost faith in Marshall, they still had a use for him. It was in their interest to delay the war's onset. Marshall could serve "as a means of relaxing tensions," giving their armies time to prepare and their political mobilization time to gain momentum. As Zhou said to his comrades, "We cannot again harbor illusions of real peace or real democracy, but it is possible that we just halt large-scale fighting for a period of time in order to consolidate our current positions and our own strength, win over new masses, and prepare for further development." With added strength, the Communists might manage some quick victories, forcing Chiang back to the negotiating table with new-found willingness to give ground. As Yenan saw it, an inevitable war still did not mean a war to the death.

The cease-fire in Manchuria had come just in time. Watchful Communist intelligence networks had been relaying updates of the north-ward progress of Nationalist armies, and Lin Biao had been preparing to abandon Harbin, the northernmost large city and the CCP's last major urban stronghold in Manchuria. With Nationalist forward units just thirty miles away, his troops were crossing to the far side of the Songhua River and blowing up bridges behind them to hinder pursuit. Mao heard about Chiang's cease-fire order and rushed off an order of his own: keep Harbin.

Yet losing Harbin would not necessarily have been a major blow to Communist prospects in Manchuria. Already, Lin's armies had been shifting back to a strategy centered not on holding cities but on occupying the area around them. The earlier stand at Siping, with Communist troops defending fixed positions for weeks, had been a deviation—one made at Mao's insistence over the skepticism of his commanders. Since then, Lin had reverted to type, dispersing troops in the countryside and readying mobile attacks and guerrilla operations as Nationalist lines stretched thinner and thinner, their overextension clear. Mao had laid all of this out months earlier, in a warning to Chiang before Marshall's arrival: "If we fight now, I cannot beat you. But I can deal with you with the same method that I used to deal with the Japanese. You can seize points and lines, and I shall occupy their sides and rural areas to surround cities." In retreat, Lin had shown his dispirited troops a film about Napoleon's defeat in Russia.

In Yenan, nothing Zhou related of Chiang's cease-fire demands, or Marshall's requisites for peace, diminished the skepticism of his comrades. As far as they could tell, Chiang was maneuvering to confine CCP troops to a few disconnected bases in Manchuria and north China, where he would try to isolate and then "annihilate" them.

Still, Zhou advocated one more push for a settlement. Although wary, Mao gave his permission. But there was a condition: as Zhou returned to talks, no military advantage was to be sacrificed in the process. Mao sent a message to his commanders in Manchuria: "While our delegates are negotiating with the KMT in Nanjing, our units in the Northeast should use this period to have a rest, to have logistics taken care of, to enhance the morale, so that we can continue to fight again."

As the cease-fire got under way, #5 Ning Hai Road turned into a madhouse. Spring had given way to a hot and sticky summer. Visitors streamed in to see Marshall, all persuaded that these fifteen days were pivotal but each with his own idea of how to take advantage of them— how to forge a fair settlement in Manchuria, how to speed military unification, how to reopen railway lines and roads. What the Nationalists and Communists intended was not entirely clear. But as Melby observed, "all other groups want peace, and every available missionary is being brought in to exert pressure in that direction."

So far Marshall had played an inside game, working privately with official representatives and only rarely resorting to more public interventions. But facing the implacability of the other players, he had begun to enlist outside actors for help. There was one he thought particularly useful, a missionary-turned-educator named John Leighton Stuart who had unique credibility across partisan lines. Hoping Stuart might be able to persuade both sides to take a more compromising stance, Marshall summoned him from Beijing, dispatching the C-54 for the trip.

They had first met in May, on the recommendation of both Chiang and Henry Luce. Born to missionary parents in Hangzhou and raised singing "Jesus Loves Me" in Chinese, Stuart had for twenty-five years presided over Yenching University (China's Harvard, said Americans), where he had educated a generation of rising leaders, Nationalist and Communist. He had championed and occasionally advised Chiang, but seeing Mao recently, Stuart had laughed about how many Yenching students had made the pilgrimage to Yenan and expressed hope that they were "proving a credit to their training." Crucially, he also knew Chiang's conservative confidant Chen Li-fu—whom Marshall had come to see as "the man most opposed to my efforts."

"I have had long experience with the Communists," Chen told a reporter in the cease-fire's opening days. "I know them and they have never forgiven me for taking 23,000 members from them." His private comments to American officials were even more bellicose. He had been fighting Communists for eighteen years, he said to Melby at a cocktail party, and would fight them for eighteen more if he had to. (Not that eighteen would be necessary: they "can easily be destroyed," Chen gloated.) He liked to tell Americans that he had first encountered Communist treachery during his time working in a Pennsylvania coal mine—incongruously, since he was small, smooth skinned, and polite. U.S. military intelligence noted his "ruthless elimination of opposition by the use of whatever means which may be available." He was equally zealous in his loyalty to Chiang.

Chen was not the only one newly brazen in his rhetoric. In Nanjing, Soviet diplomats lambasted U.S. aggression and openly speculated about the need for more active intervention. In Yenan, CCP complaints about Marshall's bias had flowered into charges of imperialist iniquity. "Is it the Chinese reactionaries, with their vicious civil war policy, who are demanding vigorous military intervention," asked *Emancipation Daily* on the first day of the cease-fire, "or is it the United States' vigorous military intervention which is demanding the Chinese reactionaries' vicious civil war policy?" A few days later, an editorial predicted that the "imperialistic elements in the United States" would turn out to be as maligned as "the Japanese imperialists before." Chiang's use of Marshall's plane while in Manchuria featured prominently in denunciations.

By now, Marshall was aware how much those eleven days had fanned suspicion and fueled propaganda. As Communist attacks on him became more virulent, he sent a top secret message to Washington, explaining that Chiang's prolonged absence "just as I had brought the two sides to the verge of an agreement . . . aroused a deep suspicion in their minds that I was favoring the Government side and was a party to the delay." It added "fat to the fire." At the same time, Marshall sensed that the criticism had a clear purpose: "to arouse U.S. opposition to any military representation out here." The Communists might see an opportunity to repel U.S. assistance entirely.

It was not just in the realm of propaganda that Communist actions belied Communist calls for peace. Fighting slowed in Manchuria itself, but in the areas around it, CCP troops maneuvered aggressively. The day the cease-fire went into effect, there were strikes on railway lines in Shandong—a broad peninsula just south of Manchuria, offering easy access to it by sea—and then days of attacks so aggressive as to raise fears of clashes with U.S. Marines posted to the port city of Tsingtao. When Marshall challenged him, Zhou brushed off the incidents as "the impertinent actions of lower level officers." But as the Executive Headquarters tracked the violations, there was too clear a pattern for Zhou's excuse to be persuasive: the Communists looked to be preserving routes between Manchuria and their other base areas, ensuring a continued ability to move troops and threaten Chiang's lines.

The cease-fire was nothing more than a "reasonable pause," Marshall acknowledged to Truman, and the question was whether he could use it to good effect. He took a characteristically methodical approach, but with a difference from before. No longer did he hope to induce reciprocal positive steps that would create a virtuous cycle of their own, each side making additional concessions in response to concessions from the other. Instead, he looked for commitments, "definite proposals," he could persuade each side to make unconditionally. That might be enough to stop most fighting and get the Executive Headquarters and truce teams working properly again. And from there, one step at a time, perhaps other issues would somehow start to look less intractable.

He pressed Zhou to stop the sabotage of railways. He tried, unsuccessfully, to sell the Communists on a Nationalist-backed proposal to give Americans the swing vote on the truce teams rather than requiring consensus. He pressed the Nationalists to give the Executive Headquarters real authority in Manchuria. Rather than rushing to reconvene the Committee of Three, he asked Zhou and a new Nationalist representative to try to make progress on their own first.

For Marshall, this frantic shuttle diplomacy proved even more grueling than the long negotiating sessions of the winter. He had his staff working "war days," as he put it to Eisenhower. Still, he projected confidence: "This is a hell of a problem but we will lick it yet, pessimists to the contrary notwithstanding."

But Katherine felt no such need to show assurance, especially after coming down with dysentery in the middle of June. "Sometimes I feel neither party really wants peace," she wrote in a letter home. "They are so bitter they want to fight it out no matter what it does to China or these poor people." Her husband was looking "thin and tired," she reported, but "still struggling manfully."

No matter how "manfully" Marshall struggled, ten days into the cease-fire "definite proposals" were just starting to take shape. Late on the morning of June 17, he sat with Zhou on the terrace, now shaded by a bamboo structure that covered much of the yard and house, cooling them in these sweltering summer months. Earlier there had been hours of heavy rain that flooded the streets, but the sun had since turned the city into a steam bath. While Marshall and Zhou talked outside, a Nationalist general was waiting inside, leaders of the Democratic League were asking for an appointment that afternoon, and Chiang was summoning Marshall to a meeting that evening. They were, noted Caughey, in "a race for time."

At this point, even Zhou seemed on edge. "Under the present rule of the Kuomintang, it is impossible to obtain true peace and democracy," he said. As Marshall pressed for actions, Zhou quibbled over words, contested the terms of the original promise of Nationalist sovereignty in Manchuria, and refused to name an acceptable breakdown of troops in the region, even though Chiang had agreed to revise the original 14-to-1 ratio. The Nationalists, Zhou scoffed, would be unsatisfied with any Communist concession, no matter how generous. He insisted that the Communists still trusted Marshall, despite their railing against American imperialism; if anything, they hoped he would stay in China "for a long time." (To Zhou's mind, one sign of good faith: Marshall had gone out of his way to return a personal notebook that Zhou had inadvertently left on the C-54, with no indication that any information inside had been extracted.) Still, Zhou refused to grant Marshall's request that the Americans get greater authority to enforce peace. "We've trusted Marshall," he said, "but to trust him and to give him arbitrary power are two different things."

At 6 p.m., Marshall visited the Generalissimo. Chiang thought Marshall's views had been moving toward his own. "Marshall's attitude is also getting more and more resolute," he recorded hopefully in his diary. He was ready to lay out his own set of demands—including the immediate withdrawal of Communist troops from the contested provinces on Manchuria's southern edge, Rehe and Chahar, a commitment to complete demobilization and integration of the two sides' armies in Manchuria by the end of 1946, and a pledge from Yenan to begin rebuilding sabotaged railway lines on June 22, the day the cease-fire was set to end. Marshall knew immediately that the CCP would never accept such conditions. He suspected Chiang knew that as well.

"We have reached an impasse," Marshall conceded to Truman the next day. The Nationalists were convinced, he explained, that the Communists "can quickly be crushed"—which he considered "a gross underestimate of the possibilities, as a long and terrible conflict would be unavoidable." Before long, the Soviets "would probably intervene openly or under cover." But he had said as much to Chiang and was not optimistic that the message had gotten through.

Marshall's pessimism about the prospects of the next five days was shared by both Chiang and Zhou. Chiang, more intent on proving that Yenan bore responsibility for the cease-fire's failure than on offering solutions of his own, dismissed Communist proposals as ruses. Zhou reported to Mao that Marshall had no real sway over Chiang, meaning it was time to "reassess the role of the United States and Marshall." Mao, in turn, dispatched a message to his cadres: "Judging from recent events, Chiang Kai-shek is preparing for large-scale war. . . . If we fight to a draw, peace may also be possible. If Chiang scores a big victory, however, it will not be possible to negotiate peace. Therefore, our army must repulse Chiang Kai-shek's attack in order to secure a peaceful future."

Caughey started sending warnings to his wife, Betty. "You and I have to think about the possibilities of another war in a few years in this place," he wrote, with concern for their two young daughters. "Mark my words, honey, about the time Pat and Nancy are ready to go to school—possibly about the time they are ready to finish school and about to be married—we will be embroiled in something that will be much worse than anything that has happened so far." Yet watching Marshall, Caughey reflected, "He sees things in a light that another man could not see them. He is philosophical about it and tries to do the best that he can and leaves the rest to destiny."

But in fact, as he contemplated the consequences of failure, Marshall was troubled. The Nationalists could not destroy the Communists, he thought, nor could the Communists destroy the Nationalists. But "between them, they could destroy China."

Marshall started warning of the "loss of China"—not necessarily to Communism, but to a terrible new war. He was operating on the assumption that if nothing had been resolved by noon on June 22, war would begin at 12:01.

On the morning of June 20, just over forty-eight hours before the cease-fire's end, Marshall received Yu Ta-wei, the Harvard-educated Nationalist general. Marshall had been struggling to persuade Chiang that there was wisdom in compromise—that the Nationalists could soften their demands and find common ground without putting themselves in danger. He had made the case through emissaries, including John Leighton Stuart, and in person. The atmosphere was growing more and more tense, rife with rumor and gossip. "Life continues to be a walking nightmare and is getting worse as the deadline approaches," wrote Melby. He wondered "whether either side can nerve itself for the final break and accept the unpredictable consequences."

With so little resolved, Marshall had only one idea: prolonging the cease-fire. But when he asked Yu how long an extension the Nationalists could offer, the answer was dispiriting: "one day." It set Marshall off. The United States "would not back a civil war," and the Nationalists were making a mistake if they assumed it would. When Yu asked what would happen if war broke out in the next few days, Marshall's answer was harsh: the Marines would be withdrawn, the navy's Seventh Fleet would sail away, and American support would be curtailed.

When Yu left, Stuart came in. Since summoning him from Beijing, Marshall had seen him daily. Stuart had held long conversations with Chiang, in Chinese, one Christian to another. He had also seen Zhou, who, after rhapsodizing about the CCP's commitment to peace, opposition to Russian influence, and desire for "American help in every way," had agreed to an extension of the cease-fire. But with Chiang, Stuart was less certain. He had come away sharing Marshall's concern that Chiang had a perilously exaggerated sense of Nationalist strength.

Next came Zhou at 3 p.m. As the end of the cease-fire approached, Marshall had found Zhou increasingly resentful. Although Zhou had agreed to an extension, he still complained about Nationalist intransigence. Meeting Chiang's demands—particularly that the Communists stand down in key parts of north China—was "impossible," he told Marshall.

But for now, an extension was the important thing: a little more time to find a way forward, to mount a "final effort to effect a peaceful solution to this situation." When Zhou left, Marshall left to see Chiang. After Marshall's outburst to Yu that morning, after all the pressure and lobbying, Chiang had spent three hours discussing the wisdom of an extension with his advisers. When Marshall arrived, Chiang announced that he would grant eight more days, until noon on June 30.

In conveying the news to Truman, Marshall was muted—but no longer despairing: "There is a wide gap to be closed but I now think I have some chance of success."

When a copy of Chiang's official announcement of the extension reached Ning Hai Road the next day, Marshall was there talking with Zhou. Even with the additional eight days, Zhou's suspicion was running high. Chiang's demands, he charged, were meant to position Nationalist forces so that "he can wipe out the Communists at any time he wishes." But Marshall pointed out that without Communist movement on military commitments—the CCP had still not submitted lists of troops for demobilization, as it was supposed to months earlier—he could not make Chiang proceed on the political front. He also noted Nationalist fears that "the Chinese Communist Party is either coordinated or dictated with or by Soviet Russia"—a claim Zhou dismissed as "completely groundless."

Marshall snapped at Zhou as well: "I do not belong to the Kuomintang Party and I do not belong to the Communist Party and I don't enjoy my job. I am merely doing the best I can."

With just over a week to put China back on a peaceful path—"this last effort, and it certainly is the last effort"—Marshall tried to revive the Committee of Three, hoping that he could get it back to its old ways. He called a meeting for the next morning, June 22. Five and a half months since the original Committee of Three had climbed the steps to Happiness Gardens, hopeful in the gray and damp of Chongqing winter, Zhou and a new Nationalist representative, Hsu Yung-Chang, arrived at #5 Ning Hai Road on a day that was, as Melby recorded, "like walking through a cloud of live steam."

The number of vexing issues had only grown since that first time.

Both sides reopened once-settled military questions—how many troops each would ultimately give up, where they would stay in the meantime, when they would become part of a national army. Both resisted the basic principle of simultaneous progress on political reform and military unification. Once intent on staying as far away from politics as he could, Marshall had come to accept that political and military considerations could not be separated. In areas currently under Communist control, especially in Manchuria, the CCP would hardly accept being cut out of governance entirely, but nor would Chiang simply cede authority. And Marshall realized that it would not be enough to stop the fighting. The two sides needed a mutually acceptable answer about what would happen after fighting had stopped.

Marshall harped on the inability of each side to understand the other's concerns: "They can only see their own fears and, therefore, draw many false conclusions." He watched each changing terms as convenient, or fixating on the other side's infractions while explaining away its own. "I think they are both wrong and that they are both alike," he said. "But they are both very human."

Marshall tried to get back into the old rhythm. He arrayed the Committee around the table. He proposed a point and then asked for assent. When he anticipated an impasse, he readied an easier point to turn to.

But this time it did not go well. They bickered over distances. They disputed basic definitions. "Hanging in the hazy atmosphere are the fears and suspicions of one side against the other," Caughey wrote while sitting at the Committee table and waiting for translation. "Bantering, elaborations, accusations are the mode." Marshall did not conceal his exasperation. For the first time, he was spotted doodling in a meeting. He cut the session short, forgetting to serve tea. When they later reconvened, Hsu—a particularly ineffective appointment by Chiang, in Marshall's view—failed even to show up, sending a substitute in his place. "We are not making much progress here," Marshall quickly concluded.

At the end of the dispiriting first day of the Committee's return to action, Marshall and Katherine, recovered from her dysentery, went to the Chiangs' for dinner. At Madame Chiang's request, it was a purely American affair—the Marshalls and some aides, a few officers, a few diplomats. "We are getting along," Chiang wrote in his diary afterward.

At 10:30 the next night, June 23, the phone rang at Marshall's house. Caughey took the call and found an aide to Zhou on the other end of the line with distressing news. At the Nanjing train station, a mob was attacking a "peace delegation" that had arrived from Shanghai, and nothing was being done to stop the beatings. Could Marshall intervene? Caughey immediately called Yu Ta-Wei, who promised that Nationalist troops would get the situation under control.

The peace delegation, a dozen distinguished intellectuals, business-people, and civic leaders, planned to meet with Marshall, the Committee of Three, and Nationalist officials in Nanjing. A crowd of 100,000 had seen the delegation off from Shanghai earlier that day with an "anti-civil war parade," chanting for peace and democracy and waving signs telling American troops, "Go Back to Your Home Sweet Home." An organization called the Shanghai National Peace Movement distributed fliers demanding American neutrality and asking, "Did you and Mr. Abraham Lincoln Like Your Civil War?"

When the delegation's train pulled into Nanjing's station, a mob was waiting. It ripped the signs and streamers from the cars, forced its way onboard, and started pummeling the activists.

After Caughey was assured that the assault would be stopped, the phone rang again. The beatings—"merciless," said reporters on the scene—were continuing, and there was still no sign of the authorities. It was after midnight by the time Nationalist troops intervened. The members of the peace delegation were covered in blood, their clothing in tatters. And it quickly emerged that Nationalist agents had been part of the mob. Even many Nationalists expressed dismay, blaming the CC Clique.

Marshall was indignant, not just about the fact of the attack but even more by Nationalist inaction, despite promises to his aides that something would be done. When he raised the incident with Chiang, Marshall heard only feeble excuses in response, as Chiang's foot went in anxious circles.

The opening days of the cease-fire had overlapped with the Washington legislative calendar in an unfortunate way. As Marshall was playing mediator in the Committee of Three, the U.S. Congress was debating details of additional assistance to Chiang's government. Since December, Marshall had tried to strike a careful balance between continuing essential help (and laying the groundwork for the much greater help that would flow to a new unified government) and not encouraging militarism by Nationalist hard-liners. The timing of this latest round sent the wrong message at a delicate time.

Congress had signed off on $52 million in Lend-Lease equipment that had been promised during the war. Then the State Department had submitted a bill committing another $100 million in military assistance following the expiration of Lend-Lease on July 1. A note of endorsement from Marshall was appended to the request: "I believe that the passage of the bill by Congress would facilitate the efforts now being made to promote peace and unity between warring factions in China." This new package came on top of other assistance over recent months—the transport of more than 400,000 Nationalist troops, the continued American troop presence, hundreds of discounted planes for the Chinese air force, a six-month supply of ammunition for Chiang's troops.

Sitting in a session of the Committee of Three, Marshall wrote Truman a hurried note, requesting that the administration issue a public clarification of what the aid was for, and what it was not for. The timing of the discussions in Congress, Marshall explained, was causing him "difficulty and embarrassment." The CCP argued that the aid package was encouraging "the government's tendency to deal with the Communists by force and thus is contributing to all out civil war," and Marshall conceded that "some die-hard Kuomintang elements in other government councils are utilizing recent American measures as a basis for pressing the Generalissimo to push forward with a campaign of determination against the Communists."

Acheson issued a statement insisting that the legislation could not "rightfully be interpreted as current support of any factional military support in China." The message was not especially persuasive. Communists did not pass up the opportunity for propaganda, and Nationalists viewed the aid as vindication no matter what they heard from Marshall or Acheson. The forces in Washington appeared to be developing in their favor.

As the days of negotiation plodded toward the June 30 deadline, the Committee of Three accomplished little. Despite progress on reopening communications and granting Americans authority on field teams, consensus remained far off on key matters—especially local governance and military demobilization. Chiang had sent Marshall a set of demands that enumerated Communist military obligations but said nothing about his political commitments. Zhou reacted sharply. His side could not give up its armies—its "bargaining power in political matters"—without the other side giving up one-party rule. "If they think that way," he said, "they are thinking war instead of peace." Marshall sighed that he was "at a loss. . . . I find the two sides so far apart and so firm in their purpose, that I do not know what to say or do."

Outside, the heat was stifling. Cholera was spreading. Chen Li-fu was blithely telling Americans that the Communists could be annihilated in three months.

With three days left before the cease-fire expired, Marshall found the two sides still "irreconcilably opposed" on key questions. That is what his weeks of "continued pressure without respite" had revealed: every discussion exposed a deeper gulf between them. He did not think another extension was viable.

He tried a last burst of shuttle diplomacy between Chiang and Zhou, ferrying ideas and pressing for concessions. He saw Chiang for two and a half hours in the morning. Then, back on Ning Hai Road, he hosted Zhou from 1:30 until 4:00, and then again at 6:30. Each side seemed convinced that the military balance would ultimately tip in its favor, meaning neither felt the need to give up any ground. There was also an ominous new dimension to the discussion. So far, ideology had arisen infrequently. But now, Zhou was suddenly stressing the fundamental ideological divide. "The Communists are protecting the rights and the social gains of the peasants in particular," he insisted. "As soon as Government troops enter those areas, those benefits will be withdrawn and the peasants put under immense exploitation and suffering." If it was a matter of ideology, of fundamental principles that allowed no compromise, the prospects for negotiation were grim. As Zhou would say, "Any concessions would constitute a failure of the Communist Party."

By this point, Zhou had already warned Mao that "negotiations are drawing close to the end." Mao slammed Marshall's mission as "a smoke-screen for strengthening Chiang Kai-shek in every way and suppressing the democratic forces in China." Even as Marshall continued his long afternoon meetings with Zhou, in Yenan *Emancipation Daily* was sharpening its attacks on the United States. "The American policy reminds us of the policy the Japanese imperialists used," declared an editorial.

As the deadline approached, Marshall saw Chiang and Zhou for hours every day—Chiang in the morning, Zhou in the afternoon. There was no clear way forward, but Marshall had his staff working late into the night, trying to concoct some new formula, some path around the multiplying deadlocks. Chiang thought it a sign of desperation: "He is terrified of warfare, as well as the Communist Party's refusal to compromise." And Chiang was not entirely wrong—Marshall was making a long-shot attempt to persuade them to stop fighting and start moving on basic commitments, agreeing to work out the details later.

On June 29, the day before the cease-fire was due to end, Marshall went to Chiang's office for a last try. The Nationalists' Nanjing headquarters was not far from Ning Hai Road, in a complex that was a studied projection of Chinese greatness, past and future. Visitors arrived through an arched gate into a Qing-era hall, passed between rows of red columns decorated in gold calligraphy, and then entered a five-story Art Deco building, with Italian light fixtures and shuttling Otis elevators and clacking typewriters. Chiang's upper-floor office was neat and unostentatious, paneled in dark wood, writing brushes lined up alongside three telephones on an otherwise spare desk.

Marshall made his case. If Chiang would show flexibility on the areas he was insisting the Communists evacuate, Marshall thought there was a chance of getting CCP compliance on other matters. Perhaps a high-level committee could solve the question of how local governance would be handled in areas evacuated by CCP troops, another contentious issue. Through a variety of channels, the Americans had been reminding the Nationalists of the benefits of flexibility—above all, a respite that would give the economy time to stabilize, but also American support, including the $500 million in financial assistance Marshall had secured but still not released. With the hours winding down, Marshall also wanted Chiang to remember the consequences of failure. Chiang and his government, Marshall said bluntly, "would be judged by the world, and certainly by American public opinion, as having unnecessarily plunged the country into chaos by implacable demands and the evident desire to pursue a policy of military settlement." When Chiang proposed that Marshall keep trying even if this cease-fire fell apart, Marshall snapped back, "I would decline to be an umpire on a battlefield."

"I can tell from his voice and tone that he is arrogant and untamable," Chiang wrote in his diary that night. "I found it very unbearable."

After leaving Chiang's office, Marshall held a last session with Zhou before the deadline, reminding him of his side's infractions—worst of all, the attacks at the start of the cease-fire, which had, in Marshall's assessment, helped provoke the Nationalists. ("Communist military supremacy in Shandong has apparently been established at least for the time being," American intelligence had since determined.) Marshall's dispiriting conclusion was that there was "no basis for optimism in the present tragic dilemma."

Zhou, for his part, exhibited a new level of bitterness, insisting, "I have made all the concessions I can." He attacked the Nationalists as "unrelenting" in their effort "to strangle the Communists." He rejected turning over territory because it would consign tens of millions of peasants to abusive landlords and "undemocratic government." He charged that everything the Nationalists did betrayed an intention to destroy the Communists.

Marshall replied wearily: "Is that all, General Zhou?"

Madame Chiang came to Ning Hai Road that evening. The Generalissimo had a party to attend and could not come himself. But in any case, there was nothing new to report. He had made his final offer.

Marshall sat down to draft a note of defeat to Truman. "A final breakdown" seemed "inevitable." Chiang would not agree to stop fighting without a full commitment to Communist demobilization, and the Communists would not commit to demobilization until there was real political reform—the same deadlock Marshall thought he had overcome months earlier. Now, Marshall reported, commanders in the field were riled, and Nationalist generals in particular seemed ready "to settle matters by force." Across China, the situation was "tense and explosive."

Yet when the cease-fire ended at noon the next day, it was with an unsettling whimper rather than a martial bang. As the clock ran out, Marshall was finishing a meeting with Chiang. At the outset, Chiang had asked if there was any chance the Communists would accept his terms at the last minute. "None at all," Marshall answered. But he wanted to reiterate his warning. Nationalist generals had been making calls for war, privately and publicly, many of them apparently intended for his ears. It suggested, he told Chiang, that the Nationalist side "was washing its hands of any democratic procedure and was pursuing a dictatorial policy of military force." Marshall offered an inflammatory analogy: it was like prewar Japan, with pugnacious military leaders dragging a country into war—and look, he needlessly emphasized, where it had gotten Japan.

But Chiang had resolved to be "stern and straight." He said he would direct his side not to go on the attack, but would make no promises beyond that. As they parted, he asked Marshall if he wanted to join him for a picnic.

Marshall's aides were not sure exactly what had happened. "There is something beneath it all that is so completely foreign to occidental mental processes that almost the whole picture is lost," said Caughey. "It seems to be based on something else than logic." Melby, however, found Chiang's logic perfectly clear. "I think if I were the Gimo I would opt for war," he wrote. "The only chance dying men have is to stake everything on a final throw before they get too weak."

CHAPTER 11

Sisyphus in China

On July 4, a few days later, Marshall was smiling. The United States had chosen that day, its own Independence Day, to grant independence to the Philippines after almost fifty years of occupation. As a young officer, Marshall had helped enforce that occupation. Now, delivering the toast at a party at the U.S. embassy in Nanjing, he was proud to say his country was giving it up.

The handover brought a frenzy of American self-congratulation. "Twice the Philippines have been liberated by the United States," crowed editorialists. Politicians hailed it as a model of what America could do for other benighted lands, starting with China. "We did not make them the first colony in a great new empire," Representative Walter Judd would brag, "but instead started immediately to help them build a republic and trained their people for the independence we promised and delivered. This is the pattern which the remainder of Asia wants."

Marshall shared in the self-congratulation, but he also drew other lessons. He had done two army tours in the Philippines, from 1902 to 1903 and 1913 to 1916. He knew what it meant to be a 21-year-old second lieutenant serving as a de facto proconsul in a de facto colony on behalf of a new global power. He had seen and studied guerrilla warfare, the last holdouts from a brutally suppressed insurgency taking the occasional shot at his jungle outpost. He had registered the toll of

long occupation on both occupied and occupier. He had witnessed the
rise of nationalism and anticolonialism—forces that the United States,
in his view, resisted at its own peril. The American government's declaration of Filipino independence, he now said, was "one of the most
honorable episodes in world history."

For Chiang it was an opportunity to reflect pride back at his American patrons. The "establishment of the Philippine republic illustrates
that the United States always is willing to help friendly neighbors realize their ideals of democracy," extolled his official statement. He hoped
that the moment would mark a new beginning for him as well. He had
maintained his resolve, and as a result, he thought, Marshall had "lost
his arrogance, aggressiveness, and disrespectfulness, and appeared
courteous, humbled, and grateful." The failure of the June cease-fire
might finally persuade him to take a different approach. "He has perhaps realized that he was over the line."

Meanwhile, Katherine and Madame Chiang were becoming
"chummy as a couple of college girls," as one of Marshall's aides
cracked. Madame Chiang was a regular presence on Ning Hai Road,
often at Katherine's invitation. One day when Marshall was sitting in
a meeting with Zhou, an aide handed him a scrap of paper. It was a
teasing note: "Madame Chiang is here and is staying for lunch.—Your
beloved wife." Marshall laughed out loud; Zhou stopped speaking and
looked up, perplexed.

The Americans did not know just what the end of the cease-fire meant.
There was no call to battle or declaration of war. On July 2, Zhou and
Chiang even met face-to-face in Nanjing for the first time, a discussion
urged by Marshall to try to overcome disagreements over local governance. "General Marshall worked incessantly seeking peace for China
and the entire world," said a Nationalist spokesman. "We should not
disappoint him." Both sides rushed to promise that, even with the
cease-fire done, their armies would fight only in self-defense.

But Marshall had come to understand how elastic a term "self-defense" could be. Each side noted matter-of-factly that if threatened it would of course have to fight back. And so he was not surprised when news of clashes started to come in. Manchuria remained relatively calm, but parts of north China were on the verge of open warfare, particularly in the Shandong territories taken by the Communists in the first days of the cease-fire. There was a flurry of reports of troop movements and attacks; newspapers printed rumors that ex-Nazis were helping the CC Clique plot the Communists' elimination.

Marshall saw what was happening: "Each side accuses the other of offensive action and therefore each side under the guise of self-defense seems to be engaging in pitted warfare." (One American officer wryly termed it "defensive annihilation.") He was unsure whom to blame more, finding himself sympathetic first to one side's accusations, then to the other's. Ultimately, he considered "both sides in the wrong," each guilty of "outrageous and stupid military actions." He quickly concluded that Chiang's promise not to strike first was nothing more than "a sop," intended to put "the government in a better position before public and probably preliminary to launching a military campaign."

For the first time since arriving in China almost seven months before, Marshall asked for Washington's guidance. "I am so closely engaged and so close to the trees that I may lack perspective," he wrote Acheson. What came back was of little use. The State Department explained that neither side seemed to want war, but could not overcome distrust to make peace; perhaps there was still a chance of persuading the Soviets not to meddle.

Although recognizing that China was on the precipice of civil war, Marshall held back. He thought it was a moment for him to stand aside and let the Chinese negotiate on their own.

"The ultimate success of my mission," he wrote a friend, "rests in the lap of the Gods."

On July 7, the Communists launched a new offensive—this one a rhetorical offensive, aimed squarely at the United States. "American imperialism is far more dangerous than Japanese imperialism," proclaimed a manifesto released by the CCP Central Committee. "Their aims are to convert our country into a corpse-filled hell, a large concentration camp or a base or colonial settlement for a new war of imperial aggression." No longer was there any suggestion that a more enlightened American course was possible. The United States was a reactionary imperial power, and could not be expected to behave otherwise. But it would never, the manifesto promised, "succeed in turning China into a colony or a 'sovereign state' of Philippine pattern."

To Chiang, the CCP's rhetorical escalation was another encouraging sign that things were going his way. It might finally make Marshall see the right path forward. To drive the message home, the Nationalists were taking every opportunity to highlight cooperation between Yenan and the Kremlin. "As if the Soviets played the music and the Communists danced," an officer told an American diplomat.

By now, the Nationalists hardly needed to belabor the point. International tension was seeping into interactions everywhere. In the field, Chinese truce team members told American colleagues that there was little hope of cooperation on the ground until Moscow and Washington had reached a real understanding. In Shanghai, American troops were instructed to avoid bars, restaurants, and clubs favored by Russians after a sailor got into a brawl in a Russian cafe.

In Washington, meanwhile, the threat from Moscow was more and more central to both strategic planning and political jockeying. The military was devising contingency plans for troops around the world in the event of war with the Soviets. The joint chiefs were compiling a report on Moscow's goal of "eventual world domination" that included the recommendation, "All nations not now within the Soviet sphere should be given generous economic assistance and political support in their opposition to Soviet penetration." A new group called the American China Policy Association was demanding an end to "pressuring the Chinese government into making further concessions to the Chinese Communists," who "have worked unremittingly to make China a satellite of the Soviet Union." George Kennan was dictating another classified analysis of Soviet strategy: "They evidently seek to weaken all centers of power they cannot dominate, in order to reduce the danger from any possible rival. . . . They will take advantage of every weakness."

Marshall had a sense of these currents. Copies of the major magazines—*Time, Life, Reader's Digest, The New Republic*—reached Nanjing, along with digests of newspapers and intelligence reports. The State-War-Navy Coordinating Committee had recently sent an analysis of Soviet ambitions in Manchuria—"a great threat to the United States as well as to China," since "Communism is in opposition to the basic Chinese way of life."

In the first week of July, Marshall got more direct exposure to the new thinking when Secretary of the Navy James Forrestal arrived in China. Few senior officials had been more focused on the Soviet threat than Forrestal. Hard-driving and pulsing with anxious intensity, he had been warning of the menace of a Russian-Chinese axis for months: "The manpower available to such a combination would be so tremendous and the indifference to the loss of life so striking that it would present a very serious problem to this country." At the cabinet lunch with Truman in November, Forrestal had seconded the suggestion that Marshall be tapped for the China mission, hoping that the arrival of so formidable a figure would be noticed in the Kremlin. In the months since, Forrestal had kept a careful lookout for any action that might lead down the "long road of appeasement." It was he who mimeographed Kennan's "long telegram" and distributed it around Washington.

On his way across the Pacific, Forrestal stopped to witness an atomic test on Bikini atoll, the mushroom clouds the most vivid display of military might in the world. He arrived in Nanjing a few days later and found Marshall clear-eyed about how much the situation had deteriorated since they had last spoken in Washington in the spring. Marshall was mulling the need for a "period of withdrawal," including of American troops, to take stock and reset U.S. policy in China.

But Forrestal left China worried. He wanted a stronger stand, and thought Marshall too intent on trying to achieve peace and not intent enough on backing Chiang. The Chinese, Forrestal concluded from his visit, "were very much like ourselves in the degree to which they prized personal liberty and the freedom of the individual, but they have not yet learned the principles of management necessary to provide a cohesive administration which would give a stable order within which individual people could really have the benefits of freedom." America's key task, accordingly, was "the training of the Chinese in the business of management and administration." Otherwise there would be civil war—and civil war would be "an invitation to some other power or group of powers to come in and dominate China."

A string of other official visitors came to town as well, from the postmaster general to agricultural specialists to gaggles of politicians. "Apparently every VIP in the world is determined that the shortest distance between any two points, even Topeka to St. Louis, is the Great Circle Route to Shanghai," grumbled an American officer. When a congressional delegation landed, most of its members seemed more interested in "after dark entertainment" than official business. "I am ashamed of my law-making country men," Caughey would say. "These jokers are a class unto themselves." But they at least brought some consequential gossip: the talk in Washington was of a Republican sweep of Congress in the coming November midterm election.

The talk in Nanjing was of Marshall's imminent departure. The end of the cease-fire had triggered another round of rumors that he would soon be gone. Many included the related detail that General Wedemeyer would take his place.

For months, Wedemeyer had been less than discreet about his promised next post. The news had been all over the papers, especially since his return to Washington for surgery in the spring. He had already discussed it widely in China, and Chiang, expecting Wedemeyer back soon, had told Marshall how pleased he would be by the appointment. Wedemeyer thought it was such a sure thing that he

made a special trip to Brooks Brothers in New York to purchase a diplomat's wardrobe—coat with tails, striped pants, silk top hat. He had
told a fellow officer in April, "General Marshall has just informed me
that my assignment as Ambassador is only a matter of nomination
and approval by the Senate."

To Marshall, the rumors were unhelpful. He was more eager than
anyone for his departure to come soon. But now that likely meant mid-
September, not immediately.

Other reservations about Wedemeyer had also come to the surface.
The next ambassador, Marshall had said, must be someone with "no
record of prejudice or advocacy which would irritate either the Chinese Nationalists or the Chinese Communists," since part of his role
might be shepherding a new government into existence. Wedemeyer
hardly fit the bill. He had served Chiang directly during the war and
was well known as a champion of Chiang's cause. In exchanges with
Marshall, Wedemeyer had emphasized that his appointment would
inflame Communist hard-liners. Marshall worried even more that it
would embolden Nationalist hard-liners, who would take it as a signal
that he was giving up for good.

Wedemeyer himself had been voicing doubts about the job. "I am
increasingly convinced that my position out there will be almost unten-
able," he wrote Luce in early July. "When I take over, I predict that the
Communists will seize upon this opportunity to abrogate agreements
and of course in the minds of the public, both in China and abroad,
they will attribute dissensions and confusions to me." He thought he
was "facing serious failure, inevitable."

Fortunately, a providential alternative had appeared. In a letter
to Acheson, Marshall described another candidate for the ambassadorship: "the most highly respected foreigner . . . Communists and
Nationalists alike trust and admire him . . . he is selfless and has only
the interest of China and America at heart." He was referring to China-
born and -bred John Leighton Stuart. As ambassador, Stuart would
"immediately create on both sides a feeling of greater confidence in the
negotiations."

Stuart had made China his life's cause and was a true believer in its promise. At 70, with a thin face and receding gray hair, he was called "Christ-like" by Chinese who knew him. Although trained as a New Testament scholar, at Yenching University he had branched out from religious roots to train students in sociology, journalism, and politics. Chiang's personal secretary was an alumnus, as were some of Zhou's young aides. He had long celebrated Chiang's "patriotic purpose" and "Christian faith," and could "talk to the Generalissimo as probably no one else can," as Melby put it. Another diplomat remarked approvingly that five decades on this side of the Pacific had made Stuart "as oblique and, when necessary, just as devious as any Chinese."

Marshall pitched Stuart on the ambassadorial post on July 4. It would not have to be a lengthy appointment, just long enough to restart negotiations and make some progress toward democratic unity—a fitting final act to his life's work. When Stuart accepted, Marshall asked the State Department to table Wedemeyer's nomination. As consolation, he allowed that Wedemeyer could return later, perhaps as the next ambassador. In the meantime, though, Marshall wanted the whole episode kept under wraps, "so as to avoid if possible insinuations that he has been sacrificed to Communist pressures." He added of Wedemeyer: "I do not need his assurances that he will willingly and cheerfully do anything I think might be helpful. I know that to be a fact."

Wedemeyer did offer his assurances—at least at first, and at least to Marshall directly. Wedemeyer had long claimed not to want the job anyway. Now, he wrote Marshall, "My principal regret about developments is that I will not be associated with you in the effort to bring about stabilization in that complex area." Wedemeyer even apologized that "continued references, misinterpretations and conjectures both in press and radio concerning my return to China have embarrassed you." As an addendum he related that an army doctor just back from China had reported that Marshall was "in excellent condition" and doing a "swell job."

What Wedemeyer said to others was entirely different. "An atomic bomb along diplomatic lines was dropped in my lap," he fumed to a

friend. Whatever his assurances, he was angry and humiliated. For
months he had blabbed about his appointment. He had promised Chiang he would return. (The Generalissimo, Wedemeyer wrote Marshall,
"indicated repeatedly how very much he needed me.") He had spent
$695 on the "funeral regalia" expected of an ambassador. A box of
Brooks Brothers shirts had already arrived in Nanjing.

Wedemeyer was as indiscreet in his pique as he had earlier been
in his pride. Soon journalists were writing that he had been indeco-
rously dumped for fear that he would "offend the Reds." In Nanjing,
the switch to Stuart had done nothing to check rumors of Marshall's
imminent departure.

"The situation is developing into a straight civil war," Marshall said to
Zhou, "and unless something is done quickly it will be too late." It was
the evening of July 16, and they were sitting on the bamboo-covered
terrace on Ning Hai Road. Summer in Nanjing was proving to be even
worse than summer in Washington, DC. The day before, the Chiangs
had fled the city for their mountain retreat, with plans to stay until
fall. Katherine had gone with them.

Since the surge in anti-Americanism among the Communists, Marshall had shown a new level of bitterness in his interactions with Zhou.
The new CCP line reflected the agility of Chinese diplomacy, personal
relationships utilized or discarded as circumstances dictated, but to
Marshall the abrupt shift was dismaying. Yenan's charges were "a rou-
tine example of Communist propaganda," he said, "a technique that is
followed regardless of the facts." Zhou insisted that Marshall was not
the intended target of the invective. Marshall did not buy it. "I am the
'reactionary party,'" he retorted. "Nobody else can be charged with this
but me, personally." Aides were taken aback.

Still, although holding back from direct negotiations, Marshall had
not stopped proffering solutions. There could be another cease-fire
order. There could be an agreement on military questions—a mutually
acceptable formula still seemed possible. They could resolve differ-

ences around local governance. "It seems to me that unless we find a basis for issuing the cease-fire order, everything will be out of control," he reminded Zhou. "All agreements will be wiped out and there will be a general civil war." As they sat on the terrace, aides passed notes flagging reports of attacks.

The C-54 tracked the Yangtze's course inland from Nanjing. The river was broad and meandering at first, but as the plane continued west, Marshall could see mountains rising from the floodplain. The Chiangs and Katherine had set off for their summer retreat in those mountains a few days earlier. He was following behind for a visit, the newly minted Ambassador Stuart in tow.

In Nanjing, departure had been slightly delayed. With Marshall and Stuart seated onboard, aides left behind on the tarmac could see why: Nationalist pilots were taking off with bombs intended for Communist targets.

After an hour and forty-five minutes, the plane landed on a grass airfield. Marshall and Stuart crossed the Yangtze on a converted Japanese gunboat, then took a jeep to the base of a steep slope. The only way up 3,500 feet was to walk or be carried. So they stepped into sedan chairs covered with fringed white awnings and resting on pine beams, and bearers in straw hats and rope sandals—Marshall had eight, most others six—hoisted the beams onto their shoulders and started the ascent. Marshall bobbed pleasantly, looking down sheer drops from the sinuous trail at the ribbon of the Yangtze below. Occasionally the bearers paused to wring sweat out of the cotton cloths that cushioned their shoulders or to rub the brown calluses underneath. ("The most undemocratic scene I have seen," said an aide.)

As they climbed, the heat of the plains gave way to bracing mountain air. There were stands of teak and bamboo, the smell of pine and chirp of cicadas. After two hours, they started to see European-style stone houses on forested slopes—a landscape Katherine compared to Switzerland. Then there was a large poster of Chiang's face hanging by the side of the road, followed by a somewhat smaller poster of Marshall's with the caption "Most Honored Angel of Peace."

The town was called Kuling, a Chinese-sounding pun on "Cooling Mountain Retreat." The British had claimed the location when China was at its weakest, and missionaries built it into a Europeanized escape from the landscape below. (Among them was an American named Absalom Sydenstricker, father of the novelist Pearl Buck, who spent idyllic childhood vacations in Kuling.) In the 1930s, Chiang had reclaimed the town and made it his summer capital. This was his first time back since the war.

For Katherine, the move could not have come too soon. The "inferno" of Nanjing was getting to her. "What with the aftermath of eight years of war, inflations, civil war, famine, and epidemics," she wrote friends, "the charm of China that I had heard so much about was certainly not evident." Nor did she find anything charming about living in a house full of her husband's aides, packed into bedrooms and crowding the table at meals. Kuling by contrast was "beautiful beyond description." The air was fresh, the temperature in the mid-70s on sunny days. There were flowers, brooks, and pleasant paths winding among stone promontories and Taoist temples.

When Marshall arrived late in the afternoon, he immediately agreed—the scenery was "magnificent" and Katherine's cottage "delightful." Down the road from a simple church, it was a gray stone bungalow surrounded by pine trees. A bucolic lawn sloped down to a swimming pool. Just across a narrow stream was the British-built villa that Chiang had renamed Mei's Cottage, after his wife. Katherine crossed the stream daily to see Madame Chiang, "who seems quite devoted to her in admiration and affection," Marshall observed.

He was feeling much less amicable, even after trading his uniform for a summer suit. Chiang's departure for Kuling had condemned negotiations to virtual paralysis. That did not strike Marshall as an unintended consequence—he was reminded of Chiang's previous prolonged absence, in Manchuria in May.

The last time they had spoken, Chiang urged patience: "Let's let time work this out." But Marshall knew what that meant. As Chiang laid it out in his diary: "I should make Marshall realize that his success does not lie only in the mediation. There are other ways, for instance, assisting my government to 'handle' the Communists militarily."

After dinner this first night in Kuling, Marshall gave Chiang an unvarnished assessment of the course events were taking and all the ways in which the Nationalists were responsible. He thought that "aggressive military action" by Nationalist generals risked causing "irredeemable chaos." The one bright spot was Stuart's presence for the first time. Afterward, Stuart shared his insight: "The Chinese Problem, as I see it, has now come in certain decisive aspects to be largely the psychology of this one man"—Chiang.

The next day, Chiang asked to see Stuart alone. When asked for his views, Stuart was as harsh as Marshall had been. Stressing that he spoke as an "old friend and as a friend of the country," he warned of the dangers of inflation and growing opposition among China's intellectuals. He urged the start of real land reform, the embrace of "true democracy," and the avoidance of the kind of "violence" and "dictatorial methods" used by the Communists. It would be the only way, Stuart told Chiang, to defeat them.

In the heat of the plains below, decay spread. The atmosphere was rife with intrigue. "The rumors around," said Melby, "are as thick as the heat." With Chiang away in Kuling, Nationalist hard-liners seemed unleashed.

One day, a bearded professor was walking home in Kunming, a city in western China, when someone shot him in the back of the head. An outspoken peace activist and member of the Democratic League third party, the professor had just denounced the Nationalists at the funeral of another scholar executed by similar means the week before. He had also studied at the Art Institute of Chicago and taught under Stuart at Yenching. Before long, it became clear that Nationalist agents had carried out the hit.

Outrage followed quickly. There was "considerable evidence," Stuart determined, "that assassinations were carefully planned and would probably continue." The Americans would not stand by—not after the beatings at the Nanjing train station, when Nationalist assurances of protection turned out to mean nothing. In an unorthodox move, the American consul in Kunming gave refuge to a number of local political activists. "Persons who at the present time criticize the Government must expect to pay with their lives," said one Nationalist official. A Nationalist general added pointedly that the security of the U.S. consulate could not be guaranteed.

Marshall was furious. He attributed the "terroristic" crackdown to Chen Li-fu. The targets of some of the most vicious repression were not Communists but liberal opposition figures trying to stake out a third way. Chiang was quick to blame resistance—whether from speechifying intellectuals, disgruntled peasants, or striking workers—on CCP incitement. He was not always wrong, but by suppressing all opposition, he only helped the Communist cause. "Those who wanted a change had but one place to go," as a U.S. diplomat would observe. And the Communists were adept at turning the outrage to their advantage. Zhou would ask, "Seeing that the Kuomintang is resorting to such actions, how can we continue the negotiations and talk about democracy?" There had been no movement on the political process in months. Chiang had recently postponed the National Assembly, originally scheduled for May, until November—leaving enough time to fight the Communists into submission.

In the meantime, China's economic plight was getting worse. According to T. V. Soong, the economy might not be able to handle another six months of instability. As it was, with more than two-thirds of the budget going to the military, inflation was rising fast. (An American financial expert who worked for Chiang pointed out that inflation had helped fertilize revolutionary sentiment in Russia before the Bolshevik takeover.) Marshall started to warn of "an economic situation the likes of which no other nation ever survived." Chiang's minister of

information publicly agreed: "General Marshall is quite right in warning that continued civil war would bankrupt China."

To add to the travails, the full extent of Soviet plunder in Manchuria was becoming clear. The Red Army had carted off an estimated
billion dollars of "war booty," including 70 percent of Manchuria's
industrial capacity. Factories had been rendered inoperable and power
plants stripped. China's industrial development was said to have been
set back a generation. Even the world-weary Melby was stunned when
he went to survey the aftermath: "It is impossible to put all this in
words, and if I had not seen myself I could not really have believed that
this sort of thing could happen." As Marshall learned of the depreda-
tion, he started advising that industrial development should from now
on be concentrated farther south, given the strategic vulnerability of
Manchuria. (He also acknowledged that Yalta hurt the United States'
ability to respond to Moscow's assertiveness there, since it had "legalized Soviet position in Manchuria and thus weakened ours.")

To Marshall, political and economic considerations bolstered the
case for Nationalist restraint. An attempt to eradicate the Communists through force would not only backfire militarily. It would also
heighten political opposition, especially among the intellectual and
professional classes, and worsen an already dire economic situation.
Marshall had begun paying closer attention to these factors. (Melby
had at first disparaged him for "seeing the situation only in terms of
things and personalities, rather than ideas and conceptions as well.")
He peppered aides with questions about land reform. He requested a
copy of a 1937 book called *400 Million Customers*, about the wondrous
potential and continually thwarted hopes of American commerce in
China. "Yes, of course," he replied when asked whether political factors
were more important than military ones.

Yet military developments were also unnerving. "The fighting
spreads here and there like a slow fire," said Melby. One summer night
in Nanjing, the boom of artillery could be heard from the other side of
the Yangtze.

Marshall's meetings with both Nationalist and Communist representatives had mostly devolved into a series of complaints about attacks and troop movements and threats, which he would wearily relay back and forth. "Each side accuses the other of exactly the same thing," he offered yet again. In relating the pattern of aggressions and retaliations to Truman, Marshall confessed that "the acts were hard to determine and the data confusing."

On July 22, the Nationalist general Yu Ta-wei asked Marshall if he thought there would be a civil war. Marshall responded that there already was. When Yu asked how outside powers would respond, Marshall told him that the Soviets would fight openly for Manchuria and covertly for the rest of China, while the American public would call for a complete withdrawal.

A few days later, T. V. Soong invited Marshall over for a movie. In a cavernous room that looked like it belonged in an English manor (a moose head was mounted over the fireplace), they watched a 1944 production of _Henry V_. Funded by the British government to boost morale during World War II, this film version abridged Shakespeare's final scene— the epilogue in which military triumph brings political and economic catastrophe on the victor.

"More meetings and more futility all the time," Caughey wrote in his diary. "I don't see how the General stands it."

Years earlier, watching Black Jack Pershing lead American forces in World War I, Marshall had grasped a lesson that stayed with him. "When conditions are difficult, the command is depressed and everyone seems critical and pessimistic, you must be especially cheerful and optimistic," he recorded. "The more alarming and disquieting the reports received or the conditions viewed in battle, the more determined must be your attitude."

Now even Katherine was taken in. "He never says die and maybe he will wear the Chinese down instead of their doing him in," she wrote from Kuling.

On July 26, the day after watching *Henry V*, Marshall repeated the five-hour journey from Nanjing. While he was gone, Kuling had been idyllic. Four thousand feet above the swelter and bloodletting of the plains, Katherine and the Chiangs had been picking mountain lilies and going on picnics. She joined them daily for a meal—chicken and waffles, tender steak—or to work in the garden with Madame Chiang. At night a fire burned invitingly in their living room, and their library had an appealing range of English books—H. G. Wells novels, *I, Claudius,* the *Encyclopaedia Britannica.* When Katherine expressed her fondness for Madame Chiang's high-necked silk dresses, a tailor was summoned to make her five. "They have been wonderful friends," Katherine said of the Chiangs.

Marshall would arrive in uniform with a stack of papers, then change into his light suit and retire to a wicker chair on the lawn for an Old Fashioned. They might play croquet or bridge—both Marshall, with his potent memory, and Madame Chiang, with her shrewdness, were fearsome opponents—or, more often, a Western board game that Katherine had recently taught the Generalissimo: Chinese checkers.

Chiang was obsessed. (The symbolism—a leader vying for the mantle of Chinese nationalism playing an ersatz Chinese game in an imperialist-built retreat with an ersatz Chinese name—was unfortunate but undeniable.) "It was one of the most pleasant experiences of late," he wrote in his diary after an evening of Chinese checkers. American officers arriving in Kuling promptly found themselves memorizing the game's rules, at the behest of Katherine or Chiang or both. Sometimes during dinner, he clapped his hands and ordered a servant to bring a board so they could play at the table. Unable to converse, Katherine and Chiang each carried on a personal monologue as they peered at the board. "He speaks no English but says now he does not need a tongue," she related.

On this second visit to Kuling, Marshall was struck by their friendship. Chiang was "her devoted admirer." At the moment, it seemed the only thing preventing a rupture. "If I was as successful in negotiations as she is in human relations," said Marshall, "all would be well."

His umbrage was at a new high. "Substitute the name of Himmler for Chen Li-fu," he exploded at one point, "and you have the same thing Germany had." His concern was not just moral; it was also strategic. Pro-Nationalist sources were telling him that abuses were making Communists out of moderates. In the American newspaper clippings he received every day, Marshall also saw what was happening to Chiang's image in the United States. Foreign correspondents were throwing around the term *gestapo* with distressing regularity. Even Luce's *Time* was predicting that the Communists were "not likely to be halted in their revolutionary tracks by anything but a good government. The present government has been dissipating, selfishly and with utter callousness, American supplies and money." Marshall told Nationalist officials that their greatest asset was Chiang's "prestige"; if that prestige crumbled, China's cause would become much more difficult. It was, Marshall said, "sheer tragedy."

Stoking the opprobrium, Sun Yat-sen's widow—and Madame Chiang's sister—had just released a searing public condemnation of her brother-in-law and his party. She denounced the violence and misrule and demanded a complete and immediate withdrawal of U.S. troops: "The American people, who are Allies and long friends of China, must be clearly told of this road to disaster." To many Americans, it was a devastating indictment.

Marshall had already cautioned Chiang about the costs of squandering public support, domestic and international. This time, Marshall hoped that Stuart might be able to deliver the message more effectively—to make the Generalissimo see "the tragedy impending" and "the overwhelming desire of the people of China for peace and their growing disapproval of the methods of the Kuomintang Party." Unfortunately, Stuart had come down with dysentery. After four days of waiting in Kuling, with Stuart laid up in bed, Marshall resorted to delivering the message himself.

When he saw Chiang on the morning of July 30, Marshall was angry about the growing power of Nationalist hard-liners. He was angry about the threats to opposition figures taking refuge in the American consulate in Kunming, and about the earlier Nanjing train station assault having continued despite promises it would be stopped. He was angry about the warped certainty of Nationalist generals that they "could liquidate within three to six months all Communist forces in China."

But Chiang was feeling confident, as he had been for weeks. During the ill-fated June cease-fire, his commander in Manchuria had assured him that the Nationalists would have no trouble wiping out Communist forces in the region. "Now let me give you my word that I will end military campaigns against the Communists in one year, and restore industrial production in two years," he had promised his party.

On the surface, such confidence seemed reasonable. Through the spring, Chiang had watched his US-trained and -equipped forces go face-to-face with the CCP's armies and triumph again and again. Communist forces numbered perhaps one-third of his own; an even smaller fraction of Chinese territory was in Communist hands. Just as important, the world was going his way. The United States needed him as an ally in an escalating contest with the Soviet Union, and there was plenty of evidence—the extension of Lend-Lease in June, the likely Republican takeover of Congress in November—that Washington would back him fully no matter how angry Marshall was. Democracy, corruption, repression: these would prove secondary to the imperatives of a larger struggle.

Coolly advising Marshall that there was no reason to be "anxious," Chiang cited a Chinese proverb: when the fruit is ripe, it will drop into your lap. Marshall left that afternoon. He thought his four days on the mountain had been useless.

On July 29, a convoy of trucks loaded with supplies for the Executive Headquarters set off from Marshall's old post of Tianjin with an escort of forty-one American Marines. Partway to Beijing, outside of a village called Anping, they encountered a roadblock of boulders and carts. The Marines stopped to investigate. As they did, gunfire suddenly tore through the rows of crops on either side of the road.

It was an ambush. Hundreds of men emerged, armed with machine guns and grenades, and surrounded the convoy. The lieutenant in charge was quickly killed. Only after four hours of fighting did the Marines manage to drive off the attackers and retreat toward Tianjin. By the end, three Americans were dead and a dozen wounded.

Although details were murky, it quickly became clear who the assailants were. "Americans don't accept this sort of thing calmly," Marshall stormed at Zhou after returning from Kuling. Zhou attempted to discredit charges of Communist culpability: maybe it was staged, part of a plot? But the attack had come amid the surge in CCP anti-Americanism. It followed another recent incident in which seven marines on a picnic were seized by Communists and held for eleven days on charges of spying. The CCP account of the Anping ambush, Marshall spat at Zhou, was "a complete, and I think a deliberate misrepresentation."

A wounded marine died the next day, bringing the death toll to four. "The mothers of these boys," said an officer, "will never understand why the U.S. should have armed forces over here."

Every few days, Marshall traveled between Nanjing and Kuling, each trip, up and down the mountain, requiring five hours and five forms of transportation. He was Sisyphus, Acheson would say, pushing his boulder up an impossible slope again and again. "He likes going up," wrote Caughey, "but only for the purpose of seeing Mrs. Marshall."

As July came to an end, Marshall recognized that the situation around China was seething. Fighting was spreading in the north, and he feared it would not be long before it spread even further.

Back in Kuling in the first days of August, Marshall continued to deplore Nationalist conduct, complaining that "narrow minded and bigoted militarists and a small nucleus of political irreconcilables pursue open civil war." He told Chiang that the current Nationalist approach was only helping the Communists. In addition to squandering Chiang's prestige, it invited prolonged chaos that would create a "fruitful breeding ground for Communism" and an "exceptional opportunity for Soviet Russia to intervene." For his part, Chiang was dismayed that Marshall was not more openly outraged by the Communist attack on the American Marines at Anping. "I figured the concessions the U.S. made will embolden the Communists to launch bigger attacks against the U.S. Army," Chiang wrote in his diary. "But, since Marshall has swallowed it I shall not fixate on that. I will just wait for it to further develop."

In fact, Marshall had ordered a special Executive Headquarters unit, Team 25, to compile evidence in the face of CCP dissembling. The Communists had been hampering the investigation and seemed, reported a senior American official in Beijing, to be "acting under higher instructions to delay, impede, and obstruct in every way possible"—turning the inquiry into "absurd farce." Between the recent kidnapping of the Marines, the Anping ambush, and now the obstruction, Marshall discerned an objective: to force American troops to withdraw. He had already heard from Navy Secretary Forrestal that such incidents "will lead to an aroused public opinion here exerting significant pressure to withdraw all Marines from China."

When Zhou came to see him in Nanjing on August 9, Marshall read the American Executive Headquarters official's complaints aloud and then issued what amounted to a threat: if the Communists did not start cooperating with the inquiry, he would issue a public denunciation. And that would not only mark the likely end of his mission. It would also bolster hard-liners on the other side. "They would convict me of agreement with them by virtue of my own statement," he said. Marshall gave Zhou twenty-four hours to change the Communist approach to the inquiry. "It must be positive action," he stressed. "I will not wait any longer."

Zhou was more interested in litigating the past—laying out a theory of failure that would reflect well on his side. He surveyed events since Marshall's arrival in China almost eight months before. "At the beginning of this period we had been devotedly pursuing the road you have proposed," he claimed, "and, even though we confronted certain difficulties, we never wavered from that course." Yet look what Washington had done in return. It had continued to fund Chiang's war machine despite a stated commitment to peace. It had transported troops and given Chiang his own air force and navy. The Nationalist military position had markedly improved. "It is easy to draw the conclusion that we are actually being 'roped in' and are in the first stage of being 'beaten up,'" Zhou continued. "We almost fell into a trap."

There had long been fundamental contradictions in U.S. policy, Zhou observed. Now, he told Marshall, "the contradictions are reflected on you."

Marshall during World War I
(Courtesy of the George C. Marshall Foundation, Lexington, Virginia)

Chiang Kai-shek, Franklin Roosevelt, and Winston Churchill at the 1943 Cairo conference, with Marshall looking on
(Courtesy of the George C. Marshall Foundation, Lexington, Virginia)

Chiang Kai-shek greets Marshall
(Associated Press)

The Committee of Three
(Associated Press)

The Chiangs toast
Marshall *(Courtesy of the
George C. Marshall Foundation,
Lexington, Virginia)*

Marshall and Nationalist General Chang Chi-chung *(Courtesy of John L. Soong Jr.)*

Crowds greet the Committee of Three during its trip across North China
(Courtesy of the George C. Marshall Foundation, Lexington, Virginia)

Marshall on the Yenan airstrip *(Courtesy of the George C. Marshall Foundation, Lexington, Virginia)*

Marshall inspects Communist troops in Yenan, with Mao Zedong, Zhou Enlai, Chang Chi-chung, and Zhu De *(Courtesy of the George C. Marshall Foundation, Lexington, Virginia)*

Marshall and Mao at Communist headquarters in Yenan *(Courtesy of the George C. Marshall Foundation, Lexington, Virginia)*

Marshall and Mao in Yenan *(Courtesy of the George C. Marshall Foundation, Lexington, Virginia)*

Marshall and Madame Mao in Yenan *(Courtesy of the George C. Marshall Foundation, Lexington, Virginia)*

Marshall's house in Nanjing *(Courtesy of the George C. Marshall Foundation, Lexington, Virginia)*

Marshall with the Chiangs and Dwight Eisenhower
(Courtesy of the George C. Marshall Foundation, Lexington, Virginia)

Katherine Marshall in Kuling *(Courtesy of the George C. Marshall Foundation, Lexington, Virginia)*

Marshall and Madame Chiang Kai-shek in Kuling *(Courtesy of the George C. Marshall Foundation, Lexington, Virginia)*

Katherine Marshall and the Chiangs play croquet in Kuling
(Courtesy of the George C. Marshall Foundation, Lexington, Virginia)

Marshall at his 66th birthday party, with John Leighton Stuart, T. V. Soong, and Chiang Kai-shek *(Courtesy of the George C. Marshall Foundation, Lexington, Virginia)*

CHAPTER 12

George Marshall Can't Walk on Water

The contradictions were clear to Marshall from the start. Eight months earlier, he had pressed the question with President Truman, with Secretary of State Byrnes, with officers and aides: what should he do if the Generalissimo did not cooperate? No one had wanted to contemplate that possibility. But Marshall did not let it go, and Truman conceded that, ultimately, Washington would have to back Chiang.

Chiang, of course, knew this detail. There had been the leak from the White House, and on top of that, the signs had become more and more clear to him as Marshall's mission ran its course. In a world split between two sides, the only thing that really mattered was which side he was on. Now he was calling Marshall's bluff.

Marshall, however, was not simply folding. On August 10, he and Stuart issued an arresting public statement, his most dramatic public gesture in China in eight months. "Fighting is daily growing more widespread and threatens to engulf the country and pass beyond the control of those responsible," it warned.

The statement's purpose, Marshall explained to Truman, "was to bring both sides, along with the public in China, to a realization of the crisis and impending chaos." Zhou deemed it an admission of failure. Nationalists grumbled that they had not been allowed to review the text. From the public, there was an outpouring of pleas for persistence.

"I know what a heart-breaking task it must have been and must be for you," wrote a man in Shanghai. "But you must not and should not be discouraged or disheartened." A group of "overseas Chinese," in San Francisco, wrote: "We entreat you to exert your final efforts to save the critical situation for the welfare of the 450 million people of China who are confronted with imminent calamity of perdition."

That same day, in Washington, a State Department official showed up at the Chinese embassy with another statement in hand. This one was from the president, for the Generalissimo's private consumption. In relaying it back to China, Chiang's ambassador cautioned that the language was "unusually strong."

Truman's letter began by stressing that Marshall spoke for the entire American government, and his warnings should be taken accordingly. From there, it described in detail how recent events in China had affected views in the United States—driving both the administration and the public toward the "conclusion that the selfish interests of extremist elements, equally in the Kuomintang as in the Communist Party, are hindering the aspirations of the Chinese people." It mentioned dismay over stalled democratization, over the influence of "militarists" and "reactionaries," and over the "cruel murders" of liberals. The conclusion could be read only as an ultimatum: "Unless convincing proof is shortly forthcoming that genuine progress is being made toward a peaceful settlement of China's internal problems, it must be expected that American opinion will not continue in its generous attitude towards your nation."

It was signed by Truman, but the text came from Marshall. Initially, Truman had intended to deliver a public message of alarm. Marshall pushed back, arguing that a "statement sufficiently strong to cause a decisive change in the Gimo's attitude and that of some of his more powerful advisers would almost inevitably so encourage the Communist Party as to change their present attitude to one of unmalleability or intransigency." The letter was his alternative, a private reinforcement of his public warning. Marshall was also adamant about one logistical detail: neither he nor Stuart should deliver the letter, out of regard for the Generalissimo's "face." The parallels between this dispatch and the one that had brought Stilwell's ejection during World War II were clear. Marshall was angry with Chiang but, unlike Vinegar Joe, saw no point in publicly humiliating him.

When Chiang read the letter, he asked Marshall to come to Kuling as soon as possible.

Mao had been working out a new theory. For the past year, Yenan had set policy on the assumption that the world situation inhibited the pursuit of armed revolution, at least as long as Moscow and Washington were talking rather than fighting. Mao's new theory said otherwise. Between the two superpowers, there was an "intermediate zone" that included China—and it was in this zone that the battle between revolution and reaction would initially be fought. Even without a US-Soviet war, there could still be war between US- and Soviet-backed armies.

Mao articulated his theory in an interview with a sympathetic American journalist named Anna Louise Strong. His new geopolitical vision was matched with newfound military brazenness. "The atom bomb is a paper tiger which the U.S. reactionaries use to scare people," he bristled as Strong transcribed. "All reactionaries are paper tigers." In a war against Washington's "running dogs," his side would surely win: "We have only millet plus rifles to rely on, but history will finally prove that our millet plus rifles is more powerful than Chiang Kai-shek's airplanes and tanks."

For months those around Mao had sensed him wrestling with the choice of whether to definitively end his party's show of cooperation. He had long been confident that in a full-scale war the Communists could at least fight to a draw. More recently, he had found cause for greater confidence. On the ground the conflict was developing along lines he had envisioned for decades. Years before, he had formulated strategies of "protracted war," with his side retreating and biding its time while internal problems weakened the adversary. He had trained commanders to "lure the enemy deep" and then direct guerrilla strikes

at the resulting vulnerabilities—or as he explained to peasant fighters, "the God of Thunder strikes the beancurd." He had imparted an
instructional verse: when the enemy advances, we withdraw; when
the enemy rests, we harass; when the enemy tires, we attack; when the
enemy withdraws, we pursue.

It was the approach he was taking now. He had made a mistake in
Manchuria in the spring, hunkering down in urban positions against
large Nationalist armies. Since then his forces had been retreating
to the countryside, building strength for counterattacks to come as
Chiang's lines stretched thin. As American intelligence assessed, "In
view of the vastness of the country and the strong hold of the Communists in extensive rural areas, the Nationalists have little or no more
prospect of eliminating them as a military factor than they had in the
futile 'extermination campaigns' of 1930-1935." Mao gave his forces a
new name: the People's Liberation Army.

One hot summer evening, CCP representatives invited Till Durdin
to dinner. Durdin had finished his stint on Marshall's staff and
returned to the *New York Times* in late July. But the message from his
hosts seemed meant for his erstwhile boss's ears: if the Nationalists
kept attacking, the Communists would not just fight back; they would
seek as much Russian help as they could get.

Then came Yenan's response to Marshall and Stuart. Far from
shocking the Communists into geniality, their statement brought a
fierce reaction. An August 14 *Emancipation Daily* editorial included the
kind of invective that had become common in the previous six weeks,
but went a step further: "General Marshall himself is not above blame."
At first he had managed some real agreements, it explained, but since
then had stood by, complicit, as Chiang tore them up. "In this way," the
editorial charged, "7 1/2 months of 'mediation' have produced large
scale civil war in China." Never before had Marshall been so directly
and publicly vilified.

At 10:45 the next morning, Marshall saw Zhou, along with Walter
Robertson and General Yeh, the CCP Executive Headquarters commissioner. Both had been summoned from Beijing to discuss the Anping

ambush. After Marshall's earlier ultimatum, the Communists had agreed to cooperate with the investigation—and then dragged it into a morass of procedural disputes. At first, in fact unaware of the circumstances of the attack, Zhou had assumed the Marines were to blame. But even as the truth emerged, he remained impenitent. "The American Marines are virtually assisting the Nationalist troops, and freak accidents are bound to occur," he threatened. "No one can be sure that no other incident will take place."

Marshall stressed to Zhou that continued obstruction would make progress impossible. "I am being deprived of almost every argument and the Government is being furnished, in its opinion, the justification of all its contentions," Marshall said. Anping risked being the shoal on which the mission ran aground, and it would be the Communists' fault.

Yet even after his own public castigation by the CCP, Marshall resisted making that warning public. It was the same quandary he faced with Chiang: saying something vehement enough to move one side in a constructive direction would encourage the other side to move in a damaging one. In this case, Nationalist hard-liners would take a blistering statement about Anping as ultimate vindication, and any remaining hope of a peaceful resolution would vanish. Marshall could not quite make that break. Although he recognized the Communists were becoming more radical, he hoped it was still a negotiating tactic rather than a permanent change.

Marshall left Ning Hai Road before the meeting ended. He had gotten Chiang's request that he set off for Kuling as soon as he could.

Chiang was no more moved by Marshall's public statement than Zhou was. "The Communists bully and insult the U.S. and Marshall like this, and yet Marshall still insists on mediating," Chiang complained in his diary. "Isn't it wishful thinking?"

When Marshall reached Kuling, it became clear that Truman's letter had not delivered the desired salutary shock either. Chiang said little about his side's infractions, and his price for a return to real negotia-tion was if anything higher than before. Marshall responded with what was becoming a litany: the "geographical weakness" of the National-ists' military position, the likelihood of political and economic col-lapse if war spread, the vulnerability of a conflict-ridden China to Soviet subversion or domination—all the consequence of a "ruinous" approach. But Marshall did not think his argument did much good.

"I have never seen anyone as stubborn as him," Chiang said after-ward. He was discouraged, summarizing in his diary: "Marshall still believes that our taking military action against the Communists will only bring about a full-scale civil war and cause our defeat. And if we will use political negotiations and try to resolve our problems by mak-ing compromises, there is greater hope for peace." It was an accurate recapitulation of Marshall's case, and Chiang did not buy it. Trying to negotiate with the CCP was, he thought, like "trying to catch a fish in a tree." He had held back his armies in the pursuit of compromise too many times before; he would not be fooled again.

Fortunately for him, Nationalist generals were still confident in their military prospects, despite Marshall's fretting. To them, such fret-ting was increasingly beside the point—as they were saying openly, even to American officials. Whatever the insistence in Truman's letter, they thought the imperatives of US-Soviet competition would ultimately override Marshall. They might have to listen to his nagging for now, murmuring acquiescence through gritted teeth. But when war came, such lofty concerns would fall away, and they would get the American help they wanted. It was a classic stratagem: borrowing the fearsome-ness of the tiger.

"I am sure that you realize that the enclosed letter contains criticism of certain individuals responsible for U.S. policy in the Far East," read a note that reached Chiang in August. The enclosed letter pronounced Marshall's approach "unsound" and endorsed the advice that Chiang was getting from hard-line advisers: "air and ground forces should be disposed so that they can quickly and effectively suppress or annihilate Communist agitators and their armed forces."

What was notable was the letter's author: would-be ambassador Wedemeyer. Back stateside, his hopes of quickly returning to China dashed, he was spreading the word about Chiang's cause. The reaction in key quarters, he related, was encouraging.

Wedemeyer's griping about the canceled appointment had gone beyond the odd comment to reporters around Washington. Almost as soon as he had finished assuring Marshall that he bore no resentment—"whatever you advise in this regard I shall accept as gospel"—Wedemeyer rushed to peddle a different message. Before long, he was writing Patrick Hurley, Marshall's predecessor as envoy, to complain about Marshall's folly. He was asking the Chinese embassy for help with public speaking. He was complaining that "Marshall's own statements concerning China are taken as equivalent to Bible texts by the U.S. people." He was claiming, to Chiang and around Washington, that "so long as our policy remains unrealistic, I want no part of the job in China." Ignoring his own indiscretion, he blamed traitorous State Department officials for the leaks about his presumed appointment.

Wedemeyer understood the changing American mood, and placed emphasis accordingly. "Exactly what happened to cause Dr. Stuart to be appointed," he wrote suggestively to one Nationalist official, "I am not at liberty to state but I feel certain that you surmise." Soon even that much restraint was gone: "Apparently there was opposition to my return on the part of certain individuals who knew that I would not tolerate half way measures in dealing with the Communist situation." If such appeasement continued, he took to warning, "all of Asia in less than a generation will come under Soviet domination by means short of war."

Wedemeyer had always concealed an element of perfidy beneath a surface of polished assurance. He had earned Marshall's regard by brilliance as a planner and tactician in the opening stretch of World War II. Even then, however, he held the America First view that the United States had been tricked into World War I and counted the pilot-turned-arch-isolationist Charles Lindbergh as a close friend. Before that, Wedemeyer had been posted to Nazi Germany and come away persuaded that "however much one disapproved of Hitler's methods, the feeling of the German people that he had raised them out of the abyss was real." After the war, he remained fixated on the dangerous influence of Jews, especially in the "money-making areas"—part of a "planned penetration by certain exponents of contrary ideologies."

By the time Marshall got around to sending a note of apology about the ambassadorial role, Wedemeyer's whisper campaign was already under way. "I am so sorry," Marshall wrote. "Altogether you have been made to suffer too much by my actions and I regret it very much." Wedemeyer sent Marshall a gift—a book called *The Great Globe Itself* by William Bullitt, a former ambassador to Moscow who had become a strident critic of the Roosevelt and Truman administrations. (Marshall despised Bullitt because of an incident during the war.) The book called for a unified anti-Soviet bloc to counter the Kremlin. Marshall read it on a summer day in Kuling.

Katherine called it his "death struggle." As summer crawled along, Marshall implored both sides to accept that their best interest lay in a different path. He reiterated to Chiang the risks—political, economic, strategic—of aggressive military action. He went back and forth from Nanjing to Kuling, up and down the mountain. He said many times that he was on the verge of giving up. He was not giving up.

The Nationalists expanded the fight and maintained unrealistically stringent conditions for another cease-fire. They talked about proceeding with political reform, but without Communist involvement. Their American-supplied planes strafed Yenan.

The Communists called cadres to battle. An order was broadcast over the radio for all to hear: supporters everywhere should prepare to "shatter Generalissimo Chiang Kai-shek's offensive." American intelligence judged it a "mobilization of all Communist forces for a full-scale civil war." Party spokesmen called the Nationalists "killers," "fascist profiteers," "cannibalistic, murderous, rotten."

The Soviets openly condemned the Generalissimo. It was a sign, the American embassy in Moscow concluded, that "Chiang cannot be counted on to serve or acquiesce in Soviet purposes" and that "the USSR had washed out in its plans the likelihood of a Chinese coalition Government."

Truce teams retreated from the field to the Executive Headquarters in Beijing, the American officers conceding that they were accomplishing nothing. Both Communist and Nationalist team members walked away and did not come back.

The subtropical summer got even more oppressive. On Ning Hai Road, it could be 90 degrees indoors during the day, and only slightly cooler at night. There was malaria in the embassy. "In the heat," said Melby, "all those with influence have fled to the hills."

But Marshall pushed on, layering demands on weary aides. "The old man is working like the devil," reported one, "but the irreconcilables on both sides are still irreconcilables."

Even as he labored, Marshall saw influence draining away from those open to compromise to those bent on fighting. He saw the Communists deliberately provoking the Nationalists into action, the Nationalists intent on "a policy of force as the only acceptable solution." He saw both sides trying to manipulate him to their own ends, playing for time and stalling as it suited them. He saw himself getting swept up in a "tornado of propaganda."

Marshall warned the Nationalists that "the Generalissimo is leading China right into Communism through his over zealous and unrealistic treatment of the present military and political situation." He warned Zhou that American intelligence had evidence of propaganda coordination between the Kremlin and CCP. He was well aware that both parties were furious with him. He stormed at Zhou one day: "I am sitting in between the two trying to be tolerant and understanding and patient. I assume I am misunderstood by many in the Government and if not misunderstood, I am bitterly resented. I don't have to tell you what the feeling is regarding me on the Communist side."

The latest front for political negotiation was a Stuart project. He aimed to launch a five-person group, composed of himself and two representatives from each side, that would set up a State Council to help govern until democratic reform moved forward. "We felt there was nothing else we could do right now," Marshall explained. He refused to return to the Committee of Three at the moment, certain it would fail. So Stuart hawked his Committee of Five, and the two sides bickered and backtracked, carped and impugned.

The negotiation took on a geometric complexity—demands layered on demands, concessions qualified by conditions, agreements eviscerated by loopholes. Marshall occasionally admitted to being confused by the course of a discussion—as did Zhou and Madame Chiang. It had become "a dizzy merry-go-round of charge, counter charge, proposal, counter proposal and committee of three or five or none," wrote Melby. "It will take a very pedantic doctoral candidate some day to unravel the threads."

It had been a year since the Americans, the Soviets, and the Chinese shared victory in World War II. At a V-J Day celebration in Nanjing, fireworks displays were canceled for fear they would be mistaken for an attack and cause panic. Chiang's anniversary message included a warning: "We must put down rebellions."

It had also been a year since the first atomic weapons were dropped on Japan. The *New Yorker* devoted an entire August issue to a report on postapocalyptic Hiroshima by John Hersey, the young reporter awed by Marshall in the spring. Bernard Baruch, a financier and statesman who was devising a plan for atomic energy, wrote to ask Marshall's thoughts. Marshall wrote back: "The turbulence in which I am involved and its tragic consequences to almost five hundred million people leads all my thinking to the urgency in this period of our civilization for finding a development without further delay of a positive means to put a stop to the probability of war." He might have a more specific response, he apologized, if only he were back in Leesburg with nothing to do but work in the garden.

Sitting on the terrace on Ning Hai Road one August afternoon, in khaki slacks and a blue blazer, Marshall thought aloud about what else he could do. There was agitation in Washington for a new approach, but opinion was polarized as to what it should be. Some called for total withdrawal and an end to support of a one-party regime that was murdering opponents, some for an unqualified embrace of Chiang as America's champion in a first battle against global Communism.

"The military situation naturally grows more serious by the day," Marshall recognized. "Each side takes the same stand with me, that the other is provoking the fighting and cannot be trusted to go through with an agreement." Neither party wanted to look responsible for snuffing out all hope, yet would do nothing to improve the odds of success.

Marshall had asked the embassy for ideas—"some elixir to give a new life to our policy," as Walton Butterworth, now the senior career diplomat, framed the task. (Butterworth had been transferred from Spain a couple months earlier on Acheson's recommendation.) The embassy's contribution focused mostly on the perils of alternate approaches. It would be too risky to "withdraw all aid from the recognized government of China and adopt a so-called policy of neutrality"; it would also be too risky to "accord all-out support to that government," since "a serious clash between the Soviet Union and the United States" might result.

A parallel inquiry in the State Department arrived at the same dilemma. "If I thought any good from our national or from an international point of view, would come from all-out support of Chiang," reasoned the China hand John Carter Vincent, "I would be for it, but I can see only trouble, trouble, trouble coming from inconclusive action." He hoped a few months of true civil war would have a "chastening effect" and cause both sides to reconsider.

If the alternatives at either extreme did not seem wise, the question was, what else could be done to improve the current approach? The embassy's analysis argued that the United States had minimal leverage over the CCP, but that there was more it could do to pressure Chiang. If his fundamental outlook would not change, at least his calculations could be shaped: "He must be convinced that there are certain limits beyond which he cannot go and still continue to receive American assistance."

In fact, Marshall had begun taking quiet steps toward that end already, in an attempt to show he was serious. The Nationalists, he said, were "encouraged by feeling dead certain the U.S. has no choice but to supply them because of our clash here with Russia." In late July, he had radioed an instruction to his rear echelon in Washington. There was a military aid bill coming up for consideration by Congress; he wanted it stalled. There was the financial assistance he had toiled to secure in the spring; he wanted most of it still withheld. In August, with the situation deteriorating further and Chiang no less intransigent, he delayed shipments of airplanes and ammunition. Nationalist officials started to notice. "It was just a matter of time before such a step would be taken," Marshall said when confronted by a general. "It confirms exactly what I have been telling you and the Generalissimo for some time." The slowdown would hardly cripple the Nationalist military effort—some $800 million in military assistance had already gone to Chiang's forces since the end of World War II, under the extension of Lend-Lease—but Marshall hoped it would focus Nationalist minds.

Still, he rejected the more draconian cutoff some in Washington wanted. He pushed noncombat aid in key sectors. Even as bombers and bullets were held back, he allowed officials to begin discussions about a major handover of "surplus property"—some $500 million in trucks, railway supplies, machinery, medical equipment, and construction materials, abandoned on Pacific islands as American troops rushed home.

The reward for balance was censure by both sides. Despite Marshall's explanation that the surplus property did not include arms or ammunition, Zhou, claiming it was "adding fuel to flame," gave a press conference in protest. "You are confusing propaganda with fact," Marshall told him, "and Chinese propaganda is far from fact."

Yet Marshall would say only so much publicly. He faced the now standard quandary: how to chasten Chiang without emboldening Yenan. The Communists, Marshall explained to Truman, "are seeking by intense propaganda and any other means available to terminate all American assistance to the Government which they claim is making possible the latter's military effort." He did not want to encourage such designs, yet he thought it necessary to show the Nationalists that intransigence carried a price.

There was a similar dilemma when it came to ongoing reductions in American troops. Pressure to bring the boys home had only intensified in recent months—especially after the death of four Marines at Anping. Secretary of the Navy Forrestal reported to Marshall that the attack had generated "significant pressure to withdraw Marines from China." Much of Truman's cabinet was urging him to do just that, while even Forrestal was recommending that the American presence in China be consolidated, to make it less vulnerable to provocation and attack. Marshall was once again getting letters from wives and mothers. "Those who have anything to do with keeping troops" in China, one charged, were "just as responsible as the men who killed those boys." Another wrote: "It may have been right for our men to die defending their own country and loved ones—but they do not need to be sacrificed needlessly in the civil strife of China."

Marshall had long been sensitive to the risks of a large ongoing military presence. He worried about both America's image and the possibility of escalation. That danger was all the greater because both the Nationalists and the Communists had an incentive to draw the Americans into the fight. "It is anticipated that the Communist Party will try every possible means to implicate the United States in the eyes of the world as fighting the civil war 'shoulder to shoulder' with the Kuomintang," reported a senior officer at the Executive Headquarters. "I am quite sure certain elements in the National Government would be extremely pleased to have us so implicated and irretrievably so."

But Marshall was also sensitive to the risks of a precipitous or poorly timed drawdown. He had been pressing for a smooth, coordinated handover from American to Nationalist forces (noting in the process that sending large armies to wage war in places like Manchuria would mean shortages of troops to hold key sites in the rest of China). Chiang's troops had been stepping sometimes shakily into the breach as the Americans withdrew.

Anping underscored the risks of both a large presence and a quick withdrawal. Marshall saw the ambush as part of a Communist effort to drive out American troops by inciting opposition on the homefront—exactly the effect it had achieved. So while he would not halt or reverse the withdrawal, Marshall slowed it down and insisted that any consolidation be done quietly. "Otherwise," he wrote Forrestal, "it would be a victory for the Communists, encourage them to more extreme propaganda and make it very hard for me to influence them." With Zhou, Marshall was explicit: more incidents like Anping would delay, not speed, the planned withdrawal of American troops.

Meanwhile, Marshall had been spending more time with figures from neither side—the third-party liberals trying to carve a middle path. Carsun Chang, the German-educated philosopher who founded the Democratic League, reassured Marshall that "there is no reason why the present conflict can not be easily solved through your mediation and a little more compromise on the part of the opposite parties." Other third-party figures were asking Marshall what they could do to help in that cause. Unite, he told them, to become a force capable of balancing the Nationalists and Communists.

The problem was that their ranks, already relatively thin, included few operators and many philosophers, more inclined to fractious debate than joint action. They "advocate discussion groups as the way out of all troubles," hoping to "stand between the two primitive giants and drive them both in the same harness, the superiority of mind and reason over naked force," Melby had scoffed after first encountering them. Now they were bearing the brunt of Chiang's repression—in many cases paying with their lives, as had the professors in Kunming. "They are learning that no party can survive here without armed force behind it," wrote Melby, "and at the same time a lot of them honestly cannot go along with either of the sides having power."

When September came, the Chiangs and Katherine were still ensconced in Kuling. Marshall was still going back and forth. After one trip, CCP propagandists mockingly speculated that he was spending his time in the mountains walking with Katherine in the moonlight. He was amused: that is exactly what he was doing.

Between those moonlit walks, Marshall tried again and again to persuade Chiang and his generals that their current course would bring chaos, destroying the economic and political foundations of Nationalist rule and offering a "formal invitation to Russia to sow the further seeds of Communism." The Generalissimo, Marshall told Madame Chiang, was operating with a sense of "false power."

But Chiang was less inclined than ever to accede to demands. He wanted Marshall to know that "pressure does not work." When especially incensed by a message, Chiang simply refused to see Marshall. When intent on letting a military offensive proceed without interference or hectoring—including a major push in Rehe, the province south of Manchuria that had almost torpedoed the first cease-fire in January—he evaded conversation. When Marshall informed Madame Chiang that Washington had blocked shipments of military aid, Chiang pledged in his diary: "He can use the sale of goods and materials as his leverage to put pressure on me and urge me to cease fire. I will just treat him with indifference and refrain from anger." Chiang's reply to Truman's letter was an unapologetic reminder of the CCP's intent to "install a totalitarian regime such as those which are now spreading over Eastern Europe." Truman promptly wrote back, expressing pointedly how eager he was to support a *unified* government with economic and military aid. "We can get along without it," T. V. Soong said of the assistance. "It would be nice to get it, but we don't absolutely need it."

Both sides remained angry at Marshall, and he remained angry at both sides. "I am not the Government of China," he snapped. "I am not the head of the Communist Party." They continued to wrangle over Stuart's Committee of Five, over the terms of a cease-fire, over the seating of a National Assembly. Every seeming breakthrough quickly proved to be another false start. The Communists demanded that fighting stop—sincerely, Marshall insisted—but refused to accept concessions Chiang wanted in exchange. A cease-fire was his trump card, he explained, so he would need to get everything he wanted before playing it, including an agreement from the Communists to take part in a National Assembly on his terms. Otherwise, he would move the political process forward without them. Only military defeat, he told Marshall, would force the Communists to truly cooperate.

Marshall thought that if there was not a cease-fire by October, the war might have spread too wide to be contained. Neither side shared his urgency. It was, Marshall wrote Truman, "a somewhat Chinese view that several months of fighting will be a necessary procedure. . . . What happens in the meantime to the hundreds of millions of oppressed people is ignored. Also what happens in the way of Soviet intervention overt or covert is also ignored." Yet he conceded to Truman that he was "stymied and can only suspend efforts while we wait and see."

Marshall was supposed to be on his way home by now. One day in Kuling, he sat Katherine down and confessed that their departure would have to be delayed. There was no hope of getting concessions from either side unless he stayed to see they were carried out. "Only he can make it stick," Madame Chiang confirmed to Katherine. Marshall wrote an aide in Washington about the timing of his return: "Disregard all press guesses and try none of your own."

Katherine was again bitter on her husband's behalf. She complained he was being treated like "a messenger boy between the Generalissimo and the Communists." She reported to a friend that he "looked as though he had been put through the wringer." It had been "a cruel year."

Marshall's aides were more philosophical. "Maybe there just ain't no answer to a problem like China," Melby quipped, as Marshall made his final trip to Kuling. Caughey wondered whether "the General was presented with a problem that is beyond the powers of one man to solve completely."

"But what did they expect?" Joe Stilwell had written as things started to come apart. "George Marshall can't walk on water."

Marshall descended from Kuling for the last time on the afternoon of September 17. Earlier that day, Chiang had received him for one more conversation in the summer capital. After Marshall left, Chiang played three games of Chinese checkers with Katherine.

When Marshall arrived back in Nanjing, by sedan chair, jeep, gunboat, airplane, and Cadillac, Zhou was no longer there. He had gone to Shanghai. And he would not return, he said, unless the Committee of Three reconvened to work out another cease-fire—doing again what it had done eight months earlier, in Marshall's hopeful first weeks in China.

Three memos from Zhou were waiting. They were extended denunciations, "on behalf of the Chinese Communist Party and the 140,000,000 population in the Communist-led liberated areas," of both the Nationalists and the United States: "War has engulfed the whole country, and the negotiation has degenerated into nothing but a camouflage for the ruthless prosecution of war." The memos appealed to Marshall to put a stop to it. At the same time, radio broadcasts from Yenan asserted that Marshall's prestige had reached a new low, his mission now just an exercise in deception as his government backed reactionary aggression.

"It is clear that he does not intend for the U.S. to mediate," Chiang said of Zhou after learning of his departure for Shanghai. Whatever Marshall's lingering "dreams of mediating," Chiang was certain of the reality: negotiation was over.

III

LIMITS OF POWER

The Rock and the Whirlpool

At the start of World War II, Marshall received a letter from a high school student in Seattle. What, the student wanted to know, was the secret of success? Marshall replied with a personal answer: "Giving the best I had to each job and not permitting myself to grow pessimistic over the slow progress or inevitable discouragements."

Over six years of world war, that determination had become renowned. Now, in China, it was being tested more than ever before.

When Marshall returned from the mountains for the last time, there were signs of fall in the September Nanjing air. A few days later, after a Cantonese lunch, he was sitting on the once-again pleasant terrace of #5 Ning Hai Road with John Beal, the communications adviser he had foisted on Chiang in the spring. As Marshall spoke of recent events, his blue eyes seemed to flash with anger. Yet Beal recorded afterward, "I suspect I have been wrong in thinking he could not stay much longer." Marshall, judged Beal, "clings so tenaciously to a seemingly hopeless job."

Others thought so as well. Melby watched him "playing against futility and despair and lack of any real hope and with nothing to go on except the conviction that somehow it must work or God help us." Melby found Marshall's pertinacity depressing; others admired it. "Here is a great man thinking of anything but himself," Caughey wrote, marveling at Marshall's renewed fervor after every setback. "He subjugates himself to a purpose."

One day in the car, a newly arrived black Cadillac, Marshall raised the matter himself. Looking out the window, he said to Caughey, "You know, whenever I get discouraged over the difficulties that I am having, I always think of the 450 million Chinese people who will suffer if I am unable to work something out."

As Marshall struggled, messages of support came from overseas. In Tokyo, General MacArthur said that no one in the world was more capable than Marshall of "bringing order out of chaos." In Washington, John Carter Vincent declared that whatever the current travails, "I'd still rather have my money on Marshall than in the stock market." General Matthew Ridgway, a hero of D-Day, sent paraphrased lines from Kipling:

> *He who digs foundations deep*
> *Fit for realms to rise upon,*
> *Little credit does he reap*
> *Of his generation,*
> *Any more than mountains gain*
> *Stature till you reach the plain.*

On September 23, as Katherine and the Chiangs prepared to return to Nanjing, Marshall radioed President Truman: "Confused and maddening as are the developments I have not lost hope at all, for maybe yet we can pull this chestnut out of the cross fire which rages around us."

"I know you can 'pull the chestnut out of the cross fire,'" Truman replied, echoing Marshall's mixed metaphor. "If it can be done at all." But in a letter to his wife, Bess, the week before, Truman had been more damning: "Looks like Marshall will fail in China."

Marshall himself would not have disputed the grim probability. Yet as Katherine wrote to friends: "As long as there is a possible chance of his stopping civil war George will not give up so heaven knows when we can come home." Marshall was still looking for that chance.

In the last days of September, Chiang settled back in Nanjing renewed and assured. The summer in Kuling, he told Katherine, had been the happiest of his life. Now, as summer came to an end, he had Marshall where he wanted him. Zhou had fled to Shanghai, and his refusal to return would leave little doubt that the Communists were playing a Russian game and plotting to drive the Americans out. Chiang reasoned that he had only to let Marshall's mission run its course and leave it to Yenan to bring about the ultimate break. Then Washington would at last stand unquestioningly and unstintingly at his back.

When Chiang saw Marshall for the first time after returning from the mountains, on the morning of September 27, they talked about the possibility of a "final rupture" between the Nationalists and Communists. Chiang was jubilant. "This is indeed in line with my intentions," he recorded.

Marshall did, however, want Chiang to extend one more cease-fire offer, to demonstrate an "attitude of tolerance." Chiang was open to the idea. It fit with his plan to maneuver the Communists into taking the blame.

But he was set on one more conquest first. The last north China city of any consequence still under Communist control was a railway depot one hundred miles northwest of Beijing called Zhangjiakou.* It was "the Communist nerve center between Yenan and Manchuria," explained American intelligence. (It was also the proposed site of Marshall's "elementary school" for Communist troops.) On September 30, the Nationalists announced a three-pronged offensive to take the city. Chiang would follow Marshall's counsel and propose a cease-fire—just as soon as Zhangjiakou was in his hands.

This was not what Marshall had in mind. "The fat's in the fire all over," he fretted. One major attack could set China aflame. Chiang had agreed to let the Communists hold on to Zhangjiakou months earlier. His insistence on seizing it now seemed to undercut his stated interest in a final push for peace.

---

* Westerners knew the city as Kalgan.

The evening after the offensive was announced, Marshall joined the Chiangs for dinner. It quickly became clear to Chiang that all was not well, despite his optimism a few days before. He fumed afterward that Marshall cared about nothing but his own success.

The next day, the first of October, Marshall stepped up the pressure. He thought it was time for a showdown. He wrote Chiang a letter: "I wish merely to state that unless a basis for agreement is found to terminate the fighting without further delays of proposals and counterproposals, I will recommend to the President that I be recalled and that the United States government terminate its efforts of mediation."

It was an ultimatum. If the attack on Zhangjiakou did not stop, Marshall would go home. And Chiang knew what that would mean: he, not the Communists, would look responsible. "This old man is too stubborn to be persuaded," he complained in his diary that night.

Yet Chiang did not give ground. He informed Marshall he would call off Nationalist armies only if the Communists abandoned Zhangjiakou without a fight. Otherwise, he would need ten or fifteen days to take it by force and then would talk peace.

The Nanjing atmosphere again turned tense. Chiang was in "a violent temper," according to Stuart. Marshall was "irritable," according to Chiang. And after a stretch of pleasant fall weather, it was once again hot. They had "entered the edge of the valley of the shadow," said Melby.

Despite the withdrawal threat, Chiang avoided Marshall while continuing the attack on Zhangjiakou. For three days after the ultimatum, the two of them did not speak. Finally Stuart persuaded Chiang that it was in his interest to take Marshall's threat seriously. Chiang accepted Stuart's argument: he had to make sure that he was not blamed if Marshall left.

On October 4, over another long dinner, Chiang laid out his case. He pronounced himself "surprised" and "disturbed" by the prospect of Marshall's departure. He invoked his "conscience as a Christian." He lavished praise on Marshall's efforts. But he did not grant the one concession Marshall demanded—an end to the attack. Chiang said he could not forfeit this opportunity, out of a sense of duty to his state.

It was 11 p.m. by the time Marshall left. Chiang thought he had gotten his point across.

In fact, Marshall had heard nothing to change his mind. The mere hint of Marshall's departure had always moved Chiang in the past; not this time. The conquest of Zhangjiakou would end any remaining hope of future negotiation, and Chiang and his generals still seemed convinced that Washington would back them as much as they wanted no matter what they did. Marshall thought he was being turned into a "stooge," his honor, and his country's, at stake.

The next morning, he drafted a message to the president: the mission was finished. "I believe that this is the only way to halt this military campaign and dispel the evident belief of the Government generals that they can drag us along while they carry through an actual campaign of force," Marshall explained. He appended suggested text for a note from Truman to Chiang. "I deplore and I know the people of the United States will deeply regret that [Marshall's] efforts to assist in bringing peace and political unity to China have proved unsuccessful," it read, "but there must not be any question regarding . . . the intentions and high purpose of the United States Government."

Sharing it only with Stuart and a few aides, Marshall submitted the message for radio transmission to Washington. All he needed was Truman's permission, and then he could go home.

With Marshall's request to be recalled on its way across the Pacific, Stuart contemplated the consequences. As much as Marshall feared for the hundreds of millions of Chinese who would pay the price of civil war, for Stuart it was more personal. Over half a century, he had devoted his life's work to a vision of Chinese renewal. If this latest bid for peaceful unity failed—and Stuart did not doubt that Marshall's departure would mark its definitive end—that vision would vanish. He worried about the toll on the Chinese people, and about his beloved students in Nationalist, Communist, and third-party ranks. And he feared for Chiang as well. Stuart had long admired Chiang's "heroic behavior," but he worried now that the Nationalists' failure to promote reform and improve the lot of China's peasants was undermining the Generalissimo's power and prestige. War would not only be terrible, Stuart thought; it might also end badly.

As these implications sank in, he panicked. The evening after Marshall dispatched his note, Stuart told one of Chiang's aides about the recall message transmitted to Washington. He got a phone call half an hour later: Chiang wanted to see him. Stuart arrived to good news. Chiang would make another offer to the Communists, including a pledge to pause the attack on Zhangjiakou. Elated, Stuart rushed to tell Marshall about the reversal.

First thing the next morning, Marshall saw Chiang. Despite the concession, the mood was more fraught than triumphant. Marshall wanted an indefinite cease-fire, Chiang a five-day pause. But Chiang gave ground, and they settled on ten days. For Marshall, it was enough. He left Chiang at 1 p.m. and rushed a telegram to Washington: withdraw the recall request. They had stepped back from the precipice.

Marshall also rushed word to Zhou in Shanghai, letting him know what Chiang was offering. He dictated the details of Chiang's proposal himself to make sure none was mangled. The Communists had been agitating for a cease-fire, and Zhou's emissaries had conveyed that if only Chiang called off the offensive against Zhangjiakou, negotiations would again be possible. There was cause for hope, however slim.

It was two days before the Communists replied: Zhou refused to return from Shanghai.

"I am completely baffled as to what your position is now," Marshall grumbled when two of Zhou's aides came to see him. They complained about the terms of Chiang's offer—the time limit on the cease-fire, the narrow scope of proposed talks, the posture of "the victor over the vanquished." After all he had done to force another cease-fire onto the table, Marshall was incensed. "I very much fear my efforts in negotiations have terminated," he told them. "That is all I have to say."

That day, Katherine was turning 64. She had not wanted to spend her birthday in China. But when she proposed going home at the end of her Kuling sojourn, Marshall had "seemed so pathetic," as she put it, that she agreed to stay. Madame Chiang was hosting a celebration for her, and Marshall joined after Zhou's aides left. At the party, the Generalissimo thought Marshall seemed repentant.

At 9 o'clock the next morning, Marshall slipped out of Nanjing. He drove to the airfield, boarded his plane, and took off as inconspicuously as possible. A short time later, he landed in Shanghai without the usual fanfare. He quietly proceeded to a house occupied by General Gillem, who was now posted in Shanghai to oversee American troops, and concealed himself behind a screen in the living room. Gillem had invited Zhou to lunch without mentioning that Marshall would be there. Marshall was going to put Zhou on the spot—an ambush that would leave him no choice but to return to Nanjing.

"Marshall is the most accomplished actor in the Army," an officer had remarked during the war. "Everybody thinks MacArthur is, but he's not. The difference between them is that you always *know* MacArthur is acting." This officer perceived what others missed: Marshall's stoic manner concealed a sense of theater that he used to his own ends. The stoicism, cultivated over many years, was itself part of the effect.

When Zhou walked into the room, Marshall stepped from behind the screen. Zhou was startled. "He damn near died," Gillem thought after watching his face. The ambush executed, Gillem left the two men to have this encounter on their own. Zhou was caught out, and Marshall was ready to go to work, the impact of a personal appeal heightened by surprise.

"I am deliberately avoiding Marshall," Zhou had written Mao after fleeing Nanjing a few weeks earlier. In justifying his refusal to return, Zhou had turned publicly vicious. The Nationalists, he charged, were rooting for World War III. Marshall's diplomacy, he told a reporter, served to "camouflage the true civil war situation in China and to black out the truth for the American and Chinese publics." In the face of such recrimination, Marshall pointedly reminded Zhou's underlings of their side's mistakes. There had been the failure to submit troop lists for demobilization after the February military unification agreement; the conquest of Changchun in April; the attacks during the June cease-fire ("you about wrecked everything I was trying to do"). Again and again, they had given Nationalist hard-liners ammunition and undercut negotiations. But what most bothered Marshall now were the attacks on his own integrity—a "stupid piece of business."

Still, Marshall wanted to try everything he could. Nearly ten months in China had sharpened his sense of failure's consequences, human and strategic. He had contemplated what a civil war would mean for the hundreds of millions of Chinese who would be caught in it. He also recognized what it would mean for American objectives: a warring China would present an easy target for Soviet influence, even if the Nationalists had an apparent military edge. And the resulting maelstrom would threaten to suck American troops into a war that the country would not support and that Marshall worried it might not win, at a time of growing demands around the world. It would not only be the wrong battle at the wrong time; it might also be a futile battle, fought at great cost.

"I don't wish to leave anything undone that I might do to try to save this situation," Marshall began after surprising Zhou. He explained how he had labored to halt the Nationalist offensive on Zhangjiakou (although he did not disclose that he had gone so far as to request his own recall). But the Communists, despite days of noisy complaints about Chiang's refusal to stop fighting, had passed up an opportunity to make the fighting stop.

After lunch, Zhou took his turn. An accomplished actor himself, he had quickly recovered from the ambush. He maintained that Chiang's offer was really just an excuse for Nationalist armies to catch their breath before resuming the attack—"tantamount to a document of surrender." He would go back only for an indefinite halt to the Zhangjiakou offensive, along with real political concessions.

Almost as soon as Zhou started talking, Marshall knew his gambit had failed. There was little point in revisiting explanations he had recited many times before. "I told you some time ago that if the Communist Party felt that they could not trust my impartiality, they had merely to say so and I would withdraw. You have now said so," he concluded abruptly. "I am leaving immediately for Nanjing. I want to thank you for coming over here to General Gillem's today and giving me this opportunity for a direct conversation with you." It had been a futile few hours.

On the flight back, Marshall reflected. Zhou had been even less cooperative than feared. His typical graciousness had been replaced by petty obstinacy. His reactions, usually clear and analytical, had turned "psychoneurotic"; they had spent half an hour quibbling over an accidental inconsistency in Marshall's phrasing.

Marshall landed in Nanjing at 6:00, unsure what to do next. The fact of the trip—"a splendid gesture," Stuart gushed privately, "the ultimate in humble, kindly-meant activity"—was revealed half an hour later in a terse statement by the embassy.

The next day, Nationalist armies marched into Zhangjiakou.

On October 13, Marshall's magnificent C-54 was taxiing down the runway when its front wheel hit a patch of soft dirt and its nose slammed into the ground, rendering it unflyable for weeks. When Caughey brought news of the accident—another diplomat had been borrowing the plane—Marshall appeared unfazed. But as usual Katherine knew otherwise. It was, she told a friend, "just another blow and a dreadful one. He was so proud of it and had planned our trip home with such interest and care."

That same day, a telegram arrived from Washington: Joe Stilwell was dead. Marshall had gotten word the week before that Stilwell was sick, and the end had come quickly. At a memorial service in Nanjing, 1,500 people showed up, including Chiang.

Stilwell had been on Chiang's mind of late. Did Marshall, Chiang wondered, harbor resentment over the Stilwell affair during the war?

In reality, Marshall had more often seen Stilwell—however gallant a fighting general, however sincere an advocate of China's cause—as a source of mistakes to be avoided. Still, it seemed darkly fitting that, as Vinegar Joe's ashes were scattered over the Pacific, Chiang was once again bridling against American exhortation.

The conquest of Zhangjiakou hardened his resolve. There had been chatter among the Americans that the Nationalists would never manage to take the city. Chiang had proved them wrong. On all fronts, Communist armies were retreating or dispersing as his armies advanced.

Chiang restarted national conscription. He announced that he would convene a National Assembly on November 12, Sun Yat-sen's birthday, with or without the Communists. (Yenan, in turn, announced it would hold a separate assembly for the "liberated areas.") On the anniversary of the overthrow of the Qing Dynasty, Chiang delivered a blistering radio address, demanding that the CCP "abandon its plot to achieve regional domination and disintegration of the country by military force." Privately, he predicted total Nationalist victory within five months.

There were reports of renewed fighting in Manchuria. The region had stayed mostly quiet since June: recognizing the risk of both overextension and Soviet reaction, Chiang had refrained from pushing farther north even without a cease-fire holding him back. But now emboldened, he had decided to wipe out the remaining CCP presence. Nationalist generals were "straining at the leash," an American officer reported, encouraged by the ease with which they were taking by force of arms what their diplomatic colleagues had struggled to get in months of negotiation.

Even the Kremlin, months after instructing Mao to fight, was anxious about his prospects. Soviet officials advised their CCP counterparts that they should consider taking part in the National Assembly Chiang had called for November. Watching from Moscow, Stalin himself was surprised by the speed of Chiang's advances.

So was Marshall. The Nationalist offensive had been more successful than he had anticipated—at least in the short term. To his mind, however, an opening burst of success did not change the Nationalists' basic strategic problem. Claiming cities was not the same as establishing control. Even driven into the hinterlands, the Communists retained "almost unlimited room in which to maneuver," judged an American military attaché. They were escaping Nationalist assaults with their armies largely intact. And as Mao had long envisioned, and Marshall could see, Nationalist lines were stretching to the point of peril.

Even in the best-case scenario, the Communists would remain able to disrupt and destabilize Nationalist power. American intelligence assessed that the fall of Zhangjiakou "has made it eminently clear that the Chinese National Government has the military capability to occupy any large city in China." But once it did, "guerrilla warfare . . . would threaten the Nationalist consolidation of communications lines and the stabilization of China's economy." In the worst case, Communist strikes might prove effective enough to reverse recent Nationalist gains, and then some.

"How exhausting," Chiang sighed as Marshall lectured him about these risks. For months, Chiang had hoped again and again that Marshall would finally see the light. Maybe Nationalist military victories would bring him around; maybe the "cold shoulder" he had gotten from Zhou in Shanghai would. Again and again, Chiang was disappointed. "Marshall's attitude has been extremely horrible and it is beyond the tolerance of many people," Chiang complained as his forces continued to take ground. "But I can tolerate the kind of embarrassment he cannot."

Indeed, Chiang was no less willful than Marshall. He had chosen his course; he did not intend to diverge from it again. Not even stopping the flow of American arms and ammunition would change that. It angered Chiang, but it did not especially constrain him. "My state and I will not be threatened by either violence or wealth," he declared to his diary. He had been well supplied over the previous year, and in the long run, he was confident that friends in Washington would take care of him, no matter what was said by Marshall and Truman and their colleagues—the "FDR party," Chiang called them. When T. V.

Soong urged him to call off an attack in order to avoid angering the Americans, Chiang rejected the advice out of hand: he "would not be influenced by Marshall's mood."

Marshall was aware that his mood was not particularly agreeable. "My endurance has about reached the limit," he snapped in one discussion. He lamented the "unhappy duty" of "the middle man" and the testy tone of every meeting. He complained about private comments and confidential letters showing up in print, sometimes in a matter of hours. (Aides joked: "If you want to have the widest possible circulation you give it to the Chinese and mark it top secret.") When he heard griping from one side about the treachery of the other, he resorted to an American idiom: "Chickens come home to roost."

With both sides, Marshall had tried his most dramatic moves yet. With Chiang, he had requested recall; Chiang gave ground, but barely. With Zhou, Marshall had made a surprise personal appeal, and it had failed. Weeks after Marshall's ambush, Zhou was still in Shanghai.

Marshall strained to keep up a good face in front of his aides. As pressure mounted, he had started getting a massage every morning, and Katherine thought he looked heartier than he had in a while. But in letters home, he did not hide his desperation to be somewhere else. "My ambitions, which grow more urgent every day, point to a quiet life in Leesburg and Pinehurst," he wrote a friend. He had heard little about the secretary of state position since his initial communication with Eisenhower; perhaps, he hoped, Truman had dropped the idea.

"The general objective of all concerned," Melby noted a few days after the Nationalist takeover of Zhangjiakou, "seems to be to end in such a way as to place the blame for the break on someone else." The dynamic had become increasingly apparent. For both Nationalists and Communists, the question was no longer whether Marshall would fail. It was how and when that failure would come, and whose fault it would appear to be. To the extent they still spoke of peace, it was meant largely as a stratagem in the growing war.

In private, Communist leaders were explicit about the endgame. "The struggle has come to the last stage, during which the focus is on the United States," Zhou had concluded. With Communist troops retreating from Zhangjiakou, Mao sent him new instructions: "You should just educate the masses, show them that the responsibility for a rupture is not ours, and resolutely expose the U.S.-Chiang Kai-shek fraud." A few days later, *Emancipation Daily* published a front-page rundown of everything the CCP had been willing to do for the sake of peace, "so that everyone could see who was responsible for this complete final break."

For the Nationalists, the concern was not just blame among their own people; it was also blame among Americans. "Marshall's attitude is serious," T. V. Soong would say. "If he goes back now he will be bitter and it could harm us." It was a point that John Beal had been trying to drive home to Chiang's advisers. He stressed that the Communist plan was "to let the government take, or refuse to take, the action which compels Marshall finally to bring his mission to an end." The Nationalists thus had to do anything necessary "to let [the Communists] break up the Marshall mission if it has come to that." Continued aggression would "give the Communists a propaganda base from which they can resurrect themselves, over a period of time, from their military defeat."

As far as Marshall was concerned, there was already plenty of blame to go around. Each side had pressed its advantage in moments of apparent success, then come back newly obliging when momentum started to reverse—"both a serious Communist mistake and a serious Government mistake," Marshall said, "a very human reaction though a very short-sighted one." Other American officials, in trying to assign responsibility for outbreaks in a widening swath of the country, threw up their hands. "It is impossible to decide, with any degree of certainty, just who started what," a military report conceded.

The fixation on blame also meant that neither side would tell Marshall definitively that his cause was hopeless—out of considerations, he was told, of saving face. "I am not interested in face," he responded. "I am only interested in peace in China."

The one faction that still seemed to share that interest was the third-party leadership. Marshall continued to look to them more and more as acrimony grew, and they urged him not to give up. The breakdown had spurred them to take the initiative, or at least to try, and Marshall encouraged them: if they acted together as one, they could become the swing vote and force both sides to come to the table and compromise. They were now, he said, "the great hope."

The views he heard from them resonated. China needed "a democratic republic of the people, for the people, and by the people"; a coalition government would constrain the worst tendencies of both sides; good governance and development would vanquish Communism for good—but "as long as there is poverty, there will be Communists in China." Acting on these premises, the third-party figures could, Marshall hoped, revive negotiations on a peaceful way forward. They had been working with Sun Fo, Sun Yat-sen's eldest son and a source of frequent liberal dissent within Nationalist ranks, to coax Zhou back from Shanghai.

While the third-party leaders lobbied Zhou, Marshall tried new arguments on the other side. Months earlier, Chiang had explained that he first had to show toughness and then could afford to show generosity. Was it time for that generosity, Marshall suggested, now that the Nationalists had taken most of the ground Chiang had insisted he needed to feel secure? Could he make a magnanimous statement to show he had tried everything for the sake of peace? Otherwise, the only thing left would be "the spirit of revenge."

What Chiang offered in response was a list of ultimatums, "jumbled in thought and provocative in nature," Marshall judged. Caughey caught him after an encounter with Chiang and found him "heart sick." As Caughey reflected, "so much depends on a few words—the fate of a Nation, the fate of Nations, in fact."

On a hot and dry late October morning, the leaves yellowing and a restless wind raising dust from Nanjing's streets, Zhou appeared unannounced on the steps of #5 Ning Hai Road. It had been more than two weeks since Marshall sprang from behind the screen in Shanghai, and they had not seen one another since. Marshall agreed to meet immediately.

Zhou had landed in Nanjing a few days before, striding across the airfield, fedora in hand and tie neatly knotted, with third-party representatives at his side. After days of pleading, they had persuaded him to return. The CCP put out a statement: it was "as ready to save the country which is on the verge of a split as a man is ready to save his deathly sick mother. Whenever there is a last ray of hope, the Communists would be ready to do their utmost."

Yet as Zhou returned, other Communists were leaving in ominous numbers. "Rapidly the Communist staff here and in Shanghai is being reduced to skeleton size," observed Melby. At the Executive Headquarters in Beijing, CCP representation had declined by almost two-thirds, leaving the operation more paralyzed than ever. "There is an increasing belief," reported the *New York Times*, "that the Communists, reluctant to enter the Government in their weakened military position and openly distrustful of American policy, are 'sitting out' General Marshall's mission in the hope that the impasse will create a situation from which they might gain new international props."

On Ning Hai Road, Zhou rejected out of hand any plausible means of achieving a pause. He seemed more interested in threats. "The Communists have never surrendered—not even in 1927 when they had no rifles in their hands," he said. "How can they expect us to surrender now?" There was no reason to, he explained to Marshall. The Nationalists might think they were winning. But many places that appeared to be under their control were in fact "weak points," which "could be very well exploited to our advantage." On that point, Marshall knew Zhou was right.

To further complicate matters, Zhou's return to Nanjing had coincided with Chiang's departure. The Generalissimo was on his first visit to Taiwan—officially an "inspection tour," although he had also taken note of the island's possibilities as a refuge. He had assured Marshall that he would be back soon, and that if summoned, he would be back within four hours. Yet just as he had in Manchuria in the spring, Chiang stayed away longer than promised. When he returned, days late, Marshall did not conceal his frustration.

"I can make no predictions favorable or unfavorable," Marshall reported to the White House as the end of October approached. "The state of peace appears at times more difficult than the state of war."

On the last day of the month, Chiang turned 60.* Chinese astrology marked it as a significant birthday, and he considered it an auspicious moment for a last great act: a final push to take care of the Communist problem once and for all.

A few days beforehand, Henry Luce had landed in Nanjing. He had come on Chiang's invitation and was received with as much pomp as any visiting dignitary. There was a procession of lavish meals, glowing toasts, and high-level briefings—all befitting Luce's status as one of Chiang's most powerful champions in the United States.

Luce had given Marshall plenty of advice and encouragement over the previous months. Just a few weeks earlier, he had invited him to address a *Time*-sponsored forum on world affairs; no one, Luce said, could better speak on the question "What Should America Do in the Far East?" (Marshall declined on the grounds that the situation was too unsettled to allow for planning anything more than five days in advance.) Luce's publications had heaped praise on Marshall and his efforts.

The day Luce arrived in Nanjing, Marshall saw him at a dinner hosted by T. V. Soong, over a table of abalone, pigeon eggs, and shark fin. Luce explained that the Nationalist position was better than any-

---

* As the Chinese counted it. By the American count, he was turning 59.

one thought. Top officials had shown him secret reports that offered a decidedly upbeat view of the military balance; the Communist problem, he related, required nothing more than mopping up. He also shared news from the United States: the Republicans were poised for a major victory in congressional elections the following week, and likely in the 1948 presidential election as well.

On Chiang's birthday a few days later, Marshall found himself with Luce again. Madame Chiang had planned a surprise excursion for her husband, amid opulent celebrations around China. (A billion firecrackers were reportedly set off, and air force planes spelled out "six ten longevity" in the sky over Nanjing.) The Chiangs, the Marshalls, Luce, and a few aides and officers boarded a private train to Tai Lake, one hundred miles east of Nanjing in the Yangtze delta. There was Chinese checkers and bridge, lunch on a barge, a stroll on a quiet island. When they returned to the train car, locals greeted the party with banners and cheers. Marshall watched Chiang. He seemed genuinely moved by the display, and said it was his happiest day in a decade.

But on the trip back to Nanjing, when Luce got going on China, Marshall changed the subject. He worried Luce had been "taken for a ride," accepting with little question what he was told and unable to separate personal sentiment from strategic judgment. "Luce has warm friendship for the Generalissimo and quite evidently is much impressed by the Generalissimo's statements," Marshall would note. "I am fond of the Generalissimo but recognize unmistakably the state of mind and governmental procedures which are the opposite of our desires. So, in effect, I stand between the rock and the whirlpool."

Yet Marshall knew that what Luce said held great appeal for Chiang and his generals. They tended to listen most carefully to those Americans whose messages they most wanted to hear.

Time soon ran a story about Chiang's birthday: "If the Generalissimo was happy, it was not because peace was in sight, but rather because the recent success of his armies has convinced many doubters that China can be unified by military means."

CHAPTER 14

At the Point of a Gun

As predicted, the November American election was a bloodbath. Democrats lost eleven seats in the Senate and fifty-four in the House. Republicans took control of both chambers of Congress for the first time since before the Great Depression, claiming commanding majorities and sweeping in a wave of brash newcomers. A young judge named Joseph McCarthy felled a moderate incumbent senator in Wisconsin. A lawyer named Richard Nixon won in California's 12th district.

Republicans framed the election as a referendum on the president. To err is Truman, the line went, and it was both potent and obvious. His approval rating had fallen from more than 80 percent to barely 30 percent in just over a year.

Yet if attacks were ardent, they were not especially coherent. Taxing and spending were the sins voters cared about most, and Republicans made much of them, promising to cut taxes by a full 20 percent. But alleged weakness in the face of Communist aggression—"appeasing Russia," charged Senator Robert Taft—also proved a rich target. Challengers called the race "a fight between Americanism and Communism." (Even candidates from Truman's own party, including John F. Kennedy, a 29-year-old Massachusetts Democrat, found advantage in this approach.) Altogether the critiques presented a picture of an administration both doing too little and spending too much.

GOP TRIUMPH SENDS A CHILL THRU VODKA SET, proclaimed a post-election headline. The new Congress's first move, however, would be to cut spending. Strength abroad might be a winning electoral maxim, but that did not make it a fiscal priority.

For months Truman had bemoaned this contradiction—the grand-standing about expansive ends while wildly slashing means. Since the war, he had been pressing Congress to slow demobilization and sustain defense spending, with little success. The run-up to the November election had only heightened his concern, as the tensions of a new age sharpened.

In late September, the tensions had exploded within Truman's own cabinet. Henry Wallace, Truman's secretary of commerce and predecessor as vice president, publicly attacked U.S. policy and called for a more conciliatory approach to Moscow, "even at the expense of risking epithets of appeasement." Truman demanded Wallace's resignation and replaced him with Averell Harriman, the former ambassador to the Soviet Union—a consolidation, it was said, of the "get tough with Russia" camp in the administration.

A few days later, the tensions exploded within the United Nations Security Council, the body conceived as a forum for the wartime Allies to keep the postwar peace. At a Council meeting in New York, Soviet representative Andrei Gromyko stood and denounced the United States as an occupying power. At the center of his denunciation was the U.S. troop presence in China.

Then, the day after that, Truman received a highly restricted report that two aides, Clark Clifford and George Elsey, had begun drafting over the summer at his request. They had gathered the thoughts of top officials and distilled them into a bleak prophecy of prolonged US-Soviet hostility. From Europe to the Middle East to Asia, Moscow was "seeking wherever possible to weaken the military position and the influence of the United States abroad as, for example, in China." They called on their country to do anything necessary, including "wage atomic and biological warfare," to demonstrate that it was "too strong to be beaten and too determined to be frightened."

It was a grim elaboration on the telegram George Kennan had dictated in bed in Moscow half a year earlier. Then Kennan had been a voice in the wilderness. Now he was the most eloquent exponent of an emerging consensus; Clifford and Elsey quoted him at length. Back in Washington, his tour in the Soviet Union over, Kennan had recently started speaking about the need "to contain [the Soviets] both militarily and politically for a long time to come."

For Truman, Kennan's call for "containment" and Clifford and Elsey's cri de coeur served as unnecessary reminders of the extent of the world's challenges. Neither, however, solved his problem of means. For now, his public concession to domestic politics would be to appoint a commission to ferret out Kremlin loyalists in government. A recent poll had asked, "What should be done about the Communists in this country?" The top response was, kill or jail them.

"War will come again, soon or later, unless the West surrenders to the Soviet Union or the Soviet Union accepts collaboration with the West," wrote Joseph Alsop, a prominent columnist. It was no longer just generals in Nanjing and revolutionaries in Yenan who were openly speculating about World War III. Churchill's Iron Curtain was coming down.

All of this was watched intently from the other side of the Pacific. Chiang knew that Truman's China policy was a key exhibit in the campaign-trail charges of appeasement. As election results came in on November 5, he asked Ambassador Stuart about their significance, and afterward requested vote tallies from specific races. (Luce had told Chiang what to look for in order to gauge Republican momentum ahead of the 1948 presidential race.) Zhou also wondered whether the Republican landslide heralded a shift in U.S. policy.

Marshall paid close attention to the currents, both political and geopolitical. He saw the analyses Kennan had dispatched from Moscow. He skimmed daily digests of press coverage of his mission, sent from Washington; when they stopped coming at one point, he sent an urgent telegram demanding they be restored: "I am at war." He had also begun quietly entering his own account into the official record— the report he had drafted Till Durdin from the *New York Times* to begin compiling months earlier. Since mid-October, aides had been sending it back to Washington piece by top secret piece, as evidence in political trials to come.

In the wake of the Democrats' electoral drubbing, the White House sent a message of reassurance, stressing that Truman "relied entirely and only on General Marshall's judgment in the China problem." That would not change, said Truman, "at least as long as I am President."

But a disquieting signal came soon after. An American businessman named Alfred Kohlberg turned up in China—"the kind of man who can spot a Communist at a thousand paces on a dark night," John Beal observed after meeting him. The American China Policy Association, which had sprung up to attack the Truman administration and lobby for Chiang's cause, was largely the work of Kohlberg. Now, in Nanjing, he was asking leading questions: he believed Marshall had been helping the Communists and was set on finding proof.

November brought a piercing chill to the Nanjing air. Daylight saving time had ended, and dusk came early. "The beauty of fall is yielding to the promise of cold and death and a sense of doom," wrote Melby.

Chiang was still waiting for the Americans to come around, but now more hopefully. He had resolved not to give in to "bullying," but also to "refrain from arguing." That way Marshall might accept on his own what Chiang for months had been trying to make him see.

On the day of the U.S. election, Chiang even proposed the sort of magnanimous gesture Marshall had been urging: a unilateral cease-fire, meant to demonstrate the Nationalist commitment to peace. As Chiang expected, Marshall approved. But when he saw a draft of the order, Marshall was disappointed again. The terms—a broad and pointed exception for "defense," generally "provocative, confusing, and irritating language"—defeated the supposed purpose. Marshall thought it was a missed opportunity, another peace offer made "at the point of a gun."

Still, on November 8, when Chiang announced that a short-term cease-fire would begin in three days, Marshall decided to do what he could with the opportunity. The alternative was "total war," and he was not yet willing to accept it. He took the offer to Zhou. "We have a saying," Marshall said. "It may be one of Confucius', I don't know—'while there's life, there's hope'—and I have been traveling on that a good many months." The cease-fire was an opportunity for the Communists, he argued, one that could restart the political process on reasonable terms. But Zhou's conditions once again seemed willfully implausible; given a chance to get what he claimed to want, he would give little in return.

When Marshall resorted to his standard lament about distrust, Zhou interrupted: "This is not a matter of suspicion or misunderstanding."

Marshall did get one concession from Zhou, an agreement to attend a meeting of the Committee of Three. But on the morning of November 11, when it gathered around a table on Ning Hai Road, like old times at Happiness Gardens in Chongqing, whatever magic there had ever been was gone. Marshall urged restraint, a cease-fire, renewed commitment to political reform and military unification—a reprise of the agreements of almost a year earlier. But his fellow Committee members were now more interested in casting blame for battles under way. The meeting amounted to little more than two hours of reciprocal accusations.

At the end of it, the Nationalists' latest cease-fire went into effect. And that evening, Chiang agreed to a three-day postponement of the National Assembly, to November 15, at the behest of third-party leaders. But Zhou dismissed Chiang's action as a "mock gesture," with nothing new in the way of compromise. When Marshall pressed on specific disagreements over the National Assembly—who would be represented, how a constitution would be ratified—Zhou brushed him off. "Chinese affairs are too complicated," he said. "I cannot give you an outline within a few minutes to make you fully understand this."

Over the three days of delay, third-party leaders, who had wrenched the postponement out of Chiang, had no more success than Marshall in hashing out mutually acceptable terms for a National Assembly. Marshall continued urging them to act together as a unified force, but the third parties were themselves riven by disunity. Some promised the CCP they would not take part in the Assembly, and others promised Chiang they would. Those leaders Chiang could not co-opt he would dismiss as Communist patsies; those Zhou could not co-opt he would chide as Nationalist stooges. The delay yielded nothing.

The National Assembly opened on the morning of Friday, November 15. Delegates arrived and bowed three times before a looming portrait of Sun Yat-sen. Chiang, in military uniform, proclaimed it the most important event in China's recent history. But it was hardly the gathering envisioned the previous January, the constitutional convention of a new Chinese democracy. No Communist representatives showed up. Nor did key third-party figures. Marshall worried the Assembly would be "an ineffective one party proposition." Not wanting his presence to imply endorsement, he skipped the opening ceremony.

There was an unsettling stillness in Nanjing as the Assembly got under way, "a feeling that nothing can be changed, that the chips have been laid down," Melby recorded in his diary. Many others agreed.

Zhou appeared on Ning Hai Road the next morning. For weeks he had been warning what would happen if the National Assembly opened on Nationalist terms: war throughout China. Since returning from Shanghai, he had seemed not just bitter, but also uncharacteristically haggard.

Zhou went right to the point. He was leaving for Yenan a few days later, and not coming back. The start of the National Assembly, without the participation of the Communists and many of the third parties, had foreclosed further talks. Chiang, Zhou charged, "is intoxicated with the idea that force can settle everything."

To Marshall, the news hardly came as a surprise, disheartening though it was. Zhou left no room for argument, and Marshall made no effort to argue. He was ready to admit that negotiation was over.

There was a final concern Zhou wanted to raise—the fate of a few dozen Communist representatives who would still be in Nanjing after he left. He wanted assurance of their safety, particularly in the event of a Nationalist attack on Yenan. Without hesitating, Marshall gave his word: American planes would evacuate them if it became necessary. They were there largely because of his mediation; he considered it his obligation to make sure they did not come to harm.

"I felt very grateful for your personal efforts despite the fact that due to various reasons (including some change in U.S. policy during the last part of this year) the negotiations have ended in vain," Zhou told Marshall. "But I feel that I still have high respect for you personally." Over the previous eleven months, they had spent hundreds of hours together, one-on-one and with the revolving cast of Nationalists who had joined them on the Committee of Three. Two men who awed those around them, who had a way of earning esteem even from adversaries, they had quickly established a rapport that brought grand promises— then gotten swept up in acrimony as those promises came apart, week by week. Yet into the fall, even as Yenan condemned Marshall as an agent of imperial reaction, Zhou had continued to refer to him as a "wise man."

The respect was reciprocated. Marshall had come to see Zhou as one of the smarter people he had ever encountered, and a scarily skillful negotiator. He had often maintained that Zhou was a relative moderate in his party, a champion of reconciliation among irreconcilables, just as Zhou hoped Marshall would. (Even some of Chiang's advisers continued to describe Zhou as a "liberal-minded man with high integrity.") But Marshall was never taken in by the notion, pushed by China hands in the American diplomatic and press corps, that Zhou was at heart a democrat, ready to shed his Communist trappings with the right signal from Washington. After all, Zhou never hesitated to identify himself as a true believer, a devoted Marxist and sincere admirer of the Soviet model, blanching at suggestions to the contrary. And Marshall had heard enough misleading propaganda from Zhou, and seen enough evidence of Soviet-CCP collusion, to recognize his capacity for deception.

Yet Zhou was also careful to avoid outright lies when he could. The protests and predictions he shared with Marshall often turned out to have more validity than those from the other side. "Every time Zhou tells me there is going to be an attack it comes off," Marshall would say.

In part this owed to Zhou's verbal and diplomatic facility. But it also owed to his skill in subterfuge and advantage in matters of intelligence. American cryptographers had labored since Marshall's arrival to break Communist codes, in order to monitor the communications between Zhou and Yenan. They rarely succeeded, not even with help from Washington, thanks to Zhou's reliance on "one-time pads," secret codes that were used once and discarded. With the Nationalists, American codebreakers heard much more. When Chiang or a general said one thing in a meeting and promptly contradicted it in orders to the field, Marshall often found out soon afterward.

Meanwhile, the CCP had planted agents throughout the Nationalists' ranks—as Marshall could tell from the accuracy of Zhou's charges. When Communists warned of an attack on Yenan, for example, they knew what they were talking about: they had a spy on the personal staff of the Nationalist general plotting it. What Marshall did not know was that his own side had been penetrated as well, not by the CCP but by the Soviets. While the young diplomats attacked earlier by Patrick Hurley as Communist agents were guilty only of telling it like they saw it (and in some cases of starry-eyed naiveté about Yenan), an economic adviser in the Nanjing embassy, Sol Adler, had passed information to KGB networks in the United States during the war, when he worked for another Soviet asset, Harry Dexter White, at the Treasury Department. Now in Nanjing, Adler was warning of the disastrous financial impact of Chiang's military spending—though he was hardly the only one making that point. Marshall had called him "indispensable."

Before Zhou left Ning Hai Road, Marshall posed one last question: Was there anything more that he could do? He asked Zhou to discuss the matter with his comrades, without regard for "face," and to get back to him with a response. "I am making a specific request of you," Marshall stressed, "and I will await your answer from Yenan." If that answer was no, he would have a definitive reason for finally going home.

Two days later, on November 18, Zhou dropped by with his wife to say good-bye to the Marshalls. The only item of business was handing over a list of Communists who would stay behind and need to be airlifted out in the event of open war. The next morning, solemn and dapper in a dark trench coat and fedora, Zhou boarded a U.S. Army plane and took off north, uncertain he would ever return to the region where he was born.

When the plane landed on the rocky Yenan airstrip, Mao stood waiting. Zhou stepped into the northern chill. Mao grasped his hand and presented him with a warm coat. To those watching, it was a signal: Zhou was still in favor.

Trading his suit for a tunic, Zhou sat down with Mao to review the events of the past eleven months. With his usual exaggerated contrition, Zhou apologized for returning "empty-handed." The self-reproach was hardly warranted. Mao had been content to sit back and see how negotiations played out. Now he and Zhou were in complete agreement: war to the death was the only way forward. "There was uncertainty as to whether or not we should fight the war," Mao had concluded. "Now, this uncertainty has been cleared up."

It was the answer to Marshall's question. There could be no more "fantasies" of peace.

The fight would be long and grueling, Mao acknowledged. Victory might take three to five years without the involvement of American troops, fifteen to twenty if the Americans fought. But he was confident he would win either way. Even if the Nationalists managed to conquer Yenan, the Communists would ultimately conquer China. He could lose battle after battle, but he would still win the war. The reactionaries, Mao told comrades, were weaker than they looked.

The dynamic he had long envisioned was already playing out in Manchuria. The Nationalists were taking territory but not destroying Communist armies. Their lines were long and vulnerable, their troops led by arrogant non-Manchurian officers, their opposition to land reform an effective recruiting tool for the CCP. (Join the revolution to protect the land, Mao's organizers directed.) And then there was Manchuria's long border with the Soviet Union, as mounting geopolitical tension promised enhanced outside support.

In the global struggle between revolution and reaction, China was destined to be a key battlefield—Mao counted on that as much as Chiang did. "The postwar world has evolved into a standoff between U.S. reactionaries and the people of the world," Mao explained. "The situation in China reflects this standoff."

Soviet policy had already started shifting accordingly. "The so-called 'mediation' mission of General Marshall is only a cover for actual interference in the internal affairs of China," the Kremlin had concluded, amid worries that Washington aimed to make China "a bridgehead for American military forces." While the extent of Soviet assistance remained a source of frustration for Mao, it was starting to increase. Recently the Kremlin had agreed to bring several hundred Chinese Communists across the border for secret military training.

Americans were starting to discern the combative new posture. As battles between the Nationalists and Communists grew in scale and scope, hostile encounters with American troops were also becoming more frequent. There had been reports of Communists firing on marines' hunting parties and railway guards, and of a raid on an ammunition dump. The American review of the Anping incident had settled on a straightforward account of the episode—an "ambush," pure and simple, "methodically planned, prepared and executed by the Communist Party Military Forces." The only question was from how high up authorization had come. "General feeling is that something nasty is about to happen," judged an American officer at the Executive Headquarters.

Melby wondered what the new posture meant for Marshall. "Very few people know how deeply hurt personally he is by the Communist attacks on his integrity," Melby thought. "Attacks on his judgment or ability or influence he does not mind, but when it is on his integrity that hurts." As Melby saw it, Marshall had bent over backward for the Communists: "He has taken from them what he has taken from no one else, and has been understanding when he has raised bloody hell with others."

But to Mao, Marshall's apparent accommodation, his overtures to peace, appeared to be part of a malevolent design. "You are swindlers," accused an *Emancipation Daily* editorial, personally blessed by Mao and directed at the Americans. He told a reporter that Marshall's mediation had been "a smoke-screen for strengthening Chiang Kai-shek in every way."

Mao's charge was overblown but not entirely off-base. Marshall, in his own words, had pushed unity as the best way, perhaps the only way, for Chiang's government to "swallow" the forces of revolution and "digest them before they became too powerful." In the process, the Communists would become part of a political opposition that could compel Chiang and those around him to accept the kind of reform that, in Marshall's view, was essential to their long-term survival. Communist participation was a means to an end: a Chinese state that could thwart a Communist takeover.

Marshall flew north a few days after Zhou. This time he was bound not for Yenan but for Tianjin, the coastal city where he served his first China tour two decades before. His purpose was not nostalgia. The American troops who remained in China were stationed in the area. What to do with them now was one of his most pressing questions.

Marshall found much unchanged in Tianjin, at least on the surface. He saw marines play football on the field where his former regiment, the Fifteenth, had played rugby matches against the French. He encountered old friends and employees—his Chinese teacher, his driver, his "number one boy." There were still frequent parties, with the same array of Russian and Chinese and European women. Yet he also noticed planes crowded onto the old polo field and tanks onto the race track. Clubhouses had been converted into barracks. For the Americans there now, little of the post's late-imperial glamor remained. The stakes had gotten too high.

From Tianjin, Marshall proceeded inland to Beijing. In a dusty late November wind, he arrived at the wood-paneled chambers of Peking Union Medical College, where in February he had hailed the progress of his Executive Headquarters, as its three-man teams fanned out across north China halting battles and refereeing disputes. This time, he found this experiment in peace-building all but finished. Fewer than one-third of the teams were still operational. The officers assigned to implement the long-postponed unification of the Communist and Nationalist armies had abandoned post. A senior American officer conceded, "We had tried an approach and it hadn't worked."

By now, the same could be said of U.S. policy more generally. The approach Marshall had helped hash out a year earlier, an extension of Washington's approach through the final years of World War II, was in ruins—that much was clear. But what to do from here was another matter. As Americans waited to see how the National Assembly would unfold, and Marshall waited for an answer from Zhou, the discussion seemed stuck.

The American election, and attendant fury over taxes and spending, had added pressure to withdraw the remaining troops, despite the apparent anger over appeasement. A poll asked Americans what their government should do in China. Just 18 percent answered to help the Nationalists, while 69 percent said to help neither side. The letters and telegrams to the White House continued: A MILLION AMERICAN MEN IN UNIFORM ARE STILL AT WAR THEY ARE BEING USED TO BOLSTER UP MERE FASCIST REGIME OF CHANG KAI SHEK INSTEAD OF PERMITTING THE CHINESE PEOPLE TO MAKE THEIR OWN DECISION. Americans wanted their boys home, and Washington worried about sustaining troop deployments elsewhere, starting with occupied Germany and Japan.

From the State Department, Dean Acheson pledged to hold off the pressure as much as he could. But Marshall recognized that further

withdrawals were a "political necessity." And more important, he saw
reasons other than domestic pressure for moving forward. Even at its
height, the troop presence had been large enough to cause serious trouble but too small to do much good—an "irritant," as Wedemeyer had
put it, with little hope of countering a real Soviet effort and thus worth
removing altogether. Marshall had long before concluded that the
Communists "could not be liquidated by National forces without full-
scale American intervention both in the movement of Chinese forces
with American equipment and the use of American personnel, possibly
even combat forces." In the 1920s, when asked how many American
troops would be needed to counter an indigenous force in China, an
American general had answered: "Half a million and it would probably
require a million more before the end of the first year." At their height
the year before, American troops had numbered a little over 100,000.

Over the course of the fall, the Marines had been consolidating
around Tianjin and Beijing, handing over guard duties at mines,
bridges, and railway depots to Nationalist forces. (These forces should
have little trouble holding important ground, Marshall pointed out,
if the best of them were not shipped off to fight in Manchuria.) Fewer
than 20,000 Marines now remained, down from three times that a
year before, along with a few hundred army personnel. (The troops'
initial charge of repatriating the Japanese was more or less complete,
with some 3 million, by the military's count, sent back to Japan.) Marshall drew up plans to cut the Marine presence first to 10,000, and then
quickly to 5,000. A drawdown would "purify" the American position as
much as possible, he told Washington. And he wanted it done quickly,
"before some new incident creates impression of reduction under hostile pressure. The numbers to be eliminated do little or no good and
really complicate the situation."

Marshall considered certain capabilities useful, and these he pressed
to maintain. The Military Advisory Group, the MAG, was up and running in Nanjing with several hundred officers, and he was also working
to ensure an ongoing American intelligence capability as troops left.
Yet he insisted on extreme care about what remaining troops did and

did not do, to avoid incidents that could easily spin out of control—especially as pressure to take a more active role mounted in certain quarters on both sides of the Pacific.

In Nanjing, Chiang wanted American officers to accompany his troops into the field. In Washington, military planners called for supporting the Nationalists "by all means short of actual armed intervention," warning that Communism would spread from China to Vietnam and Malaysia and India. Marshall resisted. He worried not just about the risks of escalation, but also, more immediately, about the message to Nationalist hard-liners. They would take enhanced military support as vindication, a sign of unconditional backing that would undercut any pressure to change their self-destructive ways. In early November, U.S. army leadership had proposed a major mapping operation, with B-29s crisscrossing China, from Taiwan to Manchuria to Tibet, and an additional 2,000 soldiers on the ground. Marshall protested emphatically on the grounds that it would "cause silent rejoicing among KMT political die-hards" in their "hope that we must become involved in backing them in possible strife with Communists, Chinese or Soviet." He also worried that it would weaken the United States' hand in contesting Soviet interference, in China and beyond.

With hindsight, Marshall could see that the collapse of his efforts the previous spring had owed as much to deterioration in the US-Soviet relationship as anything else. He had been struggling to make sense of this "year of international bickerings," and he returned to Nanjing from Tianjin and Beijing to find a memo from Acheson. "As you know," it explained, "one of our principal concerns, if not our principal concern, in endeavoring to bring about peace and unity in China, has been to forestall China's becoming a serious irritant in our relations with Russia." Acheson disavowed the once heady talk of China as a pillar of stability in Asia, but still hoped to prevent it from becoming a source of instability. "The principal problem," he stressed, "is adjustment of our relations there with the Russians without prejudice to our legitimate interests."

When Marshall arrived in China the previous December, the most acute concern had been ensuring that Red Army troops did not extend their occupation of Manchuria indefinitely. Once they were gone, to the relief of both the Nationalists and the Americans, the concern had become unhelpful Soviet meddling. Marshall hoped that withdrawing American troops would put useful pressure on Moscow, effectively shaming it into decent behavior. (A large ongoing American troop presence, by contrast, would allow Moscow to blame China's problems on Washington's interference.) Many who had spent more time around Stalin, such as Averell Harriman, deemed that hope fanciful at best.

Yet Marshall grasped Soviet objectives in China. Every analysis he requested or received sketched them in distressing terms. "Soviet intent, obvious from their current propaganda campaign, is to discredit U.S. activities in China with the hope of creating public clamor in the U.S. for withdrawal of all troops and cessation of U.S. efforts in China," he read in a War Department paper. It emphasized that the consequences of "our exclusion from China" would be dire: "Soviet power analogous to that of the Japanese in 1941." From Manchuria, American diplomats sent reports of Soviet "colonization." One complained of an "iron curtain" blocking American access to the region.

Marshall also recognized that Yenan and the Kremlin were "playing the same tune," and that cooperation had been growing in recent months. He could see their "spiritual" affinity and convergent interests. (He recalled the portraits of Lenin and Stalin in the freezing meeting hall in Yenan.) There was considerable intelligence on secret radio communication and policy coordination. Less clear to Marshall was the degree of direct Soviet support. He had put diplomats, officers, and spies on the lookout for clear evidence of military assistance, and they were finding evidence of some, but less than the Nationalists claimed. Still, if sins of commission were harder to prove, the sins of omission were obvious—and perhaps more consequential anyway. As they withdrew from Manchuria, the Soviets had abandoned Japanese arms and let the Communists take them. They had made it difficult for Nationalist troops to travel, and easy for Communists. "They could accomplish almost all their purposes by negative action," Marshall would observe. He figured Stalin realized that, with the way things were going, he could mostly sit back and let Chiang and the Americans get into trouble on their own. (Unknown to the United States, the Kremlin and Yenan were also finalizing a commercial agreement, trading Manchurian soy, sorghum, and mutton for Soviet fuel and vehicles, along with some weapons—although Stalin remained cautious about sending large numbers, and the captured Japanese stockpiles remained the more important factor.)

From Moscow, George Kennan had also speculated about the relationship between Yenan and the Kremlin. He accepted that the CCP was "subservient" to its Soviet patron. But in the long run, he thought that might change. In his analysis, the nationalism of the Chinese Communists would prove a source of comradely friction, especially given their ample cause for resentment of Soviet behavior over the years. In time, Kennan thought, those frictions could lead to fracture.

For now, however, most nascent Cold Warriors were more focused on the subservience. Wedemeyer's angry letters to American officers and Chinese officials made the case in especially stark terms. In a world "compartmented into two ideological camps," he wrote, "the Central Government of China with all its incompetence and corruption at least is opposed to the expansion of Soviet influence in the Far East."

Nationalist hard-liners had long made the same case, and the American election encouraged them to raise the pitch. A global war was coming; all that mattered was which side they were on. It was a "lesser of two evils" logic, as John Beal described it to Chiang's advisers, in the course of urging them to stop using it. He thought it "the easiest and weakest argument of all."

Marshall agreed that the logic was faulty. There was no doubt in his mind that Nationalist rule, for all its shortcomings, was far preferable to the Communist alternative. But that was not all that mattered. Without fundamental improvement, in his analysis, Chiang's "lesser evil" had little chance of averting more dire outcomes. The Nationalist approach invited more, not less, Communist influence, and more, not less, Soviet infiltration.

Marshall's hold on most American aid, in place for the previous three months, was meant to drive this point home. He wanted to disabuse hard-liners of the notion they would be backed no matter what; to get the full-fledged American support they wanted, they would have to embrace reform. Marshall continued to push through some assistance that he thought especially crucial, sometimes over the objections of economic officials in Washington, and he pressed Congress to fund ongoing humanitarian efforts. (Total aid over the previous year, between loans, funding for relief efforts, and surplus-property transfers, already amounted to several hundred million dollars.) But he continued holding the $500 million economic package he had lobbied for in the spring, instructing congressional leaders to keep it in reserve for the appropriate moment. He continued blocking shipments of weapons, ammunition, and combat gear that might end up supporting military offensives. With Nationalist officials he was frank: his country wanted to help China, but it would not forever back a repressive one-party government. The stinginess of the new Congress, he explained, only made matters worse.

"If you let this bunch know you are for them," Marshall had complained before, "you can't do anything with them."

Chiang and his advisers realized what Marshall was trying to do but refused to play along. After hearing that a request for ammunition had been denied, one Nationalist official breezily replied that it did not really matter, since the Communists would be crushed in a few months. And whatever Marshall's seeming leverage over them, they had their own American allies, who could give them leverage over Marshall. They had cultivated not just figures like Henry Luce and Alfred Kohlberg, but also the Republican politicians who were, they were being told, set to drive out "the FDR party" in the next presidential election.

They saw other allies in American business. (Kohlberg's interest in China grew out of his time producing textiles there.) Early in November, Chiang's government had signed a commercial treaty with the United States, pledging open markets and expansive opportunities for American firms, from oil and telephone companies to airlines. (At the time, more than half of China's imports came from the United States.) Communists savaged the treaty as "a new national humiliation," and even Chinese conservatives denounced it as a "new unequal treaty" that failed to protect China's "industry, economy, and livelihood against American high-speed industrial competition." But American executives, taken as ever with the potential of China's 400 million customers, were pleased.

As the end of November approached, Marshall waited and watched the National Assembly proceed. He worried that Nationalist hard-liners would have an easy time using it to cement their party's control rather than lay the groundwork for more democratic rule. Without the participation of the Communists and some of the strongest third parties, there was little countervailing pressure. That had been part of the logic of a coalition, a way of compelling reform on recalcitrant Nationalists.

Marshall had been far from alone in seeing a coalition as the best, and perhaps only, way forward. Even Chiang's staunchest advocates—Luce, Congressman Judd, the Flying Tigers commander Claire Chennault, a slew of anti-Communist officers—had called for a coalition as essential to Chiang's survival and China's renewal. Now, however, many were denying they had ever considered it.

It had been a year since Marshall had gotten Truman's phone call tapping him for this mission. After nearly as long watching him in action, Melby found Marshall wearied by the prospect of moving forward. "I think I wanted to cry," Melby wrote, "partly because he deserved a better fate than this. I know this sort of thing is the cruel logic of history, but that makes it no easier to take." The past year had been a "great experiment," Melby said, and the experiment's results were becoming dismayingly clear. He thought that at this point, "Marshall feels he made a mistake in ever thinking coalition was desirable or useful or possible."

On Thanksgiving it snowed. All day Nanjing was windy and gray. By dusk, snow sticking to the streets, it looked almost like a New England town, sending waves of nostalgia over Americans who had been in China longer than they ever thought they would.

The Marshalls spent the evening with the Chiangs. After a holiday meal, they settled in with cocktails, snow falling outside. Marshall and Madame Chiang enlisted aides for bridge. Katherine and the Generalissimo played Chinese checkers. They could still hardly communicate, though Chiang had started puckishly trying out bits of English on Katherine: "How do you do? You come back? Good-bye." The "great shine" he had taken to her, Marshall remarked, might have been the only reason the diplomatic relationship had not broken down entirely by now.

Two days later, on the last day of November, Chiang learned that Katherine would soon leave China for good. Marshall said he wanted her to spend winter in Honolulu rather than Nanjing for the sake of her health. Whatever the explanation, the news fed already rampant rumors that Marshall himself would soon go home.

That was fine with Chiang. He was mystified by what Marshall thought he was accomplishing by keeping on. The Communists got something out of it, in Chiang's assessment: as long as Marshall was around, Nationalist troops would hold back from attacking Yenan—and if an attack was delayed long enough, winter weather might intervene in the CCP's favor. But as far as Marshall's own thinking went, all Chiang could fathom was that it was a matter of pride: "Marshall is still daydreaming about continuing with the mediation so that his I-can-achieve-everything confidence is not shattered." It was the behavior, Chiang raged to his diary, of a "vindictive thug"—"unreasonable," "unethical," and "arrogant."

In fact, Marshall was waiting for one thing in particular. He had gotten no certain answer to the question he put to Zhou: could any-thing more be done? When pressed, Communist representatives left behind in Nanjing responded with hard-edged bluster. "We will not be coerced at the point of a gun," they said. But from Yenan, Zhou himself was silent.

Marshall resolved to wait until Monday, December 2. If he had heard nothing, he would accept his mission was finished.

CHAPTER 15

All of Chiang's Horses and All of Chiang's Men

On Sunday, December 1, Marshall visited Chiang. It was late in the afternoon, a day ahead of the unspoken deadline for an answer from Zhou. Before then, Marshall wanted to have a difficult conversation.

As they began to talk, Marshall warned Madame Chiang, there to translate as usual, that he intended to deliver some harsh messages, which she should feel free to frame or soften as she saw fit. No, she replied. She thought her husband should hear what Marshall had to say.

Marshall was blunt. He thought Chiang was leading China toward disaster, with an approach practically "calculated to put the Communists in power," and said so. The Nationalists were pouring money into the military, for the sake of a war they could not win, at the expense of an economy straining under spiraling inflation and a society growing more and more desperate. (The problem was not just that so much of the budget went to the military, but that corruption kept so much tax revenue from making it into the budget in the first place.) No matter how "brutal" the Nationalist attempt to annihilate the Communists, Marshall stressed, it would ultimately succeed only in sowing chaos—and chaos would play into Mao's hands.

To Marshall's mind, economic and societal collapse was the real risk for the Nationalists, and Chiang was proceeding along a course that made collapse more likely. T. V. Soong had told Marshall that the Nationalists could afford only a few more months of war without setting off financial calamity (and Soong thought that "if China collapses, the Communists will take over"). Other Nationalist officials predicted that Communism "would spread like wildfire" in the event of all-out war. The dynamic was clear in upheavals elsewhere—war was midwife to revolution.

Marshall contended that the Nationalists had squandered an opportunity to lock the CCP into a political deal months earlier, in February and March. Now they were squandering an opportunity to save themselves through economic and political reform. He saw party ranks marred by "rottenness and corruption and extortion," especially at lower levels, and dominated at higher levels by a "hard-boiled element" that has "ruined my efforts and is now ruining China." Every time he thought he had persuaded Chiang to change course, this element sabotaged any shift, having "coolly calculated on inevitable support of their party government by the United States." Marshall hoped Chiang would understand that—whatever he thought he knew of American strategy, of American politics, of deliberations in Washington—that calculation was wrong.

There was nothing uniquely astute about Marshall's insights. Chiang's own advisers could be unsparing about their side's failings, and clear-eyed about the implications. Even Wedemeyer had recently written Chiang that force would never be "the permanent solution to the Communist problem. The best antidote to the spread of Communistic ideologies is the establishment of good government, sound economy and the uniform recognition of the individual rights of human beings. . . . Only in areas of unrest, chaos, and oppression are the Communists successful in spreading their invidious propaganda."

But Marshall now wanted to be more brutally frank with Chiang than anyone had been before, forgoing the usual careful respect in hopes of scaring him straight. (One of Chiang's problems was that generals and aides and advisers rarely gave him unvarnished bad news.) Marshall recounted the past year's broken promises, lapsed agreements, missed chances. People once called Chiang a modern-day George Washington, Marshall said, but they never would again.

As Marshall spoke, Chiang listened intently to his wife's translation, his foot tracing circles in the air. When it was his turn, he spoke for over an hour.

Chiang brushed aside the warning of collapse. China's agrarian economy was less affected by war and instability than a more developed economy would be, he explained, and could survive at least long enough for his armies to destroy Mao's. And he assured Marshall that victory was no more than eight to ten months away. In Chiang's view, Communist guerrilla methods were becoming less and less effective against the Nationalists' military machine, built with American help.

The Communists had never intended to cooperate, Chiang reiterated. They were stooges set on doing the Kremlin's bidding, and always had been. No amount of Nationalist forbearance or acquiescence, no degree of democratization or reform, could have kept them from turning to rebellion in the end. The distrust Marshall so often deplored had nothing to do with it.

Chiang argued that military force was the only way the situation would be settled. That demanded a complete reconsideration not of the Nationalist approach, but of American policy. There was still time, Chiang told Marshall, to do the right thing.

Chiang's faith in the United States had been tested over the last several months. On this very day a year earlier, he had reflected on Marshall's selection and figured that American attention would work to his benefit. The leaked accounts of the Oval Office conversations before Marshall's departure had been even more encouraging, a sign that, for all the apparent evenhandedness of the Americans, for all their clamoring for democracy and reform, he would ultimately have their backing. "The Communist Party's scheme to sabotage my government's relationship with the United States turned out to benefit me," he had determined when Marshall arrived. But Marshall had done much to call that certainty into question—his prodding, his criticism, his slowdown in assistance, his persistence in mediation. In moments of exasperation, Chiang had to remind himself, "If I were to give up on the United States the ramifications are unimaginable."

In recent weeks, Chiang had been trying to sell Marshall on a new role, one that might put him firmly on Chiang's side: Marshall could stay in Nanjing as a personal adviser. Chiang repeated the invitation now.

Marshall had turned the offer down before and did again. He had watched others take up similar charges, fired by the hope that with the right advice, the right blueprint for success, Chiang, and China, would live up to American aspirations. They came with technocratic assessments and high-minded reforms, only to be thwarted by the realities of power and politics and chaos on the ground. Over the past year, Marshall had seen his own counsel ignored again and again, and that was even though he had the U.S. government behind him. He had fully registered Chiang's "customary willingness to say 'yes' without, however, accepting the advice given." Was there any reason to believe he would be more effective as a mere adviser? He figured that the real purpose of Chiang's offer was to attract more American support.

Marshall had increasingly focused on this quandary—how to help a partner do what the United States thought was necessary when that partner had other ideas. No matter how badly Washington wanted to support Chiang, no matter how big its stake in ensuring his survival and blocking Communist advances, it could help only insofar as Chiang and those around him were willing and able to help themselves. Otherwise all the money and weapons and advice in the world would be for naught.

"There are few harder stunts of statesmanship," an American official would note, "than at one and the same time to sustain a foreign government and to alter it against its fears and inclinations." Or as Marshall would put it, "The question is to what extent you can crack the whip." He wanted to help Chiang—after all, he had spent weeks in Washington wrenching a massive assistance package out of a stingy, skeptical Congress—but could do so effectively only "if he gives us the opportunity." The United States could not want it more than he did.

Chiang had bet these reservations would fall away amid global hostilities. What he heard from his sources in Washington gave him plenty of reason to think this bet would turn out right. But such confidence only infuriated Marshall. Chiang's advisers were making a "serious error," he said; the United States would not "be dragged through the mud by these reactionaries." He had asked that a message be delivered to the "militarists" in Nationalist ranks: "The army is draining 80 to 90 percent of the budget and if you think the U.S. taxpayer is going to step into the vacuum this creates, you can go to hell."

Ultimately, Marshall's frustration with Chiang's failings was not just a matter of moral outrage, or of principle for principle's sake. To Marshall, the principles were crucial to a strategic objective, part of the means to a desired end. The financial mismanagement, the suppression of dissent, the carpetbagging and abuse—these were consequential errors, not secondary considerations.

And yet Marshall retained a basic respect for Chiang. Unlike Stilwell and others before, Marshall did not let frustration curdle into contempt. He would say he was fond of the Generalissimo, and aides were struck by their mutual graciousness even as the mission foundered. Despite tolerating so much corruption in the party, "his personal integrity is on a high level," Marshall believed of Chiang, his commitment to his country sincere no matter how frequently wrongheaded his approach. Chiang would often do the right thing in the end, Marshall once said, but "always too late."

After converting to Christianity two decades earlier, Chiang had underlined a passage in a religious volume: "God never uses anybody to a large degree until after He breaks that one all to pieces." He had borne that sense of destiny for much of his life. He could speak of democracy when he needed to. He had recently stood before the National Assembly and declared his readiness "to return to the people of the entire nation the responsibility of government." But at bottom, he saw his duty in Confucian terms—renewal would come through the leadership of a proud, upright, noble leader. Madame Chiang told Marshall that she had tried for years to make her husband understand democracy, but with only two percent success.

As their conversation neared its end, Chiang told Marshall that he was ready to give up his burden and retire. He had just to complete this final act—defeating the Communist threat for good.

The exchange had lasted three hours, into the evening. When Marshall left, Chiang reflected on their discussion and thought he had persuaded Marshall. Marshall reflected and thought it revealed just how wide the gulf between their respective visions was. Over almost a year of meetings and meals, parties and outings with their wives, games of croquet and cards and Chinese checkers, neither of them had been swayed.

Both men had gotten where they were through sheer will, each renowned for tenacity and resolve. Marshall had come to see stubbornness as Chiang's greatest strength and greatest weakness—the fatal flaw of a tragic hero. Chiang might have said the same of Marshall.

This was not the first time Marshall had watched a society spiral into chaos, militarism, and revolution. Conditions like these had opened the way to Nazism and Fascism in Europe in the 1930s, a fresh memory that lay behind his pleas to Americans at the end of World War II. "Along with the great problem of maintaining the peace we must solve the problem of the pittance of food, of clothing and coal and homes," he exhorted. "Neither of these problems can be solved alone." As important as events on the battlefield were other questions—"where the mouthful of food will come from, where they will find shelter tonight and where they will find warmth from the cold of winter." Now more than ever, wars would not be won by arms alone.

In China, the warnings of collapse were not hyperbolic. Its currency was plummeting, inflation surging. The Shanghai cost-of-living index had doubled in a matter of months. As prices rose, merchants hoarded rice. In city after city, strapped workers went on strike. Protesters shouted, "We are begging food from the mouth of guns!"

Chiang and the Nationalists hardly deserved sole blame. Even the most enlightened ruler or most capable administration would have struggled to reverse the toll from years of war and foreign exploitation. Yet in holding himself up as China's preeminent national leader, Chiang had taken on unsupportable expectations of what he could deliver. Fury over stalled postwar revival, over food shortages, over hyperinflation, over centuries-old landlord depredations and official corruptions and peasant agonies, easily became fury at his rule—especially with a little encouragement from savvy Communist organizers. It was a domestic replay of the diplomatic resentments of World War II, when unmet promises of China's potential bred antipathy in Allied capitals. Chiang once again struggled to live up to a fatally heroic image. His stature was a curse.

The judgments were harsh, the forecasts dire. An American financial adviser to the Nationalists assessed that they were already years behind in implementing a serious financial reform to check inflation. The "ancient evils," worried Ambassador Stuart, had "reasserted their hold." There was talk of the Mandate of Heaven ceasing to grace Chiang's rule.

A former aide sent Marshall a series of *New Yorker* articles by John Hersey, the young Tianjin-born reporter so heartened by Marshall's progress the previous winter (and since then made famous by his dispatch from Hiroshima). "China has fallen apart once more," Hersey wrote, "and it looks now as if all of Chiang's horses and all of Chiang's men would have a very, very hard time putting her together again."

The day after his long discussion with Chiang, Marshall radioed an unvarnished account of their exchange to Washington. When his rear echelon delivered it to the Oval Office, Truman responded not just with his standard message of vague encouragement, but also with a note of permission: whenever Marshall thought it was time for him to come home, he could. The timing, the telegram specified, "is yours and yours alone to determine."

That was also the day, December 2, Marshall had set as his own deadline for an answer from Zhou. Since returning to Yenan, Zhou had given damning statements to journalists. Planeload after planeload of Communists had taken off from Nanjing and Shanghai and Beijing, headed north. But Marshall had asked for a straightforward answer to his straightforward question of whether anything more could be done. By December 3, he had still not gotten one.

A brief note arrived from Yenan two days later. Rather than a direct answer, it set out conditions for restarting negotiations. Zhou's demands—reverting to the troop positions of a year earlier, dissolving the National Assembly—were so flagrantly implausible that they made the answer to Marshall's question inescapably clear. The Communists as much as the Nationalists were committed to settling China's future by force.

Marshall got the point. The Communists were "beyond our reach." The only good he could do now was to stay in Nanjing as the National Assembly proceeded, in the hope that his presence would ensure as constructive an outcome as possible. The assembly would be a test of whether Chiang's regime could find a path to reform even without the pressure of Communist participation, and become the kind of partner Washington could fully back. So Marshall waited and watched. Nanjing was wet, windy, and cold.

On the evening of December 7—five years to the day since the Japanese attack on Pearl Harbor—the Chiangs came to #5 Ning Hai Road. Katherine, sinuses in rough shape, had decided to fly the following morning. Although she regretted leaving Marshall, especially with Christmas coming, he was insistent. She did not know how long she would be waiting for him in Honolulu. Madame Chiang and the Generalissimo said their good-byes, all promising to stay in touch.

Katherine took off early the next day. Marshall pestered aides for updates on her trip, unable to hide his concern. That afternoon, he joined Madame Chiang for a long walk on the slopes of Purple Mountain. (Marshall's hill walks could be strenuous enough to wear out young officers.) Madame Chiang had been a friend and a generous host to Katherine, and Marshall was grateful. He was equally grateful for Madame Chiang's help with his official efforts. Despite how things had turned out, he considered her a force for good. He thought Chiang would be "lost without her."

Katherine's departure set off another flurry of rumors that Marshall's would soon follow. Aides in both Washington and Nanjing fielded a barrage of phone calls from reporters demanding to know if the rumors were true. Chinese newspapers announced that Marshall would go home any day now—and continued to announce it day after day. The rumors were summarily denied. Caughey instructed his wife to ignore the apparent good news in the press (good at least as far as the family was concerned, since it would mean he was coming home).

"The General came out here for sixty days and he has been here for a year and he literally does not know when he will leave," Melby speculated. "Never having failed before, he cannot yet bring himself to admit he has failed this time."

But after a few days of rumor and denial, Marshall sent a note to Acheson: "It appears now very likely that I should return to Washington in the near future, though this possibility should not leak out."

His exit would be his last chance. As Marshall could see, neither side had been particularly interested in his mission succeeding for the past few months at least. They had been interested only in how it would end, and how that ending would be perceived, in China, in the United States, and by the rest of the world. A departure on the right note, with the right flourish, would usefully shape those perceptions.

On December 15, he wrote out a long message by hand—the first draft of a statement he would issue when he left. He had been discussing it with aides for a few days, wondering how he could both call out the Communists for their obstructionism and make "reactionary elements" in Nationalist ranks "see the handwriting on the wall," while bolstering the remaining liberals, of all parties, who might still be able to right China's course.

There was also the debate back home to consider. Since the midterm election, it had grown even more heated. Leading the campaign on one side was Luce. *Time* called for ending Marshall's efforts and letting Chiang finish off the Communists once and for all. Nationalist victories, it brightly proclaimed, made negotiation unnecessary. (Undercutting its own assurance, the magazine also warned: "If the U.S. does not openly and quickly give full material and economic support to the Nationalist Government, China must pass into the Russian orbit. This could only mean a U.S. strategic retreat to the line of the Mariana Islands.") Luce followed up with a private telegram, which Marshall found "shallow, if not completely biased" by personal connections.

Other recently laudatory voices turned derisive. "If George Marshall remains in China until he is as old as Methuselah, he won't make peace," General MacArthur told an adviser to the Nationalists. "Marshall, you know, will be running with Truman in the next campaign and he may even be number one." Marshall sensed not just the more sharply personal edge to the criticism, but also the damage it was doing to his efforts to encourage Chiang on a better path—and by extension, to Chiang's own prospects. The drumbeaters would stoke the militarists' fervor for a final showdown and, Marshall deplored, "seriously weaken my hand because of encouragement to the controlling clique."

Yet the pro-Nationalist view was not the only one gaining currency in the United States. Even as Luce and his allies called for all-out support of Chiang, other voices, equally strident, called for Washington to wash its hands of China altogether. "Chiang Kai-shek's brand of democracy is not ours, any more than is Mao Tse-tung's," wrote the Harvard scholar John Fairbank, who had done wartime intelligence work in China. "We have let our fears of Russia and of communism, on which the right-Kuomintang plays so skillfully, drive the Chinese revolution further into dependence on Russia and upon communism."

A new book about China was making American bestseller and Book-of-the-Month Club lists, and when it arrived in Nanjing, it caused a stir there as well. The young *Time* correspondent Teddy White had broken definitively from his boss and published (with another Luce reporter, Annalee Jacoby) a powerfully reported broadside called *Thunder Out of China*. It was the counterpoint to the visions of the Luce empire, with

Chiang not as Confucian-Christian savior but as lord of misrule. "We are left as the patrons of the decadent and corrupt, and the Russians become the patrons of the vigorous and dynamic," White and Jacoby wrote. "Americans must now realize one of the hard facts of Chinese politics—that in the eyes of millions of Chinese their civil war was made in America."

White had kind things to say about Marshall, praising his "integrity, wisdom, and devotion." Yet even he could not "reconcile a policy of peaceful words and warlike deeds." In Washington, according to White, the standard response to hard questions about that policy was "wait till Marshall gets back."

Acheson wrote Marshall to update him on the growing stateside contentiousness, with "extremists on one side calling for all-out support of Chiang and those on the other side advocating complete withdrawal of support." There was also a rising chorus of complaint from "impartial observers that they have not been kept fully informed of our actions in China," Acheson related. ("In a sense," wrote White, "all relations between the U.S. and China exist in the vest pocket of George Marshall.")

To address that complaint, Truman released a policy statement on December 18, ostensibly an update of the one timed with Marshall's initial departure for China. It clarified little, in Nanjing or Washington, mostly serving to reveal how many dilemmas had remained unresolved since Marshall had first waded into the policy debates the previous December. Reprising many of the same exhortations and elisions, along with a slew of new ones, it traced Marshall's efforts over the past year. "While avoiding involvement in their civil strife we will persevere with our policy of helping the Chinese people to bring about peace and economic recovery in their country," it proclaimed. In stressing an American commitment to a "united and democratic China," Truman omitted the third word in the old mantra—strong.

By now, that mantra—a strong, united, and democratic China—had taken on an ironic edge. Wits in the American embassy had taken to standing impudently at attention every time they heard the three words.

It reflected a general ill temper in Nanjing's official circles as the holidays approached. The cocktail parties and receptions started up again, but with little of the hope or good feeling of the year before in Chongqing. On Ning Hai Road, Katherine's absence was felt by all. Marshall was coming down with a cold, canceling social engagements and avoiding visitors. Madame Chiang sent fruit and candy and cheerily told him to get well by Christmas.

From Yenan, Truman's statement occasioned another blast of scorn. "If America wants to show respect for Chinese independence, she must withdraw troops from China," said a CCP spokesman. Until recently the face of conciliation, Zhou was now the most prominent voice of denunciation. Was it not clear, he asked, "that the United States and Chiang Kai-shek are working hand in glove to give free rein to large-scale hostilities?" Fliers scattered in the streets of Nanjing accused Marshall and MacArthur of colluding with Japanese militarists; Communist outlets compared Americans to Nazis.

Chiang, meanwhile, hoped to make Truman's statement play in his favor. He had already been concertedly cultivating Marshall, aware that his mission must be approaching its end. Noting rumors of a presidential run, Chiang repeated his request that Marshall stay as an adviser, insisting he could do more good in Nanjing than Washington. He asked for Marshall's advice on Chinese democracy. The substance of Truman's statement suggested that such appeals were doing some good. "What is important is that he put the blame for the failure of the mediation on the Communists," Chiang judged. "Marshall should be credited for this. He is perhaps moved by my sincerity."

Marshall was well aware that "blame for failure" was the paramount concern of both sides at this point. While Chiang searched for promising signals between the lines of Truman's statement, the Communists insisted they could not be said to have given up on talks, since Zhou's aides were still in Nanjing. (Marshall had come to have high regard for the skill of these Communist propagandists: "Their publicity campaign is without any regard to the facts but has a well defined purpose," while "the Government publicity has the same disregard for the facts but lacks clever direction.")

Marshall had been struggling over his own ongoing dilemmas—how to support the Nationalists without encouraging hard-liners and undercutting reform, how to spur reform without publicly tearing down the Nationalists and thus playing directly into the hands of the Communists. He did not want to "destroy the foundation" of Chiang's government, but he also considered it "useless to expect the United States to pour money into a Government dominated by a completely reactionary clique bent on exclusive control of governmental power." He would not give up entirely on the notion that a unified government might some day be possible—he even continued to speculate offhandedly that Mao could be de facto prime minister under a President Chiang Kai-shek—but it was abundantly clear that such a prospect was at best a long way off.

"At the present," Marshall reported to Washington, "I have been using all of my influence to force the adoption of a constitution in keeping with the PCC resolutions"—one that lived up to the high-minded political agreements struck over his first weeks in China, "a genuine democratic document" rather than "a hollow instrument of dictatorship." With the right constitution, the door back to a peaceful solution might, over the long run, remain open.

Initial signals from the National Assembly had been worrying. The absence of the Communists and key third parties meant that Nationalist delegates had the power to turn the proceedings into a "steamroller" rather than a deliberative body. (In a moment of frustration, Marshall had wondered out loud whether any of the Chinese even understood democracy.) But recent reports were more promising. The assembly was the biggest gathering of its kind that the world, not just China, had ever seen, and the lively give-and-take persuaded even some skeptical observers that it was more than just a charade. The draft constitution opened with a call for "a democratic republic of the people, for the people, and by the people."

What gave Marshall pause was his belief that, in the long run, political progress would depend on the existence of an opposition party to keep the Nationalists in check. He thought one-party control accounted for much of the decay over the years—"what happens when one group stands in continuous power without anybody to attack their motives and procedures." A coalition government, with the Communists functioning as "a constructive opposition party," would have created helpful pressure. With that possibility off the table, Chiang and the Nationalists would have to push forward toward democracy on their own. The conniving of the hard-liners so far, especially the previous spring when Marshall was in Washington, made unnervingly clear how hard that would be. "I did not expect the Kuomintang to surrender its power without a struggle," Marshall complained, "but I also did not expect the kind of chicanery which they have practiced since February." The party, he declared, "cannot reform itself."

That is where the third-party leaders and other liberals came in, or so Marshall, and others, hoped. If bringing the Communists into government was implausible, this small band, disjointed and often ineffectual as it was, could form the basis of a true middle in Chinese politics, checking extremists on both sides. The problem, as Marshall could see, was that rather than joining together, the "liberal elements" continued to bicker and take sides. Nationalist repression—the Nanjing train-station beating in June and the Kunming murders in July still loomed large—was driving many of them away.

"It is an ugly sight to watch a country increasingly being forced into one extreme or the other," observed Melby. "It makes any form of decent liberalism seem hopeless."

On Christmas Eve, the Chiangs hosted a small party. Marshall was the last to arrive. His cold had gotten worse, and he had canceled plans to attend Christmas services at St. Paul's, the local Episcopal church. But the Chiangs had worked hard to generate some good cheer for the Americans, and Marshall entered to find officers in dress uniforms and diplomats in dinner jackets standing around on a panda-skin rug, drinking martinis and Old Fashioneds as Christmas music played. After roast turkey and brandied fruitcake, a portly Nationalist official wearing a Santa Claus costume and hoisting a sack of presents emerged from behind a screen. He gave Marshall a reading stand to use in bed (his reading habits were well known) and joked, "You know, when I came past Honolulu I saw Katherine and she said to be sure to say hi to George." Marshall left as soon as he could, and the party broke up immediately afterward.

Around the same time, another Christmas party broke up six hundred miles to the north, in Beijing. Two U.S. marines had been drinking heavily at the Manhattan Club for most of the night. On their way to the next party, they came upon a 19-year-old woman, a Peking University student named Shen Chung. Later that night, police found them on the nearby Polo Grounds, Shen crying out that she had been raped. As the news made its way around China, protesters began heading into the streets, fury trained on the United States.

In Nanjing the next afternoon, Christmas Day, the National Assembly held its closing session. (Marshall declined an invitation to attend, instructing that no explanation be given for his absence.) Chiang presided over the ratification of a new Chinese constitution and walked off stage to cries of "Long live China!" The Communists, surprising no one, dismissed the text as a "fake constitution." But the assessments passed to Marshall were encouraging. Chiang had stood firm against the scheming and dissent of the CC Clique and other conservatives in his ranks. The final document promised national elections in 1947, governmental reform, and the return of the capital to Beijing. Whether any of this would actually be implemented, whether it would prove to be more than a "collection of words" without pressure from a strong opposition, was another question. But it was a start. Inside the hall, there was a notable feeling of accomplishment.

Outside, there were growing demonstrations. "Yanks, go home," students shouted at American troops. "Get out you beasts," read the signs. This time, rather than suppressing protests, Nationalist authorities ordered police protection for protesters. They knew the anger was real. "Every major turning point in modern Chinese history," Teddy White and Annalee Jacoby had written in *Thunder Out of China*, "has been signalized by student uprisings."

On the afternoon of December 28, Marshall visited Chiang for another difficult conversation. In Marshall's view, the risks to Chiang's rule were not just political and social and economic; they were also military.

Even many Americans were saying that "the Commies don't have a chance." The Nationalists had American planes and rifles and artillery, sometimes matched against Communist spears and sickles and pig knives. They had two or three times as many troops, and three or four times as many guns. Communist units were in retreat almost everywhere, including from many of their "liberated areas." Chiang's forces had claimed control of more of China than ever before, upwards of 80 percent, from perhaps 15 percent a little over a year earlier. The Communists "fight like babies," a Nationalist commander scoffed.

Chiang was readying his final offensive, certain that total victory would come at some point in 1947. The irritations of managing Marshall's mission would no longer be a drag on his ability to fight (or, for that matter, to suppress dissent). According to Chiang's plan, two large pincers of the best Nationalist divisions would cut off Mao's forces. Before the Soviets could effectively intervene to save them, the Communists would be annihilated.

Chiang had ordered attacks on remaining pockets of Communist strength. He had troops massing to take Yenan (despite promises to the contrary to Marshall, who no longer placed much stock in such promises anyway). He had even started extending his writ beyond Chinese shores, preparing to send decommissioned American Navy ships to seize islands in the South China Sea, based on a map of an expansive

U-shaped claim to the contested waters drawn up by his officials. He was confident: total victory was within reach, and it was time for a last burst of action.

"You can sometimes win a great victory by a very dashing action," Marshall would say. "But often, or most frequently, the very dashing action exposes you to a very fatal result if it is not successful." That was the danger he sought to get across now. Nationalist confidence in a great victory was in fact overconfidence, and overconfidence could be fatal. He wanted Chiang to recognize that his power, seemingly so vast, had limits.

Marshall reminded Chiang that Nationalist generals had been guaranteeing imminent victory since the spring, based on continual "faulty and optimistic estimates" of their strength. Again and again, they had predicted quick success; again and again, their predictions had proved wrong.

Marshall had served in his country's army for four decades. He had charted victories in two world wars. He had also witnessed the strange power of rebellion on his first tour in the Philippines, where an outgunned but spirited insurgent army inflicted great damage on a more modern force. When Marshall assessed that Chiang's "seeming success" was in reality "great weakness," it was with this long military experience in mind, along with everything he had seen in China over the past twelve months. In his assessment, Chiang's army was capable of neither "destroying the Communist Party by force," nor of "defending itself against the guerrilla tactics of the Communists." The Nationalists might appear to have control, but appearances could be deceiving. As American intelligence reports warned, "The military position of the Chinese Nationalists is actually much less improved than would appear on the surface."

Marshall and Chiang had discussed the risks of overextension for months, and Chiang was aware of the danger. But Marshall now saw prudence falling away in the fervor of final victory. Nationalist lines stretched and Nationalist forces spread themselves thin. And Marshall was far from the only one to identify the peril. "China is simply too vast," Wedemeyer had recently written in one of his missives to Nanjing. "It is obvious that we should not dissipate our resources all over China and Manchuria."

The extent of the Nationalists' advantage in weaponry, with hundreds of millions of dollars in modern arms sent by Washington, was also deceptive. In pursuit of fast-moving Communist troops, heavy American vehicles bogged down in the mud. Antitank guns got marooned miles from the front. American snow boots were too big for Chinese feet. And troubling numbers of the Nationalists' weapons were ending up in Communist hands, some captured, some bought from corrupt officers. "We do not know how much the Government is losing," Marshall admitted, but his sources suggested that the number was considerable. Communist troops sang: "We have no rifles, we have no cannon; the enemy makes them for us!"

When Chiang's forces won battles, victory often came at a steep price, steep enough to call into question whether they were really victories at all. A Nationalist general estimated that recent forward movement had consumed one-fifth of total strength and enough American ammunition and weaponry to supply tens of thousands of troops. To Marshall's dismay, Chiang continued to send army after army into Manchuria, many of them with little or no training, peasant boys sent to the slaughter with guns they barely knew how to fire.

The quality of Nationalist command was a big part of the problem. Marshall would rate Chiang "the worst advised military commander in history." Generals more interested in court politics than battlefield imperatives gave calamitously misleading assessments of military realities. Leadership positions went to "those politically acceptable rather than those qualified," noted an embassy analysis. (Until that changed, it added, "all efforts to strengthen the present army by increasing its technical and material means will result in no more than a temporary and superficial benefit.") Marshall had pressed Chiang to cashier the worst offenders—after all, a purged and rebuilt officer corps was key to American victory in World War II—but with little success.

The lapses went deeper than bad advice. Nationalist generals could be so suspicious of one another that they thwarted coordination and hoarded resources. Many were guilty of, in Chiang's words, "corruption and degeneracy," including selling supplies for profit. ("Jeeps had a habit of walking off if unwatched for a few minutes," Marshall would point out.) They abused their troops—ruining morale and driving junior enlisted men into Communist armies, where they were said to get better treatment—and also local populations in regions where it mattered most. In Manchuria, residents started to complain that life had been better under the Japanese.

Nationalist lapses played right into Communist strategy. As Marshall had pointed out to Chiang, the Communists had "no intention of making a stand or of fighting to a finish at any place"; they "lost cities and towns but they have not lost their armies." (Chiang's own experience gave him reason to recognize the potency of this strategy: he had done much the same to the Japanese.) As Chiang's forces advanced, Communist troops continued to recede into the hinterland, "luring the enemy in deep," where they waited to strike weak points in roads and rails and logistics networks. They were also well indoctrinated, fired with the belief that they were fighting for something right—especially those peasants who had benefited from land reform, a "gallant peasant army," the CCP proclaimed, "the best guarantee of our final victory." The Communists, White and Jacoby had written, "knew precisely what the peasants' grievances were and how those grievances could be transmuted into action."

For the past year, when he contemplated the consequences of his mission's failure, Marshall had thought of prolonged chaos and civil war, perhaps a return to "the dark ages of warlordism." Even Stalin, even Mao at many points, had considered total Communist victory as far-fetched as total Nationalist victory. But Marshall was starting to play out the string of consequences that flowed from his warnings. He had seen how impressive Communist command could be, how cunning a strategist Mao was. He realized that collapse was a real possibility, and collapse would be a boon to Communist prospects and an opening to Soviet infiltration. Where would that end? An earlier summary by an aide emphasized: "General Marshall concluded that so long as there remained in existence an independent Communist Government and independent Communist Army, China was highly vulnerable to undercover Soviet infiltration, which would result in the Communists overthrowing the Generalissimo by force of arms."

Thus his plea to Chiang now. Be farsighted, Marshall urged. His own mission, his attempt to cement peace and political democratization and military unification, may have failed. But it was not too late, Marshall said, for Chiang to change China. He could throw himself into winning over the Chinese people, into leading them along a better path, into building a liberal party, rather than risking everything on the battlefield. It would make him "the father of the country."

They had talked for two hours. As soon as he was back on Ning Hai Road, Marshall wrote a message to Truman. "It is quite clear to me that my usefulness will soon be at an end for a variety of reasons," Marshall conceded. He had become "persona non grata."

He still wanted to fire his last salvo, calling out both Nationalist reactionaries and the Communists. But beyond that, Marshall told the president, the mission was finished: "It is now going to be necessary for the Chinese, themselves, to do the things I endeavored to lead them into."

CHAPTER 16

Into the Fire

On the first day of 1947, just as on the first day of 1946, Hart Caughey was awakened early and ordered to get to Marshall's room as soon as he could. Caughey had spent nearly every day for a year at the great man's side, in awe throughout despite going from despair to dogged hope and back to despair about the mission's prospects. "I don't know when I've been so depressed," he wrote his wife on Christmas Eve. Sixteen months since the end of the war he was sent to China to fight, he still did not know when he could go home.

When Caughey reported, Marshall was in bed. The evening before, the Chiangs had thrown a party for his 66th birthday. Marshall showed up in their living room in dress uniform and was greeted by fifty guests—the usual array of officers and diplomats, but also Nationalist figures such as Chen Li-fu. Madame Chiang, fur draped over her shoulders, presented him a red-and-gold long-life candle. The Generalissimo toasted his labors in the cause of peace. (Other guests knew nothing of the request for recall Marshall had sent three days earlier and found his response strangely restrained.) He left at 9 p.m., not early enough to stave off a relapse of his lingering cold.

Sick in bed this New Year's morning, he had summoned Caughey for a change in plans. Marshall was supposed to fly to Shanghai for an Army-Navy football game and string of receptions. His cold gave him reason to skip the trip. But there was an added benefit to his not going. Protests over the Christmas Eve rape were getting bigger and angrier, and his arrival in Shanghai risked adding fuel to fire. Both Chiang and the city's mayor had requested that Marshall stay away. He would be a lightning rod for anti-American ire—demonstrations that day were being called "anti-US-brutality marches"—and they worried about what might happen.

Even in Nanjing, under tighter control, protests were growing. A crowd of 1,500 students massed outside the new American embassy— in an unfortunate resonance, the building had previously belonged to the Japanese puppet president—and spewed invective at every American they saw. "Bloody GI, Get out Before We Kick You Out," said banners. Marshall's aides took circuitous routes through the city to avoid hostile encounters with rock-throwing demonstrators. Elsewhere, the protests were larger. Crowds screamed that Washington was plotting to turn China into a colony; that Americans were worse than the Japanese; that just as American marines were violating Chinese women, the American government was violating Chinese sovereignty. Ambassador Stuart met with a delegation of students and tried to be conciliatory. But other American officers and officials argued, privately and publicly, that the incident had been blown out of proportion or even trumped up entirely, "the Dreyfus case of North China," perhaps a Communist setup. Such denials only made things worse.

For Chiang, the protests required a delicate response. A leader vying for the mantle of nationalism, he could hardly stand against them. Yet demands for American withdrawal threatened his interest in more military help. In a radio broadcast, he walked a fine line, hailing Chinese sovereignty while warning that the young were "too easily influenced and deceived."

Yenan could be more categorical. It spotted opportunity and was quick to take advantage, hailing the protesters' "struggle to the death" against "American imperialists and their running dogs." The rape of Shen Chung, it pronounced, was the rape of the entire Chinese nation.

The popular outrage was hardly of Communist manufacture, or the protests of Communist instigation. But it was just the kind of sentiment and circumstance that CCP leaders were adept at turning to their own revolutionary ends—particularly Zhou, who had long recognized that patriotic students could be made into useful allies. "Confused, frustrated and faithless," wrote Till Durdin in the *New York Times*, "the young people of China are in a mood that makes them ready tools for a campaign rooted in the already existing dissatisfaction with the government and with another country that has done much to support it."

Anti-Americanism had been on the rise for months, just waiting for the right spark to set off a nationalist conflagration. A little more than a year earlier, Chinese crowds could be heard chanting, "America is the very best." But before long, they were instead cursing the United States for fomenting war and thwarting peace. A Shanghai newspaper had recently polled 18,907 locals and claimed that 98.9 percent wanted American troops gone. Canadian shopkeepers started writing "Canada" on their front doors.

American officials could explain away the anger as a sublimation of other grievances. "Widespread resentment against Government which cannot be openly expressed is being turned almost entirely against the U.S.," rationalized an embassy report. Marshall detected CCP propaganda, "successful in stirring up an active and unreasoning anti-American feeling," especially among a "naive" Chinese intelligentsia, all with the aim of driving out the United States.

While there was some truth to such analysis, a string of other outrages involving American troops had preceded the rape. There were seemingly endless stories of bar fights and beaten prostitutes and black-marketeering. A drunk sailor thrashed a Shanghai rickshaw-puller to death. There were so many traffic accidents involving American military jeeps—"city tigers," some Chinese called them—that residents hinted darkly that these might not really be accidents. To add insult to injury, U.S. officers had negotiated a deal allowing their troops to be tried in U.S. military courts, evoking the impositions of imperialists past.

"The fund of Chinese good-will toward the United States is a tangible asset to our credit in this country and a factor which exists outside the realm of ideologies and political parties," Marshall had observed earlier. Now, he feared, that good-will risked being "tossed to the winds in the destruction of the great respect in which the world has held the American Army."

To an unsettling degree, it had happened already. The United States, Melby assessed, "has lost an amount of goodwill and friendliness that is equaled only by the amount of goodwill the Russians have lost. I think it would be difficult to exaggerate the hatred in which we are both held."

On January 3, Marshall, still sick, received two confidential messages from Washington. The first, a telegram from Secretary of State Byrnes, was a response to Marshall's admission that there was nothing left to do. "We are in hearty accord with the course you have pursued and the views you express as to future action," the telegram read. It ended with a request from the president that Marshall return to the United States for consultations on China and "other matters."

The second was from the president himself. He had summoned Marshall's rear echelon to the Oval Office for a message that was to be conveyed to Nanjing in "utmost secrecy." Truman wanted Marshall back as soon as possible, for reasons related to those "other matters"— "the project the President has previously discussed with you." Marshall did not need further clarification. Truman had not dropped the idea of replacing Secretary of State Byrnes after all. Marshall's worries were about to expand in both scale and scope, his retirement put off a while longer.

"Your country is fortunate in having the benefit of your counsel at this critical time," Truman had written a few days earlier in a birthday note. The fact that "the Chinese have fallen short of acting upon your wise counsels" had done nothing to alter that judgment.

Both the Nationalists and the Communists had chosen to act on those counsels only when it suited them. Marshall looked back at the seeming miracles and subsequent disappointments of his mission's opening act and judged: "They were both so frequently in the wrong that there was never a clear case for either side, except possibly in last February when I felt the Communists had played the game with cleaner hands than the Government." To the extent the Communists had, it was only insofar as they thought a successful negotiation was in their interest—they had their own reasons to cooperate. As those reasons changed, as a result of both Nationalist reactions and, even more, Soviet encouragement, they had stopped playing along. At critical moments throughout the mission, each side had cause to put off a settlement in order to press its advantage—stringing Marshall along until it decided his services as a mediator might once again be of value. Ultimately, both sides were right to be suspicious of the other.

For all the sense of China as some exotic other, Americans tended to project their own country's experience onto China's struggles. Was the divide between Nationalists and Communists really so different from the divide between Republicans and Democrats? (If Democrats and Republicans had independent armies, Wedemeyer had quipped, they would be at war as well.) Marshall was not immune to the temptations of American analogy. He had talked about baseball umpires and Benjamin Franklin, about American rights and freedoms. He had pointed out that Americans were still arguing about their own civil war—supposedly evidence that two sides did not have to agree on history to coexist in a government. (The American civil war was not mere history to Marshall: his own family had been split by it, and he had been the only northerner in his class at the Virginia Military Institute at a time when the war was a fresh wound for southern cadets.) Of course, the analogy could be turned on its head: if it took a civil war for Americans to work out fundamental political questions, perhaps the Chinese needed a civil war as well. Still, such projections made it easy to imagine China, with the right advice or assistance or exhortation, quickly becoming the great power America wanted it to be.

Marshall would sometimes speak of China's potential for greatness. Its resources, its economic promise, its population—"all should combine to free the people from their present distress and lift China to its rightful position among the nations of the world." But the vision had become vague and aspirational; Marshall did not think it would happen any time soon.

To most Americans, that whole line of speculation seemed fanciful at this point. Their concern was less China's potential for world leadership than China's relevance to US-Soviet competition. As Marshall thought about how best to end his mission, the embassy worked on its own reassessment of the U.S. position. The end result, dispatched to Washington, emphasized that the Kremlin was intent on using "confusion and chaos . . . to precipitate a collapse which can be fully exploited," and that "the most logical instrument for the accomplishment of this objective is the Chinese Communist Party." The embassy saw little cause for hope that the government would reverse the deterioration, by showing the Chinese people "that it can give them a life at least as good, if not better, than the Communists hold out." The Nationalists, "if left unmolested, will surely dig their own graves and prepare confirmation of the Communist thesis."

On January 5, two days after receiving Truman's request, Marshall replied with a message for the president: "I think I fully understand the matter to be discussed. My answer is in affirmative if that continues to be his desire. My personal reaction is something else."

He began choreographing his exit, with the precision of a director and the flair of an actor, for maximal impact on his audience. He would tell almost no one, not even most aides, until a couple of days before. He would time the public announcement to get the news into the press just a day in advance. He would put out a bracing statement as he left. And then he would let the impact of his valedictory rebuke sink in for a few days—before revealing that he was taking over as secretary of state, the shock of his appointment compounding the shock of his departure.

He hoped the sequence would, somehow, spur a constructive

rethinking in Nationalist circles that would, someday, allow a return to peaceful unification. In giving up he might achieve what he had been unable to by keeping on, a jolt to set things on a better course. Either way, it would be his mission's final move.

To maintain surprise, Marshall accepted invitations for dates when he would be long gone. He asked aides in Washington to stop forwarding mail, but to tell no one they were doing so. Since most of the staff living at #5 Ning Hai Road had no idea what was coming, he delayed packing. Caughey, one of the few in the know, had to resist settling outstanding debts from his games of darts.

On January 6, at dusk, Marshall went to see Chiang. It had been a dreary weekend in Nanjing, and it was rainy and windy as Marshall passed through wet and darkening streets. He had decided the day before that he would fly on the morning of January 8.

Marshall promptly delivered the news, and Chiang responded with a disquisition on past American slights: the Yalta accords in February 1945, the Moscow summit the following December, various risible proposals for US-Soviet-British cooperation in China. It was Chiang in proud Nationalist mode, and Marshall was not sure what to make of it at this particular moment. Ever since concluding that further mediation was futile, Marshall had struggled to make Chiang see that he must embrace change on his own, constructing a more open China that would give the Communists a stark choice between cooperating and being marginalized. Marshall held out hope that Chiang would come around, whatever the objections of his most trusted hard-line advisers and other self-serving sycophants around him. In that regard, this response was not especially encouraging.

Marshall omitted a detail from their conversation—the coming secretary of state nomination. Not even Chiang would know beforehand. Each of them had spoken of this current undertaking as a final act: Chiang said he would defeat Mao and then step down, responsibilities finished; Marshall would fulfill his China mission and get back to his aborted retirement. Each, however, was coming to sense that, far from a final act, he was in the first stage of an even greater challenge. It was not turning out to be the ending either of them hoped.

On his last day in China, Marshall had a full schedule. He wanted to avoid a flood of lavish events and formal obligations—an added reason for the last-minute announcement—but people scrambled to get a few minutes of his time, just as they had upon his arrival thirteen months before.

He saw Nationalist figures he regarded as forces for good, reminding them that "courage and patriotism" among liberals was key to China's future. He understood the weaknesses of these squabbling factions, in both Nationalist ranks and third parties. Yet the only way forward was for them to join together to push Chiang, and China, in the right direction.

He saw one of the Communist representatives left behind by Zhou, who had never given him the courtesy of a direct answer to his question. Marshall recognized that it had become "almost impossible to deal with the Communists."

He saw T. V. Soong and warned of the "disagreeable" statement to come, explaining that he felt compelled to deliver it, in an effort to "arouse bitterness and anger" among the "radicals, reactionaries, and irreconcilables."

He left letters of recommendation for his driver ("careful, understands motor cars") and masseur ("an excellent masseur"). He invited a group of children to Ning Hai Road for ice cream and let them stay to watch a movie as he continued his meetings. He received a gift from the embassy staff, a watch like one he had recently admired on Walton Butterworth's wrist.

In the evening, he saw Chiang. Over Marshall's last Chinese meal, each delivered a warm toast. Marshall praised Chiang's thoughtfulness and sincerity; that Chiang had remained courteous and composed even in harsh moments was, Marshall thought, the sign of a "really big man." Chiang also made a last bid for unqualified American support—

and thought he may have made the case at last. That night he wrote of Marshall: "He was grateful for my hospitality and patience. This is attributable to me holding my tongue and bearing insults for the past year. Whether he will assist me or not, it will be a success for me if he leaves without holding any grudges against me."

The Chiangs had scrambled to get parting gifts together. For Caughey, there was a silk robe to take to his wife, decorated in plum blossoms—"symbolic of the triumph of the spirit in adversity," Madame Chiang explained. For Marshall, there was a note signed by Chiang to pass to President Truman: "In her hour of crisis, my country has been most fortunate in having General Marshall with us."

Marshall's final statement was meant to insult, but it was not a surly outburst. It was a carefully aimed parting shot.

Marshall had worked on the text for almost a month. He had exact specifications for its release, everything from header ("personal statement by General Marshall") to timing (no more than twenty-four hours after the announcement of his departure). His words were chosen to provoke radicals on both sides. Seeing him gone, they would attack him as viciously in public as they did in private. And then, later, the announcement of his new position would come. In the case of the Communists, the vitriol would be clarifying. In the case of the Nationalists, it would sideline hard-liners—since Chiang, the thinking went, could not afford to keep close advisers who had openly maligned the new secretary of state. Marshall hoped the result would be to "strengthen the position and influence of the better elements."

The final text opened with a litany of denunciations. "Sincere efforts to achieve settlement have been frustrated time and again by extremist elements of both sides," Marshall wrote. He denounced the Nationalists' "dominant group of reactionaries who have been opposed, in my opinion, to almost every effort I have made to influence the formation of a genuine coalition government" yet were banking "on substantial American support regardless of their actions." He denounced the

Communists' "unwillingness to make a fair compromise," "wholesale disregard of facts," and readiness to inflict great hardship on the Chinese people in pursuit of "an economic collapse to bring about the fall of the Government, accelerated by guerrilla action." (He also, at last, openly derided Yenan's excuses for the Anping ambush that killed four Marines in July as "almost pure fabrication.") He denounced both sides' "overwhelming suspicion"—"they each seemed only to take counsel of their own fears"—even while acknowledging the fundamental conflict between their visions. The Communists, he specified, "frankly state that they are Marxists and intend to work toward establishing a communistic form of government."

Caught in the crossfire, Marshall lamented, was "the long suffering and presently inarticulate mass of the people of China." Yet after the litany of denunciation, his solution sounded almost plaintive: "The salvation of the situation—as I see it—would be the assumption of leadership by the liberals in the Government and in the minority parties, a splendid group of men, who as yet lack the political power to exercise a controlling influence. Successful action on their part under the leadership of Generalissimo Chiang Kai-shek would, I believe, lead to unity through good government."

Among Marshall's 1,800 words, any interested party could find something to fix on for its own purposes.

Chiang would insist that the statement was "friendly and constructive" and appeal to his party to "accept good-naturedly any well-intentioned criticisms."

Chen Li-fu would thank Marshall for "calling our attention to the fact that the Chinese Communists are Marxists of the pure breed," yet protest that the Nationalists accused of being "reactionaries" were simply more sophisticated in their understanding of Communist tactics.

Some Nationalist officials would bite their tongues and merely acknowledge that the statement was "unusually frank." One would score it "55 percent for the government, 45 percent for the Communists."

Zhou would condemn Marshall's entire mission as treachery and mock Marshall's belief that "this rotten government, still headed by the same Chiang Kai-shek, can suddenly be transformed into a good one." Mao would proclaim: "We are now on the eve of revolution."

Both Nationalist and Communist newspapers would censor key portions of the statement. One military-backed Nationalist outlet would quote just the parts about the Communists and claim that Marshall was calling for their complete extermination. Others would delete the word "reactionary."

The third parties, their unity Marshall's only remaining hope, would be divided in their response. "That General Marshall has not accomplished his mission in China," the Democratic League would conclude, "is not a personal failure but is a failure of American policy."

Henry Luce, though privately judging the statement fair, would wonder whether it was time to "blow the whistle" on Marshall.

The Soviets would turn openly hostile, the once genial ambassador to China accusing Marshall of playing the "ugly role of Chiang Kai-shek's herald" and doing the bidding of "reactionary Republicans."

"Marshall's farewell 'a plague on both your houses' statement has the Chinese vacillating between stunned silence and anguished screams," Melby would sum up. "American interest in China," he figured, "is now gone for a while. Later it will be different."

Yet for all the furor, the reaction amounted to less than Marshall had intended. Events far away would upend his choreography.

On January 8, just before 8 o'clock in the morning, Marshall stepped out of a black Cadillac and onto the gravel at Nanjing's airfield. It was here that, thirteen months earlier, the Chiangs had first welcomed him to China. It was here that, in the spring, Eisenhower had landed with a secret request from the president. It was from here that Marshall had set out on eight summertime trips to Kuling, going up and down the mountain as things fell apart below.

On this morning the airfield was slick with snowmelt. Marshall, in trench coat and peaked cap, shook hands with those who had come to see him off. There were assorted American diplomats and officers,

Ambassador Stuart smiling in a fedora, and a stone-faced Communist. The Generalissimo's bulletproof limousine pulled up a few minutes late, and the Chiangs accompanied Marshall up the stairway and onto his plane to say good-bye. "Come back," Madame Chiang told him, "come back soon." Chiang looked into Marshall's eyes as they shook hands.

The plane took off shortly after 8:00. It would make its way, island by island, to Honolulu, where Marshall was due a week of rest. He was leaving China with little, just as he had arrived. Most of the gifts he had received—watercolors, tea sets, ivory carvings—had either been quietly shipped back already or left behind in the frenzied departure. As when coming, he was returning with just three aides: a clerk; his cook and orderly, Richard Wing; and Hart Caughey, who was glad to be both going home and extending his time with Marshall. "Adequate words are not within me to give you a true idea of how great a man I think he is," Caughey, sitting on the plane as they began the trip, wrote in a letter to his wife. "If General Marshall can't, no one can."

John Melby watched from the ground, noting that he was the only official who had been in China for Marshall's arrival and was still there now. "It was a gallant cause, perhaps doomed to failure from the start, but worth the try," he reflected in a letter to his mistress, Lillian Hellman. Doomed or not, failure had bleak implications: "Lacking any external restraint the boys are now quite naturally getting down to the really grim business of fighting a civil war as she is fought in China. . . . The really ugly part of this business is just getting under way."

Chiang also took the opportunity to reflect. When saying good-bye on the plane, he thought there had been tears in Marshall's eyes and concluded, "I can see that he is a man of sentiments." Going forward, Chiang believed Marshall would be on his side, through the next and final phase of operations against the Communists. "He and I ending like this is the biggest achievement of the past year," Chiang wrote in his diary, with both triumph and relief. "It occurred to me," he added, "that Marshall's wife had once told him that Chairman Chiang would do whatever needs to be done if he thinks what he does is right or necessary. I think his wife is more astute than him."

Three hours after taking off, Marshall's plane was over Okinawa. The island—where more than 100,000 American and Japanese troops had been killed in battle two years earlier, and which was now fast becoming a citadel of American military power—was visible below. All of a sudden, the pilot stepped into the cabin and addressed Marshall: "Congratulations, Mr. Secretary."

News of the appointment had come in over the cockpit radio. A leak had forced Truman to make the announcement early. Far from going home to ride and garden and read, Marshall was in fact about to, as he put it, "step from the frying pan and into the fire."

Caughey opened a bottle of scotch, a parting gift from another officer, and gushed about Marshall's singular value to the country. Marshall shook his head and sighed, "Poor Mrs. Marshall."

Losing China

On June 5, 1947, five months after leaving Nanjing, Secretary of State Marshall traveled to Cambridge, Massachusetts, to receive a twice-postponed honorary degree from Harvard. Two years before, war had forced him to forgo it; one year before, the China mission had. Finally at Harvard, he took the opportunity to share a few words. They would become the most famous of his life.

In his matter-of-fact way, Marshall described Europe's devastation and what it meant for America. He highlighted the menace of "hunger, poverty, desperation, and chaos." He outlined the imperative of "breaking the vicious circle and restoring the confidence of the European people." He called on his country to "do whatever it is able to do to assist in the return of normal economic health in the world, without which there can be no political stability and no assured peace." Yet there was a catch: America could achieve little on its own. It should be willing to offer assistance on a previously unthinkable scale, but only if the recipients themselves took certain steps. "The initiative," Marshall said, "must come from Europe."

Truman decided to call the aid effort the Marshall Plan, since only naming it after Marshall gave it any hope of clearing Congress. It would be the largest foreign-assistance package in history, nearly $13 billion in total*—a spur to European recovery, a check on Soviet expansion, a shining example of American leadership. As in China, Marshall saw the dangers of chaos and desperation. As in China, he saw overcoming those dangers as the precondition to overcoming a Communist threat. Unlike in China, he saw partners willing to do what only they could to make assistance work.

Marshall had arrived back in Washington in January. Ahead of his return, the Senate had unanimously confirmed him as secretary of state, and messages of congratulations and offers of help had poured in (including from, of all people, Patrick Hurley). When he reached Washington, Katherine and Caughey along, Marshall took care of one persistent rumor before taking up his new task. He reiterated to reporters that he would not run for president in 1948, or ever. A tense, unsettled world gave him enough to catch up on without political distractions.

There were challenges everywhere, and for thirteen months Marshall had thought of little besides China. It did not take long for him to start repeating the warnings and exhortations of his final days as army chief of staff, now with new urgency and perspective. "Peace has yet to be secured," he told students weeks into the job, "and how this is accomplished will depend very much upon the American people"—a "heavy responsibility," but shirked at great peril. "We can act for our own good," he would declare, "by acting for the world's good."

When Marshall first went before Congress as secretary of state, however, his previous mission dominated discussion. Behind closed doors, he was as blunt as he had been with Chiang. He laid out the dilemmas and what it would take for American help to make a real difference in China. "Certain things have to happen over there," he said. "The great problem is how much deterioration sets in before those things do happen."

Since Marshall's departure, every last agreement had collapsed. The Executive Headquarters and Committee of Three had officially dis-

---

* Equivalent to $130 billion in real dollars today, and roughly $900 billion today measured as a percentage of GDP.

solved. As promised, the Americans were flying Communist personnel to Yenan, and the remaining members of the Dixie Mission were
boarding return flights out. The equipment for Marshall's aborted
"elementary school" for Communists had been repurposed to train
Nationalists. Chiang had taken Marshall's exit as his opportunity
to fight without restraint, more confident than ever in his prospects.
(He took Marshall's apology for not mentioning the secretary of state
appointment beforehand as a sign that there was no lingering ill will.)
Melby, staying on in Nanjing, was more pessimistic than ever: "All
over and in all directions the signs of deterioration are deepening and
accelerating."

"One of the saddest, or rather the most inexcusable, things is to say
'I told you so,'" Marshall testified before Congress. "But this was all
foreseen and all stated again and again and again."

As China continued on its course, global tensions sharpened. In
March, Marshall attended another Moscow great-power summit, where
any lingering hope for concord definitively ended. While Marshall was
there, Truman called for assistance to Greece and Turkey in their fights
against Communist insurgency and Soviet infiltration. "It must be the
policy of the United States to support free peoples who are resisting
attempted subjugation by armed minorities or outside pressures," he
pronounced—what soon became known as the Truman Doctrine.

Two days later, the Nationalist assault on Yenan began. Chiang's
chief of staff said the Communists would be finished in three months.

Marshall supported Truman's call to assist Greece and Turkey, but
found its language too sweeping, too resistant to prioritization, too
uniform in approach. For aid to work, there would have to be a shared
commitment. "No amount of assistance can prove effective or of lasting benefit unless the Greek people themselves are prepared to work
together resolutely for their own salvation," he said. That meant freeing
political prisoners. It meant rejecting "armed extremists of whatever
political complexion." Perceptive observers pointed out that Marshall's
message was "strikingly similar in spirit to his now famous statement
on the Chinese situation."

Marshall also knew that Greece and Turkey were just the beginning. As he registered desperation throughout Europe, he returned to dilemmas that had occupied him before—how to reverse the chaos and collapse that invited Communist success; how to engender faith in democratic societies; how to help to the greatest extent possible without obscuring the fact that "basic responsibility for European recovery rests on the European countries themselves." If the effort in Europe was to work, it had to overcome those dilemmas in ways that Marshall could not in China.

To come up with a plan, he summoned George Kennan, the diplomat whose telegrams from Moscow he had read over the prior year. Marshall wanted Kennan to head up a new State Department strategy outfit, the Policy Planning Staff, and make European assistance its first task. When Kennan received the charge and requested instructions, Marshall offered just one: "avoid trivia."

Almost as soon as the Marshall Plan was announced, the appeals began. There should be a Marshall Plan for China, said Chiang's ambassador in Washington. There should be a Marshall Plan for Latin America, said South American governments. There should be a Marshall Plan for the entire Far East, said intelligence reports. So began a venerable tradition in American statecraft: for every problem, a Marshall Plan was the solution.

Marshall himself disagreed. Even if one great challenge consumed strategists, he resisted pressure for one great solution. The best approach, he would say, comprised "not big things but many little things."

During World War II, Marshall had struggled to manage "the hungry table"—the continual clamor of needy allies and "localitis"-afflicted commanders for more support. As secretary of state, he presided over another hungry table. American power was vast, vaster than any other nation's and at any other time, but not limitless. He had to weigh proliferating needs, to distinguish the vital from the secondary, vital and achievable from vital but futile. Otherwise, the Communists' aptitude for chaos could disperse American effort across so many fronts that all might be lost. "There is a tendency to feel that wherever the Communist influence is brought to bear . . . we should immediately meet it, head on as it were," Marshall cautioned. "I think this would be a most unwise procedure for the reason that we would be, in effect, handing over the initiative to the Communists."

A few months after Marshall's return, the Nationalists took Yenan. As CCP forces retreated, Mao decreed: "fight no battle unprepared, fight no battle you are not sure of winning."

To Marshall, in the new global struggle, the battle for Europe was not just most vital but also the one he could be most confident of winning. Soviet domination of the continent, given its resources and relative proximity, was America's "strategic nightmare." A Kremlin-controlled Europe would, Marshall assessed, "impose incalculable burdens upon this country and force serious readjustments in our traditional way of life." Fortunately, prospects for holding the line in Western Europe were decent, as long as Europeans proved willing to do their part. On this score, Marshall was quickly heartened. While he had pledged never to campaign for the presidency, he was soon flying around the United States campaigning for his aid plan with all the fervor of a candidate. It was "the greatest decision in our history," he proclaimed, crucial to "the survival of the kind of world in which democracy, individual liberty, economic stability, and peace can be maintained."

Marshall repeated at every turn: "Only the Europeans themselves can finally solve their problems." Of China he said the same: "the main part of the solution of China's problems is largely one for the Chinese themselves."

For American security, the stakes in China were high, but not as high as in Europe. "China does not itself possess the raw material and industrial resources which would enable it to become a first-class military power within the foreseeable future," Marshall argued, especially in its present state of "social and political revolution." Western Europe had industrial capacity that, if harnessed by a Soviet military machine, would constitute a mortal threat; China did not. Turkey would offer a crucial base in a war against Moscow; China would not. When the Joint Chiefs of Staff ranked countries by the importance of their defense to national security, China was thirteenth—behind even Korea and Japan, to the chagrin of Nationalist officials.

Yet for Marshall, as ever, preliminary to the question of should was the question of could. If the answer to the latter was no, the former was academic. His thirteen months in China gave him ample cause for skepticism, at a time when every dollar, officer, or weapon sent to Chiang was a dollar, officer, or weapon not available elsewhere.

Even leaving aside governance, China presented challenges. There was growing anti-Western nationalism, ferociously clear in the protests ahead of Marshall's departure. There was sheer scale—as Kennan's Policy Planning Staff noted, "an area twice the size of Europe and with a population three times that of Europe is afflicted with most of the ills of Europe, including ideological conflict, plus those arising from a precipitate and concentrated transition from medievalism to modernism." Calls to back Chiang to the same extent as Greece ignored that greater Shanghai alone was roughly the size of Greece.

Above all, there was the fact of Chiang and his party needing to change in profound ways for aid to have the desired effect. In Europe, a few years of assistance were likely to get economies working again; the same could not be said for China. Militarily, Chiang continued the self-defeating practices Marshall had deplored—retaining bad generals, neglecting training and morale, overextending lines, and alienating local populations. No amount of aid or advice could counteract those shortcomings. The Nationalists already had the advantage in weapons and troops, as well as a surfeit of counsel, as Marshall knew from unhappy experience: "They greeted me in the most sympathetic fashion and did nothing."

As the Truman Doctrine and Marshall Plan took hold, Chiang and his champions fixed on Washington's supposed double standard. The situations in Europe and Asia were "identical," they asserted. To approach the two differently, charged Representative Walter Judd, was both "racist and naive"; Chiang speculated that Marshall was driven by antipathy toward the "yellow-skinned." If the United States was set on containing Communism, the argument went, China deserved as unstinting a commitment as any other country. (Kennan, the progenitor of containment, countered: "If I thought for a moment that the precedent of Greece and Turkey obliged us to try to do the same thing in China, I would throw up my hands and say we had better have a whole new approach to the affairs of the world.")

For Marshall, realism about what could be done in China did not mean giving up and doing nothing. He rejected calls to end aid—Truman grumbled about "pouring sand in a rathole"—or renounce Chiang. (That would put the United States in the lousy position of administering the "coup de grace" to the Nationalists.) He asked colleagues for ideas and solicited proposals for "what we can conceivably do." He pushed piecemeal assistance, hoping to "provide a breathing space" for reform. He also loosened the arms embargo in place since the last months of his mission. At the time it was implemented, Nationalist armies had been well supplied, as Chiang's disregard of the embargo made clear. But once concerns over potential shortages arose, Marshall let up, allowing munitions dumps to be "abandoned" to the Nationalists and, by May 1947, scrapping the embargo altogether.

"I have tortured my brain," Marshall said in June, shortly after giving his Harvard speech, "and I can't now see the answer."

He even turned to General Wedemeyer, sending him temporarily back to China in July. "A Marshall Plan for China?" headlines speculated. But after several weeks on the ground, Wedemeyer was despairing. His reports painted a grim picture of "apathy and bewilderment," "pathetic" troops, and police suppression of "the mildest forms of political disagreement." Without sweeping change, all-out assistance "would merely make rich men richer and the Chinese Communists would march on successfully." He recommended more military and economic aid, arguing Washington should try to save the situation no matter how long the odds. But nothing in his analysis—this from one of Chiang's most ardent advocates—suggested that even a major increase would do much good. Before returning, he excoriated Nationalist officials for every failing Marshall identified, and more. ("The insult imposed upon us by Wedemeyer is even worse than that of Marshall and Stilwell," Chiang lamented.) The Communists were in "excellent spirit," Wedemeyer concluded, the Nationalists "spiritually insolvent."

Amid the push to get the Marshall Plan through Congress, Marshall also backed a $500 million China Aid bill (in part to head off opposition to European assistance by Chiang's advocates among American legislators). At 10 percent of what would go over the same period to Western Europe, an economy more than five times larger, the package was hardly insignificant. But it was less than the Nationalists wanted, in scale and kind, and Marshall knew it was likely to achieve little other than "buying time."

His position changed in another regard as well: if a coalition government had ever been a viable idea, Marshall conceded it was no longer. Instructions went to American diplomats in Nanjing: "overlook no suitable opportunity to emphasize the pattern of engulfment which has resulted from coalition governments in eastern Europe." What had appeared essential in 1945, even to Chiang's American champions, appeared dangerously fanciful in the world that had taken shape since.

Through 1948 and into 1949, the situation deteriorated along lines many predicted, and then abruptly got much worse.

Although his forces had retreated everywhere, Mao promised victory in five years. Less than two years later, on October 1, 1949, he stood on Beijing's Gate of Heavenly Peace and, Zhou beside him, declared the founding of the People's Republic of China. Two months after that, Chiang fled to Taiwan, never to return.

Much about how this happened was, as Marshall put it, "foretold." The undoing began in Manchuria, where overextended Nationalist armies led by high-handed commanders made for easy targets. (American advisers urged Chiang to cut his losses and consolidate his position farther south, but he demurred.) The Communists captured huge quantities of American arms and turned them back on their intended beneficiaries. ("He is losing about 40 percent of his supplies to the enemy," Marshall said of Chiang. "If the percentage should reach 50 percent he will have to decide whether it is wise to supply his own troops.") Nationalist forces switched sides en masse—including, as the end neared, former Committee of Three member Chang Chi-chung. City dwellers and liberals increasingly backed the CCP as well, as inflation spiraled upward, political repression intensified, and Chiang retracted promises of reform.

As the CCP advanced, it was no longer waging a war of daring guerrilla strikes, as its mythology held, but of massive battles. Its decisive campaign, starting in late 1948, approached world-war scale, with encounters involving hundreds of thousands of troops and spanning hundreds of miles. And as Mao tallied wins, Stalin took another look at his Chinese comrades and conceded he had been wrong to doubt them. Realizing revolution had a chance, he increased the flow of weapons and assistance. CCP griping about Soviet stinginess, though never allayed entirely, started to ease. (Mao still could not get a face-to-face meeting with Stalin.) A new American intelligence operation, the Central Intelligence Agency, reported that, while hard evidence was difficult to come by, Soviet support was undoubtedly growing.

In Washington, warnings got more strident. If China fell, Communism would proceed like "a snowball rolling down into the valley of despair and destruction," said Wedemeyer. Congressman Judd used a baseball analogy: Communism would reach first base in China, second base in the rest of Asia, third base in Africa, and home in America.

As warnings escalated and the Communists advanced, so did calls to do something to stop them. General Douglas MacArthur, not known for prudence, quipped that anyone advocating ground troops for China "should have his head examined." Yet various proposals sought to heighten American commitment in ways that Marshall feared would lead dangerously in that direction. Wedemeyer wanted to send 10,000 advisers, with leeway to get more closely involved. James Forrestal, in the new post of secretary of defense, promoted a plan to revive the Flying Tigers. Senior army officers wanted to take command of ten Nationalist divisions. Naval officers wanted a joint American-Nationalist force, to "stand and hold, come hell or high water." Nationalist officials proposed placing American advisers throughout their ranks and American bases on Chinese soil. Henry Luce published a slashing essay in *Life* by former ambassador William Bullitt urging American oversight of Chiang's armies, with MacArthur in charge. ("The independence of the U.S. will not live a generation longer than the independence of China," Bullitt declared.) At the other extreme were schemes to unseat Chiang and install someone more pliant.

Marshall resisted the push, intervening with Truman when necessary. He supported assistance but opposed anything suggesting "direct responsibility for the conduct of civil war in China, or for the Chinese economy, or both." He backed military advice but blocked steps that raised the risk of "getting sucked in" along an unpredictable path of intervention and escalation. Failed half-measures could too easily necessitate larger commitments. Ultimately, he warned, the United States would "have to be prepared to take over the Chinese Government, practically, and administer its economic, military, and government affairs." That would not just spur a nationalist backlash among Chinese, likely negating any benefits. "It would involve this Government in a continuing commitment from which it would be practically impossible to withdraw."

The price of that commitment would be high. It would mean less for "more vital regions where we now have a reasonable opportunity of meeting or thwarting the Communist threat," and a "dissipation of resources" that would "inevitably play into the hands of the Russians." Yet it was not just about resources. A full-scale military commitment would, Marshall warned, involve "obligations and responsibilities . . . which, I am convinced, the American people would never knowingly accept. We cannot escape the fact that the deliberate entry of this country into the armed effort in China involved possible consequences in which the financial costs, though tremendous, would be insignificant when compared to the other liabilities involved." In his assessment, to have even a hope of destroying the CCP by force, Chiang would need "full-scale American intervention"—at a minimum several hundred thousand troops. And loose talk of World War III only heightened Marshall's leeriness. "The Chinese have long been intent on the U.S. going to war with Soviet Union," he noted, "with the expectation that the U.S. would drag the Chinese Government out of its difficulties."

Marshall's position infuriated Chiang. "Every time I see soldiers without wisdom, troops in disorder, and youngsters being rude," he fumed, "it reminds me that all of this is Marshall's fault." Yet as ever, Chiang was resolute: "Since God loves me and entrusted me with a mission, I will not quit halfway. What can the likes of Marshall and Stalin do to me?"

His salvation was supposed to come with the 1948 American presidential election. Chiang had been hearing for years that Truman and Marshall would be driven out by more sympathetic Republicans. "If Marshall does not change his insulting policies towards China he will without a doubt lose momentum," Chiang reassured himself. "The American people will not be controlled by a warlord." On the campaign trail, Thomas Dewey, the Republican nominee, pledged additional advisers and weapons and, according to messages from Wedemeyer, would be open to even more once in the White House. Chen Li-fu crossed the Pacific to hand a letter to Dewey—seeing Marshall in Washington, Chen claimed to be there observing democracy in action—and returned with promises of a significant military commitment. The assurances reinforced Chiang's "almost mystical" faith, as Stuart put it, that America would rescue him; there were reports of his troops withdrawing into cities and hunkering down until Dewey won. As election day in November approached, Dewey led in the polls by double digits.

Truman's victory was a shock for many, but an especially unpleasant one for Chiang. "The diplomatic situation will become even worse," he bemoaned. His armies lost Manchuria the same day.

Marshall had been looking forward to the election as well. He had been putting off kidney surgery, and a new presidential term would be his moment to finally step down. The resurrection of Western Europe was under way; a transatlantic alliance was taking shape; American pilots were valiantly subverting a Soviet blockade in the Berlin airlift. For his role in all of this, for giving "hope to those who desperately needed it," *Time* again named Marshall its man of the year.

In China, however, assessments were more dire than ever. (Marshall had expected that American success in the West might bring increased Soviet mischief in the East.) "The long-anticipated crisis in China has unmistakably arrived," the CIA reported. "Its main features conform approximately to the pattern that was anticipated—military defeats, economic collapse, political defections, and a general sense of the desirability of peace at any compromise." Pessimistic strategists were turning their attention to options for limiting the fallout, by holding the line against Communism in Japan, South Korea, and Vietnam, and to speculation that the CCP would soon enough prove an unreliable partner for the Kremlin. "When the issue of subservience to Moscow has become more immediate than that of 'U.S. Imperialism,' Chinese nationalism will prove stronger than international Communism," the CIA prophesied hopefully.

As Marshall prepared to hand the State Department's reins to Dean Acheson, the Nationalists made final appeals. Chen Li-fu called on Marshall to be a sick China's doctor, an embattled China's Lafayette. One official would issue another request for "an extension of the Marshall plan to the Far East." Another would acknowledge that because of Nationalist failure "to make appropriate political, economic, and military reforms, your assistance has not produced the desired effect," by way of promising to better utilize assistance going forward. (Total American aid since World War II already amounted to some $3 billion, more than half military.*) But at his last National Security Council meeting, on November 23, 1948, Marshall warned once more against "dispersion of U.S. resources, in response to the many demands upon them, over so many areas that no conclusive result will be obtained anywhere."

---

* Equivalent to $30 billion in real dollars today, and roughly $200 billion today measured as a percentage of GDP.

At the start of December, as he checked into Walter Reed Hospital for surgery, Madame Chiang arrived in town to make an appeal in person. She had kept up frequent, friendly correspondence with the Marshalls, sending Katherine updates on weather and doctor's visits and current events—"all the American women have been rushing out of Shanghai and Nanjing the past week"—and teasingly addressing Marshall by a childhood nickname, General Flicker. She still ranked just below Eleanor Roosevelt on lists of the women Americans most admired. Yet now newspapers referred to Madame Chiang not as China's Florence Nightingale or Joan of Arc, but as an "embarrassing guest." Staying with Katherine in Leesburg, she visited Marshall in the hospital and pleaded for increased assistance, stressing that the fights in China and in Berlin were one and the same. It did not take her long to see that her plea had failed.

Just before Chiang's defeat, Marshall looked back on the challenges in China over the previous four years. "I have never known any problem that had so much complexity in it," he reflected. He also recognized that this observation, no matter its accuracy, would mean little in the frenzy of recrimination to come: "People want action and they want it today. That is the way democracy goes and you cannot get away from it."

Soon they would start asking the barbed question: Who lost China? Chiang, at least, had a ready answer. He blamed Marshall, "who lost us and lost China." Looking back, Chiang wished he had prevented Marshall's mission from ever happening.

At other times, Chiang acknowledged his own errors: he had scattered his forces, overcommitted in Manchuria, relied on "muddle-headed" generals and "degenerate" officials. As the end came, he wrote in his diary: "I increasingly realize that it was unwise for us to not heed Marshall's and Russia's attempt to mediate our problems with the Communists. . . . but I did not expect Marshall to be this stubborn."

Marshall had said before: Chiang was always too late.

For Americans, 1949 was a year of nasty shocks. Communists took China. Moscow tested an atomic bomb. American officials were charged with spying on their own government—some rightly, many wrongly. Tension and terror, mounting steadily since the war, spiked to new highs. The Cold War had fully arrived.

The Truman administration rushed to tell its version of how China was "lost," in the form of a white paper detailing American efforts and Nationalist shortcomings. "The unfortunate but inescapable fact is that the ominous result of the civil war in China was beyond the control of the government of the United States," Secretary of State Acheson wrote in a prefatory note. "Nothing that this country did or could have done within the reasonable limits of its capabilities could have changed that result."

What followed was unique in the annals of American foreign policy: a lengthy, sophisticated attempt, with freshly declassified documentation, to explain to the public why events unfolded the way they did. Politically, it was an abysmal failure.

In the angry debate and prolonged panic just beginning, the white paper incited many and persuaded few. (Acheson's takeaway was that explanations to the American people must be "clearer than the truth.") Chiang condemned it as "a heavy blow to our people." Mao held it up as proof of "intervention" by the "neurotic United States imperialist group—Truman, Marshall, Acheson." (The very premise fanned Mao's paranoia: if Americans believed China was lost, surely they would try to win it back.) Congressional Republicans mocked it as a "whitewash of a wishful do-nothing policy."

Politics had never really stopped at the water's edge, as the adage claimed. But insofar as Marshall had succeeded in attracting broad support for his efforts as secretary of state, comity disintegrated in the vitriol of the China debate. "There is no such thing as a bipartisan foreign policy," declared Republican senator Robert Taft. Chiang's advocates in the "China Lobby" launched a "full-dress attack" on the administration. Editorialists denounced America's "moral retreat."

John F. Kennedy—speaking in Salem, Massachusetts, of witch trials fame—rued the "tragic story of China" and derided Marshall's role in it. Under pressure to demonstrate a strong stand on China's periphery, Truman committed $10 million in military aid to fight Communism in Vietnam. (Marshall, now from the sidelines, warned against being "plunged by political momentary pressures into action that we may find later was highly inadvisable.")

American policymakers held out hope for nationalism-fueled friction between the Soviets and Chinese. When the State Department gathered officials and academics, including a now-retired Marshall, for advice after Mao's victory, they stressed the need to "exploit . . . any rifts" between the two Communist camps. "Even if the devil himself runs China," Acheson would conclude, at least he should be "an independent devil."

Mao went out of his way to dash those hopes. He responded to American feelers about a relationship by imprisoning diplomats. "It is not possible to sit on the fence," he reassured Stalin, who was as wary of CCP independence as Americans were wishful. Truman would concede, "The Russians cannot dominate [the Chinese] forever, but that is a long-range view and does not help us just now."

By now Mao had reason to be grateful to Moscow, despite frustrations with its restrained approach through the first years of civil war. Although Soviet aid to Mao never matched American aid to Chiang, it reached substantial levels in the fight's final phase. More important, Mao and his comrades were true believers in the cause they shared with Moscow. "They were Communists, they were Marxists," Marshall had recognized, and "they did not make any pretense of not being associated with the Communists of Russia."

In the wake of victory, Mao's actions at home were similarly unambiguous. Within a few years, more than a million actual or suspected enemies of the revolution would be killed, often by flagrantly cruel means, and many more imprisoned. Businesses would be shuttered, free speech suppressed, a Soviet-style legal system established. Predictions by American diplomats and journalists that the Chinese Communists would turn into mere "agrarian democrats" proved laughable.

For Stalin, Mao's victory induced a surge of revolutionary euphoria. When the Communist leader of North Korea, Kim Il Sung, asked for permission to invade South Korea, Stalin, despite having said no before, said yes. What had changed was China. Now Mao could help Kim if necessary. (Proving that hopes of Sino-Soviet strain were not entirely unreasonable, some Chinese Communists thought Stalin was deliberately entrapping Mao in a quagmire.) And American refusal to intervene in China (and a recent speech by Acheson) suggested Washington would stay out of Korea as well.

Stalin's calculation turned out to be wrong. When North Korean troops attacked in June 1950, the United States quickly sent troops to defend the South, as part of a multinational force under United Nations auspices but with MacArthur in command.* Not only were circumstances different from those in China—on the Korean peninsula, one country had invaded another—but the shocks of the previous year had brought about a new American posture.

A few days later, Truman appeared in person at Marshall's door in Leesburg. He needed to drag Marshall out of retirement again, this time to oversee America's nascent war effort as secretary of defense. Whatever his personal feelings, Marshall's sense of duty kicked in once again. ("When the President motors down and sits under our oaks and tells me of his difficulties, he has me at a disadvantage.") Yet Marshall hesitated to accept for another reason. "They are still charging me with the downfall of Chiang's government in China," he cautioned the president. "I want to help, not hurt you." When that failed to dissuade Truman, Marshall agreed to serve for six months.

As he feared, his selection this time was met not with universal acclaim, but with acrimony. "It should be remembered that as a diplomat Marshall did much to lose the war which as a soldier he had done so much to win," charged Senator Joseph McCarthy. "General

---

* A United Nations force was possible only because the Soviets were boycotting the Security Council to protest the fact that Chiang's government, rather than Mao's, still controlled China's seat.

George C. Marshall is a living lie," declared Senator William Jenner, "a front man for traitors." (Marshall's response: "Jenner? Jenner? I do not believe I know the man.") Yet Marshall was ultimately confirmed, and in September 1950, his 70th birthday approaching, he found himself presiding over another war. Before long, there would be more than 200,000 American troops in Korea.

The fight against North Korea was immediately hard going, as Marshall knew a land war in Asia would be. Soon it became even tougher. MacArthur, emboldened by an audacious amphibious landing behind enemy lines, rushed troops northward toward the border with Manchuria (despite orders not to provoke the Soviets or Chinese). Mao did not stand by, and just weeks after Marshall's return to the Pentagon, tens of thousands of Chinese troops poured into Korea to support their comrades. Less than five years since the two of them toasted peace in Yenan, Marshall's army was at war with Mao's.

There was also strife on the home front. The rush northward had been one in a string of actions by MacArthur that contravened Washington's orders. He had complained openly about the scope of his mission. He had told reporters that defeating the Chinese Communists would be easy if only the politicians would let him take the fight to Chinese territory. The last straw was a letter read on the floor of Congress (calling for, among other things, unleashing Chiang's Nationalist armies on the People's Republic). Truman fired him for insubordination—promptly setting off another round of recrimination. For the China Lobby, Korea had become another battle in the "unfinished China war," in Congressman Judd's words, and MacArthur was now its martyr.

"If we lose this war to Communism in Asia the fall of Europe is inevitable," MacArthur wrote in the letter that brought his downfall. "There is no substitute for victory."

It was the kind of rousing slogan Marshall considered alluring but treacherous, calls to win a single battle at any price undercutting the "cold-blooded calculation and wisdom and foresight" needed to win the bigger war. Even while overseeing the effort in Korea, Marshall was adamant in his reminders to keep the global picture in mind. (Korea was "a very small peninsula," he would note, and "the Soviet Union's activities cover pretty much the whole world.") When China joined the fight, he suspected "a carefully laid Russian trap" meant to draw the United States into a quagmire and open the way for Soviet moves on other fronts. Countering demands to extend the fight to "Red China" itself, Marshall shared the view that it would be "the wrong war, at the wrong place, at the wrong time, and with the wrong enemy."

MacArthur's response was to savage the China mission. Despite his praise of Marshall's efforts at the time, now MacArthur pronounced it "one of the greatest blunders in American diplomatic history for which the free world is now paying in blood and disaster and will in all probability continue to do so indefinitely."

On a fall day in 1951, Marshall returned to his house in Leesburg. He had arrived here six years earlier on another fall day, only to have his hours-old retirement interrupted by a phone call from the president. Since that call, he had spent thirteen months struggling to bring unity out of chaos in China; two years refashioning America's global role as secretary of state; and a year overseeing another terrible war as secretary of defense.

Four decades in the army, spanning two global conflicts, had taught Marshall that there was no such thing as an easy war. These past six years had taught him that there was no such thing as an easy peace. The next great war, he warned, would bring only the "empty triumph of inheriting the responsibility for a shattered world." Yet a peace that was merely the absence of war could not hold. Peace had to be a "dynamic force," reinforced by both awareness of war's costs and readiness to fight should fighting become necessary.

A sustained peace also meant reckoning with the deeper currents that Marshall had come to see. As he would write: "The benighted people, the little people of the earth, have begun to realize how tragic their situation is, how unfair. The Communists seize this growing revolt as a spring-board for their own purposes. They use it. We have largely ignored it through the years, with all our kindly and generous feelings toward our fellow men. Much of our present troubles spring from this source."

But those troubles would no longer be Marshall's to manage. "You have earned your retirement many fold," Truman wrote him. This time there would be no interruption. From here on, Marshall would spend his days working in the garden, and riding in the hills, and reading beneath landscapes painted by Madame Chiang in her Taiwanese exile. He would lead a delegation to Queen Elizabeth's coronation, and, in 1953, become the first American military man to win the Nobel Peace Prize. ("This does not seem as remarkable to me as it quite evidently appears to others," he said in his address. "I know a great deal of the horrors and tragedies of war.") But he would never return to government service. And he would never write his memoirs, despite lucrative offers from publishers. He was too concerned about the people he would hurt if he wrote the truth.

Yet as Marshall gradually withdrew from public life, American politics took a dark turn—spurred in significant part by the "loss" of China. Marshall was far from spared. Even before he stepped down from the Pentagon, Joe McCarthy had taken to the floor of the Senate to spin a tale of Marshall's treason, with "the criminal folly of the disastrous Marshall Mission" at its center. "If Marshall were merely stupid," McCarthy sneered, "the laws of probability would dictate that part of his decisions would serve this country's interest." The only explanation, accordingly, was "a conspiracy so immense and an infamy so black as to dwarf any previous venture in the history of man." (McCarthy thought so highly of his three-hour ghostwritten rant that he had it published as a book, *America's Retreat from Victory: The Story of George Catlett Marshall*.)

The charges were risible—the greatest of the Greatest Generation half-knowingly involved in a Communist plot—but in the fervid atmosphere of the day, they got traction. McCarthy saw traitors everywhere: in academia, in Hollywood, throughout the U.S. government. Some of those named were guilty of passing information to Moscow; many more were not, especially among the China hands who had earlier incurred Patrick Hurley's wrath and now found themselves targets of McCarthy's inquisition. That included John Melby, who after a prolonged investigation (focused largely on his affair with Lillian Hellman, the recipient of his love letters from China and an outspoken leftist) was expelled from the foreign service.

Others joined in McCarthy's crusade. Wedemeyer helped quietly at first, and then, having whispered darkly about Marshall ever since the canceled ambassadorship, went public. Wedemeyer's self-congratulatory memoir alleged that exhaustion and intellectual shortcomings had made Marshall "easy prey to crypto-Communists, or Communist sympathizing sycophants, who played on his vanity to accomplish their own ends." Marshall's China mission, according to Wedemeyer, caused the Nationalists to become "so disheartened and demoralized by our attitude that they finally ceased to resist the Communists." No matter that much in this narrative contradicted what he said at the time, whether in his own sycophantic letters to Marshall or his own report about Chiang's prospects. The memoir was meant, said Wedemeyer's former deputy in an inadvertently damning defense, "as an apology and not to be completely factual."

The more surprising betrayal came from Eisenhower, who had been recruited by the Republican Party to run in the 1952 presidential election. When it came time to campaign in Wisconsin alongside Joe McCarthy, Eisenhower had his speechwriter prepare a denunciation of McCarthyism—"a sobering lesson in the way freedom should *not* defend itself"—but then lost courage and left the material out. When he got in front of the crowd, he shook hands with McCarthy and blamed the "loss" of China on "men whose brains were confused by the opiate of this deceit," doing nothing to defend the man to whom he owed his rise against a demagogue's charges of treason. "General Marshall was responsible for his whole career," an incensed Truman would say. "Eisenhower sold him out."

Marshall himself did not get angry enough to have to forgive. He knew politics was a "dirty business." He wrote Eisenhower: "I felt because of the vigorous attacks on me by various Republicans any communication with you might be . . . detrimental to your cause." Upon Eisenhower's victory, Marshall wrote a gracious note, with one piece of advice: "I pray especially for you in the choice of those to be near you. That choice, more than anything else, will determine the problems of the years and the record of history. Make them measure up to your standards."

Only Katherine could detect any underlying hurt in her stoic husband; she conspired with one of his former aides, Frank McCarthy, who contacted the new president and suggested saying something in defense of Marshall. ("I know how sensitive General Marshall is to activities of his friends," McCarthy reported back to Katherine, "so I am sending these messages directly to you with the suggestion that you show them to General Marshall only if you think he would like to see them.") From the White House, Eisenhower would praise Marshall lavishly. And before long, Eisenhower, too, would be savaged for being weak on Communism.

To Marshall, engaging accusations at all, even in self-defense, would serve only to dignify his accusers and demean himself. He was not rattled by the rantings of men like McCarthy and Jenner, or the fictions of onetime acolytes like Wedemeyer. "If I have to explain at this point that I am not a traitor to the United States," he would say, "I hardly think it's worth it." Only when it was necessary to stand up for others did he enter the fight. Vouching for former aides and colleagues charged with disloyalty, Marshall issued a warning: McCarthy's accusations and insinuations "confuse our friends abroad, undermine and weaken our position before the world and actually lend assistance to the powers that would destroy us."

At the height of the McCarthyist fury, one of the most renowned anti-Communist voices in America rose to Marshall's defense. The theologian Reinhold Niebuhr cautioned against "desperation on our side which would tempt us to confront Communism in Asia primarily in military terms and thus play into the hands of the Communist

political propaganda by which it would expand still further into Asia."
It was "difficult to sit by with folded hands," he wrote. "Yet we may have
to learn to fold our hands."

Niebuhr was best known for his Serenity Prayer: grant me the serenity to accept the things I cannot change, courage to change the things
I can, and wisdom to know the difference. In a sense, Marshall's core
strategic principle echoed Niebuhr's invocation.

Yet both Niebuhr and Marshall knew that the fact that something
could not be changed did not make it any less terrible: that was the tragic
implication of both the principle and the prayer. Within a few years of
Communist victory in China, any remaining illusions about Mao—his
ideology, his cruelty, his revolutionary ambition—had been stripped
away entirely. War in Korea had dragged on into 1953, leaving millions of
Chinese and Koreans (and 37,000 Americans) dead. Within China's borders, Mao's victims also numbered in the millions; his nascent attempt
at forced industrialization and collectivization, the Great Leap Forward,
would lead to a famine that killed tens of millions more.

In retirement, Marshall heard often from Madame Chiang, who sent
both personal and political updates. He worked to help refugees from
Communist China, and pushed for asylum for friends and contacts
forced to flee Mao. (Katherine brought her maid and nurse from Nanjing to Leesburg, and helped her get American citizenship a few years
later.) He signed a petition against Communist China's admission to
the United Nations, his name appearing alongside those of some of his
most slanderous accusers. From the U.S. perspective, the only bright
spot was that, less than a decade since Mao's victory, the relationship
between the Soviets and the Chinese had already soured. But the Cold
War delirium made it hard for most Americans to see the split, and
impossible for those who did see to capitalize on it.

The question—who lost China?—echoed through American politics
for years. The China Lobby remained forceful and feared. A right-wing
fringe found its namesake in John Birch, the young OSS agent killed
in an encounter with Chinese Communists weeks after the end of
World War II, and the John Birch Society became the country's primary

purveyor of conspiracy theory and fevered accusation. (In the imag-
inings of the Birchers, even Eisenhower was "a dedicated, conscious
agent of the Communist conspiracy.") Swaths of the U.S. government
remained gutted by McCarthyism, almost anyone with regional exper-
tise driven out in a cloud of suspicion; when Averell Harriman took
over the State Department's Asia section as the American effort in
Vietnam expanded, he found it a "wasteland." U.S. officials made trips
to Vietnam and returned to recommend a few thousand more military
"advisers," then a few thousand more. Meanwhile, leaders fretted over
the political fallout of "losing" another Asian country to Communism.
"God almighty," said Lyndon Johnson as he agonized over Vietnam,
"what they said about us leaving China would just be warming up
compared to what they'd say now."

Marshall died on October 16, 1959, following a long deterioration
punctuated by two strokes. In obituaries, the tally of achievements was
long: building the modern American army and leading it to victory in
World War II; forging the Marshall Plan and a model of global leadership that would long outlast him; standing as an exemplar of decency
and dignity in one of the American body politic's lowest moments.
President Truman called Marshall "the greatest of the great in our
time." President Eisenhower spoke of his "steadfast courage and wise
decision." George Kennan praised him as "the American gentleman at
his best—honorable, courteous, devoid of arrogance, exacting of others
but even more of himself."

When Chiang heard the news, he reflected on Marshall's "stubbornness" and speculated that Marshall's demise was a by-product of
guilt. "Is his death a good thing for the revival of the Chinese nation?"
Chiang wondered. He initially refused to sign a condolence note
drafted by Madame Chiang. But then he read what she had written
about Marshall. "She only tries to console his wife, but does not mention the good or bad deeds of the deceased," Chiang recorded in his
diary. "So we sent the letter in both of our names."

Substitutes for Victory?

Foreign policy is made by analogy. The stories we tell matter. How we tell them matters.

When considering their country's role in the world, Americans like stories of heroism or villainy, of clear triumph or utter catastrophe. In the standard telling, the years covered in this book are a prime exhibit of heroism and triumph. They mark the start of the American era, a period of visionary leadership that supplied doctrines and models still invoked today. The Marshall Plan, the transatlantic alliance, the democratic renovation of Japan and Germany, the self-sacrifice of the Greatest Generation and foresight of the Wise Men: all fit into a narrative of power and purpose reshaping the world and ultimately winning the Cold War.

More than any other figure in that narrative, George Marshall embodies the conception of American leadership at its best—strong, generous, bold. The Greatest Generation venerated his greatness, the Wise Men his wisdom. Politicians, policymakers, and military officers in every decade since have claimed to be carrying on his legacy. The tradition that began soon after his Harvard speech continues: every great challenge, whether in the Middle East or middle America, still seems to be met with calls for a new Marshall Plan.

The China mission cuts against the conception of American power that Marshall and his era have been taken to represent. It is a story not of possibility and ambition, but of limit and restraint; not of a victory achieved at any cost, but of a kind of failure ultimately accepted as the best of terrible options. Perhaps not surprisingly, the common under-standing of Marshall and his accomplishments has tended to leave out his time in China altogether.

But Marshall would not have told the story that way. The China mis-sion was as integral to the record of those years as any of his justly sto-ried achievements. It loomed large in his lived experience—the debate over the "loss" of China, after all, became one of the most poisonous in American politics—and also powerfully shaped his approach to the Cold War world taking shape. To Marshall, failure could not be sepa-rated from the broader record; reckoning with limits, "trying to keep to the things we could do" and focusing on those battles that could be won, was essential to overall success. Neither his story nor his coun-try's was as straightforwardly triumphant as the mythology would come to hold.

"You are dealing all the time with the Monday quarterback," Mar-shall, near the end of his life, commented to his biographer Forrest Pogue. "In many cases, most cases, he wouldn't have dared to do the things he talks about. But after it is all clear and all is seen, he can tell you pretty well how it ought to have been done."

Marshall was leery of retrospective judgments. To him, hindsight was not 20/20; it obscured as much as it clarified. Even when carried out earnestly, without self-serving aims, the "Monday-quarterback business" rarely captured the true choices at the time of action, what was known and what was not, what resources were at hand and what constraints were in place. ("When you judge decisions," Marshall beseeched Congress as McCarthyism gained steam, "you have to judge them in light of what there was available to do it.") Veiled counterfac-tuals could too easily assume the benefits of an alternate course while ignoring the attendant risks, costs, and trade-offs. The supposed clar-ity of hindsight was often just comforting myth—or low opportunism, with many who had advocated something in the moment of decision claiming bitter opposition or brilliant foresight later on. "Their later states of mind don't accord with what they had in mind at the time," Marshall observed. "They are sort of 'backed out' by the political recriminations and accusations." He did not name names.

Over the thirteen months of Marshall's mission, an unsettled world was changing fast. At the start, American policymakers still hoped that Allied unity in the war could be extended into the postwar. They pushed a series of "one-world" initiatives, as the historian John Lewis Gaddis has put it, aimed at sustaining great-power cooperation and collective problem-solving, with the Soviets (and the Chinese) at the table. There was the United Nations, joint humanitarian relief, the new Bretton Woods economic structure of the World Bank and International Monetary Fund—and also the common effort to avert breakdown in China. In time this changed, making early hopes for comity look naïve. The opportunists denied ever having shared them, and those one-world visions were refashioned for a divided Cold War world.

Marshall, like most Americans, never fully grasped the negative capability the Chinese brought (and continue to bring) to diplomacy. For all his efforts to see the world through negotiating partners' eyes, he did not quite bridge the divide in worldviews, with clashing notions of power that were in the end irreconcilable. Marshall knew both sides were set on playing him for their own ends—not just at the negotiating table, but also during the parties and picnics, over the cocktails and card games. Even with that awareness, their moves sometimes baffled him, particularly as the end came. He could not always help projecting an American understanding of political contest onto their more existential fights, failing to fathom just how far they were willing to go.

Marshall could have given the Nationalists the full-scale support they wanted, military and economic, without pushing restraint or cease-fires. Or he could have refused to fulfill World War II–era agreements to assist the Nationalists into 1946, cutting them off more quickly and sharply than he did, and made a decisive turn toward Mao, banking on underlying structural tensions between him and the Soviets.

In the years after the mission, Marshall's critics fixed on the first alternative: China was America's to save, and it was Marshall's failure to have lost it. The policymakers of the early Cold War, Lyndon Johnson argued in justifying his escalation in Asia, "had lost their effectiveness from the day that the Communists took over in China. . . . And I knew that all these problems, taken together, were chickenshit compared with what might happen if we lost Vietnam." Some political figures went a step further, calling Vietnam an opportunity to pursue the course that should have been pursued in China a decade and a half before. Even into the 1980s, the analogy would maintain its grip, with the "loss" of China invoked as an argument for intervention elsewhere. (In a sense, the China mission was Washington's first encounter with a lesson learned repeatedly through the Cold War and beyond: the near-impossibility of resolving somebody else's civil war.) Reflecting on such arguments and what they wrought, the historian Ernest May proposed "that the whole course of the subsequent Cold War would have proceeded differently, abroad and at home, if Marshall had not personally acted to bar involvement in the Chinese civil war. Pressures for involvement were so strong that, had another person been President Truman's principal adviser on national security policy, they could have been irresistible."

Later, critics skeptical of hardened Cold War categories fixed on the second alternative approach. A more enlightened policy toward the Communists, the argument went, could have won them over as anti-Soviet allies a quarter century before Nixon ultimately did, with the help of Zhou Enlai. (Other key CCP figures from the time of the China mission also went on to play central roles in subsequent events, including Deng Xiaoping, China's great economic reformer, and Xi Zhongxun, father of current Chinese president Xi Jinping.)

The historian Odd Arne Westad has called these the myths of the "loss" and the "lost chance," both fanciful, both of them reassuring in their affirmation of American omnipotence. "It would not have been possible for the United States to prevent a Communist victory in China by military force, covert operations, or diplomatic initiatives," Westad wrote. Nor, given everything known of Mao, was a more conciliatory U.S. policy likely to have transformed him into an ally in the immediate aftermath of revolution.

Marshall came away with a more limited sense of America's place in the story. A master of self-control, here he came to terms with what could not be controlled; a can-do man in a can-do era, here he learned what could not be done—the hardest part of strategy. Yet that did not mean settling into fatalism. Marshall also returned home with a deeper sense of what it would take to succeed in the larger struggle just beginning. In ways both positive and negative, the China mission would leave its mark on the model of American leadership he went on to build.

Again and again, Marshall was urged to tell his own story, to polish history so it reflected the record the way he wanted—as Churchill famously remarked, to ensure it would be kind. Again and again, Marshall refused, even when publishers offered him outlandish sums. Only with some persuasion, and late in his life, did he agree to give a series of interviews to a biographer.

For a leader so attentive to public debate when he was in the midst of a fight, military or diplomatic, this refusal might seem surprising. Marshall thought a memoir would have to be either disingenuous or gratuitously hurtful, and neither of those courses interested him. But even more important, he had long believed that fixating on judgments in the future would pervert his judgment in the present. During World War II, one particularly adamant suggestion that he keep a personal record for later use came from a Robert E. Lee biographer, who noted that Lee's failure to define a legacy had allowed others to define it instead. Marshall wrote back to explain his reasons for not doing so:

> It continually introduces the factor of one's own reputation, the
> future appreciation of one's daily decisions, which leads, I feel, sub-
> consciously to self-deception or hesitations in reaching decisions. I
> realize that in the future I will probably be embarrassed by the lack

of factual evidence or contemporary notes regarding this or that phase of the war as influenced from my office. If I in any way propagated such thoughts, it would inevitably affect the clarity and logic of my daily approach to the changing situation.

Marshall's refusal to craft history is doubly striking because he so highly valued its study. It was the only subject at which he excelled in school. Even in the middle of the war, he read thick volumes on Napoleon and ancient Rome, and asked newspaper publishers to encourage Americans to study history's "great lessons pertinent to the tragic problems of today." Decades later, in a classic study of how decision makers use (and misuse) history, Richard Neustadt and Ernest May would single out Marshall for his ability to think in "time-streams"—drawing a web of connections between the present and the past in order to illuminate possible paths into the future. "By looking back," they wrote, "Marshall looked ahead."

Marshall knew history's lessons were never clean or simple. He had seen how crudely or misleadingly they could be applied. "There always seem to be too many conflicting and disturbing factors for a calm appraisement, too much special pleading, too much violent prejudice," he noted. Over and over he had watched other leaders act on "impressions retained from schooling in biased histories, poorly taught." And yet history was, Marshall believed, of "great value in broadening my perspective and tempering my disposition." It could serve as a corrective to the nostalgia-laden selective memory that sustains myth and warps perspective in the present by excising the wrenching choices and struggles of the past.

Today, as Americans agonize and argue over fears of national decline, the story of the China mission is in one sense sobering. Even at the height of its power, when it had just led the Allies to victory in World War II and accounted for nearly half of the global economy, America could not solve every problem. But the story should also be reassuring. In its moment of greatest leadership, America did not have to solve every problem to show that it was strong.

A NOTE ON NAMES AND QUOTATIONS

For the sake of the reader's ease, I have tried to use whichever English version of a Chinese name is most familiar to most Western readers. In some cases, this has resulted in an inconsistency or anachronism. (For example, Beijing at the time was known as Beiping—"northern wind" rather than "northern capital"—yet I use Beijing here.)

The material on and quotations from Marshall and his circle come largely from their own contemporaneous records—meeting notes, telegrams, memos, letters, and diary entries, all listed in the notes. In many cases, I have corrected misspellings and typos that are not telling in their own right. The central perspective of the narrative is an American one, and for the rest of the story I have relied on the many excellent historians who have written on the Chinese Civil War and early Cold War, and the many excellent biographers of other key figures in the story (as well as of Marshall). A full register of their works appears in the notes and bibliography.

ACKNOWLEDGMENTS

Over five years of research and writing, I accumulated a long list of debts, most of which will never be properly repaid.

At the George C. Marshall Foundation, I'm grateful to Paul Barron and Jeffrey Kozak for their advice and help in the archives, as well as to Brian Shaw and Rob Havers for their support. Mark Stoler of the University of Vermont and Barry Machado of Washington & Lee generously shared their wisdom and deep knowledge whenever I asked. A number of excellent researchers—Nikki Weiner, Terry Sun, Jacob Glenn, Yanping Liu, John Chen, Chen Gong, Josh Hochman, and Rhys Dubin—provided crucial help at various points along the way. Thomas Sung, Rebecca Soong, and John L. Soong Jr. vividly recounted their personal experiences.

In China, I relied on the help of some people I knew already and many more that I was meeting for the first time, all of them exceedingly generous. Peter Hessler, Jeff Wasserstrom, Emma Oxford, Maura Cunningham, Nicole Barnes, Charlie Edel, Ren Xiao Shan, and John Pomfret offered valuable contacts and advice. In Beijing, I had fascinating discussions with Niu Jun and Zhang Baijia, and benefited from the hospitality of Liu Gang. In Chongqing, Chen Guangmeng, Qian Feng, and Han Qing were immensely helpful, as were He Wen in Shaanxi and Xiong Hua Wu in Kuling. In Nanjing, Michael Zhang, Guo Biqiang, Xiao Zhencai, Dong Guoqiang, and Edmond Yang all gave lavishly of their time, knowledge, and enthusiasm. William Chan was a tremendous fellow traveler and intellectual partner—and deserves many additional thank-yous for his ongoing friendship and advocacy.

At New America, I'm thankful to Steve Coll, Anne-Marie Slaughter, Andres Martinez, Peter Bergen, Becky Shafer, and Kirsten Berg for building an unparalleled infrastructure and fostering an unparalleled environment for writers trying to make progress on first books. At NYU, Mike Williams supported the final stages. Jose Fernandez and Andrea Gabor lent me a beautiful place to write.

A long list of friends, mentors, and colleagues talked through or read some or all of the manuscript (in a few cases more than once): Alan Schoenfeld, Patrick Radden Keefe, Mira Rapp-Hooper, Kurt Campbell, Harold Tanner, Gideon Rose, Jonathan Tepperman, Stuart Reid, Rebecca Lissner, Jacob Freedman, Jake Sullivan, John Gaddis, Mike Fuchs, Marc Dunkelman, Katharine Smyth, Dan Brook, Richard Feinberg, Tom Meaney, Dan Schwerin, Jim Kurtz-Phelan, Jared Leboff, Chris Heaney, Ryan Floyd, Liaquat Ahamed, Joshua Cooper Ramo, Arne Westad, Barry Machado, Mark Stoler, Lincoln Caplan, and Paul Barron.

My justly storied editor, Star Lawrence, got what I was trying to do from the beginning and patiently and expertly saw it through the end. Thanks also to Emma Hitchcock and Rachel Salzman at Norton. And the fantastic Tina Bennett not only relentlessly championed the book at every turn; she also seemed to always have a great idea or reassuring word at just the right moment.

My wonderful in-laws, Jessie and Jim, have been supportive and encouraging in countless ways, including by providing an idyllic Nova Scotia refuge for reading and writing. My sisters, Rachel and Abby, bolstered me when I needed bolstering. I owe my parents, Phyllis and Jim, more appreciation for more reasons than I can start to articulate (or even recognize)—but anyway, as they know, ingratitude may be the truest testament to good parenting.

Finally, and most of all, thank you to Darin, who talked me through every travail, read every word twice, and gave me the fortitude to start in the first place.

NOTES

Abbreviations in Notes

AW	Albert Wedemeyer	JHC	John Hart Caughey
CKS	Chiang Kai-shek	JM	John Melby
Final report	George C. Marshall, *Marshall's Mission to China, December 1945–January 1947: The Report and Appended Documents*	KTM	Katherine Tupper Marshall
		LOC	Library of Congress
		Marshall interviews	*George C. Marshall Interview and Reminiscences for Forrest C. Pogue,* edited by Larry I. Bland
FRUS	United States Department of State, *Foreign Relations of the United States*		
		MC	Marshall Carter
GCM	George C. Marshall	MHI	Military History Institute
GCMRL	George C. Marshall Research Library		
		NARA	National Archives
Hoover	Hoover Institution Archives	Papers	*The Papers of George Catlett Marshall,* Vols. 1–6 edited by Larry I. Bland et al.; Vol. 7 edited by Mark A. Stoler
HST	Harry S. Truman		
HSTL	Harry S. Truman Library		

Prologue: Oh! General Marshall, We Communists Honor You

1   **"I can tell"** Forrest C. Pogue, *George C. Marshall: Statesman,* 102; **"The entire people"** Li Tien-Min, *Chou En-Lai,* 261–262.

1-2   **lost** Gillem diary, 4 March 1946, Alvan Gillem Papers, MHI; **side of a mountain** Memoirs of Ivan D. Yeaton, 120, Ivan D. Yeaton Papers 1, Hoover; **"long peace"** Alexander V. Pantsov, *Mao*, 305.

2   **6,000 people** *Emancipation Daily* 5 March 1946.

2   **five hundred** *Emancipation Daily* 5 March 1946; **"Oh! General Marshall"** Li, *Chou*, 261–262.

2   **"sits and masks"** Gillem diary, 4 March 1946, Alvan Gillem Papers, MHI; **"All were satisfied"** *Emancipation Daily* 5 March 1946; **He had sat** Gillem diary, 4 March 1946, Alvan Gillem Papers, MHI; **fail to notice** Transcript of GCM comments, Conference on Problems of United States Policy in China, Secretary's Files 152/4, HST Papers, HSTL; **model of vehicle** Katherine Marshall, *Together*, 60; **Mao would ride** JHC letter, 23 March 1946, JHC Papers 2/8, GCMRL.

3   **"armies called"** Ed Cray, *General of the Army*, 515.

3   **"strong, united"** *FRUS* 1945 Vol. 7, 770.

3   **a miracle** Marshall cable, 25 January 1946, GCM Papers 24/1, GCMRL; **Benjamin Franklin** *New Yorker* 16 March 1946; **"a new stage"** Odd Arne Westad, *Decisive Encounters*, 32.

4   **"god of peace"** Marshall cable, 25 January 1946, GCM Papers 24/1, GCMRL; **"peace will"** GCM to HST, 16 January 146, Naval Aide Files 8/9, HST Papers, HSTL.

5   **"next war"** Papers Vol. 5, 273.

1. Peace Is Hell

9-10   **"In a war"** Papers Vol. 5, 365; **"greatest military man"** Statement by the President, 20 November 1945, Secretary's Files 197/12, HST Papers, HSTL; **"finest soldier"** Henry L. Stimson, *On Active Service in Peace and War*, 664; **"strongest man"** Cray, *General*, 398; *Time* magazine Cray, *General*, 442; **Stalin said** Averell W. Harriman, *Special Envoy to Churchill and Stalin*, 445.

10   **"At breakfast"** Marshall, *Together*, 118; **Atlas** List of aliases, John Paton Davies Papers 11/4, HSTL; **"We are off"** Papers Vol. 5, 367.

10   **a true home** Marshall, *Together*, 118; **"My ambitions"** GCM to Merrill Meigs, 2 February 1946, GCM Papers 123/21, GCMRL.

10-11   **"General Marshall speaking"** Dean Acheson, *Sketches from Life*, 147; **"Yes, Mr. President"** Papers Vol. 5, 372.

11   **Katherine . . . relax** Marshall, *Together*, 282.

11   **"Son-of-a-bitch"** Robert J. Donovan, *Conflict and Crisis*, 149.

11   **thought to send him across the Pacific** GCM to Joseph Stilwell, 3 August 1944, GCM Papers 60/56, GCMRL.

12   **"Mexicans"** Carrolle J. Carter, *Mission to Yenan*, 131; **"motherfucker"** Dieter Heinzig, *The Soviet Union and Communist China*, 43; **lewd joke** Gra-

ham Peck, *Two Kinds of Time*, 612; **"being leaked on"** Robert Edwin Herzstein in Larry I. Bland, *George C. Marshall's Mediation Mission to China*, 123; **Clown, Big Wind** S. C. M. Paine, *The Wars for Asia*, 235.

13   **he told his fellow cabinet members** Townsend Hoopes, *Driven Patriot*, 304; **Hurley resignation** Donovan, *Conflict*, 149-151.

13   **discussion over lunch** Donovan, *Conflict*, 150.

14   **came in a suggestion** Walter Millis, *Forrestal Diaries*, 113.

14   **"Truman's eyes"** Matthew Connelly Oral History, HSTL; **"reverence"** Averell Harriman Oral History, GCMRL; **"earned a rest"** Millis, *Forrestal Diaries*, 238; **temporary appointment** Millis, *Forrestal Diaries*, 113; **Red Room** David McCullough, *Truman*, 475.

14   **Fort Necessity** Papers Vol. 7, 844.

15   **"Ike" . . . cross-channel invasion** Forrest C. Pogue, *George C. Marshall: Organizer of Victory*, 303; **Stimson recorded** Pogue, *Organizer*, 325; **"I could not sleep"** Mark A. Stoler, *George C. Marshall*, 108.

16   **his presence** Acheson, *Sketches*, 147; **"abject humility"** Papers Vol. 5, 555; **command, decision** Mark Perry, *Partners in Command*, 103; **"Don't fight the problem"** Acheson, *Sketches*, 156; **"To say what makes greatness"** Acheson to GCM, 10 January 1949, GCM Papers 56/4, GCMRL.

16   **"first-name business"** John Robinson Beal, *Marshall in China*, 325; **"I have no feelings"** Acheson, *Sketches*, 154.

16   **"Those who stand up"** Thomas Ricks, *The Generals*, 35; **little black book, "to relieve him"** Forrest C. Pogue, *George C. Marshall: Ordeal and Hope*, 94–95; **"You give"** McCullough, *Truman*, 861.

16-17 **"Modern warfare"** Papers Vol. 1, 621; **"It becomes more and more"** Papers Vol. 1, 705; *in principle* Dean Rusk, *As I Saw It*, 132.

17   **"brilliant planner"** Ricks, *Generals*, 23; **"appalling proposition"** Papers Vol. 1, 160; **aluminum and antifreeze** Papers Vol. 2, 595; **netting** Papers Vol. 3, 82; **59,000 miles** Cray, *General*, 374; **"The future effort"** Papers Vol. 3, 106; **out of gas** Perry, *Partners*, 332.

17-18 **"The destinies"** Perry, *Partners*, 283; **"organizer of victory"** Cray, *General*, 515; **taken a gentlemanly army** Pogue, *Ordeal*, 1; **had produced** Cray, *General*, 554; **citation** Papers Vol. 5, 365.

18   **"best man"** Cray, *General*, 9; **"massive brain"** Charles F. Brower, *George C. Marshall*, 17; **in an argument, prompting Roosevelt** Jean Edward Smith, *Eisenhower in War and Peace*, 312; **"Persuade by accomplishment"** Cray, *General*, 341.

18-19 **"It will take history"** Papers Vol. 4, 383; **"unnatural genius"** Cray, *General*, 297; **unlikely formulation** Philip D. Sprouse Oral History, HSTL; **bestseller list** Marshall, *Together*, 275-276; **"The Democratic Party owes it to the people"** Cray, *General*, 403; **"I have never voted"** Papers Vol. 2, 616.

19   **"The hour war"** Papers Vol. 1, 596; **"peace of the entire world"** Thomas

G. Paterson, "If Europe, Why Not China?," 23; **"waste the victory"** "Marshall's Mission," JHC Papers 2/8, GCMRL.

19   **"terrific toll"** Marshall, *Together*, 259.

19-20   **casualty lists** Papers Vol. 5, 223; **graphic reports** Stoler, *George C. Marshall*, 121; **"I loathe war"** Papers Vol. 5, 224.

20   **commanders rest** Pogue, *Organizer*, 326; **by 10:30 a.m.** Statement by Secretary Ross, 27 November 1945, Secretary's Files 197/12, HSTL; **"devil to pay"** Papers Vol. 5, 372.

20   **too old** McCullough, *Truman*, 255; **"if you ever pray"** McCullough, *Truman*, 353; **unsettled** Marshall interviews, 331.

20   **"Peace is hell"** Donovan, *Conflict*, 125.

21   **meat** Donovan, *Conflict*, 229; **wheat** Donovan, *Conflict*, 203; **"great emergency"** Donovan, *Conflict*, 112; **"drink Coke"** Walter Isaacson, *The Wise Men*, 19; **In a survey** George H. Gallup, *The Gallup Poll*, 535; **Hitler** Gallup, *Gallup*, 527.

21   **global economic activity, gold reserves** Melvyn P. Leffler, *A Preponderance of Power*, 2; **"We have virtually been elected"** Papers Vol. 5, 362.

21   **"political counterstroke"** *New Republic* 10 December 1945; **"stroke of genius"** Clark to HST, Personal File 2996, HST Papers, HSTL; **"I do not need to tell you"** Luce to GCM, 29 November 1945, GCM Papers 74/44, GCMRL.

22   **"Kansas City"** T. Christopher Jespersen, *American Images of China*, 164.

22   **"The inherent weakness in our position"** Odd Arne Westad, *Restless Empire*, 131.

23   **"not worth a cent"** Michael H. Hunt, *The Genesis of Chinese Communist Foreign Policy*, 66; **"exploitable"** Warren I. Cohen, *America's Response to China*, 23.

23   **"our difficulties in China"** Papers Vol. 3, 422; **"our loyal ally in China"** Michael Schaller, *The U.S. Crusade In China*, 87; **"democratic traditions"** Jespersen, *American Images*, 51; **"How to Tell Japs"** *Life* 22 December 1941; **"airport-warphanage-dugout," shacks and beggars cleared** Peck, *Two Kinds*, 428-429.

24   **"giant pincer"** Barbara W. Tuchman, *Stilwell and the American Experience in China*, 238; **"The determination"** GCM to CKS, 1 July 1942, GCM Papers 60/42, GCMRL.

24   **Churchill** Maochun Yu, *OSS in China*, 242; **"a new epoch"** Herbert Feis, *The China Tangle*, 62.

24-25   **"unconquerable China"** Tuchman, *Stilwell*, 291; **"no possibility"** John Paton Davies, *Dragon by the Tail*, 276; **"three-power alliance"** Kenneth S. Chern, *Dilemma in China*, 51; **"most important factor"** Akira Iriye, *American, Chinese, and Japanese Perspectives on Wartime Asia*, 288-289; **balance Russia** John Lewis Gaddis, *Strategies of Containment*, 11.

25   **"great American illusion"** Feis, *China*, 284; **"If I can epitomize"** Robert Dallek, *The Lost Peace*, 90; **The Soviets** Wm. Roger Louis, *Imperialism at Bay*, 284; **"the white man's position"** Yu, *OSS*, 198.

26 **"manure pile"** Tuchman, *Stilwell*, 372; **"distorted view," "in the dark"** Tuchman, *Stilwell*, 197; **"stupid leadership"** Tuchman, *Stilwell*, 194; **"The cure"** Jay Taylor, *Generalissimo*, 278.

26 **Marshall chided** Taylor, *Generalissimo*, 244; **"Sultan"** Tuchman, *Stilwell*, 360; **summon him home** Feis, *China*, 79; **"your profane message"** Tuchman, *Stilwell*, 345.

27 **"most severe humiliation"** Taylor, *Generalissimo*, 289; **lyric** Taylor, *Generalissimo*, 290.

27 **"the bursting"** Tuchman, *Stilwell*, 506.

27 **"China could not lose"** Theodore H. White, *Thunder Out of China*, 77.

28 **"decorative object"** Rana Mitter, *Forgotten Ally*, 298; **"really laughable"** Mitter, *Forgotten*, 353; **stab of humiliation** Pogue, *Ordeal*, 365; **share of global Lend-Lease** Mitter, *Forgotten*, 245; **Chiang threatened** Tuchman, *Stilwell*, 312.

28 **Skyway to Hell** White, *Thunder*, 154; **"much sound"** Davies to Hopkins, 21 October 1944, John Paton Davies Papers 11/4, HSTL.

28-29 **"Because the Pacific"** Mitter, *Forgotten*, 254; **"I thought these were American planes"** Marshall interviews, 374; **Every piece of equipment** Hannah Pakula, *The Last Empress*, 398; **"maintaining China in the war"** Pogue, *Organizer*, 210.

29 **Chinese soldiers eating a puppy** White, *Thunder*, 133; **Uncle Chump** White, *Thunder*, 160; **Chinese recruits** David D. Barrett, *Dixie Mission*, 60; **"We Americans here"** AW to Embick, 7 December 1944, AW Papers 81/14, Hoover; **"not fighting"** AW to Hull, 25 November 1944, AW Papers 81/35, Hoover.

29 **"confining themselves"** Cray, *General*, 411.

30 **"three generations"** Cray, *General*, 506.

30 **military planners** James F. Schnabel, *The Joint Chiefs of Staff and National Policy*, 92; **Marshall expected** Marc S. Gallicchio, *The Scramble for Asia*, 22; **Mao was predicting** Chen Jian, *Mao's China and the Cold War*, 26.

30 **"If peace comes"** Jonathan D. Spence, *To Change China*, 276.

31 **"I am delighted"** CKS to GCM, 30 November 1945, GCM Papers 60/51, GCMRL; **Marshall replied** GCM to Wei, 1 December 1945, GCM Papers 60/51, GCMRL.

2. Horrid Dilemmas

32 **"Hollywood's idea"** *New Republic* December 1945; **"tried for losing"** *Washington Post* 18 December 1945.

32 **depart for China by December 7** GCM to Wei, 1 December 1945, GCM Papers 60/51, GCMRL.

33 **"I prefer to rest"** *New York Times* 7 December 1945; **"If we had failed"** *New York Times* 7 December 1945; **"a tragedy"** "Marshall as Witness," GCM Papers 24/11, GCMRL.

33 **twenty-four hours** *New York Times* 14 December 1945.

33 **"God bless democracy"** Papers Vol. 6, 484.

33 **"race of supermen"** Marshall cable, 11 December 1945, GCM Papers 124/40, GCMRL.

34 **In his telling . . ."urgency to succeed"** Marshall interviews, 40.

34 **"I do not feel it right"** Papers Vol. 1, 94.

34–35 **still curse** Marshall interviews, 548; **"I've never seen a man"** Cray, *General*, 306; **relaxing "completely"** Stoler, *George C. Marshall*, 28; *went to bed* Cray, *General*, 452; **"lived outside of himself"** Marshall, *Together*, 110; **a proverb** Papers Vol. 3, 501.

35 **challenged the top American general** Papers Vol. 1, 122; **"Mr. President, I am sorry"** Marshall interviews, 109; **"You said 'yes' pleasantly"** Cray, *General*, 139.

35 **State Department's policy paper** GCM to Leahy, 30 November 1945, GCM Papers 124/27, GCMRL.

35 **"For the past week"** Papers Vol. 5, 391.

36 **"we could expect Russia"** War Department Memo for Record, 10 December 1945, John E. Hull Papers, MHI.

36 **"I am still trying to find where the war left off"** Caraway to Paige, 13 December 1945, Paul Caraway Papers, MHI.

37 **"puppet of the Soviet"** AW report on developments in China, 20 November 1945, AW Papers 86/4, Hoover; **"de facto protectorate"** FRUS 1945 Vol. 7, 615; **"should Chiang attempt"** John Paton Davies, *China Hand*, 215.

37 **"horrid dilemma"** *Washington Post* 4 December 1945.

38 **"sufficient weapons"** War Department Memo for Record, 10 December 1945, John E. Hull Papers, MHI; **Marshall had asked, before the State Department reworked** Hull to GCM, 30 June 1951, John E. Hull Papers, MHI.

38 **Byrnes conceded** War Department Memo for Record, 10 December 1945, John E. Hull Papers, MHI; **A man of his caliber** Vincent to Byrnes, 10 December 1945, Marshall Mission Records 1, NARA.

38 **Order Number One** HST to CKS, 15 August 1945, Naval Aide Files 8/11, HST Papers, HSTL; **"largest troop movement"** Richard Bernstein, *China 1945*, 308; **"angeles of peace"** Ronald H. Spector, *In the Ruins of Empire*, 52.

39 **"incidental"** JHC letter, 11 November 1945, JHC Papers 2/6; **the main purpose was** Spector, *In the Ruins*, 7, 26.

39 **"How do you draw"** Gallicchio, *Scramble*, 92; **"conflicting orders"** FRUS 1945 Vol. 7, 684; **"Under the present circumstances"** AW report on developments in China, 20 November 1945, AW Papers 86/4, Hoover; **"an important contribution"** FRUS 1945 Vol. 7, 532.

39–40 **Wedemeyer advised** Davies, *China Hand*, 266; **more urgent priorities** Spector, *In the Ruins*, 39; **recently boasted** Davies, *China Hand*, 309.

40 **a million troops, party members** Paine, *Wars*, 224; **100 million people** Christopher R. Lew, *The Third Chinese Revolutionary Civil War*, 2; **"China's destiny"** Davies, *China Hand*, 215.

40 **"Without Soviet assistance"** *FRUS* 1945 Vol. 7, 630.

40 **"Soviet Russia's connivance"** CKS to HST, 23 November 1945, Naval Aide File 7/4, HST Papers, HSTL; **"collaborate with the Chinese Communists"** *FRUS* 1945 Vol. 7, 653.

41 **"delaying tactics"** *FRUS* 1945 Vol. 7, 759; **"block all progress"** GCM to Leahy, 30 November 1945, GCM Papers 124/27, GCMRL.

41 **"I do not anticipate any difficulty"** Feis, *China Tangle*, 397; **"If the unification"** AW report, 23 November 1945, AW Papers 91/1, Hoover.

42 **brash former missionary** Theodore H. White, *In Search of History*, 239; **Communists cut his throat** Yu, *OSS*, 239.

42 **Mao was apologetic, "very unfortunate"** Minutes of meeting with Mao and Zhou, 30 August 1945, AW Papers 87/6, Hoover; **provocative** Schaller, *U.S. Crusade*, 269; **"disturbing effect"** Minutes of meeting with Mao and Zhou, 30 August 1945, AW Papers 87/6, Hoover; **"doing their utmost"** Schaller, *U.S. Crusade*, 285.

43 **"As I see it"** *FRUS* 1945 Vol. 7, 1375; **"a reduction in the"** Steven I. Levine, *Anvil of Victory*, 75; **"stabilize the situation"** AW report on developments in China, 20 November 1945, AW Papers 86/4, Hoover; **"the policy of Byrnes"** Robert E. Herzstein, *Henry R. Luce, Time, and the American Crusade in Asia*, 53.

43 **"not yet capable"** AW report on developments in China, 20 November 1945, AW Papers 86/4, Hoover.

43 **"A divided China"** *FRUS* 1945 Vol. 7, 630.

44 **"unfortunate eventuality"** . . . **"war in the Pacific"** Notes on a meeting with the President, Mr. Byrnes, and Admiral Leahy, 11 December 1945, GCM Papers 124/27, GCMRL.

44 **"in the event"** Papers Vol. 5, 393.

45 **"The fact that"** HST to GCM, Secretary's Files 112/6, HST Papers, HSTL.

45 **"horns of a dilemma"** GCM to Leahy, 30 November 1945, GCM Papers 124/27, GCMRL; **"U.S. support"** U.S. Department of State, *China White Paper*, 608; **"prejudice the objectives"** *FRUS* 1945 Vol. 7, 772.

45 **"Events of this century"** U.S. Policy Toward China, GCM Papers 124/27, GCMRL; **"they will be"** *FRUS* 1945 Vol. 7, 773.

45 **"would make full use"** Bernstein, *China*, 281; **frustration with Mao** Averell Harriman Oral History, GCMRL; **"use of words"** Kennan to Harriman, 23 April 1945, Naval Aide Files 8/4, HST Papers, HSTL; **been spooked** Odd Arne Westad, *Cold War and Revolution*, 76.

45 **"no permanently safe international relations"** Donovan, *Conflict*, 93; **"decide to give active support"** Feis, *China*, 389.

47 **Acheson, would make sure** Papers Vol. 5, 376; **"rear echelon"** Acheson, *Sketches*, 150.

47 **one other assurance** Papers Vol. 5, 395.

47 **"might by some chance"** Papers Vol. 5, 384.

47   **National airport** GCMRL newsreels.

48   **"the most difficult"** Marshall cable, 10 December 1945, GCM Papers
        124/40, GCMRL; **"Upon General Marshall"** *Washington Post* 11 Decem-
        ber 1945; **"armed for years"** *Time* 10 December 1945; **"The situation in
        China"** Marshall cable, 4 December 1945, GCM Papers 124/40, GCMRL.

48   **"bitter blow," "I give a sickly smile"** KTM to McCarthy, Frank McCar-
        thy Papers 1, GCMRL.

48   **sense of duty** James Shepley Oral History, GCMRL; **"a great honor"** Wil-
        son to GCM, 20 December 1945, GCM Papers 124/12, GCMRL; **"one-man
        task"** Page to GCM, 5 June 1946, GCM Papers 123/29, GCMRL; **"grave-
        yard for American officials"** Spence, *To Change*, 266.

48   **Stilwell visit** Henry Byroade Oral History, GCMRL.

48-49   **a few months** Marshall, *Together*, 283; **departure** GCMRL newsreels.

49   **"the bravest man"** E. J. Kahn Jr., *The China Hands*, 184.

3. Marshall Is Too Big

50   **"walking in the fog"** John F. Melby, *The Mandate of Heaven*, 52; **"so many
        threads"** JM to Hellman, 28 November 1945, JM Papers 36, HSTL.

50   **rained, clouds** Melby, *Mandate*, 67; **"Everybody scurrying"** JM to Hell-
        man, 19 December 1945, JM Papers 36, HSTL.

51   **he thought back** Marshall interviews, 132.

51   **on long flights** Frank McCarthy Oral History, GCMRL; **"plushest"** JHC
        to Betty Caughey, 2 May 1946, JHC Papers 2/8, GCMRL; **fast-rising** AW
        to GCM, 2 December 1945, Marshall Mission Records 1, NARA; **"never
        at a loss"** JM to Hellman, 3 January 1946, JM Papers 36, HSTL; **"without
        anyone"** Papers Vol. 5, 406.

51   **rough plan** *FRUS* 1945 Vol. 7, 776-777; **odds** Henry Byroade Oral History,
        GCMRL.

51-52   **Shanghai arrival** GCMRL newsreels, *Chicago Tribune* 21 December 1945;
        Wedemeyer conversation Wedemeyer later became associated with the
        McCarthyite right and, shortly before Marshall's death, published a vicious
        attack on his former chief in a book called *Wedemeyer Reports!* Among other
        things, he reported that he had found Marshall exhausted and not up to the
        task, and told him that it could not be done—supposedly eliciting a tantrum
        from Marshall. While Marshall was certainly tired, and others in meetings
        agree that Marshall had been warned about the difficulty of success (as if
        he were not already well aware of it), the story as Wedemeyer later told it is
        contradicted by considerable evidence, including Wedemeyer's own words
        from the time and others' firsthand accounts, such as that of Walter Robert-
        son. Wedemeyer's report became a widely repeated part of the story, but his
        charges are mostly fanciful, concocted for the sake of a political takedown
        after the fact.

52   **"source of energy," "role model"** Orville Schell, *Wealth and Power*, 178; **unpresentable** CKS diary, 22 December 1945, Hoover.

52   **back of the car** GCMRL photographs; **almost midnight** CKS diary, 22 December 1945, Hoover.

52–53   **"same stake"** CKS diary, 21 December 1945, Hoover; **"cannot emulate"** CKS diary, 21 December 1945, Hoover; **Marshall wanted** Marshall interviews, 607; **Marshall statements** GCM-CKS meeting notes, 21 December 1945, Marshall Mission Records 20, NARA.

53   **"excellent impression"** AW to Hurley, 24 December 1945, AW Papers 81/36, Hoover; **"deference"** Spector, *In the Ruins*, 215; **"deceptive propaganda"** CKS diary, 21 December 1945, Hoover; **"The more deferential"** CKS diary, 22 December 1945, Hoover.

53   **mood** Melby, *Mandate*, 67; **"fix everything"** JM to Hellman, 4 December 1945, JM Papers 36, HSTL; **instantaneous lull** *Washington Post* 22 December 1945; **optimistic statements** *New York Times* 23 December 1945.

53   **national anthems** *New York Times* 23 December 1945.

53   **"Is Marshall"** JM to Hellman, 19 December 1945, JM Papers 36, HSTL.

54   **"prince-of-the-blood"** Papers Vol. 1, 263; **"unbelievable luxury"** Papers Vol. 1, 235; **"cheap liquor"** Papers Vol. 1, 273; **venereal disease** Luther D. Miller Oral History, GCMRL.

54   **"interesting events"** Papers Vol. 1, 274.

54–55   **"in the midst"** Papers Vol. 1, 270; **"very lucky"** Papers Vol. 1, 271; **guns** Papers Vol. 1, 283; **rail lines, blockades** Papers Vol. 1, 286; **maintaining order** Marshall interviews, 119; **"Can Do"** Tuchman, *Stilwell*, 99; **"leadership and ability"** Papers Vol. 1, 271; **"A Chinese soldier"** Papers Vol. 1, 272; **watched refugees** Papers Vol. 1, 284.

55   **ordered other officers** Newell to Allen, 16 March 1926, GCM Papers 8/27, GCMRL; **"without provoking"** Papers Vol. 1, 299; **2,500 characters** Papers Vol. 1, 294; **"grunt and whine"** Papers Vol. 1, 275; **"treaty rights," "wranglings"** Papers Vol. 1, 281; **"quite a Chinaman"** Papers Vol. 1, 277.

55   **"rarely judge"** Papers Vol. 1, 274; **"no one ventures"** Papers Vol. 1, 266.

55   **ominous implications** Papers Vol. 1, 277; **"strong man"** Papers Vol. 1, 271.

55   **"Profound change"** Taylor, *Generalissimo*, 48.

56   **his flaws** Taylor, *Generalissimo*, 30; **"meticulous self-control"** Jonathan Fenby, *Chiang Kai-shek*, 69; **Every morning** Taylor, *Generalissimo*, 17; **"loved to make decisions"** Mitter, *Forgotten*, 33.

56   **upright stone** Taylor, *Generalissimo*, 11; **"utter depression"** Fenby, *Chiang*, 43; **prostitutes** Taylor, *Generalissimo*, 18; **sterile** Taylor, *Generalissimo*, 34; **eating simply,** Taylor, *Generalissimo*, 40; **"From this day on"** Schell, *Wealth*, 188–189.

57   **Ho Chi Minh** Westad, *Restless*, 200; **Soviet advisers,** Taylor, *Generalissimo*, 54.

57   **"I treat them"** Taylor, *Generalissimo*, 55; **"a peculiar person"** Spence, *To*

Change, 195; **"like a lemon"** Philip Short, *Mao*, 178; **$80,000** Gao Wenqian, *Zhou Enlai*, 57.

57　　**"The Japanese"** Thomas D. Lutze, *China's Inevitable Revolution*, 22; **Hemingway** Peter Moreira, *Hemingway on the China Front*, 204.

58　　**pieces of a modern state** Lloyd E. Eastman, *Seeds of Destruction*, 1; **Unity rested on deals** Taylor, *Generalissimo*, 86; **Supposed commitments** Taylor, *Generalissimo*, 107; **"After a long waiting"** Lloyd D. Eastman, *Abortive Revolution*, 266.

58–59　　**imperfect Mandarin** Schell, *Wealth*, 173; **"traditional virtues"** Schell, *Wealth*, 187; **bible daily** Pakula, *Last*, 214; **"bear the cross"** Taylor, *Generalissimo*, 109; **"He has come"** Jespersen, *American Images*, 37.

59　　**15 million dead, 80 million displaced** Mitter, *Forgotten*, 5; **"trusting no one"** Tuchman, *Stilwell*, 480; **sacrificed little** Eastman, *Seeds*, 64; **"manmade famine"** Eastman, *Seeds*, 68; **Yellow River dikes** Mitter, *Forgotten*, 163; **cholera, plague, malaria** Paine, *Wars*, 137; **"seething with unrest"** Eastman, *Seeds*, 70.

59　·　**Chiang reflected** Fenby, *Chiang*, 452.

60　　**"Marshall is too big"** Westad, *Decisive*, 52.

60　　**China important** CKS diary, 28 November 1945, Hoover; **Stalin must think** CKS diary, 3 December 1945, Hoover; **"not in line"** CKS diary, 18 December 1945, Hoover.

60　　**"When Marshall asked"** Harold M. Tanner, *The Battle for Manchuria and the Fate of China*, 83.

60–61　　**"utterly feudal"** Mitter, *Forgotten*, 173; **high officials** Peck, *Two Kinds*, 51; **"a county seat"** White, *Thunder Out of China*, 8; **population** Paine, *Wars*, 135.

61　　**Madame Chiang wrote** Pakula, *Last*, 354; **"most bombed out"** Pocket Guide to China, AW Papers 87/3, Hoover; **wash their clothes** Peck, *Two Kinds*, 87; **"unbeatable"** Pocket Guide to China, AW Papers 87/3, Hoover.

61　　**"The prevailing"** Harold M. Tanner, *Where Chiang Kai-shek Lost China*, 37; **"rather medieval court intrigue"** Somervell to GCM, 24 October 1943, GCM Papers 60/54, GCMRL; **"yells, bells, and smells"** Gillem journal notes, 7 February 1946, Alvan Gillem Papers, MHI.

61–62　　**charged with keeping tabs** Melby, *Mandate*, 22; **"dreary expanse"** JM to Hellman, 12 November 1945, JM Papers 36, HSTL; **"you feel"** JM to Hellman, 30 November 1945, JM Papers 36, HSTL; **"a local gin"** JM to Hellman, 5 November 1945, JM Papers 36, HSTL; **navy doctor** JM to Hellman, 31 December 1945, JM Papers 36, HSTL; **"the most foul"** Gillem diary, 15 March 1946, Alvan Gillem Papers, MHI; **rats, peddlers, and power outages** Ralph Clough Oral History, Foreign Service Oral History Program, LOC; **squeals of pigs** JHC to Betty Caughey, 4 December 1945, JHC Papers 2/6, GCMRL; **"Sing Sing"** Melby, *Mandate*, 40; **"Time means"** Melby, *Mandate*, 53.

62   **deep brown mud** Melby, *Mandate*, 28; **Happiness Gardens** Taylor, *Generalissimo*, 333; **water heater** Eng to Caraway, 25 December 1945, Paul Caraway Papers, MHI; **house** Description based on personal visit.

62   **white hope** Roger B. Jeans, *The Marshall Mission to China*, 236; **press speculation** *South China Morning Post* 3 December 1945; **official chatter** JM to Hellman, 19 December 1945, JM Papers 36, HSTL.

62–63   **"You arrive here"** Hu to GCM, 14 January 1946, GCM Papers 123/36, GCMRL; **"mad with joy"** National Central University students to GCM, 23 April 1946, GCM Papers 123/24, GCMRL; **"sincere Christians"** Chang et al. to GCM, 1 January 1946, GCM Papers 122/15, GCMRL; **Others denounced** Antung representatives to GCM, GCM Papers 123/16, GCMRL; **postal . . . "poorly educated"** Embassy summary of letters to GCM, GCM Papers 123/24, GCMRL; **"number one boy"** GCM to Hsieh, 10 May 1946, GCM Papers 123/4, GCMRL; **former cook** GCM to Rockey, 6 February 1946, GCM Papers 123/35, GCMRL; **discarded novels** Group letter to GCM, 29 April 1946, GCM Papers 124, GCMRL; **borrow his airplane** Chang to GCM, 27 April 1946, GCM Papers 122/15, GCMRL.

63   **"great Christian republic"** Clovelly to GCM, 12 January 1947, GCM Papers 122/45, GCMRL; **Churchill** Churchill to GCM, 4 April 1946, GCM Papers 122/25, GCMRL; **clover** Stark to GCM, 15 December 1945, GCM Papers 123/42, GCMRL.

63   **relevant files** *FRUS* 1945 Vol. 7, 776; **"pungent collection"** Yu, *OSS*, 109; **"gestapo atmosphere"** JM to Hellman, 2 November 1945, JM Papers 36, HSTL; **"Just fiddling"** JM to Hellman, 14 November 1945, JM Papers 36, HSTL.

64   **trailed or bugged** JM to Hellman, 13 December 1945, JM Papers 36, HSTL; **"I wish to Christ"** JM to Hellman, 18 February 1946, JM Papers 36, HSTL.

64   **"a natural"** JM to Hellman, 28 November 1945, JM Papers 36, HSTL; **"a national hero"** Yeaton to AW, 16 December 1945, AW Papers 91/8, Hoover.

64   **Marshall wanted** *FRUS* 1945 Vol. 7, 804; **"All Fighting Ceases"** *Washington Post* 18 December 1945.

64–65   **"We are gratified"** *New York Times* 17 December 1945; **Chiang asserted** GCM-CKS meeting notes, 21 December 1945, Marshall Mission Records 20, NARA; **Communist spokesmen** *New York Times* 15 December 1945; **The government praised . . . the Communists** *New York Times* 16 December 1945; **"All official attitudes"** JM to Hellman, 17 December 1945, JM Papers 36, HSTL.

65   **"decided not to"** Zhang Baijia in Bland, *George C. Marshall's*, 210; **CCP's strategy** Niu Jun in Bland, *George C. Marshall's*, 242; **"Russian-style Communism"** Marshall cable, 6 December 1945, GCM Papers 124/40, GCMRL; **"Communist attitude"** *FRUS* 1945 Vol. 7, 705; **"If Marshall uses"** Westad, *Cold War*, 138.

65–66   **Marshall-Zhou meeting** GCM-Zhou meeting notes, 25 December 1945, Marshall Mission Records 20, NARA; **delightful** Han Suyin, *Eldest Son*, 192.

66   **"a genuine interest"** Papers Vol. 5, 404; **"we have called"** *New York Times*, 17 December 1945; **string of questions** GCM-Soong meeting notes, 24 December 1945, Marshall Mission Records 20, NARA; **dissident government figures, women** GCM Memorandum on China for HST, 18 May 1954, GCM Papers 241/5, GCMRL; **"listen more"** *FRUS* 1945 Vol. 7, 804.

66–67   **meet with reporters** GCM press conference transcript, 24 December 1945, Marshall Mission Records 20, NARA; **"foolish"** *New York Times* 25 December 1945; **"it will be some time"** *Washington Post* 25 December 1945; **rain-slicked** JM to Hellman, 23 December 1945, JM Papers 36, HSTL; **number of steps** *New York Times* 25 December 1945; **"no opinion"** *New York Times* 23 December 1945; **cease-fire by Christmas** *New York Times* 23 December 1945; **"special fancy"** News summary in JM to Hellman, 30 December 1945, JM Papers 36, HSTL.

67   **"Marshall has"** JM to Hellman, 28 December 1945, JM Papers 36, HSTL.

67   **"Women Communists"** *New York Times* 23 December 1945; **eggnog** JM to Hellman, 23 December 1945, JM Papers 36, HSTL; **fifteen-minute conversation** *Washington Post* 25 December 1945; **the Zhous** Melby, *Mandate*, 69; **"handle the Communists"** Melby, *Mandate*, 69.

67–68   **Christmas Day at the Chiangs'** Melby, *Mandate*, 144; **"a good show"** Caraway personal correspondence, 27 April 1947, Paul Caraway Papers, MHI.

68   **Martha Washington, Cleopatra, Joan of Arc, Florence Nightingale** Pakula, *Last*, 304–305, 379; **Zeus, Snow White** List of aliases, John Paton Davies Papers 11/4, HSTL.

68   **"*Vogue* cover"** Jespersen, *American Images*, 100; **"suppressed neigh"** Pakula, *Last*, 471; **"lovely legs"** Moreira, *Hemingway*, 142; **"so delightful"** Pakula, *Last*, 326; **"sex appeal"** Pakula, *Last*, 440; **"charm the birds"** Pakula, *Last*, 326; **"a man's job"** Tuchman, *Stilwell*, 281; **minister of war** Jack Belden, *China Shakes the World*, 435.

69   **Gettysburg Address** Pakula, *Last*, 52.

69   **"Scarlett O'Hara accent"** Pakula, *Last*, 24; **"masculine brain"** Jespersen, *American Images*, 82; **"charm and poise"** W. H. Auden, *Journey to a War*, 55.

69   **"Our wedding"** Pakula, *Last*, 183; **half his achievements** Pakula, *Last*, 199; **Book of Jeremiah** Taylor, *Generalissimo*, 133; **"da"** Taylor, *Generalissimo*, 76.

69–70   **"Madame's body"** Jespersen, *American Images*, 82; **"forthright American"** Jespersen, *American Images*, 54; **30,000, 17,000** Jespersen, *American Images*, 99; **Hayworth, Temple, Bergman** Pakula, *Last*, 438; **China market** Pakula, *Last*, 437; **"Lord helps"** Pakula, *Last*, 423; **Congress, "We welcome"** Pakula, *Last*, 422; **"most powerful"** Pakula, *Last*, 277.

70   **"prima donna … live democracy"** Marshall cable, 5 December 1945, GCM Papers 124/40, GCMRL; **greed and corruption** Peck, *Two Kinds*, 81; **"greatest crook"** Beal, *Marshall*, 5; **gossip** Decades later, someone who

had gone on a wartime goodwill tour with the rakish former presidential candidate Wendell Willkie wrote that Willkie and Madame Chiang spent a night together, with Willkie emerging to tell giddy tales after the Generalissimo and a coterie of guards interrupted them. True or not, it does indicate the place she occupied in the minds of men like Willkie at the time, and the nature of the gossip; **vase** Taylor, *Generalissimo*, 276; **impregnated** John S. Service, *Lost Chance in China*, 94.

70 **influence over Chiang** Marshall interviews, 607; **Chiang wanted her** Beal, *Marshall*, 247.

70-71 **Chiang felt at ease** CKS diary, 26 December 1945, Hoover; **"delightful smile"** Henry A. Wallace, *The Price of Vision*, 279; **"massage his ego"** Peter Chen-Main Wang, "Revisiting U.S.-China Wartime Relations," 241; **insufficiently skeptical** CKS diary, 26 December 1945, Hoover.

71 **took the time to write the report himself** Jeans, *Marshall Mission*, 13; **"possibility of a leak"** GCM to HST, 1 January 1946, Naval Aide Files 8/9, HST Papers, HSTL.

71 **Marshall's message** GCM to HST, 1 January 1946, Naval Aide Files 8/9, HST Papers, HSTL.

72 **"Soviet intent"** GCM to Byrnes, 26 December 1945, Marshall Mission Records 1, NARA; **Stalin belittled** *FRUS* 1945 Vol. 7, 841; **"boasters"** Harriman, *Special Envoy*, 527; **"not real Communists"** Feis, *China*, 140; **"not intentionally"** Westad, *Cold War*, 163.

72 **likely to follow** *FRUS* 1945 Vol. 7, 825; **Marshall could** James F. Byrnes, *Speaking Frankly*, 227-228; **statesman** *FRUS* 1945 Vol. 7, 850.

4. The Committee of Three

73 **left side of the road to the right** AW to Dade Wedemeyer, 24 December 1945, AW Papers 80/19, Hoover.

73 **"He just sits"** Melby, *Mandate*, 76; **150 guests** Undated clipping, GCM Papers 24/12, GCMRL; **told his staff** Tanner, *Battle*, 86; **took offense** Chen Li-fu Oral History, Columbia University Library.

74 **"the next war"** JHC to Betty Caughey, 29 December 1945, JHC Papers 2/7, GCMRL; **"a lonely man"** JHC to Betty Caughey, 1 January 1946, JHC Papers 2/7, GCMRL.

74 **"I've never seen"** JHC to Betty Caughey, 4 January 1946, JHC Papers 2/7, GCMRL; **maybe sick** JM to Hellman, 24 December 1945, JM Papers 36, HSTL; **On the contrary** Others, including David Barrett and Wang Shih-chieh in their oral history interviews with Forrest Pogue, also reject the notion that Marshall was too exhausted to be effective. This assertion became part of later attacks. Wedemeyer would make the charge, though his letters from the time contradict it, with commentary on Marshall's energy and drive; **"ball of fire"** Jeans, *Marshall Mission*, 71.

75   **"You are only conscious"** JHC to Betty Caughey, 4 January 1946, JHC
        Papers 2/7, GCMRL; **wicked memory** Marshall, *Together*, 9; **skim a memo**
        John E. Hull Oral History, GCMRL; **nine newspapers** Marshall inter-
        views, 486; **impatient** Reuben Jenkins Oral History, GCMRL; **"one mis-
        take"** JM to Hellman, 20 March 1946, JM Papers 36, HSTL; **"a bald eagle"**
        David D. Barrett Oral History, GCMRL.

75   **veterans warned** Henry Byroade Oral History, GCMRL; **"He does not
        like"** JHC to Betty Caughey, 2 February 1946, JHC Papers 2/7, GCMRL; **"I
        must have"** Ricks, *Generals*, 47.

75–76   **directness, indefinite pronoun** JHC to Betty Caughey, 16 November
        1946, JHC Papers 2/11, GCMRL; **"greatest course"** George V. Underwood
        Oral History, GCMRL; **"The General will"** JHC to Betty Caughey, 6 June
        1946, JHC Papers 2/9, GCMRL; **smoking** Melby, *Mandate*, 186.

76   **"varsity ball"** Carter to JHC, 30 July 1946, JHC Papers 1/2, GCMRL; **"to
        learn at firsthand"** Papers Vol. 5, 697; **"Formidable yes"** JHC to Betty
        Caughey, 6 June 1946, JHC Papers 2/9, GCMRL.

76   **"promise for the future"** JHC to Betty Caughey, 4 January 1946, JHC
        Papers 2/7, GCMRL.

76   **Chang Chun description** Howard L. Boorman, *Biographical Dictionary of
        Republican China*, Vol. 1, 47.

77   **actor, female roles** Gao, *Zhou*, 29; **even Chiang** Fenby, *Chiang*, 340.

77   **Gellhorn, Hemingway** Moreira, *Hemingway*, 129; **expressive eyebrows**
        Davies, *Dragon*, 347.

77   **"run-down aristocratic"** Gao, *Zhou*, 87; **his parents** Dick Wilson, *Zhou
        Enlai*, 20; **"Paris is beautiful"** Wilson, *Zhou*, 57; **discussion groups, read
        Marx** Wilson, *Zhou*, 55.

77   **turning cadets** Gao, *Zhou*, 51; **during this crackdown** Gao, *Zhou*, 54.

78   **savage father** Short, *Mao*, 30; **Zhou conceded** Gao, *Zhou*, 87; **"good little
        children"** Short, *Mao*, 392.

78   **"Mao's housekeeper"** Wilson, *Zhou*, 123; **"conditions outside"** Wil-
        son, *Zhou*, 138; **"A revolution"** Taylor, *Generalissimo*, 61; **Zhou took notes**
        White, *In Search*, 186.

78–79   **inkwell** Han, *Eldest*, 141; **five assassins** Pantsov, *Mao*, 247.

79   **Reporters in need of copy** Edgar Snow, *Red Star Over China*, 76; **govern-
        ment spokesmen** Stephen R. MacKinnon, *China Reporting*, 82; **Even when
        . . . he was lying** Henry Byroade Oral History, Foreign Service Oral History
        Program, LOC; **code name** List of aliases, John Paton Davies Papers 11/4,
        HSTL.

79   **Over dinner** John Melby Oral History, HSTL; **tentative English conver-
        sation** Wilson, *Zhou*, 144; **flirtatious streak** Gao, *Zhou*, 47; **never seemed
        to get drunk** Han, *Eldest*, 202; **called him Joe** Henry Byroade Oral His-
        tory, Foreign Service Oral History Program, LOC; **When he wanted to
        flatter them** White, *In Search*, 84.

79   **"They are vigorous"** John King Fairbank, *Chinabound*, 307; **"not the clothes"** Han, *Eldest*, 191; **"Don't be impatient"** Kai-yu Hsu, *Chou En-Lai*, 167.

79   **"Expose the darkness"** Michael M. Sheng, "America's Lost Chance in China?," 150.

80   **Mao dispensed advice on handling Chiang** Service, *Lost*, 302; **more cooperative** Service, *Lost*, 307; **shrank from combat** Michael M. Sheng, *Battling Western Imperialism*, 49; **"If you land"** Sheng, *Battling*, 90; **visit Roosevelt** Barbara W. Tuchman, "If Mao Had Come to Washington," 44.

80   **"The KMT tries"** Heinzig, *Soviet Union*, 40; **a crafty merchant** Heinzig, *Soviet Union*, 41; **Monopoly, the situation** John S. Service Oral History, Foreign Service Oral History Program, LOC; **"a unified group"** Service, *Lost*, 198.

80–81   **signed off on Dixie** Carter, *Mission*, 19; **radio gear** Yu, *OSS*, 166; **lessons in spycraft** Yu, *OSS*, 188; **would have equipped** Carter, *Mission*, 145.

81   **on a flight** Barrett, *Dixie*, 65.

81   **Roosevelt got a copy** Schaller, *U.S. Crusade*, 21; **"fired by the belief"** Snow, *Red Star*, 125; **"rural equalitarianism"** Snow, *Red Star*, 219.

81–82   **"cave Marxists"** Pantsov, *Mao*, 4; **peasant armies** Odd Arne Westad, *Brothers in Arms*, 49; **"a cross between"** Belden, *China Shakes*, 168; **"Eagle Scout behavior"** Davies, *China Hand*, 26; **"gung ho"** Davies, *China Hand*, 27; **Mao mused** Sheng, *Battling*, 82; **"the most conservative"** Service, *Lost*, 307; **"The Communist political program"** Sheng, *Battling*, 77; **even avowed haters of Communism** Leahy diary, 11 December 1945, William D. Leahy Papers, LOC.

82   **"bill of goods"** Taylor, *Generalissimo*, 299; **"sinister intentions"** Stilwell to GCM, 30 March 1944, GCM Papers 60/55, GCMRL.

82   **"Not that I like"** Carter, *Mission*, 139; **"Chiang could not whip"** Service, *Lost*, 384.

82   **military intelligence** Lyman P. Van Slyke, *The Chinese Communist Movement*.

83   **first encounter with Stalin** Marshall, *Together*, 167.

83–84   **"President's attitude"** Wallace, *Price*, 520; **"anti-Russian"** Stoler, *George C. Marshall*, 159; **Dexter White** Pogue, *Statesman*, 152; **hard-liners** Harriman, *Special Envoy*, 503.

84   **"created conditions"** AW to GCM, 8 September 1945, GCM Papers 90/22, GCMRL; **"effective machine"** Ernest R. May, *The Truman Administration and China*, 8.

84   **"Soviet policy"** Cohen, *America's Response*, 149.

84   **"as serfs"** Short, *Mao*, 195; **"bloc within"** Michael H. Hunt, *The Genesis of Chinese Communist Foreign Policy*, 108; **"babble"** Heinzig, *Soviet Union*, 220; **his death** Westad, *Brothers in Arms*, 15.

84–85   **forbade his execution** Pantsov, *Mao*, 301; **Soviet weapons** Paine, *Wars*, 344; **Soviets grumbled** Heinzig, *Soviet Union*, 34; **questionably Commu-**

nist Westad, *Cold War*, 38; **"obviously too weak"** Niu Jun, *From Yan'an to the World*, 77; **without much Soviet support** Westad, *Brothers in Arms*, 6; **"over to Moscow"** Heinzig, *Soviet Union*, 8.

85   **"We should listen"** Heinzig, *Soviet Union*, 33; **"voice from the remote place"** Sheng, *Battling*, 23.

85   **"Stalin's pupils"** Bernstein, *China*, 251; **ready to fight** Sheng, *Battling*, 101; **Sino-Soviet Treaty** Mitter, *Forgotten Ally*, 355; **orders to Mao** Niu, *From Yan'an*, 196.

85–86   **set a new course, directive** Chen, *Mao's*, 28; **"way of France"** Heinzig, *Soviet Union*, 77; **"a good washing"** Taylor, *Generalissimo*, 317.

86   **contorted analysis** Sheng, *Battling*, 105; **pointed out that overt Soviet support** Chen, *Mao's*, 28; **"Third world war"** Sheng, *Battling*, 104; **his own execution** Pantsov, *Mao*, 346.

86   **Communist infiltration** Tanner, *Where*, 31; **staged firefight** Tanner, *Battle*, 55; **"diplomatic embarrassment"** Tony Saich, *The Rise to Power of the Chinese Communist Party*, 1270; **The Soviets also** Heinzig, *Soviet Union*, 90; **considerable benefit** Bruce A. Elleman in Bruce A. Elleman, *Naval Coalition Warfare*, 127.

86   **"greater the current victory"** Niu, *From Yan'an*, 229.

86–87   **recalled Soviet representatives** Westad, *Decisive*, 31; **threatened to use tanks** Westad, *Cold War*, 125; **refused to hand over** Harold M. Tanner, "Guerrilla, Mobile, and Base Warfare in Communist Military Operations in Manchuria," 1189; **"puzzled and disappointed"** Spector, *In the Ruins*, 42; **hammer-and-sickle tattoo** Tanner, "Guerrilla," 1189; **Soviets stood by** Heinzig, *Soviet Union*, 91.

87   **After ten days** GCM to HST, 1 January 1946, Naval Aide Files 8/9, HST Papers, HSTL.

87   **resistant, quickly amenable** GCM to HST, 1 January 1946, Naval Aide Files 8/9, HST Papers, HSTL; **public call for Marshall** *Washington Post* 1 January 1946.

87   **"prospects for domestic peace"** Marshall cables, 3 January 1946, GCM Papers 24/1, GCMRL; **"no hope for unity"** JM to Hellman, 9 November 1945, JM Papers 36, HSTL; **"a sort of truce"** JM to Hellman, 3 January 1946, JM Papers 36, HSTL.

87   **Communists were persuaded** Zhang in Bland, *George C. Marshall's*, 214; **"He holds that the Communist army"** Qin Xiaoyi, *The Chronicles of President Chiang*, Vol. 5.2, 2750.

88   **"role of referee"** *New York Times* 1 January 1946; **"I was here"** FRUS 1946 Vol. 9, 790; **Recent negotiations** Lutze, *China's*, 35; **"worse than beasts"** Jung Chang, *Mao*, 297; **"gangster"** Service, *Lost*, 302; **"turtle's egg"** Barrett, *Dixie*, 74; **"Fascist chieftain"** James Reardon-Anderson, *Yenan and the Great Powers*, 100; **"stubborn heart"** Belden, *China Shakes*, 263.

88   **Stalin had explicitly warned** Heinzig, *Soviet Union*, 67; **worse than fac-**

ing Japan Taylor, *Generalissimo*, 310; **"we cannot use"** Simei Qing, *From Allies to Enemies*, 66; **"We are striving sincerely"** *FRUS* 1945 Vol. 7, 566; **radio broadcast** *New York Times* 1 January 1946.

88–89   **"fed up with war"** Zhang in Bland, *George C. Marshall's*, 207; **Stalin told them** Odd Arne Westad, "Losses, Chances, and Myths," 107; **too weak** Levine, *Anvil*, 42.

89   **"the sympathy"** He Di in Bland, *George C. Marshall's*, 182; **path of negotiation** Zhang in Bland, *George C. Marshall's*, 207; **"new democracy"** Niu, *From Yan'an*, 133; **"big chance"** Niu, *From Yan'an*, 160; **"people's consciousness"** He in Bland, *George C. Marshall's*, 180; **prospects good** Sheng, *Battling*, 85.

89   **"two-sided policy"** Hunt, *Genesis*, 138; **"Every single rifle"** He in Bland, *George C. Marshall's*, 183; **"strategy of peace"** Zhang in Bland, *George C. Marshall's*, 207.

89   **Communist spokesmen** Niu, *From Yan'an*, 246; **Cadres were told** Westad, *Cold War*, 131; **"Ideas of friendship"** Westad, *Cold War*, 128.

90   **"unified and democratic"** Heinzig, *Soviet Union*, 104; **"the most hopeful"** Marshall cables, 29 December 1945, GCM Papers 24/1, GCMRL; **need for cooperation** Westad, *Cold War*, 137; **"unforgettable insult"** Edmund S. Wehrle in Bland, *George C. Marshall's*, 70; **using barbarian** Westad, *Brothers in Arms*, 59; **leave it to the Americans** Sheng, *Battling*, 128.

90   **government's position** Marc S. Gallicchio, *The Cold War Begins in Asia*, 110; **"Generalissimo's military strength"** Yenan Observer Group analysis, 25 December 1945, AW Papers 90/6, Hoover.

90   **Chennault** Davies, *Dragon*, 370; **"solution of China's problems"** War Department, *Chinese Communist*, 243.

91   **Yeaton** Yenan Observer Group analysis, 25 December 1945, AW Papers 90/6, Hoover.

91   **Paris . . . Shanghai** Donovan, *Conflict*, 165; *SERFDOM NEVER* New York Times 7 January 1946.

91   **"emotional crisis"** Schnabel, *Joint Chiefs*, 99; **"isolation fever"** Xiaoyuan Liu, *Partnership for Disorder*, 288; **Fifteen thousand a day, still savaged** Thomas J. Christensen, *Useful Adversaries*, 39; **"as soon as possible"** HST to GCM, Secretary's Files 112/6, HST Papers, HSTL; **reminding Chiang** Soong to CKS, 10 November 1945, T. V. Soong Papers 37/25, Hoover.

91   **"invasion of a foreign shore"** Military Advisory Group welcome booklet, Virginia Lee Papers, GCMRL; **"White Russian girls"** Spector, *In the Ruins*, 52.

92   **"as human beings"** Pocket Guide to China, AW Papers 87/3, Hoover; **"starch in rain"** *Life* 24 December 1945; **"If I were Chinese"** JHC to Betty Caughey, 19 December 1945, JHC Papers 2/7, GCMRL; **Americans mocked** AW to Lucas, 24 August 1947, AW Papers 93/40, Hoover; **"chinks"** *New Yorker* 18 May 1946; **"slopies"** Goodfriend to GCM, 19 December 1945, GCM Papers 122/41, GCMRL; **careening American jeeps** *New*

Yorker 9 February 1946; **Troops looked upon the Chinese** Goodfriend to GCM, 19 December 1945, GCM Papers 122/41, GCMRL.

92 **"It beats me"** Goodfriend to GCM, 19 December 1945, GCM Papers 122/41, GCMRL; **"If anybody had meddled"** Mark F. Wilkinson in Bland, *George C. Marshall's*, 333.

92 **Mothers accused Truman** Summary of letter to HST, 5 December 1945, White House Central Files 757/13, HST Papers, HSTL; **"my son's life"** Chern, *Dilemma*, 163; **2,000 postcards** White House mailroom to Smith, 11 January 1946, White House Central Files 757/12, HST Papers, HSTL; **AFL and CIO** *Washington Post* 15 December 1945; **"Chiang Kai-shek supported us"** HST to Delacy, 12 January 1946, Secretary's Files 151/9, HST Papers, HSTL.

93 **homeward-bound ships** *New York Times* 21 December 1945; **Parents wrote** GCM to Rumage, 2 February 1946, GCM Papers 123/36, GCMRL; **an older couple** Rumage to GCM, 5 March 1946, GCM Papers 123/36, GCMRL; **"You got out"** Andrews to GCM, 1 February 1946, GCM Papers 122/4, GCMRL.

93 **Mao was a disciple** Pantsov, *Mao*, 279; **well-thumbed translation** Barry Machado of Washington & Lee found and examined Marshall's copy, a 1929 edition that was once part of his library in Leesburg.

93 **maps of troops** *FRUS* 1946 Vol. 9, 38; **waved gently** GCMRL newsreels.

93–94 **neutral ground** James Shepley Oral History, GCMRL; **determine strategy** CKS diary, 6 January 1946, Hoover; **be friendly** He in Bland, *George C. Marshall's*, 193; **directive on diplomacy** Saich, *Rise*, 1215; **"For the sake"** Wilson, *Zhou*, 89; **"plain capitalist"** Zhang in Bland, *George C. Marshall's*, 219.

94 **time, space, and good faith** Committee of Three minutes, 10 January 1946, Marshall Mission Records 19, NARA.

94 **He had claimed** *FRUS* 1945 Vol. 7, 801; **it was the only way** Marshall interviews, 210.

94–95 **draft order aloud** *FRUS* 1946 Vol. 9, 56; **"What does 'these'"** *FRUS* 1946 Vol. 9, 45; **he interrupted** *FRUS* 1946 Vol. 9, 102; **relying on** JHC Oral History, GCMRL; **"mandatory"** JHC to Betty Caughey, 12 February 1946, JHC Papers 2/7, GCMRL; **tactics** JHC to Betty Caughey, 23 February 1946, JHC Papers 2/7, GCMRL; *this* **month** Beal, *Marshall*, 59.

95 **"Things are going"** Marshall cables, 8 January 1946, GCM Papers 24/1, GCMRL.

95 **"Now, Gentlemen"** *FRUS* 1946 Vol. 9, 65; **Soong sometimes swapped** Interview with Rebecca Soong, 22 December 2014.

95–96 **"As a negotiator"** AW to Hutchin, 1 September 1946, Paul Caraway Papers, MHI; **"pleasure to watch"** JHC to Betty Caughey, 4 January 1946, JHC Papers 2/7, GCMRL; **"guiding spirit"** JM to Hellman, 7 January 1946, JM Papers 36, HSTL.

96 **"The promise of peace in China"** *New York Times* 9 January 1946; **"Are hostilities"** *FRUS* 1946 Vol. 9, 68.

96 **Rehe and Chahar dispute** *FRUS* 1946 Vol. 9, 61–73.

96–97 **"Gentlemen, it appears to me"** Committee of Three minutes, 10 January 1946, Marshall Mission Records 19, NARA; **ended the session early** GCM to HST, 10 January 1946, Naval Aide Files 8/9, HST Papers, HSTL.

97 **10 o'clock that evening** GCM to HST, 10 January 1946, Naval Aide Files 8/9, HST Papers, HSTL; **the only way** Wehrle in Bland, *George C. Marshall's*, 73.

97 **on Chiang's orders** CKS diary, 9 January 1946, Hoover; **battling to take control** *Washington Post* 3 January 1946; **two provinces** He in Bland, *George C. Marshall's*, 186; **"must completely control"** Saich, *Rise*, 1270.

97 **respectfully acknowledged** CKS diary, 9 January 1946, Hoover; **major gains** CKS diary, 5 January 1946, Hoover; **did not have to cede** GCM to HST, 10 January 1946, Naval Aide Files 8/9, HST Papers, HSTL; **a declaration of peace** Wehrle in Bland, *George C. Marshall's*, 73; **provide Chiang the . . . aid** Shepley to HST, 26 February 1946, GCM Papers 124/28, GCMRL.

98 **after midnight** *New York Times* 11 January 1946; **Committee of Three signing** Committee of Three minutes, 10 January 1946, Marshall Mission Records 19, NARA; **uniform, suit, tunic** GCMRL newsreels.

98 **leaflets** *New Yorker* 4 May 1946 and Marshall cables, 15 January 1946, GCM Papers 24/1, GCMRL.

5. Unity Out of Chaos

99 **roar of applause** *Time* 21 January 1946; **"long stride"** Herzstein in Bland, *George C. Marshall's*, 128; **"important gain"** *South China Morning Post* 11 January 1946; **"phase of peaceful development"** Bernstein, *China*, 358; **"mission is complete"** Marshall cables, 11 January 1946, GCM Papers 24/1, GCMRL.

99 **"historic," "pause for deliberation"** Committee of Three minutes, 10 January 1946, Marshall Mission Records 19, NARA.

99–100 **blueprints** GCM to HST, 1 January 1946, Naval Aide Files 8/9, HST Papers, HSTL; **trucks and radios** Papers Vol. 5, 407; **late-night conferences, Beijing hotel** History of the Executive Headquarters, Alvan Gillem Papers, MHI.

100 **Marshall worried** Committee of Three minutes, 10 January 1946, Marshall Mission Records 19, NARA; **more violence, exaggerating** *FRUS* 1946 Vol. 9, 373.

100 **"my full confidence"** GCM to Byroade, 14 January 1946, GCM Papers 122/8, GCMRL; **"an impartial source"** GCM to HST, 1 January 1946, Naval Aide Files 8/9, HST Papers, HSTL; **his C-54** *FRUS* 1946 Vol. 9, 127; **one hundred colonels** War Department Personnel memo, 16 March 1946, GCM

Papers 124/34, GCMRL; **promoted to Brigadier General** Royall to HST, 15 January 1946, White House Central Files 840, HST Papers, HSTL; **rules, kit** History of the Executive Headquarters, Alvan Gillem Papers, MHI.

101   **"to go home"** Walter Robertson Oral History, GCMRL; **"solely"** Committee of Three minutes, 10 January 1946, Marshall Mission Records 19, NARA; **the American served** History of the Executive Headquarters, Alvan Gillem Papers, MHI.

101   **"less fighting"** *FRUS* 1946 Vol. 9, 377; **"a courageous experiment"** History of the Executive Headquarters, Alvan Gillem Papers, MHI.

101   **"good faith"** *FRUS* 1946 Vol. 9, 115; **"hardest problem"** GCM to HST, 10 January 1946, Naval Aide Files 8/9, HST Papers, HSTL; **"fundamental requirement"** GCM to HST, 16 January 1946, Marshall Mission Records 15, NARA; **Chiang proposed** CKS diary, 16 January 1946, Hoover; **"This will make us"** *FRUS* 1946 Vol. 9, 364.

101   **"Conducting war"** Papers Vol. 6, 74.

102   **Zhou and Chang** JHC to Betty Caughey, 19 January 1946, JHC Papers 2/7, GCMRL; *True Victory* GCM appointment list, 16 January 1946, Marshall Mission Records 7, NARA; **"Hard to believe," transfixed** JHC to Betty Caughey, 19 January 1946, JHC Papers 2/7, GCMRL.

102   **come to relish** JHC to Betty Caughey, 8 February 1946, GCMRL; **Marshall told stories** JHC to Betty Caughey, 12 October 1946, JHC Papers 2/10, GCMRL, JM to Hellman, 9 January 1946, JM Papers 36, HSTL, and Beal, *Marshall*, 63; **"He can pull"** JHC to Betty Caughey, 10 December 1946, JHC Papers 2/11, GCMRL.

102-3   **"the way he relaxes"** JHC to Betty Caughey, 19 January 1946, JHC Papers 2/7, GCMRL; **Marshall had learned that lesson** Marshall, *Together*, 110; **napped** JHC to Betty Caughey, 8 February 1946, JHC Papers 2/7, GCMRL, JHC Oral History, GCMRL; **sightseeing walks** Jeans, *Marshall Mission*, 241; **"cheap fiction"** JM to Hellman, 6 January 1946, JM Papers 36, HSTL; **stream of movies** Carter to Army Motion Picture Service, 21 October 1946, GCM Papers 124, GCMRL; *The Atom Strikes* JHC to Betty Caughey, 13 February 1946, JHC Papers 2/7, GCMRL; *Tarzan* GCM appointment list, 2 August 1946, Marshall Mission Records 7, NARA; **concentrated as intently** George V. Underwood Oral History, GCMRL; **ice cream** Melby, *Mandate*, 186.

103   **"I long for"** GCM to Wilson, 11 January 1946, GCM Papers 124/12, GCMRL.

103   **to strategize** JHC to Betty Caughey, 16 March 1946, JHC Papers 2/8, GCMRL; **cocktail shaker** Madame CKS to AW, 6 February 1946, AW Papers 83/27, Hoover; **corrected American staff** George V. Underwood Oral history, GCMRL; **cultivated his aides** George V. Underwood Oral history, GCMRL; **birthday presents** JHC to Madame CKS, 16 November 1946, JHC Papers 1/5, GCMRL; **long-standing Chinese practice** Henry Kissinger, *On China*, 51; **"color into your cheeks"** Madame CKS to GCM,

8 February 1946, GCM Papers 122/20, GCMRL; **leafy complex, Marshall cottage** Visit to Huanshan.

103   **Over dinner and vodka** JM to Hellman, 9 January 1946, JM Papers 36, HSTL; **talked amiably** Andrei M. Ledovsky in Bland, *George C. Marshall's*, 428; **Petrov had no idea** Ledovsky in Bland, *George C. Marshall's*, 427.

103–4   **beer, gin, brandy** Melby, *Mandate*, 146; *baiju* JM to Hellman, 12 January 1946, JM Papers 36, HSTL; **"right-wing KMT"** JM to Hellman, 10 February 1946, JM Papers 36, HSTL; **Communist officers** Melby, *Mandate*, 66.

104   **"city of rumors"** JM to Hellman, 14 January 1946, JM Papers 36, HSTL; **"lack of secrecy"** GCM to Arnold, 11 February 1942, GCM Papers 60/52, GCMRL; **Nationalist stooge** JM to Hellman, 26 February 1946, JM Papers 36, HSTL; **false names** Beal, *Marshall*, 167; **"have to assume"** Melby, *Mandate*, 92; **Jeeps** JM to Hellman, 9 July 1946, JM Papers 36, HSTL; **Marshall's clothes** *New York Times* 14 January 1946; **scores of moles** Frederic Wakeman Jr., *Spymaster*, 340; **codebook** Wakeman, *Spymaster*, 273.

104   **military surveillance** Papers Vol. 5, 420; **"world matters as they affect China"** Papers Vol. 5, 420; **Nationalist codes, more challenging** Papers Vol. 5, 420, and James Shepley Oral History, GCMRL.

104   **encrypted messages** Carter to JHC, 14 November 1946, Marshall Mission Records 2, NARA; **frequent reminders** GCM to HST, 24 January 1946, Marshall Mission Records 15, NARA; **"no slip"** Papers Vol. 5, 554; **infamously indiscreet** George V. Underwood Oral History, GCMRL; **"as a sieve"** Dean Acheson Oral History, GCMRL; **William Leahy** Carter to JHC, 14 November 1946, Marshall Mission Records 2, NARA, and Marshall Carter Oral History, GCMRL.

105   **drilled discretion** John Melby Oral History, GCMRL; **Stilwell's great sin** Marshall interviews, 605; **"I am carefully refraining"** Papers Vol. 5, 432; **State Department spokesman** Papers Vol. 5, 399; **"frequent leaks"** Papers Vol. 5, 435; **few trusted reporters** George V. Underwood Oral History, GCMRL.

105   **"nobody nothing"** JM to Hellman, 14 January 1946, JM Papers 36, HSTL; **"all bluffed"** JM to Hellman, 25 January 1946, JM Papers 36, HSTL.

106   **"ancient battle"** JM to Hellman, 9 January 1946, JM Papers 36, HSTL.

106   **"persuade the Chinese Government"** HST to GCM, 14 December 1946, Secretary's Files 112/7, HST Papers, HSTL; **only after Marshall's arrival** Final report 10, and Peck, *Two Kinds*, 673; **Chiang went on** *New York Times* 11 January 1946; **"If we remember"** CKS speech to PCC opening, 10 January 1946, JM Papers 1, HSTL; **Zhou followed** Wilson, *Zhou*, 168; **"going full blast"** Melby, *Mandate*, 91.

106   **landlord exploitation and warlord domination** Frederic Wakeman Jr., *Reappraising Republican China*, 104; **inflation, railways** Westad, *Decisive*, 29; **could read** Westad, *Decisive*, 17; **in the fields** Wakeman, *Reappraising*, 28; **Life expectancy** Westad, *Decisive*, 20.

106   **"We can thank"** "Extracts from Harry's letter written at Shanghai, China," 11 April 1946, P. Frank Price Papers 6, GCMRL; **Old Testament** Jespersen, *American Images*, 67.

107   **American-educated daughters** Boorman, *Biographical Dictionary*, Vol. 2, 149; **"Foreigner"** Westad, *Cold War*, 47; **imperious strut** Beal, *Marshall*, 19; **"I have never associated"** Frank Dikötter, *The Age of Openness*, 38; **Harvard Club** White, *In Search*, 73.

107   **"a monopoly"** *FRUS* 1946 Vol. 10, 568; **"Chinese fascism"** Melby, *Mandate*, 162; **Blackshirts** Wakeman, *Reappraising*, 148; **"Himmler"** Gillem to Palmer, 23 March 1946, Alvan Gillem Papers, MHI; **"any time, any place"** Wakeman, *Spymaster*, 4; **Wedemeyer decried** AW to CKS, 10 January 1946, AW Papers 86/1, Hoover; **"Chinese Gestapo"** JM to Hellman, 3 November 1945, JM Papers 36, HSTL.

107–8 **"thousands of incompetents"** AW to GCM, 8 September 1945, GCM Papers 90/22, GCMRL; **head of Chiang's military council** Memorandum on Lung, 12 February 1946, GCM Papers 123/15, GCMRL; **landowners** Belden, *China Shakes*, 100; **"One is faced"** *FRUS* 1946 Vol. 9, 1351.

108   **"flaming revolutionaries"** JM to Hellman, 19 December 1945, JM Papers 36, HSTL.

108   **"weak and rotten"** Eastman, *Seeds*, 91; **"ease and pleasure"** Taylor, *Generalissimo*, 157; **"hatred and repugnance"** Pakula, *Last*, 213; **"inefficiency and corruption"** Taylor, *Generalissimo*, 99; **"If we do not weed"** Eastman, *Abortive Revolution*, 277.

108   **"most astute politician"** Tuchman, *Stilwell*, 262; **personally corrupt** Peck, *Two Kinds*, 480; **ignored abuses** Taylor, *Generalissimo*, 107; **"most fundamental problem"** Taylor, *Generalissimo*, 100; **envoy from Nazi Germany** Eastman, *Abortive Revolution*, 40.

108   **"Considering his background"** Evaluation of military situation in China, 20 November 1945, AW Papers 86/4, Hoover.

109   **"pull the plug"** Paine, *Wars*, 234; **"cut the ground"** Qing, *From Allies*, 61.

109   **"If the Nationalist Party"** *FRUS* 1946 Vol. 10, 165; **"The Communists of course prefer"** JM to Hellman, 12 January 1946, JM Papers 36, HSTL.

109   **"who wins"** JM to Hellman, 12 November 1945, JM Papers 36, HSTL.

110   **"fundamental requirements"** Papers Vol. 5, 404; **"most powerful thing"** GCM Statement to Chinese Editors, 23 February 1946, GCM Papers 122/30, GCMRL; **Benjamin Franklin's speeches** *New Yorker* 16 March 1946, and *Time* 25 March 1946; **"backward and colonial peoples"** GCM Encyclopaedia Britannica draft, GCM Papers 123/34, GCMRL.

110   **Marshall did not see much he could do** Papers Vol. 5, 417; **"Marshall needs help"** JM to Hellman, 14 January 1946, JM Papers 36, HSTL; **"scrounging around in odd corners"** JM to Hellman, 18 January 1946, JM Papers 36, HSTL.

110   **January 22 meeting, bill of rights** GCM to HST, 24 January 1946, Naval Aide Files 8/9, HST Papers, HSTL.

110   **"Even the Communists"** Ramon H. Myers in Bland, *George C. Marshall's*, 154; **"too tolerant"** Qin, *Chronicles*, Vol. 6.1, 2776.

110   **pale sunshine** JM to Hellman, 20 January 1946, JM Papers 36, HSTL; **The Communists** CKS diary, 23 January 1946; **But to Marshall** GCM to HST, 24 January 1946, Naval Aide Files 8/9, HST Papers, HSTL.

111   **"a dose of American medicine"** GCM to HST, 24 January 1946, Naval Aide Files 8/9, HST Papers, HSTL; **"the Stilwell era"** Qin, *Chronicles*, Vol. 6.1, 2778.

111   **"face"** Shepley to HST, 26 February 1946, GCM Papers 124/28, GCMRL; **message stamped EYES ONLY** GCM to HST, 24 January 1946, Naval Aide Files 8/9, HST Papers, HSTL.

111   **"meat ax"** Beal, *Marshall*, 328; **"You may state"** HST to GCM, 14 December 1946, Secretary's Files 112/7, HST Papers, HSTL; **railroad supplies** *FRUS* 1946 Vol. 10, 944; **ships** *FRUS* 1945 Vol. 7, 1202; **ammunition** Papers Vol. 5, 410; **incentive for both sides** *FRUS* 1945 Vol. 7, 1203; **"huge amount of capital"** Qing, *From Allies*, 68; **the only country** Hunt, *Genesis*, 156.

111   **half a billion** *FRUS* 1946 Vol. 10, 737; **Lend-Lease** There had been some disagreement about just how much Washington had committed. U.S. officials thought they were on the hook for equipping 39 divisions. In Cairo, however, Roosevelt had apparently made breezy reference to making that 90 divisions in a meeting with Chiang. Chiang, not unreasonably, took this as a commitment, while FDR had not bothered to make a record or inform anyone else of what he had said. Others present could remember something "vague and loose," while Chiang took this as yet another broken commitment.

112   **bulk of American troops** Final report 382–383; **some Marines** Papers Vol. 5, 423; **China's air force** Memo to GCM on Chinese Air Force, AW Papers 82/23, Hoover.

112   **Stravinsky** Shanghai Municipal Symphony Orchestra Program, 6 January 1946, Paul Caraway Papers, MHI; **"Moonlight Sonata"** La Ballet Russe Program, 1945–46, Paul Caraway Papers, MHI; **"One part is slick"** Melby, *Mandate*, 148; **"treacherously Westernized"** JHC to Betty Caughey, 4 January 1946, JHC Papers 2/7, GCMRL.

112   **no one was there** JHC to Betty Caughey, 28 January 1946, JHC Papers 2/7, GCMRL; **roads slick with mud** JM to Hellman, 31 January 1946, JM Papers 36, HSTL.

112–13 **assurance** Isaacson, *Wise Men*, 42; **Sino-Soviet Treaty** Harriman to HST, 14 August 1945, Naval Aide Files 14/8, HST Papers, HSTL; **farewell meeting** Harriman-Stalin meeting notes, 23 January 1946, GCM Papers 122/46, GCMRL.

113   **Kennan memo** *FRUS* 1946 Vol. 9, 116–119.

113   **"Both his thoughts"** CKS diary, 25 January 1946, Hoover; **Harriman seemed to share** Wehrle in Bland, *George C. Marshall's*, 82.

113   **appeared tense** Jeans, *Marshall Mission*, 76; **dining room** Jeans, *Marshall Mission*, 7; **said too much** CKS diary, 29 January 1946, Hoover.

113–14   **eleven Soviet armies** Gallicchio, *Scramble*, 43; **300,000 Soviet troops** Heinzig, *Soviet Union*, 88; **he wanted more time** Westad, *Cold War*, 141; **stated reason** Marshall cables, 31 January 1946, GCM Papers 24/1, GCMRL; **mounting protest** Summary of telegrams, 21 January 1946, Naval Aide Files 22/1, HST Papers, HSTL.

114   **Factories, power plants, and railways** Tanner, *Battle*, 31, 102; **appalled** Brian Murray, "Stalin, the Cold War, and the Division of China," 3; **inability to distinguish** Tanner, *Battle*, 31; **"capacity to drink"** Spector, *In the Ruins*, 46; **"trophies"** FRUS 1946, Vol. 10, 1112.

114   **"trembling inside"** Leffler, *Preponderance*, 99; **vulnerable east** Leffler, *Preponderance*, 88; **"showcase"** Heinzig, *Soviet Union*, 53.

114–15   **Stalin told them** Zhang Suchu in Bland, *George C. Marshall's*, 57; **gave him leverage** Westad, "Losses," 107; **would not tolerate** Heinzig, *Soviet Union*, 67; **provoke American intervention** Heinzig, *Soviet Union*, 96.

115   **offered Stalin** Tanner, *Battle*, 50, and Murray, "Stalin," 4; **"liquidate"** Heinzig, *Soviet Union*, 107; **"dominant position"** Heinzig, *Soviet Union*, 112; **American troops** Heinzig, *Soviet Union*, 109; **Kremlin's price** Tanner, *Battle*, 39.

115   **"vandalism and theft"** Harriman, *Special*, 539.

115–16   **at midnight** CKS diary, 30 January 1946, Hoover; **"He thought"** Harriman, *Special*, 539; **cautionary message** Wehrle in Bland, *George C. Marshall's*, 83.

116   *Das Kapital* AW to GCM, 3 February 1946, GCM Papers 124/8, GCMRL.

116   **Peace was truly** Westad, *Cold War*, 147; **Others wondered** Niu, *From Yan'an*, 253; **Zhou thought** Westad, *Cold War*, 149.

116   **Zhou-GCM conversation** GCM to HST, 1 February 1946, Naval Aide Files 8/9, HST Papers, HSTL; **Marshall's aides** GCM to HST, 31 January 1946, Secretary's Files 151/9, HST Papers, HSTL.

116   **Mao letter** GCM to HST, 1 February 1946, Naval Aide Files 8/9, HST Papers, HSTL.

117   **"political strife"** CKS speech to PCC closing, 31 January 1946, JM Papers 1, HSTL; **"a charter"** Marshall cables, 5 February 1946, GCM Papers 24/2, GCMRL; **"big political gains"** Marshall cables, 2 February 1946, GCM Papers 24/2, GCMRL; **"national leadership"** Taylor, *Generalissimo*, 342.

117   **"true and great friend"** Student Organizations to GCM, 31 January 1946, GCM Papers 122/23, GCMRL; **"no longer any doubt"** *New York Times* 2 February 1946; **Lippmann** *Los Angeles Times* 7 February 1946.

117–18   **He detected. . . . what they were** CKS diary, 2 February 1946, Hoover; **"bonding"** CKS diary, 9 February 1946, Hoover; **might retire** *Washington Post* 6 February 1946; **George Washington** Marshall cables, 7 February 1946, GCM Papers 24/2, GCMRL.

118   **"current situation"** Niu, *From Yan'an*, 254; **dictates** Saich, *Rise*, 1278; **closed-doorism** Saich, *Rise*, 1280; **"not only represents"** Sheng, *Battling*, 124.

118   **Communist officials ordered** Sheng, *Battling*, 123; **"this new stage"** Westad, *Cold War*, 148; **"isolate"** Qing, *From Allies*, 79; **"our party"** Saich, *Rise*, 1280; **Mao himself sent instructions** Westad, *Cold War*, 148.

118   **"China has stepped"** Sheng, *Battling*, 126; **buoyantly** Short, *Mao*, 404; **"indelible contribution"** He in Bland, *George C. Marshall's*, 186; **Liu Shaoqi** Ariyoshi Yenan Observer Group memo, 3 February 1946, JM Papers 1, HSTL; **CCP started making plans** Sheng, *Battling*, 125–126.

118-19   **message in Harriman's** Papers Vol. 5, 440; **"words, words, words"** JM to Hellman, 31 January 1946, JM Papers 36, HSTL; **"I do not now"** GCM to Acheson, 5 February 1946, GCM Papers 122/3, GCMRL.

119   **skies were clearing** Melby, *Mandate*, 103; **"It looks as if"** HST to GCM, 2 February 1946, Secretary's Files 160/10, HST Papers, HSTL.

119   **"unity out of chaos"** KTM to McCarthy, Frank McCarthy Papers, GCMRL.

119   **outrage in Chongqing** Heinzig, *Soviet Union*, 59.

119-20   **small price** Harriman, *Special*, 399; **military assessment** Stoler, *George C. Marshall*, 137–138; **stay a surprise** Harriman to HST, 15 June 1945, Naval Aide Files 14/7, HST Papers, HSTL; **Stalin did not** Chen, *Mao's*, 25.

120   **"American diplomacy"** Mitter, *Forgotten*, 355; **"maximum sacrifice"** William C. Kirby, "The Internationalization of China," 439; **"ache in the joints"** Niu, *From Yan'an*, 203.

120   **"Down with imperialism"** *New York Times* 23 February 1946; **signs** Sheng, *Battling*, 131; **Mobs** *New York Times* 23 February 1946; **Nationalist toughs** Taylor, *Generalissimo*, 344.

120   **Marshall update** GCM to HST, 9 February 1946, Naval Aide Files 8/9, HST Papers, HSTL.

121   **sun, plum trees** Melby, *Mandate*, 102; **"Things today"** GCM to Acheson, 5 February 1946, GCM Papers 122/3, GCMRL; **General Chang** Boorman, *Biographical Dictionary*, Vol. 1, 41; **intrigue** Seymour Topping, *Journey Between Two Chinas*, 53; **matchmaker** FRUS 1946 Vol. 9, 196.

121   **"Political power"** Short, *Mao*, 203; **"Our armies"** *New York Times* 16 December 1946; **"If I control"** Pakula, *Last*, 133; **"tiger for his skin"** Heinzig, *Soviet Union*, 115; **"pure illusion"** Melby, *Mandate*, 116.

121-22   **Other officers** Papers Vol. 5, 440; **Wedemeyer plotted** FRUS 1946 Vol. 9, 192; **"digestible"** Henry Byroade Oral History, GCMRL; **three million** Military intelligence review, 28 February 1946, Naval Aide Files 17/1, HST Papers, HSTL; **one million** Military intelligence review, 14 February 1946, Naval Aide Files 17/1, HST Papers, HSTL.

122   **"You are accepting"** Papers Vol. 5, 480.

122   **frivolous chatter** JHC to Betty Caughey, 12 February 1946, JHC Papers 2/7, GCMRL; **"the Professor"** FRUS 1946 Vol. 9, 311; **party** JHC to Betty Caughey, 19 February 1946, JHC Papers 2/7, GCMRL.

122   **table** JHC to Betty Caughey, 23 February 1946, JHC Papers 2/7, GCMRL; **"war of papers"** Committee of Three minutes, 10 January 1946, Mar-

shall Mission Records 19, NARA; **they would start** JHC to Betty Caughey, 23 February 1946, JHC Papers 2/7, GCMRL; **Translation** JHC to Betty Caughey, 23 February 1946, JHC Papers 2/7, GCMRL; **write letters** Jeans, *Marshall Mission*, 124; **"long and extremely delicate"** GCM to Andrews, 14 February 1946, GCM Papers 122/4, GCMRL; **they would break** JHC to Betty Caughey, 23 February 1946, JHC Papers 2/7, GCMRL.

123   **"a definite paper"** Papers Vol. 5, 604; **"the quickest way"** *FRUS* 1946 Vol. 9, 258; **Some recommendations** *FRUS* 1946 Vol. 9, 222; **"That is the way"** *FRUS* 1946 Vol. 9, 288; **American military thought** *FRUS* 1946 Vol. 9, 203; **"education in this"** *FRUS* 1946 Vol. 9, 323.

123   **pleasant afternoon** JM to Hellman, 18 February 1946, JM Papers 36, HSTL; **"You as umpire"** *FRUS* 1946 Vol. 9, 254; **"We must fully realize"** *FRUS* 1946 Vol. 9, 238.

123   **"gestures," "personality"** Davies, *China Hand*, 218; **sixteen-hour days, "anything new"** Han, *Eldest*, 191; **"General Motors"** George V. Underwood Oral History, GCMRL.

123-24 **any delay** Papers Vol. 5, 462; **"elementary school"** GCM to MacArthur, 22 February 1946, Marshall Mission Records 11, NARA.

124   **"loss of face"** *FRUS* 1946 Vol. 9, 786; **"unorganized swarms"** Papers Vol. 5, 493; **"presentable manner"** *FRUS* 1946 Vol. 9, 786; **"to sneer"** Caraway to AW, 19 February 1946, Paul Caraway Papers, MHI; **"speeding the end"** Gillem journal notes, 25–28 February 1946, Alvan Gillem Papers, MHI; **"Russian infiltration"** Papers Vol. 5, 493.

124-25 **"Nobody thought"** *FRUS* 1946 Vol. 9, 277; **In Manchuria** Taylor, *Generalissimo*, 343; **"Since agreement"** CKS diary, 2 March 1946, Hoover.

125   **how to title** *FRUS* 1946 Vol. 9, 276.

125   **"We want unification"** Sheng, *Battling*, 126.

125   **"the conservatives"** GCM to HST, 19 February 1946, Naval Aide Files 8/9, HST Papers, HSTL; **hard-liners were striking back** Sheng, *Battling*, 127.

125   **meeting with editors** GCM Statement to Chinese Editors, 23 February 1946, GCM Papers 122/30, GCMRL.

126   **haircut** *FRUS* 1946 Vol. 9, 292; **leather briefcase** GCM to Chang, 23 February 1946, GCM Papers 122/14, GCMRL.

126   **"I will hang"** *FRUS* 1946 Vol. 9, 285; **sixty reporters** *FRUS* 1946 Vol. 9, 295; **brush, pen** *New York Times* 26 February 1946.

126   **"The signatures"** *FRUS* 1946 Vol. 9, 293; **"We will completely"** *FRUS* 1946 Vol. 9, 295; **epithets** *FRUS* 1946 Vol. 9, 294.

126   **"This agreement"** *FRUS* 1946 Vol. 9, 295; **"on notice"** GCM to HST, 26 February 1946, Marshall Mission Records 15, NARA.

6. First Lord of the Warlords

127   **morning sky** JM to Hellman, 26 February 1946, JM Papers 36, HSTL; **"At the top"** Belden, *China Shakes*, 13.

127   **spread over three floors** McElway report, GCM Papers 24/5, GCMRL.

127   **Executive Headquarters visit and remarks** GCM remarks at Executive Headquarters, 28 February 1946, Marshall Mission Records 15, NARA.

128   **"heavy stick"** Caraway note, January 1946, GCM Papers 122/9, GCMRL; **"My time"** GCM to HST, 24 January 1946, Naval Aide Files 8/9, HST Papers, HSTL.

128   **propaganda truce** *FRUS* 1946 Vol. 9, 375; **cash and radio gear** Papers Vol. 5, 431; **directed the Americans** JHC to Byroade, 18 February 1946, JHC Papers 1/1, GCMRL.

128   **"Both sides"** *FRUS* 1946 Vol. 9, 369; **Rehe and Chahar** Tanner, *Battle*, 44; **Communist team member** *FRUS* 1946 Vol. 9, 382; **"unfortunate precedents"** *FRUS* 1946 Vol. 9, 387.

129   **frequently stalled** *FRUS* 1946 Vol. 9, 377; **"guerrilla nature"** *FRUS* 1946 Vol. 9, 369; **"degree of cooperation"** *FRUS* 1946 Vol. 9, 393.

129   **Chiang wanted** CKS diary, 26 February 1946, Hoover.

129   **"most important instrument"** Papers Vol. 5, 505; **number of truce teams** History of the Executive Headquarters, Alvan Gillem Papers, MHI; **"pleasant dreams"** McElway report, GCM Papers 24/5, GCMRL; **half a million** *FRUS* 1946 Vol. 9, 462; **task was immense** GCM to HST, 10 February 1946, Naval Aide Files 8/9, HST Papers, HSTL; **"The prosperity of China"** Papers Vol. 5, 505.

129-30 **an assistance package** GCM to Byrnes, 25 February 1946, Marshall Mission Records 15, NARA; **"great deal longer"** GCM to Robertson, 21 February 1946, GCM Papers 123/35 GCMRL.

130   **Smiling families** GCMRL photographs; **Bands, School groups** Gillem diary, 3 March 1946, Gillem Papers, MHI; **painting** *New York Times* 5 March 1946; **homemade signs** *Time* 25 March 1946.

130   **west Texas, Dust Bowl** Gillem diary, 3 March 1946, Alvan Gillem Papers, MHI; **Chicago of China** Gillem diary, 5 March 1946, Alvan Gillem Papers, MHI; **"most encouraging"** *South China Morning Post* 9 March 1946; **"the ganbei circuit"** Gillem journal notes, 25-28 February 1946, Alvan Gillem Papers, MHI.

130   **He lauded** Papers Vol. 5, 488; **He appealed** *FRUS* 1946 Vol. 9, 472; **baseball** *FRUS* 1946 Vol. 9, 473.

130-31 **a thousand years** Melby, *Mandate*, 130; **"rough and thankless"** GCM to Churchill, 18 June 1946, GCM Papers 122/9, GCMRL; **chided Byroade** GCM to Byroade, 8 March 1946, Marshall Mission Records 15, NARA; **a struggle** Gillem journal notes, 25 May 1946, Alvan Gillem Papers, MHI; **"From evaluation"** Minutes of Executive Headquarters meeting, 20 January 1946, Alvan Gillem Papers, MHI; **"I looked down"** *FRUS* 1946 Vol. 9, 468.

131   **"an amazing task"** GCM to HST, 6 March 1946, Naval Aide Files 8/9, HST Papers, HSTL; **"The biggest problem"** *FRUS* 1946 Vol. 9, 470.

131   **"new opportunity"** *FRUS* 1946 Vol. 9, 262; **There were commanders**

Papers Vol. 5, 506; **florid accounts** Gillem diary, 2 March 1946, Alvan Gillem Papers, MHI; **"The team meets"** FRUS 1946 Vol. 9, 466.

131   **"larger issues"** GCM to HST, 6 March 1946, Naval Aide Files 8/9, HST Papers, HST; **"If reiteration"** Papers Vol. 5, 489.

132   **A turbulent flight over desolate terrain** Gillem diary, 3 March 1946, Gillem Papers, MHI; **"glasses of water"** Committee of Three meeting notes, 3 March 1946, Marshall Mission Records 25, NARA; **"Marshall made"** Gillem diary, 4 March 1946, Gillem Papers, MHI.

132   **Yenan preparations** Memoirs of Ivan D. Yeaton, 120, Ivan D. Yeaton Papers 1, Hoover.

132   **"He likes things," "war room"** Yeaton to AW, 10 March 1946, AW Papers 91/8, Hoover.

132   **"Things locally"** Yeaton to AW, 6 February 1946, AW Papers 91/8, Hoover; **a distinction** He in Bland, George C. Marshall's, 176; **a progressive** Spector, In the Ruins, 217; **Zhou compared him** Taylor, Generalissimo, 343.

133   **showing up at dances, had been withdrawn** Yeaton to AW, 6 February 1946, AW Papers 91/8, Hoover; **"diplomatic illness"** Pantsov, Mao, 270; **Mao was lying in bed** Short, Mao, 403.

133   **flaws** Pantsov, Mao, 99; **"Why should you obey"** Pantsov, Mao, 41; **"His force"** Short, Mao, 60; **"The will," rivers, mountains** Pantsov, Mao, 42; **biographies** He Di, "The Most Respected Enemy," 145; **Theodore Roosevelt** Hunt, Genesis, 210; **"We need"** He, "Most Respected Enemy," 145.

133   **heard of America** Lucien Bianco, Origins of the Chinese Revolution, 79; **map of the world** Pantsov, Mao, 26; **He called forth** Pantsov, Mao, 172; **Avenge the Shame** Pantsov, Mao, 145.

134   **the Long March** Pantsov, Mao, 288.

134   **counterrevolutionary sins** Short, Mao, 309; **Kang Sheng** Mitter, Forgotten, 282; **"Leniency"** David E. Apter, Revolutionary Discourse in Mao's Republic, 290.

134   **grass-paper** Topping, Journey, 94; **Standard Oil drums** Short, Mao, 354; **unbuckling his pants** Jonathan D. Spence, Mao Zedong, 98; **introduced her to Mao** Pantsov, Mao, 327; **she raged** Pantsov, Mao, 310.

134-35 **"Dogma"** Bianco, Origins, 79; **opium** Paine, Wars, 158; **seek truth** Pantsov, Mao, 238; **from bloodthirsty revolutionary to advocate of peace** Westad, Cold War, 168.

135   **"glorious success"** Yu Shen in Bland, George C. Marshall's, 256; **discipline in diplomacy** Chen, Mao's, 12; **"Diplomatic attitudes"** Saich, Rise, 1215.

135   **pilot searching, parachute drop, "It's easy to see," terraced fields** Gillem diary, 4 March 1946, Alvan Gillem Papers, MHI; **drop into the valley** Davies, Dragon, 344.

135   **Mao stood** Memoirs of Ivan D. Yeaton, 133, Ivan D. Yeaton Papers 1, Hoover; **Marshall came down** GCMRL photos.

135   **"gaunt"** Snow, Red Star, 90; **pudgy, losing his hair, soft** White, In Search,

195; **handshake** Henry Byroade Oral History, Foreign Service Oral History Program, LOC.

135–36 **Mao of Edgar Snow's** Snow, *Red Star*, 92–93; **"megalomania"** Snow, *Red Star*, 94; **"force of destiny"** Snow, *Red Star*, 90; **"uncanny faculty"** Pantsov, *Mao*, 320; **A diplomat** Davies, *Dragon*, 347.

136   **After reviewing** GCMRL photographs; **for a holiday** *Emancipation Daily* 5 March 1946; **A banner** GCMRL photographs.

136   **Dignitaries** Sidney Rittenberg, *The Man Who Stayed Behind*, 78; **Heat** Gillem diary, 4 March 1946, Alvan Gillem Papers, MHI.

136   **Marshall kept, Mao sat** GCMRL photographs; **He thanked Marshall** *FRUS* 1946 Vol. 9, 501; **He wanted to convey** Final report, 53.

136   **Marshall praised** *FRUS* 1946 Vol. 9, 502.

137   **his host's face** Gillem diary, 4 March 1946, Alvan Gillem Papers, MHI; **Mao toasted Marshall's** Hsu, *Chou*, 172; **simple meal** Gillem diary, 4 March 1946, Alvan Gillem Papers, MHI; **A Communist who had attended** GCMRL photographs.

137   **straw** Davies, *China Hand*, 217; **screenings** Barrett, *Dixie*, 51; **howls of wolves** Rittenberg, *The Man*, 78; **lights bobbed** Topping, *Journey*, 3; **The next morning** Gillem diary, 5 March 1946, Alvan Gillem Papers, MHI; **griddle** Memoirs of Ivan D. Yeaton, 104, Ivan D. Yeaton Papers 1, Hoover.

137   **Marshall's departure** GCMRL photographs, and *Emancipation Daily* 5 March 1946.

137–38 **"We completely agree"** *Emancipation Daily* 5 March 1946; **Mao remained** Transcript of GCM comments, Conference on Problems of United States Policy in China, Secretary's Files 152/4, HST Papers, HSTL.

138   **tracking Churchill's visit** Sheng, *Battling*, 137.

138   **doctors** Serge N. Goncharov, *Uncertain Partners*, 15; **physical and political** Gillem diary, 5 March 1946, Alvan Gillem Papers, MHI; **The symbolism** Tanner, *Battle*, 104.

138   **note from Marshall** GCM to HST, 6 March 1946, Naval Aide Files 8/9, HST Papers, HSTL.

138   **Truman replied** HST to GCM, 7 March 1946, Naval Aide Files 8/9, HST Papers, HSTL.

138   **"If things continue"** HST to Delacy, 15 February 1946, Secretary's Files 151/9, HST Papers, HSTL; **"anxiety to get"** HST to GCM, Naval Aide Files 8/9, HST Papers, HSTL.

139   **Chiang wanted to keep armed and in place** Spector, *In the Ruins*, 42; **"who are we neutral against"** Henry Aplington, "Sunset in the East," 172.

139   **He had seen occupation before** Marshall interviews, 140; **"hard-drinking"** Marshall interviews, 133; **"Why don't you go home"** Marshall cables, 15 January 1946, GCM Papers 24/1, GCMRL.

139   **"Never fire"** Sheng, *Battling*, 116; **"retreat"** Niu, *From Yan'an*, 245; **several**

confrontations Westad, *Cold War*, 113; **Wedemeyer complained** AW to Hurley, 24 December 1945, AW Papers 81/36, Hoover.

139 **Marshall admitted** Shepley to HST, 26 February 1946, GCM Papers 124/28, GCMRL.

140 **"We must clear"** GCM to HST, 9 February 1946, Naval Aide Files 8/9, HST Papers, HSTL; **reassure Stalin** Steven I. Levine, "A New Look at American Mediation in the Chinese Civil War," 356; **"General Marshall feels"** AW to Eisenhower, 11 March 1946, AW Papers 81/13, Hoover; **"eyes of the world"** GCM to HST, 9 February 1946, Naval Aide Files 8/9, HST Papers, HSTL.

140 **ammunition** Papers Vol. 5, 410; **air force** Memo to GCM on Chinese Air Force, AW Papers 82/23, Hoover; **"middle men"** GCM to HST, 6 March 1946, Naval Aide Files 8/9, HST Papers, HSTL.

140 **4,000-man** Gallicchio, *Scramble*, 90; **into the field** McClure to AW, 7 April 1946, AW Papers 82/18, Hoover; **navy forces** AW to GCM, 4 May 1946, GCM Papers 124/8, GCMRL; **raising suspicions** Gallicchio, *Scramble*, 176.

140–41 **commercial advantages** *FRUS* 1946 Vol. 10, 814; **other offers** *FRUS* 1946 Vol. 10, 815; **"aimed to create"** Schaller, *Crusade*, 285; **"sell out his heritage"** AW to GCM, 24 January 1946, GCM Papers 124/8, GCMRL; **African American troops** War Department to Wedemeyer, 9 February 1946, Marshall Mission Records 20, NARA; **Chiang had allowed** AW Memo to CKS, 11 February 1946, AW Papers 86/1, Hoover.

141 **Marshall's prodding** Papers Vol. 5, 486; **"This participation"** *FRUS* 1946 Vol. 10, 818.

141 **sodden afternoon, heavy cold** Papers Vol. 5, 501; **he was feeling good** GCM to Chamberlin, 7 March 1946, GCM Papers 17/21, GCMRL; **"His praise"** Shepley to GCM, 28 February 1946, GCM Papers 124/34, GCMRL.

141 **"American assistance"** *FRUS* 1946 Vol. 9, 513; **"I get the impression"** Shepley to GCM, 28 February 1946, GCM Papers 124/34, GCMRL.

141 **dismayed by ongoing** GCM to HST, 9 February 1946, Naval Aide Files 8/9, HST Papers, HSTL; **"all you have accomplished"** Shepley to GCM, 28 February 1946, GCM Papers 124/34, GCMRL; **Secretary of State Byrnes** *Washington Post* 6 March 1946.

142 **unity** Harriman, *Special*, 539; **first formal protest** Westad, *Cold War*, 152.

142 **"General M."** Jeans, *Marshall Mission*, 244; **"angry man"** JM to Hellman, 26 February 1946, JM Papers 36, HSTL; **"If no peaceful solution"** Chang to GCM, 11 March 1946, GCM Papers 122/15, GCMRL.

142 **sumptuous dinner** JHC to Betty Caughey, 16 March 1946, JHC Papers 2/8, GCMRL.

142 **evening prayer** CKS diary, 10 March 1946, Hoover; **"His impression"** Qin, *Chronicles*, Vol. 6.1, 2842; **as Marshall had noticed** Shepley to HST, 26 February 1946, GCM Papers 124/28, GCMRL; **In a war** CKS diary, 9 March 1946, Hoover.

142 **stated rationale** CKS statement to GCM, 10 March 1946, Marshall Mission Records 1, NARA; **real fear** Westad, *Cold War*, 154.

143 **"reestablishment"** Papers Vol. 5, 497; **secret instruction** GCM to Robertson, 11 March 1946, Marshall Mission Records 15, NARA.

143 **Chiang was also worried about mounting resistance** GCM to HST, 18 March 1946, GCM Papers 124, GCMRL; **heavy secrecy** JM to Hellman, 7 March 1946, JM Papers 36, HSTL; **"power, prestige"** JM to Hellman, 18 February 1946, JM Papers 36, HSTL; **"greatest purges"** JM to Hellman, 20 March 1946, JM Papers 36, HSTL; **"Most of the people"** Westad, *Cold War*, 150.

143 **Marshall sensed** GCM to HST, 13 March 1946, Marshall Mission Records 1, NARA; **bring irreconcilables** *FRUS* 1946 Vol. 9, 513; **Chiang had even asked** *FRUS* 1946 Vol. 9, 445.

143-44 **"considerable change"** *FRUS* 1946 Vol. 9, 513; **"worried gang"** JM to Hellman, 21 February 1946, JM Papers 36, HSTL; **"caves and ditches"** JM to Hellman, 24 February 1946, JM Papers 36, HSTL; **"provocations"** Zhou statement to GCM, 10 March 1946, AW Papers 89/4, Hoover; **forbearance** *FRUS* 1946 Vol. 10, 246; **"dirty work"** JM to Hellman, 7 March 1946, JM Papers 36, HSTL.

144 **"your subordinates"** Jean Edward Smith, *Eisenhower in War and Peace*, 314; **told General Gillem** Gillem diary, 6 March 1946, Alvan Gillem Papers, MHI.

144 **"I could have been"** Gillem diary, 6 March 1946, Alvan Gillem Papers, MHI.

144 **"easy mind"** *FRUS* 1946 Vol. 9, 551.

144 **correspondents rushed** *New York Times* 12 March 1946; **"He gave me"** *New Yorker* 16 March 1946.

145 **"I succeeded"** GCM to HST, 13 March 1946, Marshall Mission Records 1, NARA; **Red Army commander** Levine, *Anvil*, 4.

145 **another winter** Shepley to GCM, 28 February 1946, GCM Papers 124/34, GCMRL; **Marshall and Chiang had talked** CKS diary, 11 March 1946, Hoover; **one request, American policy** CKS statement to GCM, 10 March 1946, Marshall Mission Records 1, NARA; **"What General Marshall"** *FRUS* 1945 Vol. 9, 540.

145 **Marshall and Madame Chiang** McElway report, GCM Papers 24/5, GCMRL.

145 **radio to Shepley** Papers Vol. 5, 489.

7. If the World Wants Peace

149 **"A tall man"** *Time* 25 March 1946; **Katherine was waiting** *New York Times* 16 March 1946.

149 **kept his return quiet** GCM to Spencer, 22 March 1946, GCM Papers 60/18, GCMRL; **his cold** GCM to Spencer, 22 March 1946, GCM Papers 60/18, GCMRL; **hoarse** *Washington Post* 17 March 1946; **"We now need him"** Upton to KTM, 10 May 1946, GCM Papers 124/6, GCMRL.

149–50 **"a stupendous accomplishment"** AW to Eisenhower, 11 March 1946, AW Papers 81/13, Hoover; **Henry Luce** Luce to GCM, 27 February 1946, GCM Papers 74/44, GCMRL; **Carsun Chang** Chang to GCM, 11 March 1946, GCM Papers 122/15, GCMRL; **"Ever since his arrival"** Army Liaison to War Department, 18 March 1946, GCM Papers 124/36, GCMRL; **A journalist made much** Marshall cables, 25 January 1946, GCM Papers 24/1, GCMRL.

150 **two brief stops** Papers Vol. 5, 491; **hoped to borrow** Papers Vol. 5, 465; **troops to Japan in return** GCM to AW, 16 March 1946, GCM Papers 124/34, GCMRL; **national pride** FRUS 1946 Vol. 9, 429.

150 **Capra's help** Papers Vol. 5, 501.

150 **keep Truman informed** John Melby Oral History, HSTL; **"I know very little"** HST to Wallace, 25 January 1946, Secretary's Files 151/9, HST Papers, HSTL; **Byrnes** HST to Byrnes, 5 January 1946, Secretary's Files 283/26, HST Papers, HSTL; **shaky ground** Dean Acheson, *Present at the Creation*, 135.

151 **What Marshall had seen . . . the best hope** Shepley to HST, 26 February 1946, GCM Papers 124/28, GCMRL.

151 **brow furrowed** *Time* 25 March 1946; **Marshall press comments** GCM Press conference transcript, 16 March 1946, Marshall Mission Records 3, NARA.

151–52 **"Marshall's presence"** Jeans, *Marshall Mission*, 245; **"The permanence"** AW to Eisenhower, 11 March 1946, AW Papers 81/13, Hoover.

152 **a genial man** Melby, *Mandate*, 131; **his temper** Alvan Gillem Oral History, GCMRL.

152 **"definitely not a Marshall"** McClure to AW, 7 April 1946, AW Papers 82/18, Hoover; **Gillem hardly needed reminding** Gillem to Palmer, 23 March 1946, Alvan Gillem Papers, MHI; **"Well she is worth seeing"** Gillem diary, 10 March 1946, Alvan Gillem Papers, MHI; **wished he were on it** Gillem diary, 12 March 1946, Alvan Gillem Papers, MHI; **press had trouble** *South China Morning Post* 11 March 1946 and 15 March 1946.

152 **"Kuomintang thing"** Melby, *Mandate*, 125; **Gillem conceded** Gillem diary, 12 March 1946, Alvan Gillem Papers, MHI; **spent the day** Gillem diary, 12 March 1946, Alvan Gillem Papers, MHI; **"poker game"** Minutes of Military Sub-Committee meeting, 13 March 1946, Alvan Gillem Papers, MHI; **slept poorly** Gillem diary, 13 March 1946, Alvan Gillem Papers, MHI.

152 **war booty** Tanner, *Battle*, 102; **"Too rapid"** FRUS 1946 Vol. 9, 601; **"The Russians are pretty cute"** JM to Hellman, 16 March 1946, JM Papers 36, HSTL.

153 **"softening"** Gillem to GCM, 28 March 1946, GCM Papers 124/30, GCMRL; **Soviets alerted** Westad, *Cold War*, 158; **American resolve** Gillem to GCM, 28 March 1946, GCM Papers 124/30, GCMRL.

153   **"Further delay"** GCM to Gillem, 18 March 1946, GCM Papers 124/34, GCMRL; **"Force the issue"** GCM to Gillem, 21 March 1946, GCM Papers 124/34, GCMRL.

153   **"Now we have"** FRUS 1946 Vol. 9, 578; **responsibilities** FRUS 1946 Vol. 9, 582; **"The Army"** FRUS 1946 Vol. 9, 577.

153   **without permission** Directive covering destruction of military works along railroad lines, 15 April 1946, Alvan Gillem Papers, MHI; **"my responsibility"** FRUS 1946 Vol. 9, 590; **making contact** FRUS 1946 Vol. 9, 587; **he was touched** JHC notes of meeting with Zhou, 23 March 1946, JHC Papers 1/3, GCMRL; **"I have Zhou"** FRUS 1946 Vol. 9, 599; **"point of conflict"** History of the Executive Headquarters, Alvan Gillem Papers, MHI.

153   **"United States policy"** Army Liaison to War Department, 18 March 1946, GCM Papers 124/36, GCMRL; **"need not worry"** GCM to HST, 18 March 1946, Secretary's Files 151/9, HST Papers, HSTL.

154   **Marshall was as busy** GCM to Churchill, 18 June 1946, GCM Papers 122/9, GCMRL; **"still Chief of Staff"** Gallicchio, Scramble, 172.

154   **"old isolationism"** GCM Statement to Chinese Editors, 23 February 1946, GCM Papers 122/30, GCMRL; **that pressure** Papers Vol. 5, 506.

154   **memo from his staff** Shepley to HST, 26 February 1946, GCM Papers 124/28, GCMRL.

154–55 **a fraction of what was necessary** FRUS 1946 Vol. 10, 963; **restoring communications** New York Times 2 February 1946; **after freezing talks** FRUS 1946 Vol. 10, 911; **quietly prepare** FRUS 1946 Vol. 10, 935; **withering skepticism** Acheson, Present, 148; **"a loan"** FRUS 1946 Vol. 10, 926; **T. V. Soong complained** FRUS 1946 Vol. 10, 948.

155   **multiple representatives** GCM to AW, 29 March 1946, GCM Papers 124/34, GCMRL; **surplus equipment** GCM to Gillem, 27 March 1946, GCM Papers 124/34, GCMRL; **"famine conditions"** GCM to HST, 26 February 1946, Naval Aide Files 8/9, HST Papers, HSTL; **"favorable terms"** FRUS 1946 Vol. 10, 950; **C-54** AW to GCM, 25 April 1946, AW Papers 82/23, Hoover; **"substantial advances"** GCM to Gillem, 27 March 1946, GCM Papers 124/34, GCMRL.

155   **communications adviser** GCM to Gillem, 18 March 1946, GCM Papers 124/34, GCMRL; **"Your mission"** Beal, Marshall, 4.

155–56 **Marshall pressed** Vincent to GCM, 11 April 1946, GCM Papers 124/4, GCMRL; **recruited officers** GCM to Gillem, 27 March 1946, GCM Papers 124/34, GCMRL; **congressional approval** FRUS 1946 Vol. 10, 827; **by 20,000** Papers Vol. 5, 514; **"really an irritant"** Spector, In the Ruins, 267; **"reduce the scale"** Nimitz to Eisenhower, 4 April 1946, GCM Papers 124/30, GCMRL; **enough troops** GCM to AW, 29 March 1946, GCM Papers 124/34, GCMRL; **Chiang's armies** AW to CKS, 12 April 1946, AW Papers 81/2, Hoover.

156 **"most difficult problem"** Papers Vol. 3, 547; **"localitis"** Perry, *Partners,* 256; **"priority of this theater"** Papers Vol. 4, 132; **"no localitis involved"** Papers Vol. 5, 493.

156 **Congress** *New York Times* 11 April 1946; **Truman speech** *Chicago Tribune* 7 April 1946.

156–57 **"Rebuffs," "police the world"** *Chicago Tribune,* 8 April 1946; **voted down** *Chicago Tribune* 9 April 1946; **"the quarrel in China"** Mansfield to HST, 7 November 1945, White House Central File 111/2, HST Papers, HSTL; **administration was charged** *Chicago Tribune* 5 April 1946; **whiskey distilleries** *Chicago Tribune* 12 April 1946.

157 **goddaughter's baptism** Rose Page Wilson, *General Marshall Remembered,* 314; **"so overcrowded"** GCM to Pierce, 28 May 1946, GCM Papers 123/33, GCMRL; **Churchill** GCM to Churchill, 18 June 1946, GCM Papers 122/9, GCMRL.

157 **"World War III"** Niu, *From Yan'an,* 269; **"Churchill now takes"** *Chicago Tribune* 14 March 1946.

157 **war with Russia** Shepley to GCM, 28 February 1946, GCM Papers 124/34, GCMRL; **"appeasement"** *FRUS* 1945 Vol. 7, 713; **pinkos** *Chicago Tribune* 17 March 1946; **J. Edgar Hoover** Donovan, *Conflict,* 173; **Soviet conduct** Gallup, *Gallup,* 567; **Moscow could be trusted** Leffler, *Preponderance,* 106.

158 **Kennan telegram** George F. Kennan, *Memoirs 1925–1950,* 505.

158 **Forrestal** Donovan, *Conflict,* 188.

158 **Stalin's speech** Melby memo on Stalin 9 February speech, 5 March 1946, GCM Papers 123/21, GCMRL; **"hard whiskey glasses"** GCM Statement to Chinese Editors, 23 February 1946, GCM Papers 122/30, GCMRL.

159 **"completely immobilized"** *FRUS* 1946 Vol. 9, 740; **delaying tactics** Tanner, *Battle,* 150; **Marshall told Gillem** GCM to Gillem, 6 April 1946, GCM Papers 124/35, GCMRL; **procedural disputes** *FRUS* 1946 Vol. 9, 738.

159 **"national suicide"** *Washington Post* 8 March 1946; **"diehard elements"** Shepley to HST, 26 February 1946, GCM Papers 124/28, GCMRL; **"revisions"** Westad, *Cold War,* 157; **American intelligence reported** Military intelligence review, 11 April 1946, Naval Aide Files 17/3, HST Papers, HSTL.

159 **"working schedule"** Zhou to Gillem, 20 March 1946, JHC Papers 1/3, GCMRL; **public complaints** Zhou statement, 4 April 1946, Alvan Gillem Papers, MHI; **"civil war"** Zhou statement, 4 April 1946, Alvan Gillem Papers, MHI; **abetting it** *FRUS* 1946 Vol. 9, 722; **"Without simultaneous resolution"** Tanner, *Battle,* 108.

160 **spurious charges** History of the Executive Headquarters, Alvan Gillem Papers, MHI; **new nickname** Topping, *Journey,* 274; **railway lines** Robertson to Gillem, 26 March 1946, Alvan Gillem Papers, MHI; **Chiang expressed** Gillem journal notes, 25–28 February 1946, Alvan Gillem Papers, MHI.

160 **Tai himself** Wakeman, *Spymaster*, 355; **Communists, Americans** Melby, *Mandate*, 163; **spirit of Sun** Wakeman, *Spymaster*, 357; **staged his own death** Wakeman, *Spymaster*, 355; **American plane** JHC to Betty Caughey, 11 April 1946, JHC Papers 2/8, GCMRL; **friends of Zhou** JM to Hellman, 26 April 1946, JM Papers 36, HSTL; **suspected sabotage** Boorman, *Biographical Dictionary* Vol. 1, 398; **13-year-old daughter** Jeans, *Marshall Mission*, 247.

160-61 **"can fix it"** JHC to Betty Caughey, 8 April 1946, JHC Papers 2/8, GCMRL; **"appalling"** JM to Hellman, 6 April 1946, JM Papers 36, HSTL; **"desire for early return"** Summary of telegrams, 13 April 1946, Naval Aide Files 22/1, HST Papers, HSTL.

161 **"immediate return"** FRUS 1946 Vol. 9, 736; **Madame Chiang** Madame CKS to GCM, 2 April 1946, GCM Papers 60/44, GCMRL.

161 **"hard battle," "sold China"** GCM to AW, 29 March 1946, GCM Papers 124/34, GCMRL; **in his assessment** GCM to Gillem, 5 April 1946, GCM Papers 124/35, GCMRL; **single day off** AW to Chiang, 25 April 1946, AW Papers 81/2, Hoover.

161 **by early fall** AW to Eisenhower, 11 March 1946, AW Papers 81/13, Hoover; **Wedemeyer had** Shepley to HST, 26 February 1946, GCM Papers 124/28, GCMRL; **"I will serve"** AW to GCM, 17 February 1946, GCM Papers 124/8, GCMRL.

161-62 **speculation** *Washington Post* 6 March 1946, and JM to Hellman, 28 March 1946, JM Papers 36, HSTL; **"I'm tired"** HST to Byrnes, 5 January 1946, Secretary's Files 283/30, HST Papers, HSTL; **talked it over** Jeans, *Marshall Mission*, 248.

162 **Marshall must take Truman's offer** AW to GCM, 17 February 1946, GCM Papers 124/8, GCMRL; **"When the time comes"** AW to GCM, 25 April 1946, AW Papers 82/23, Hoover.

162 **"She says George"** KTM to McCarthy, 19 February 1946, Frank McCarthy Papers 31/23, GCMRL.

162 **"lust for"** Army Liaison to War Department, 10 April 1946, GCM Papers 124/36, GCMRL; **speeches and interviews** FRUS 1946 Vol. 9, 742; **"seriously weaken"** FRUS 1946 Vol. 10, 980.

163 **"We don't know how long"** *New York Times* 15 April 1946.

8. Balance of Mistrusts

164 **Manchuria account** Marshall, "Forgotten Scenes of Heroism," GCM Papers 1/9, GCMRL.

164 **any foreign officer before** Marshall, "Report of visit to Manchurian battlefields, with recommendations," GCM Papers 1/9, GCMRL.

165 **"Chinese Manchuria"** Westad, *Restless*, 117; **coal, electricity** Paine, *Wars*, 28; **"Ruhr"** AW to GCM, 13 June 1946, GCM Papers 124, GCMRL; **"cockpit"** Melby, *Mandate*, 103.

165 **made a recommendation to his army superiors** Marshall, "Report of visit to Manchurian battlefields, with recommendations," GCM Papers 1/9, GCMRL.

165–66 **Tokyo** Eichelberger to GCM, 15 April 1946, GCM Papers 122/31, GCMRL; **Beijing** Papers Vol. 5, 525; **she peered down . . . ever seen** Papers Vol. 5, 525.

166 **welcome Katherine** *New York Times* 19 April 1946; **100 degrees, humidity, heat, dust, and smells** Papers Vol. 5, 525.

166 **"With your wisdom"** Chang to GCM, 22 April 1946, GCM Papers 122/14, GCMRL; **"Marshall will take"** *Chicago Tribune* 15 April 1946; **"disgusted"** JHC to Betty Caughey, 10 April 1946, JHC Papers 2/8, GCMRL; **"out of the fire"** JHC to Caraway, 14 April 1946, Paul Caraway Papers, MHI; **"About time"** Melby, *Mandate*, 138.

166 **"It is about like it was"** *New York Times* 19 April 1946.

166 **"out of hand"** *FRUS* 1946 Vol. 9, 788; **CCP troops waged** Military intelligence review, 25 April 1946, Naval Aide Files 17/3, HST Papers, HSTL; **ragged Nationalist force** Tanner, *Battle*, 123; **American officer there** *FRUS* 1946 Vol. 9, 823.

167 **From the airfield** *New York Times* 19 April 1946; **At first pleased** CKS diary, 23 March 1946, Hoover; **galling** CKS diary, 2 April 1946, Hoover; **"every effort to ruin"** Qin, *Chronicles*, Vol. 6.1, 2842; **Zhou had been** *Chicago Tribune* 5 April 1946; **"America needs"** Tanner, *Battle*, 111.

167 **"tragedy"** *FRUS* 1946 Vol. 9, 793.

167 **Yu had** Yu Ta-wei Oral History, GCMRL; **fully trusted** Alvan Gillem Oral History, GCMRL; **forthright** GCM-Yu meeting notes, 14 June 1946, Marshall Mission Records 4, NARA.

167–68 **Marshall erupted** *FRUS* 1946 Vol. 9, 788–789; **Nationalist fighters** Gillem journal notes, 17 April 1946, Alvan Gillem Papers, MHI.

168 **avoiding him** Tanner, *Battle*, 152; **Marshall's anger** *FRUS* 1946 Vol. 9, 1305; **"Marshall probably"** Sheng, *Battling*, 139; **Zhou seemed worried** JM to Hellman, 26 April 1946, JM Papers 36, HSTL.

168 **dreadful** Marshall, *Together*, 284; **crowds** Papers Vol. 5, 526; **a lyric** Spence, *To Change*, 251; **Katherine wrote home** Bland, *George C. Marshall's*, 574.

169 **aides had wondered** JHC to Betty Caughey, 10 April 1946, JHC Papers 2/8, GCMRL; **"I have forced"** GCM to McCarthy, 22 February 1946, Frank McCarthy Papers 31/20, GCMRL; **he quickly recognized** GCM to Churchill, 18 June 1946, GCM Papers 122/25, GCMRL.

169 **"most extreme position"** JM to Hellman, 13 April 1946, JM Papers 36, HSTL.

170 **"coup"** Qing, *From Allies*, 77; **Nationalist hands** Westad, *Cold War*, 157; **His ambassador** Westad, *Cold War*, 157; **"I should wait"** Wehrle in Bland, *George C. Marshall's*, 89.

170 **sharp misgivings** Sheng, *Battling*, 127; **backtrack and stall** Victor Shiu Chiang Chen, "Imagining China's Madrid in Manchuria," 92; **"substan-**

tial concessions" Qing, *From Allies*, 81; **"We can neither"** He in Bland, *George C. Marshall's*, 191.

170–71 **global concord** Westad, *Cold War*, 69; **"counterrevolutionary tide"** Sheng, *Battling*, 138; **fascist plot** Sheng, *Battling*, 127; **imperial designs** Yang Kuisong, "The Soviet Factor and the CCP's Policy toward the United States in the 1940s," 26; **"too courteous"** Sheng, *Battling*, 132; **expand contacts** Westad in Bland, *George C. Marshall's*, 611; **American military assessment** China theater memo, 25 April 1946, AW Papers 87/6, Hoover.

171 **punishing Chiang** Westad, "Losses," 108; **American aims** Westad in Bland, *George C. Marshall's*, 512.

171 **"democratic forces"** Niu, *From Yan'an*, 278.

171 **Kennan had written another** Hopkins to HST, 29 May 1945, Naval Aide Files 9/6, HST Papers, HSTL.

172 **breakfast, Caughey was newly confident** JHC to Betty Caughey, 23 April 1946, JHC Papers 2/8, GCMRL.

172 **"war in the making"** JHC to Betty Caughey, 11 April 1946, JHC Papers 2/8, GCMRL; **"strangest things"** JHC to Betty Caughey, 19 April 1946, JHC Papers 2/8, GCMRL; **"Maybe everybody"** JHC to Betty Caughey, 19 April 1946, JHC Papers 2/8, GCMRL.

173 **less capable replacements** *FRUS* 1946 Vol. 9, 737; **no accident** Final Report, 76; **shot at by Communists** *FRUS* 1946 Vol. 9, 807.

173 **Chiangs' country house, prosecute a case, Marshall's anger** CKS diary, 20 April 1946, Hoover; **had sabotaged** Final Report 103; **"all blame"** Qin, *Chronicles*, Vol. 6.1, 2868.

173 **terms of military unification** Final Report, 104.

174 **"radicals and militarists"** *FRUS* 1946 Vol. 9, 831; **attack on Changchun** Tanner, *Battle*, 156; **he had advocated** Zhang in Bland, *George C. Marshall's*, 222; **"maintain friendly relations"** He in Bland, *George C. Marshall's*, 193.

174 **wrote the university's president** GCM to Conant, 20 April 1946, GCM Papers 122/25, GCMRL.

174 **"I've exhausted"** Papers Vol. 5, 534; **"difficult man"** *FRUS* 1946 Vol. 9, 804.

175 **"watch a city die"** JM to Hellman, 2 February 1946, JM Papers 36, HSTL.

175 **"Minor civil war"** Gillem to GCM, JHC Papers 1/7, GCMRL.

175 **his party's survival** Tanner, *Where Chiang*, 29; **"expansion of Soviet power"** May, *Truman*, 66–67.

175–76 **"completely unprepared for occupation"** *FRUS* 1945 Vol. 7, 628; **Kremlin would respond** Levine, "New Look," 354; **Moscow had long warned** Heinzig, *Soviet Union*, 67; **Wedemeyer** AW Memorandum for CKS, 10 November 1945, AW Papers 81/2, Hoover.

176 **would likely win** Tanner, *Battle*, 60; **prudent move** CKS diary, 20 April 1946 and 23 April 1946, Hoover; **"a unified country"** Spector, *In the Ruins*, 225; **"no choice"** *Life* 24 December 1945.

176 **"waste paper"** FRUS 1946 Vol. 9, 720; **Marshall pointed out** Final Report, 104.

176-77 **Soviets threatened** Heinzig, *Soviet Union*, 93; **American dominance** Yang, "Soviet Union," 26; **"fight without restraint"** Westad, *Brothers*, 60; **Communist commanders** Sheng, *Battling*, 132; **boats and trains** Tanner, *Battle*, 109.

177 **OSS detachments** Yu, *OSS*, 24; **Strategic Services Unit** Revised plan for SSU operations, 20 April 1946, AW Papers 91/2, Hoover; **"lookouts"** FRUS 1946 Vol. 10, 1134; **persuasive evidence** Papers Vol. 5, 421; **Byroade assessed** FRUS 1946 Vol. 9, 727; **Marshall had pressed** Papers Vol. 5, 500; **"Russian game"** JM to Hellman, 9 March 1946, JM Papers 36, HSTL.

177 **"Due to their"** Military intelligence review, 25 April 1946, Naval Aide Files 17/3, HST Papers, HSTL; **"facts on the ground"** Tanner, *Battle*, 100; **"cocky"** Papers Vol. 5, 526; **300,000, "high morale"** Lau to Byroade, "Situation in Manchuria," 17 April 1946, Alvan Gillem Papers, MHI; **Lin Biao** Tanner, *Where*, 33; **"Everything is decided"** Westad, *Cold War*, 160.

178 **they were sure** Qing, *From Allies*, 81; **"Chiang has no choice"** Tanner, *Battle*, 111.

178 **sadistic methods** Iris Chang, *The Rape of Nanking*, 6. **W. H. Auden sonnet** "In Time of War," *The Collected Poetry of W. H. Auden.*

179 **"greatest shame"** Mitter, *Forgotten*, 202.

179 **Ming emperor's** Schell, *Wealth*, 119; **"coiling dragon"** Chang, *Rape*, 62.

179 **overcrowded that planes** Melby, *Mandate*, 41; **refugees sleeping** Topping, *Journey*, 15; **American diplomats** Ralph Clough Oral History, Foreign Service Oral History Program, LOC; **"barracks existence"** JM to Hellman, 26 April 1946, JM Papers 36, HSTL; **electricity, pillows** Melby, *Mandate*, 145; **two vehicles** Papers Vol. 5, 537; **"Basic foodstuffs"** Papers Vol. 5, 545.

179 **failed to follow through** FRUS 1946 Vol. 9, 795; **lent his own plane** FRUS 1946 Vol. 9, 802.

180 **"Being too eager"** FRUS 1946 Vol. 9, 812; **"Lincoln's idea"** *New York Times* 5 May 1946; **Yet in Manchuria** Zhou statement, 4 April 1946, Alvan Gillem Papers, MHI.

180 **both sides stepping back** FRUS 1946 Vol. 9, 814; **empowering the Committee of Three** FRUS 1946 Vol. 9, 798; **provocative and exceptionally unwise** Final Report, 101; **Both sides** FRUS 1946 Vol. 9, 740.

180 **"shameful"** CKS diary, 27 April 1946, Hoover.

180-81 **"prepare for war"** Westad, *Decisive*, 42; **"afraid and helpless"** Myers in Bland, *George C. Marshall's*, 158; **"terrified"** Qin, *Chronicles*, Vol. 6.1, 2876; **"poisoned"** CKS diary, 28 February 1946, Hoover; **"appeasement and compromise"** CKS diary, 20 April 1946, Hoover; **World War II** CKS diary, 29 April 1946, Hoover.

181 **asked rhetorically** Qin, *Chronicles*, Vol. 6.1, 2878; **America would have no choice** Westad in Bland, *George C. Marshall's*, 509.

181   **clear blue sky** JM to Hellman, 5 May 1946, JM Papers 36, HSTL; **"people's government"** *FRUS* 1945 Vol. 7, 1458.

181   **"to deal with"** Qin, *Chronicles*, Vol. 6.1, 2884; **"be pressured"** CKS diary, 4 May 1946, Hoover.

181–82 **Chiang's satisfaction** CKS diary, 4 May 1946, Hoover; **solution in Manchuria** Jeans, *Marshall Mission*, 250; **Soviets' departure** Tanner, *Battle*, 147.

182   **Marshall wrote Truman** Papers Vol. 5, 540–544.

9. Fighting While Talking

183   **His mood** JHC to Betty Caughey, 20 April 1946, JHC Papers 2/8, GCMRL; **"Oh, George"** JHC to Betty Caughey, 7 May 1946, JHC Papers 2/8, GCMRL; **"A wife"** GCM to McCarthy, 22 February 1946, Frank McCarthy Papers 31/20, GCMRL; **"The affection"** JM to Hellman, 29 September 1946, JM Papers 36, HSTL; **"very pleasant"** GCM to Bright, 4 May 1946, GCM Papers 122/7, GCMRL; **those moments** Stoler, *George C. Marshall*, 54.

183   **"all fungus"** Bland, *George C. Marshall's*, 574; **"patience of Job"** Bland, *George C. Marshall's*, 575; **Marshall continued to find himself as busy** GCM to Bright, 4 May 1946, GCM Papers 122/7, GCMRL; **"tempers the General's formidability"** JHC to Betty Caughey, 10 May 1946, JHC Papers 2/8, GCMRL; **"General's wife"** Jeans, *Marshall Mission*, 255.

184   **luxurious** Papers Vol. 5, 555; **air conditioners** Connors to JHC, 20 June 1947, JHC Papers 1/16, GCMRL; **former ambassador** JHC to Betty Caughey, 21 June 1946, JHC Papers 2/9, GCMRL; **croquet** JHC to Connors, 5 June 1947, JHC Papers 1/16, GCMRL.

184   **back terrace, Old Fashioned** Alvan Gillem Oral History, GCMRL; **Richard Wing** JHC to Connors, 5 June 1947, JHC Papers 1/16, GCMRL; **"best looking girls"** JHC to Betty Caughey, 6 June 1946, JHC Papers 2/9, GCMRL.

184   **Bullfrogs, birds** JM to Hellman, 27 April 1946, JM Papers 36, HSTL.

184–85 **choice night spot** Beal, *Marshall*, 120; **Tosca** Melby, *Mandate*, 151; **Officers' Club** Topping, *Journey*, 81, and Military Advisory Group welcome booklet, Virginia Lee Papers, GCMRL; **Arriving American women** Military Advisory Group welcome booklet, Virginia Lee Papers, GCMRL; **social commentator** *South China Morning Post* 26 August 1946; **evening gatherings** Melby, *Mandate*, 209; **fighting while talking** He in Bland, *George C. Marshall's*, 184.

185   **biggest battle** Reardon-Anderson, *Yenan*, 155; **"Do not fear"** Tanner, *Battle*, 141.

185   **Siping** Tanner, *Battle*, 1.

185   **"one blow"** Tanner, *Battle*, 132; **troops, weapons** Tanner, *Battle*, 168.

185   **"Battle of Madrid"** Cheng, "Imagining," 99; **will to fight** Tanner, *Battle*, 136.

185   **"Politics is war"** Short, *Mao*, 646.

186   **"The year after V-E Day"** Jeans, *Marshall Mission*, 250.

186   **sunshine** GCMRL newsreels; **"that of a father"** Stoler, *George C. Marshall*, 113.

186   **"influence Russia"** Perry, *Partners*, 12; **350 more senior officers** Perry, *Partners*, 29; **Eisenhower was so disturbed** Perry, *Partners*, 229.

186   **more aggressive stance** CKS diary, 9 May 1946, Hoover; **Eisenhower had been summoned** Robert H. Ferrell, *The Eisenhower Diaries*, 363; **presidential succession** Smith, *Eisenhower*, 463; **"ace in the hole"** Papers Vol. 5, 547.

186–87 **Marshall quipped** Smith, *Eisenhower*, 463; **at least September** Papers Vol. 5, 547; **code on a scrap of paper** Ferrell, *Eisenhower Diaries*, 363.

187   **Metropolitan Hotel** Beal, *Marshall*, 21; **Peking duck,** Henry Aplington, "Sunset in the East," 163; **unhelpful signal** GCM to HST, 9 February 1946, Naval Aide Files 8/9, HST Papers, HSTL; **so many troops to Manchuria** *FRUS* 1946 Vol. 10, 867; **one of his tasks** GCM-Zhou meeting notes, 3 June, Marshall Mission Records 4, NARA.

187   **railroad equipment** *FRUS* 1946 Vol. 10, 983; **surplus American property** *FRUS* 1946 Vol. 10, 1038; **"The Chinese problem"** *FRUS* 1946 Vol. 10, 794.

188   **imminent departure** GCM to Byrnes, 11 May 1946, GCM Papers 124/31, GCMRL.

188   **official account** GCM to War Department, 28 April 1946, Marshall Mission Records 47, NARA; **Durdin** Topping, *Journey*, 204; **"He will be tackling"** *New York Times* 16 December 1945; **"Would you be"** Papers Vol. 5, 555; **Durdin joined Marshall's staff** GCM to Acheson, 15 July 1946, Marshall Mission Records 7, NARA.

188   **Eisenhower's note** Papers Vol. 5, 547.

188   **land reform** Westad, *Decisive*, 38.

188   **sign on a shop** Peck, *Two Kinds*, 715.

189   **"Several hundred million persons"** Pantsov, *Mao*, 172.

189   **"battle for China"** Westad, *Decisive*, 62; **landlord retribution** Pantsov, *Mao*, 186.

189   **"personal property"** Spector, *In the Ruins*, 60; **Chiang railed** Suzanne Pepper, *Civil War in China*, 20; **Loyal southerners, Manchurian elites** Levine, *Anvil*, 245; **Wedemeyer lamented** AW to McClure, 22 August 1947, AW Papers 93/45, Hoover.

189   **rice market** Melby, *Mandate*, 143; **intelligence report relayed alarm** Summary of telegrams, 21 June 1946, Naval Aide Files 22/2, HST Papers, HSTL.

190   **what power had done** GCM Memorandum on China for HST, 18 May 1954, GCM Papers 241/5, GCMRL.

190   **"strategy of force"** *FRUS* 1946 Vol. 9, 975; **Stalin had invited** GCM-CKS meeting notes, 12 May 1946, Marshall Mission Records 20, NARA; **Although Marshall thought** GCM to HST, 12 May 1946, GCM Papers 124/31, GCMRL; **bargain for Stalin's help** Tanner, *Battle*, 169.

190   **hours into a northward retreat** Tanner, *Battle*, 162.

190   **Lin thought of Napoleon** Tanner, *Battle*, 180.

190–91 **When Marshall got angry** Cray, *General*, 57; **"save your ammunition"** Papers Vol. 2, 396; **"I don't believe"** JM to Hellman, 18 February 1946, JM Papers 36, HSTL.

191   **lunch on the sunny terrace** Beal, *Marshall*, 51.

191   **The Communists** *FRUS* 1946 Vol. 9, 807; **outside help** Beal, *Marshall*, 28; **alert from Zhou** Taylor, *Generalissimo*, 349; **"Marshall has gained"** CKS diary, 16 May 1946, Hoover.

191–92 **He was hesitant** *FRUS* 1946 Vol. 9, 857; **"so many violations"** *New York Times* 12 May 1946; **"keep the ship trim"** Papers Vol. 5, 558; **"trembling on the verge"** *FRUS* 1946 Vol. 9, 827.

192   **"never was enviable"** *New York Times* 12 May 1946.

192   **"fire and enthusiasm"** JHC to Betty Caughey, 4 May 1946, JHC Papers 2/8, GCMRL; **"each side consulted"** *FRUS* 1946 Vol. 9, 860; **every potential threat** *FRUS* 1946 Vol. 9, 861.

192   **"propaganda blast"** Jeans, *Marshall Mission*, 252; **"reckless propaganda"** Papers Vol. 5, 561; **Marshall knew the message** Papers Vol. 5, 564; **Nanjing was buzzing** JHC to Betty Caughey, 20 May 1946, JHC Papers 2/9, GCMRL; **"something had to be done"** GCM to HST, 22 May 1946, Secretary's Files 160/10, HST Papers, HSTL.

193   **"We are confronted"** Papers Vol. 5, 551.

193   **Chiang had a concern** *FRUS* 1946 Vol. 9, 880; **"terminate all hope"** Papers Vol. 5, 563; **offered his plane** GCM to Carter, 10 June 1946, GCM Papers 122/9, GCMRL.

194   **"quite hopeful"** GCM to HST, 22 May 1946, Secretary's Files 160/10, HST Papers, HSTL.

194   **He told Marshall he would be back** GCM-Zhou meeting notes, 23 May 1946, Marshall Mission Records 20, NARA.

194   **Zhou visit** GCM-Zhou meeting notes, 23 May 1946, Marshall Mission Records 20, NARA.

194   **story about the Marshalls** GCM to Eisenhower, 11 June 1946, GCM Papers 122/32, GCMRL.

194   **"die-hard government political boys"** GCM to Eisenhower, 11 June 1946, GCM Papers 122/32, GCMRL.

194   **"weaken my influence"** GCM to Eisenhower, 11 June 1946, GCM Papers 122/32, GCMRL; **senior Nationalist officials said openly** Beal, *Marshall*, 61.

195   **"serious undercover rumor campaign"** Shepley to GCM, 23 May 1946, Marshall Mission Records 47, NARA; **"sold out to the Communists"** Beal, *Marshall*, 58; **also been leaks** *Washington Post* 13 May 1946.

195   *Life* **editorial** *Washington Post* 28 May 1946; **"That becomes 'appeasement'"** *Chicago Tribune* 22 May 1946.

195   **kept Marshall abreast of the chatter** AW to GCM, 29 May 1946, GCM Papers 124/9, GCMRL.

195-96 **letters to Marshall** AW to GCM, 29 May 1946, GCM Papers 124/9, GCMRL; **Luce's reporters** Herzstein, *Luce*, 59; **"Communists will take over"** AW to Harriman, 20 May 1946, AW Papers 81/24, Hoover.

196   **pro-Communist ruse** Carter to GCM, 23 May 1946, Marshall Mission Records 2, NARA; **"anti-American forces," "emanate from Moscow"** Gallicchio in Bland, *George C. Marshall's*, 403.

196   **"symbolic gesture against the actual power"** Papers Vol. 5, 554.

197   **Zhou himself bristled** *FRUS* 1946 Vol. 10, 552; **"Direct positive proof"** Final report of Yenan Observer Group, 15 April 1946, Marshall Mission Records 27, NARA; **"irrefutable deductive proof"** Military intelligence review, 23 May 1946, Naval Aide Files 17/4, HST Papers, HSTL.

197   **"The destruction of the Communist military forces in Manchuria"** Tanner, *Battle*, 155; **a million Nationalist troops** Paine, *Wars*, 75.

197-98 **vied for position** Westad, *Decisive*, 149; **"we take it away from them"** JM to Hellman, 18 November 1945, JM Papers 36, HSTL; **"disregard of truth"** Tuchman, *Stilwell*, 514.

198   **political factors** *FRUS* 1946 Vol. 9, 1424.

198   **"We all want peace"** *FRUS* 1946 Vol. 9, 1424; **"exorbitant"** *FRUS* 1946 Vol. 9, 340; **formula for success** Taylor, *Generalissimo*, 100.

198   **"means of educating"** Ronald Keith, *The Diplomacy of Zhou Enlai*, 31; **public calls for a peaceful solution** *New York Times* 26 May 1946.

198   **pleasant spring day** JM to Hellman, 24 May 1946, JM Papers 36, HSTL; **seemed within reach** GCM-Zhou meeting notes, 23 May 1946, Marshall Mission Records 20, NARA; **improved attitudes in the field** *FRUS* 1946 Vol. 9, 893.

199   **Marshall set into a tirade** Beal, *Marshall*, 58.

199   **thought about halting** Tanner, *Battle*, 166; **"a truce"** Tanner, *Battle*, 170; **changed his mind** Taylor, *Generalissimo*, 352; **"protection of God"** Tanner, *Battle*, 171; **"shows no regard"** Qin, *Chronicles*, Vol. 6.1, 2702.

200   **Zhou had requested permission** Westad, *Decisive*, 41; **Mao even instructed** Tanner, *Battle*, 159; **Americans immediately noticed** Robertson to GCM, 1 June 1946, GCM Papers 123/35.

200   **relinquish momentum** Levine, "A New Look," 367.

200   **"middle of a fight"** Papers Vol. 5, 571.

200   **stated desire for peace** Madame CKS to GCM, 24 May 1946, Marshall Mission Records 5, NARA; **"It is best if the mediation"** Tanner, *Battle*, 171.

200-201 **Communication between him and Marshall** *FRUS* 1946 Vol. 9, 993; **"continued advances"** GCM to Soong, 29 May 1946, Marshall Mission Records 5, NARA; **"integrity of my position"** Papers Vol. 5, 577.

201   **take another plane** GCM-Zhou meeting notes, 3 June 1946, Marshall Mission Records 4, NARA; **give up** Wehrle in Bland, *George C. Marshall's*, 19; **Marshall did not say** JM to Hellman, 31 May 1946, JM Papers 36, HSTL; **"such a conflict"** GCM Memorial Day remarks, 30 May 1946, GCM Papers 123/17, GCMRL.

201   "**turning point in history**" GCM-Zhou meeting notes, 30 May 1946, Marshall Mission Records 20, NARA; **talk all day** GCM-Zhou meeting notes, 3 June, Marshall Mission Records 4, NARA; **as a friend** Papers Vol. 5, 573; "**total war**" GCM-Zhou meeting notes, 30 May 1946, Marshall Mission Records 20, NARA; "**bright side**," "**gloomy side**" Papers Vol. 5, 573.

202   "**aggressive action**," "**foolishly idealistic**" GCM-Zhou meeting notes, 3 June, Marshall Mission Records 4, NARA.

202   "**The boss man is beginning to get the idea**" JM to Hellman, 3 June 1946, JM Papers 36, HSTL.

202   "**other U.S. circles**" JM to Hellman, 3 June 1946, JM Papers 36, HSTL.

202   "**My endurance**" CKS diary, 31 May 1946, Hoover.

202–3   "**force a truce**" Jeans, *Marshall Mission*, 253; **Chiang anxious** Taylor, *Generalissimo*, 353; **right foot** Marshall interviews, 607; **shaved head** Beal, *Marshall*, 81.

203   **Chiang had made his decision** Tanner, *Battle*, 188; **recognized the prudence** CKS diary, 20 April 1946, Hoover, and Taylor, *Generalissimo*, 354; **a Soviet response** Summary of telegrams, 29 November 1946, Naval Aide Files 22/3, HST Papers, HSTL; **position of strength** Tanner, *Battle*, 188.

203   "**temporary advantage**" GCM to AW, 1 June 1946, GCM Papers 124/31, GCMRL; "**crushing blow**" Tanner, *Battle*, 179; "**killed and wounded**" Tanner, *Battle*, 180; "**voluntary**" FRUS 1946 Vol. 9, 975.

203   "**not to fail**" Tanner, *Battle*, 188.

203   **Chaing rejected it** CKS diary, 5 June 1946, Hoover.

204   **Chiang drafting order** CKS diary, 6 June 1946, Hoover.

204   **letter for Marshall** CKS to GCM, 6 June 1946, Marshall Mission Records 2, NARA.

204   "**final effort at doing business**" Papers Vol. 5, 578.

10. Umpire on a Battlefield

205   **last chance** GCM to Patterson, 19 June 1946, GCM Papers 123/30, GCMRL; "**China's destiny**" Jeans, *Marshall Mission*, 253; "**little breather**" JM to Hellman, 7 June 1946, JM Papers 36, HSTL.

205   "**an opportunity to demonstrate in good faith**" FRUS 1946 Vol. 9, 982.

205   "**the persistence**" FRUS 1946 Vol. 9, 983; "**no opportunity for the realization of peace**" *New York Times* 7 June 1946; "**amicable atmosphere**" GCM-Zhou meeting notes, 6 June 1946, Marshall Mission Records 4, NARA.

206   **Marshall was ready** GCM-Zhou meeting notes, 6 June 1946, Marshall Mission Records 4, NARA.

206   **box of candy** GCM-Zhou meeting notes, 10 June 1946, Marshall Mission Records 4, NARA; **half a million troops** *New York Times* 8 June 1946.

206   "**Marshall's efforts to mediate**" Zhang in Bland, *George C. Marshall's*, 225; **winking support** Tanner, *Battle*, 153; **Mao resolved not to be fooled** He, "Most respected," 147.

207   **"relaxing tensions"** Niu, *From Yan'an*, 282; **"We cannot again harbor illusions"** Tanner, *Battle*, 168.

207   **hinder pursuit** Lew, *Third Chinese*, 42; **keep Harbin** Chang, *Mao*, 306.

207–8 **Yet losing Harbin** Levine, *Anvil*, 130; **Nationalist lines stretched thinner and thinner** Sheng, *Battling*, 141; **"If we fight now"** Liu, *Partnership*, 291; **a film about Napoleon's defeat** Tanner, *Battle*, 197.

208   **Chiang was maneuvering to confine CCP troops** Lew, *Third Chinese*, 40.

208   **"While our delegates are negotiating"** Sheng, *Battling*, 142.

208   **madhouse** Bland, *George C. Marshall's*, 142; **hot and sticky summer** JM to Hellman, 7 June 1946 and 10 June 1946, JM Papers 36, HSTL; **"all other groups"** Melby, *Mandate*, 164.

208   **Hoping Stuart might be able to persuade** *FRUS* 1946 Vol. 9, 1023.

209   **recommendation of both Chiang** John Leighton Stuart, *Fifty Years in China*, 163; **and Henry Luce** Herzstein in Bland, *George C. Marshall's*, 133; **"Jesus Loves Me"** Stuart, *Fifty Years*, 17; **China's Harvard** Topping, *Journey*, 19; **He had championed** Yu-Ming Shaw, *An American Missionary in China*, 104; **"proving a credit to their training"** Stuart, *Fifty Years*, 155; **"man most opposed"** Papers Vol. 5, 634.

209   **"I have had long experience"** *New York Times* 17 June 1946; **eighteen years** *FRUS* 1946 Vol. 9, 1046; **"easily be destroyed"** Melby, *Mandate*, 161; **Pennsylvania coal mine** *FRUS* 1946 Vol. 9, 1046; **smooth skinned** Beal, *Marshall*, 72; **polite** JM to Hellman, 4 February 1947, JM Papers 36, HSTL; **"ruthless elimination"** Analysis of KMT, AW Papers 87/6, Hoover; **loyalty to Chiang** Boorman, *Biographical Dictionary*, Vol. 1, 206.

209   **Soviet diplomats lambasted U.S. aggression** Papers Vol. 5, 600, and Beal, *Marshall*, 84; **"Chinese reactionaries"** *New York Times* 8 June 1946; **"imperialistic elements"** *New York Times* 10 June 1946.

210   **"just as I had brought the two sides"** GCM to Carter, 10 June 1946, GCM Papers 122/9, GCMRL; **"to arouse United States opposition"** Papers Vol. 5, 590.

210   **railway lines** History of the Executive Headquarters, Alvan Gillem Papers, MHI; **attacks so aggressive** *New York Times* 14 June 1946; **"impertinent actions"** *FRUS* 1946 Vol. 9, 1024; **routes between Manchuria** *FRUS* 1946 Vol. 9, 867.

210   **"reasonable pause"** Papers Vol. 5, 590; **"definite proposals"** GCM-Zhou meeting notes, 10 June 1946, Marshall Mission Records 4, NARA.

211   **sabotage of railways** GCM-Zhou meeting notes, 12 June 1946, Marshall Mission Records 4, NARA; **progress on their own** *FRUS* 1946 Vol. 9, 1004.

211   **more grueling, "war days"** GCM to Eisenhower, 11 June 1946, GCM Papers 122/32, GCMRL; **"hell of a problem"** Papers Vol. 5, 586.

211   **Katherine dysentery and letter** Papers Vol. 5, 589.

211   **rain, steam bath** JM to Hellman, 17 June 1946, JM Papers 36, HSTL; **While Marshall and Zhou** JHC to Byroade, JHC Papers 1/1, GCMRL;

"race for time" JHC to Betty Caughey, 17 June 1946, JHC Papers 2/9, GCMRL.

211–12   on edge JHC to Betty Caughey, 17 June 1946, JHC Papers 2/9, GCMRL; "Under the present rule" Papers Vol. 5, 583; "for a long time" GCM-Zhou meeting notes, 10 June 1946, Marshall Mission Records 4, NARA; notebook A memoir from one of Zhou's aides later said that the notebook had included information about CCP secret agents, and that while Zhou had feared Marshall would pass the information to the Nationalists, there was no evidence he ever had. See Yu, *OSS*, 254; "trusted Marshall" *Time* 17 June 1946.

212   Chiang thought CKS diary, 14 June 1946, Hoover; "Marshall's attitude" CKS diary, 15 June 1946, Hoover; Marshall knew immediately Beal, *Marshall*, 84.

212   "We have reached an impasse" Papers Vol. 5, 599; said as much to Chiang *FRUS* 1946 Vol. 9, 1043.

213   dismissed Communist proposals Beal, *Marshall*, 81; Zhou reported, message to his cadres He in Bland, *George C. Marshall's*, 195.

213   Caughey started sending warnings JHC to Betty Caughey, 18 June 1946, JHC Papers 2/9, GCMRL.

213   "destroy China" GCM-Zhou meeting notes, 21 May 1946, Marshall Mission Records 20, NARA.

213   "loss of China" *FRUS* 1946 Vol. 9, 878; war would begin GCM to Carter, 16 June 1946, White House Confidential File 38/1, HST Papers, HSTL.

214   "a walking nightmare" JM to Hellman, 21 June 1946, JM Papers 36, HSTL.

214   Marshall-Yu *FRUS* 1946 Vol. 9, 1105.

214   Marshall-Stuart *FRUS* 1946 Vol. 9, 1108–1109.

214   "impossible" *FRUS* 1946 Vol. 9, 1088.

214–15   "final effort" GCM to Patterson, 19 June 1946, GCM Papers 123/30, GCMRL; Chiang had spent three hours CKS diary, 20 June 1946, Hoover.

215   "chance of success" GCM to HST, 20 June 1946, Secretary's Files 160/10, HST Papers, HSTL.

215   Marshall-Zhou *FRUS* 1946 Vol. 9, 1129–1131.

215   "last effort" *FRUS* 1946 Vol. 9, 1129; "walking through a cloud" JM to Hellman, 24 June 1946, JM Papers 36, HSTL.

216   Marshall had come to accept GCM-Yu meeting notes, 14 June 1946, Marshall Mission Records 4, NARA.

216   inability of each side to understand *FRUS* 1946 Vol. 9, 1129–1131.

216   "Hanging in the hazy atmosphere" JHC to Betty Caughey, 23 June 1946, JHC Papers 2/9, GCMRL; doodling Jeans, *Marshall Mission*, 254; particularly ineffective *FRUS* 1946 Vol. 10, 185; "We are not making" *FRUS* 1946 Vol. 9, 1173.

217   Chiangs' for dinner JHC to Betty Caughey, 23 June 1946, JHC Papers 2/9, GCMRL; "We are getting along" CKS diary, 22 June 1946, Hoover.

217   **Caughey took the call** JHC to Betty Caughey, 27 June 1946, JHC Papers 2/9, GCMRL.

217   **crowd of 100,000** Qing, *From Allies*, 88; **"Home Sweet Home"** *New York Times* 24 June 1946; **"Your Civil War"** Shanghai National Peace Movement pamphlet, 22 June 1946, Alvan Gillem Papers, MHI.

217   **It ripped the signs and streamers** Lutze, *China's*, 49.

217   **"merciless"** *New York Times* 24 June 1946; **after midnight** JHC to Betty Caughey, 27 June 1946, JHC Papers 2/9, GCMRL; **members of the peace delegation** *New York Times* 24 June 1946; **Even many Nationalists expressed dismay** Beal, *Marshall*, 93.

217-18 **indignant** Beal, *Marshall*, 95; **When he raised the incident** Marshall interviews, 575.

218   **"I believe that the passage"** Papers Vol. 5, 598; **discounted planes** Papers Vol. 5, 562; **ammunition** Papers Vol. 5, 566.

218   **Marshall note to Truman** GCM to HST, 26 June 1946, Secretary's Files 160/10, HST Papers, HSTL.

219   **Acheson issued a statement** Acheson press conference transcript, 28 June 1946, Secretary's Files 151/9, HST Papers, HSTL.

219   **key matters** GCM to HST, 26 June 1946, Secretary's Files 160/10, HST Papers, HSTL; **Zhou reacted** GCM-Zhou meeting notes, 29 June 1946, Marshall Mission Records 4, NARA; **at a loss** Papers Vol. 5, 609.

219   **heat, Cholera** JM to Hellman, 24 June 1946, JM Papers 36, HSTL; **Chen Li-fu** Beal, *Marshall*, 88.

219   **Marshall found the two sides "irreconcilably opposed"** *FRUS* 1946 Vol. 9, 1213.

220   **give up any ground** *FRUS* 1946 Vol. 9, 1038; **ideological divide** GCM-Zhou meeting notes, 29 June 1946, Marshall Mission Records 4, NARA.

220   **"negotiations are drawing"** Sheng, *Battling*, 142; **"a smokescreen"** Hunt, *Genesis*, 170; ***Emancipation Daily*** *New York Times* 29 June 1946.

220   **staff working late into the night** Jeans, *Marshall Mission*, 255; **"He is terrified"** Qin, *Chronicles*, Vol. 6.1, 2947.

220   **Chiang's office** Personal visit, and Beal, *Marshall*, 230.

221   **benefits of flexibility** Beal, *Marshall*, 96; **"judged by the world," "umpire on a battlefield"** GCM-CKS meeting notes, 29 June 1946, Marshall Mission Records 4, NARA.

221   **"I can tell from his voice"** CKS diary, 29 June 1946, Hoover.

221   **his side's infractions** *FRUS* 1946 Vol. 9, 1260; **provoke the Nationalists** Beal, *Marshall*, 109; **"Communist military supremacy"** Summary of telegrams, 21 June 1946, Naval Aide Files 22/2, HST Papers, HSTL; **"tragic dilemma"** Papers Vol. 5, 613.

222   **bitterness** Jeans, *Marshall Mission*, 255; **"all the concessions"** *FRUS* 1946 Vol. 9, 1259; **"unrelenting"** *FRUS* 1946 Vol. 9, 1250; **"undemocratic government"** *FRUS* 1946 Vol. 9, 1256.

222   **"Is that all"** *FRUS* 1946 Vol. 9, 1259.

222   **note of defeat** Papers Vol. 5, 613.

222   **Marshall-Chiang** GCM-CKS meeting notes, 30 June 1946, Marshall Mission Records 20, NARA.

223   **"stern and straight"** CKS diary, 30 June 1946, Hoover; **join him for a picnic** JHC to Betty Caughey, 29/30 June 1946, JHC Papers 2/9, GCMRL.

223   **"There is something beneath it all"** JHC to Betty Caughey, 29 June 1946, JHC Papers 2/9, GCMRL; **"If I were the Gimo"** JM to Hellman, 21 June 1946, JM Papers 36, HSTL.

11. Sisyphus in China

224   **July 4** JM to Hellman, 8 July 1946, JM Papers 36, HSTL.

224   **editorialists** *Chicago Tribune* 4 July 1946; **Walter Judd** *Chicago Tribune* 6 January 1947.

224–25 **guerrilla warfare** Marshall interviews, 126; **toll of long occupation** Marshall interviews, 140; **"most honorable episodes"** *FRUS* 1946 Vol. 10, 372.

225   **"ideals of democracy"** *Chicago Tribune* 5 July 1946; **"lost his arrogance"** CKS diary, 30 June 1946, Hoover; **"He has perhaps realized"** CKS diary, 3 July 1946, Hoover.

225   **"chummy as a couple of college girls"** Hickey to McCarthy, 17 October 1946, Frank McCarthy Papers 30/6, GCMRL; **"Madame Chiang is here"** KTM to GCM, JHC Papers 1/8, GCMRL; **Marshall laughed, Zhou stopped** JHC to Betty Caughey, 25 July 1946, JHC Papers 2/10, GCMRL.

225   **did not know** Leahy to HST, 26 July 1946, Naval Aide Files 22/2, HST Papers, HSTL, and *New York Times* 1 July 1946; **"General Marshall worked incessantly"** *Washington Post* 1 July 1946.

226   **he was not surprised when news of clashes** GCM to Acheson, 5 July 1946, AW Papers 82/23, Hoover; **rumors that ex-Nazis** *South China Morning Post* 2 July 1946.

226   **"Each side accuses"** *FRUS* 1946 Vol. 9, 1317; **"defensive annihilation"** Gillem journal notes, 14 November 1946, Alvan Gillem Papers, MHI; **He was unsure** *FRUS* 1946 Vol. 9, 1275; **"both sides"** *FRUS* 1946 Vol. 9, 1306; **Chiang's promise not to strike first** Papers Vol. 5, 615.

226   **"I am so closely engaged"** Papers Vol. 5, 615; **The State Department explained that** *FRUS* 1946 Vol. 9, 1296.

226   **a moment for him to stand aside** *FRUS* 1946 Vol. 9, 1283.

226   **"lap of the Gods"** Papers Vol. 5, 618.

226–27 **"American imperialism is far more dangerous"** *FRUS* 1946 Vol. 9, 1313; **"Philippine pattern"** CCP Central Committee Manifesto, 7 July 1946, JM Papers 1, HSTL.

227   **To Chiang** CKS diary, 9 July 1946, Hoover; **make Marshall see the right path** CKS diary, 16 July 1946, Hoover; **the Nationalists were taking**

every opportunity Westad, *Decisive*, 45; **"As if the Soviets played"** *FRUS* 1946 Vol. 9, 1294.

227   **In the field, Chinese truce team members** *FRUS* 1946 Vol. 9, 1355; **In Shanghai, American troops were instructed** *Chicago Tribune* 5 July 1946.

227   **military was devising contingency plans** Leahy to HST, 26 July 1946, Naval Aide Files 22/2, HST Papers, HSTL; **joint chiefs were compiling a report** Schnabel, *Joint Chiefs*, 50; **American-China Policy Association** *Washington Post* 26 July 1946; **Kennan** Draft of Information Policy on Relations with Russia, 22 July 1946, Dean Acheson Papers 27/4, HSTL.

228   **Copies of the major magazines** JM to Hellman, 3 February 1946, JM Papers 36, HSTL; **"great threat to the United States"** Papers Vol. 5, 617.

228   **"manpower available to such a combination"** Millis, *Forrestal Diaries*, 108; **"road of appeasement"** Millis, *Forrestal Diaries*, 141.

228   **"period of withdrawal"** Millis, *Forrestal Diaries*, 174.

229   **thought Marshall too intent** Millis, *Forrestal Diaries*, 188; **"very much like ourselves"** Millis, *Forrestal Diaries*, 176; **"an invitation to some other power"** Millis, *Forrestal Diaries*, 190.

229   **other official visitors** GCM to Chamberlin, 6 July 1946, GCM Papers 17/21; **"every VIP"** Caraway to Carr, 1 February 1946, Paul Caraway Papers, MHI; **"after dark entertainment"** Gillem to Handy, 12 August 1946, Alvan Gillem Papers, MHI; **"I am ashamed"** JHC to Betty Caughey, 8 September 1946, JHC Papers 2/10, GCMRL; **Republican sweep** Beal, *Marshall*, 116.

229   **another round of rumors** *FRUS* 1946 Vol. 9, 1277, and Jeans, *Marshall Mission*, 255.

229–30   **all over the papers** *Washington Post* 5 May 1946; **how pleased he would be by the appointment** Papers Vol. 5, 461; **a special trip to Brooks Brothers** AW to Caraway, 24 October 1946, Paul Caraway Papers, MHI; **"General Marshall"** AW to McClure, 12 April 1946, AW Papers 82/18, Hoover.

230   **the rumors were unhelpful** GCM to Acheson, 5 July 1946, AW Papers 82/23, Hoover; **mid-September** Papers Vol. 5, 628.

230   **"no record"** Shepley to HST, 26 February 1946, GCM Papers 124/28, GCMRL; **inflame Communist** AW to GCM, 29 May 1946, GCM Papers 124, GCMRL; **embolden Nationalist hard-liners** Papers Vol. 5, 572.

230   **"I am increasingly convinced"** AW to Luce, 2 July 1946, AW Papers 82/14, Hoover; **"serious failure"** AW to McClure, 12 April 1946, AW Papers 82/18, Hoover.

230   **letter to Acheson** GCM to Acheson, 5 July 1946, AW Papers 82/23, Hoover.

231   **"Christ-like"** Topping, *Journey*, 19; **Chiang's personal secretary** GCM to HST, 22 July 1946, Secretary's Files 160/10, HST Papers, HSTL; **Zhou's young aides** Beal, *Marshall*, 216; **"patriotic purpose"** Stuart, *Fifty Years*, 120; **"Christian faith"** Shaw, *American*, 140; **"talk to the Generalissimo"** Melby, *Mandate*, 166; **"devious as any Chinese"** May, *Truman*, 13.

231 **allowed that Wedemeyer** Papers Vol. 5, 572; **"possible insinuations"** Papers Vol. 5, 628; **"I do not need his assurances"** Papers Vol. 5, 628.

231 **Wedemeyer had long claimed** AW to JHC, 1 May 1946, JHC Papers 1/9, GCMRL, and AW to McClure, 1 July 1946, AW Papers 82/18, Hoover; **he wrote Marshall** AW to GCM, 12 July 1946, GCM Papers 124, GCMRL.

231–32 **"atomic bomb"** AW to Eng, 10 July 1946, AW Papers 81/15, Hoover; **promised Chiang** AW to GCM, 12 July 1946, GCM Papers 124, GCMRL; **"he needed me"** AW to GCM, 25 April 1946, AW Papers 82/23, Hoover; **$695** AW to Caraway, 24 October 1946, Paul Caraway Papers, MHI; **"funeral regalia"** AW to GCM, 12 July 1946, GCM Papers 124, GCMRL; **box of Brooks Brothers shirts** AW to JHC, 5 February 1947, JHC Papers 1/9, GCMRL.

232 **"offend the reds"** *Chicago Tribune* 17 July 1946; **rumors of Marshall's imminent departure** JM to Hellman, 10 July 1946, JM Papers 36, HSTL.

232 **"straight civil war"** *FRUS* 1946 Vol. 9, 1369; **Summer in Nanjing** GCM to Bryden, 14 September 1946, GCM Papers 122/7, GCMRL.

232 **Yenan's charges** GCM-Zhou meeting notes, 11 July 1946, Marshall Mission Records 4, NARA; **Zhou insisted that Marshall** *FRUS* 1946 Vol. 9, 1327; **"I am the 'reactionary party'"** Papers Vol. 5, 627; **Aides were taken aback** Melby, *Mandate*, 170.

233 **"It seems to me that unless we find a basis"** *FRUS* 1946 Vol. 9, 1368.

233 **bombs** JHC to Betty Caughey, 18 July 1946, JHC Papers 2/10, GCMRL.

233 **hour and forty-five** GCM to Bryden, 14 September 1946, GCM Papers 122/7, GCMRL; **grass airfield** GCMRL photographs; **sedan chairs** GCMRL photographs; **ascent** GCM to Eisenhower, 17 September 1946, GCM Papers 122/32, GCMRL; **bearers paused** Beal, *Marshall*, 145; **calluses** White, *In Search*, 66; **"most undemocratic"** Eng to Caraway, 26 July 1946, Paul Caraway Papers, MHI.

233–34 **As they climbed** JHC photograph caption, JHC papers 5/5, GCMRL; **two hours** GCM to Eisenhower, 17 September 1946, GCM Papers 122/32, GCMRL; **Switzerland** Bland, *George C. Marshall's*, 580; **posters** JHC photograph caption, JHC papers 5/5, GCMRL.

234 **immediately agreed** Papers Vol. 5, 650; **"quite devoted"** GCM to Bryden, 14 September 1946, GCM Papers 122/7, GCMRL.

234 **unintended consequence** Beal, *Marshall*, 122.

235 **"time work this out"** Jeans, *Marshall Mission*, 256; **"make Marshall realize"** Qin, *Chronicles*, Vol. 6.1, 2969.

235 **"aggressive military action"** *FRUS* 1946 Vol. 9, 1355; **"The Chinese Problem"** *FRUS* 1946 Vol. 9, 1389.

235 **Stuart to Chiang** *FRUS* 1946 Vol. 9, 1390.

235 **"rumors around"** JM to Hellman, 23 July 1946, JM Papers 36, HSTL.

235 **bearded professor** Taylor, *Generalissimo*, 357, and Boorman, *Biographical Dictionary*, Vol. 3, 411; **Art Institute of Chicago** Fairbank, *Chinabound*, 315; **Yenching** Shaw, *American*, 172; **Nationalist agents** Tanner, *Where Chiang*, 50.

236   **"considerable evidence"** *FRUS* 1946 Vol. 9, 1381; **"pay with their lives"** *FRUS* 1946 Vol. 9, 1400.

236   **"terroristic" crackdown** GCM to HST, 2 August 1946, Secretary's Files 160/10, HST Papers, HSTL; **not always wrong** Westad, *Decisive*, 82; **"Those who wanted"** Paine, *Wars*, 263; **"Seeing that"** *FRUS* 1946 Vol. 9, 1362.

236–37 **American financial expert** Arthur Young Oral History, HSTL; **Marshall started to warn** Papers Vol. 5, 630; **"bankrupt China"** *New York Times* 20 June 1946.

237   **industrial capacity** Paine, *Wars*, 241; **back a generation** Spector, *In the Ruins*, 35; **"It is impossible"** JM to Hellman, 18 August 1946, JM Papers 36, HSTL; **As Marshall learned** Papers Vol. 5, 616; **acknowledged that Yalta** Papers Vol. 5, 616.

237   **"seeing the situation"** JM to Hellman, 9 January 1946, JM Papers 36, HSTL; **questions about land reform** JM to Hellman, 10 February 1946, JM Papers 36, HSTL; *400 Million Customers* McWilliams to GCM, 22 April 1946, GCM Papers 123/20, GCMRL; **"Yes, of course"** *FRUS* 1946 Vol. 9, 1424.

237   **"fighting spreads"** JM to Hellman, 9 July 1946, JM Papers 36, HSTL; **boom of artillery** JM to Hellman, 23 July 1946, JM Papers 36, HSTL.

238   **"Each side accuses"** Papers Vol. 5, 631; **"the acts were hard to determine"** GCM to HST, 30 July 1946, Secretary's Files 160/10, HST Papers, HSTL.

238   **Marshall-Yu** GCM-Yu meeting notes, 22 July 1946, Marshall Mission Records 4, NARA.

238   **T. V. Soong invited** GCM appointment list, 25 July 1946, Marshall Mission Records 7, NARA; **English manor,** *Henry V* Beal, *Marshall*, 135.

238   **"More meetings"** Jeans, *Marshall Mission*, 256.

238   **"When conditions are difficult"** George C. Marshall, *Memoirs of My Services in the World War*, 1.

238   **"never says die"** Papers Vol. 5, 631.

239   **mountain lilies** JHC clipping, JHC Papers 2/11, GCMRL; **picnics** Bland, *George C. Marshall's*, 586; **tender steak** Beal, *Marshall*, 168; **chicken and waffles** Jeans, *Marshall Mission*, 258; **work in the garden** Papers Vol. 5, 669; **a fire burned** Beal, *Marshall*, 149; **their library** Fenby, *Chiang*, 255; **silk dresses** Papers Vol. 5, 669; **"wonderful friends"** Papers Vol. 5, 668.

239   **wicker chair, Old Fashioned** Beal, *Marshall*, 149; **fearsome opponents** Jeans, *Marshall Mission*, 29.

239   **"most pleasant experiences"** CKS diary, 2 August 1946, Hoover; **game's rules** Gillem journal notes, 7–10 September 1946, Alvan Gillem Papers, MHI; **Sometimes during dinner** John Hart Caughey Oral History, GCMRL; **personal monologue** Stuart, *Fifty Years*, 278; **"He speaks no English"** Bland, *George C. Marshall's*, 588.

239   **"her devoted admirer"** Papers Vol. 5, 697; **"If I was as"** GCM to AW, 30 September 1946, GCM Papers 124, GCMRL.

240   **Himmler, Pro-Nationalist sources** Beal, *Marshall*, 177; **newspaper clippings** *FRUS*, 1946 Vol. 9, 1423; **"gestapo"** Beal, *Marshall*, 173; **"not likely to be halted"** *Time* 10 June 1946; **"sheer tragedy"** Papers Vol. 5, 640.

240   **"The American people"** Papers Vol. 5, 638.

240   **"the tragedy impending"** *FRUS* 1946 Vol. 9, 1420.

241   **"could liquidate within three to six months"** GCM-Yu meeting notes, 16 July 1946, Marshall Mission Records 4, NARA.

241   **wiping out Communist forces** Levine, *Anvil*, 84; **"Now let me give you my word"** Qing, *From Allies*, 83.

241   **triumph again and again** Lew, *Third*, 39; **Communist forces numbered** Qing, *From Allies*, 87; **Washington would back him fully** Westad, *Decisive*, 45; **would prove secondary** Beal, *Marshall*, 114.

241   **"anxious"** CKS diary, 11 July 1946, Hoover; **Chinese proverb** GCM to HST, 30 July 1946, Secretary's Files 160/10, HST Papers, HSTL; **four days on the mountain had been useless** Papers Vol. 5, 639.

241   **Anping** Henry I. Shaw, *The United States Marines in North China*, 17.

242   **quickly became clear** Beal, *Marshall*, 140; **"Americans don't accept"** *FRUS* 1946 Vol. 9, 1433; **"deliberate misrepresentation"** *FRUS* 1946 Vol. 9, 1432.

242   **"mothers of these boys"** Note to Caraway, 29 August 1946, Paul Caraway Papers, MHI.

242   **Sisyphus** Acheson, *Present*, 204; **"He likes going up"** Jeans, *Marshall Mission*, 259.

242   **Marshall recognized that the situation** *FRUS* 1946 Vol. 10, 1045.

242–43 **"narrow minded"** Papers Vol. 5, 646; helping the Communists GCM-CKS meeting notes, 5 August 1946, Marshall Mission Records 4, NARA; **"fruitful breeding ground"** Papers Vol. 5, 651; **"exceptional opportunity"** *FRUS* 1946 Vol. 9, 1469; **"I figured the concessions"** Qin, *Chronicles*, Vol. 6.1, 2981.

243   **Team 25** History of the Executive Headquarters, Alvan Gillem Papers, MHI; **"absurd farce"** *FRUS* 1946 Vol. 9, 1491; **"lead to an aroused"** *FRUS* 1946 Vol. 10, 873.

243   **GCM-Zhou meeting** *FRUS* 1946 Vol. 9, 1475–1476.

243   **Zhou was more interested** *FRUS* 1946 Vol. 9, 1484–1486.

244   **"the contradictions"** *FRUS* 1946 Vol. 9, 1483.

12. George Marshall Can't Walk on Water

245–46 **statement's purpose** GCM to HST, 16 August 1946, GCM Papers 124/31, GCMRL; **Zhou deemed it** *FRUS* 1946 Vol. 10, 8; **Nationalists grumbled** Beal, *Marshall*, 155; **"heart-breaking task"** Liang to GCM, 12 August 1946, GCM Papers 123/10, GCMRL; **"We entreat you"** Lee to GCM and Stuart, 12 August 1946, GCM Papers 123/10, GCMRL.

246   **"unusually strong"** Koo to Soong, 12 August 1946, T. V. Soong Papers, Hoover.

246   **Truman's letter** HST to CKS, 10 August 1946, Secretary's Files 151/9, HST Papers, HSTL.

246–47   **"statement sufficiently strong"** FRUS 1946 Vol. 9, 1450; **Generalissimo's "face"** Papers Vol. 5, 651.

247   **Mao's new theory** He in Bland, *George C. Marshall's*, 196; **Even without a US-Soviet war** Westad, *Brothers*, 61.

247   **Mao interview with Strong** Pantsov, *Mao*, 351.

247–48   **those around Mao had sensed him wrestling** Qing, *From Allies*, 87; **long been confident** Andrew Bingham Kennedy, "Can the Weak Defeat the Strong?," 894; **"protracted war"** Short, *Mao*, 255; **"God of Thunder"** Short, *Mao*, 214; **instructional verse** Short, *Mao*, 222.

248   **approach he was taking now** Tanner, *Battle*, 196; **American intelligence** Military intelligence review, 18 July 1946, Naval Aide Files 18/2, HST Papers, HSTL.

248   **Durdin had finished** Carter to Sulzberger, 16 July 1946, GCM Papers 124, GCMRL; **message from his hosts** Durdin to GCM, 31 July 1946, GCM Papers 122/28, GCMRL.

248   *Emancipation Daily* **editorial** FRUS 1946 Vol. 10, 48.

249   **Zhou had assumed** Spector, *In the Ruins*, 253; **"The American Marines"** FRUS 1946 Vol. 10, 16.

249   **"I am being deprived"** GCM-Zhou meeting notes, 15 August 1946, Marshall Mission Records 4, NARA.

249   **Nationalist hard-liners** GCM to HST, 16 August 1946, Secretary's Files 160/10, HST Papers, HSTL; **still a negotiating tactic** FRUS 1946 Vol. 10, 70–71.

249   **"Isn't it wishful thinking"** CKS diary, 15 August 1946, Hoover.

249   **Marshall-Chiang meeting** GCM to HST, 17 August 1946, Secretary's Files 160/10, HST Papers, HSTL.

250   **"I have never seen"** Qin, *Chronicles*, Vol. 6.1, 2989; **"Marshall still believes"** Myers in Bland, *George C. Marshall's*, 157–158; **"fish in a tree"** Taylor, *Generalissimo*, 359.

250   **borrowing the fearsomeness of the tiger** John W. Garver, *Chinese-Soviet Relations*, 210.

250   **"I am sure that you realize"** AW to CKS, 2 August 1946, T. V. Soong Papers, Hoover; **The enclosed letter pronounced** AW to CKS, 2 August 1946, AW Papers 81/2, Hoover.

251   **reaction in key quarters** AW to CKS, 25 April 1946, AW Papers 81/2, Hoover.

251   **"I shall accept as gospel"** AW to GCM, 4 May 1946, GCM Papers 124/8, GCMRL; **Marshall's folly** AW to Hurley, 31 December 1946, AW Papers 93/6, Hoover; **asking the Chinese embassy** AW to Counselor, Chinese Embassy, 24 April 1946, AW Papers 92/28, Hoover; **"Marshall's own statements"** AW memo on "Chinese problem," 10 August 1946, AW Papers

90/6, Hoover; **to Chiang** AW to CKS, 2 August 1946, AW Papers 81/2, Hoover; **"so long as our policy"** AW to Yeaton, 8 August 1946, AW Papers 83/36, Hoover; **he blamed traitorous State Department** AW to Caraway, 24 October 1946, AW Papers 80/19, Hoover.

251   **"Exactly what happened"** AW to Wei, 9 August 1946, AW Papers 83/30, Hoover; **"Apparently there was opposition"** AW to Chen, 13 August 1946, AW Papers 80/22, Hoover; **"all of Asia"** AW memo on "Chinese problem," 10 August 1946, AW Papers 90/6, Hoover.

251-52 **America First view** Pogue, *Ordeal*, 141; **Charles Lindbergh** AW to CKS/Madame CKS, 15 December 1947, AW Papers 98/17, Hoover; **"Hitler's methods"** Spence, *To Change*, 266; **"money-making areas," "planned penetration"** AW to Hurley, 2 December 1947, AW Papers 98/41, Hoover.

252   **"I am so sorry"** Keith E. Eiler in Bland, *George C. Marshall's*, 106; **Marshall despised Bullitt** Pogue, *Organizer*, 476; **Marshall read it** GCM to AW, 28 August 1946, GCM Papers 124, GCMRL.

252   **"death struggle"** Papers Vol. 5, 645; **He reiterated to Chiang the risks** GCM-CKS meeting notes, 16 August 1946, Marshall Mission Records 4, NARA.

252   **strafed Yenan** History of the Executive Headquarters, Alvan Gillem Papers, MHI.

252   **An order was broadcast** *New York Times* 20 August 1946; **American intelligence judged** Military intelligence review, 22 August 1946, Naval Aide Files 18/3, HST Papers, HSTL; **Party spokesmen called the Nationalists** *New York Times* 17 August 1946.

253   **"Chiang cannot be counted on"** Summary of telegrams, 19 August 1946, Naval Aide Files 22/2, HST Papers, HSTL.

253   **Truce teams** History of the Executive Headquarters, Alvan Gillem Papers, MHI.

253   **subtropical summer** GCM to Spencer, 14 August 1946, GCM Papers 123/41, GCMRL; **90 degrees** Papers Vol. 5, 650; **only slightly cooler** JHC to Betty Caughey, 23 August 1946, JHC Papers 2/10, GCMRL; **malaria** JM to Hellman, 29 September 1946, JM Papers 36, HSTL; **"In the heat"** JM to Hellman, 6 August 1946, JM Papers 36, HSTL.

253   **"The old man"** Carter to Davis, 13 August 1946, Marshall Carter Papers, GCMRL.

253   **"policy of force"** GCM to HST, 17 August 1946, Secretary's Files 160/10, HST Papers, HSTL; **He saw both sides** Beal, *Marshall*, 164; **"tornado of propaganda"** FRUS 1946 Vol. 10, 249.

253   **"The Generalissimo is leading"** Papers Vol. 5, 663; **He warned Zhou, "I am sitting"** GCM-Zhou meeting notes, 29 August 1946, Marshall Mission Records 4, NARA.

254   **"We felt there was nothing else"** GCM-Yu meeting notes, 30 August 1946, Marshall Mission Records 4, NARA; **He refused to return** FRUS 1946 Vol. 10, 255.

254   **admitted to being confused** GCM-Zhou meeting notes, 11 September 1946, Marshall Mission Records 4, NARA; **as did Zhou** FRUS 1946 Vol. 10, 145; **and Madame Chiang** FRUS 1946 Vol. 10, 172; **"dizzy merry-go-round"** Melby, *Mandate*, 190–191.

254   **fireworks displays were canceled** Jeans, *Marshall Mission*, 148; **"put down rebellions"** *New York Times* 14 August 1946.

254   **Marshall wrote back** Papers Vol. 5, 661.

255   **slacks, blazer** Beal, *Marshall*, 163.

255   **"The military situation"** GCM to HST, 30 August 1946, Secretary's Files 160/10, HST Papers, HSTL.

255   **"some elixir"** FRUS 1946 Vol. 10, 152; **embassy's contribution** FRUS 1946 Vol. 10, 148.

255   **parallel inquiry in the State Department** FRUS 1946 Vol. 10, 58.

256   **"encouraged by feeling dead certain"** Beal, *Marshall*, 198; **wanted it stalled** FRUS 1946 Vol. 10, 753; **wanted most of it still withheld** FRUS 1946 Vol. 10, 996; **shipments of airplanes** Carter to Deputy Chief of Staff, 13 August 1946, GCM Papers 124/25, GCMRL; **ammunition** FRUS 1946 Vol. 10, 757; **Nationalist officials** GCM-Yu meeting notes, 5 September 1946, Marshall Mission Records 4, NARA; **"It was just a matter"** GCM-Yu meeting notes, 30 August 1946, Marshall Mission Records 4, NARA; **slow-down would hardly cripple** Westad, *Decisive*, 49; **$800 million** Chinese Embassy analysis, 2 March 1948, AW Papers 99/11, Hoover.

256   **"surplus property"** Military intelligence review, 5 September 1946, Naval Aide Files 18/4, HST Papers, HSTL.

256   **"adding fuel"** FRUS 1946 Vol. 10, 1053; **press conference** *New York Times* 2 September 1946; **"You are confusing"** GCM-Zhou meeting notes, 29 August 1946, Marshall Mission Records 4, NARA.

257   **"are seeking by intense"** GCM to HST, 30 August 1946, Secretary's Files 160/10, HST Papers, HSTL.

257   **"significant pressure"** FRUS 1946 Vol. 10, 873; **Much of Truman's cabinet** Wallace, *Price*, 608; **even Forrestal was recommending** Forrestal to HST, 15 August 1946, Secretary's Files 151/9, HST Papers, HSTL; **"Those who have anything"** Lynch to GCM, 2 August 1946, GCM Papers 123/15, GCMRL; **"It may have been right"** Torkel to GCM, 30 July 1946, GCM Papers 124/2, GCMRL.

257   **"It is anticipated"** Timberman to McConnell, 23 August 1946, Timberman-Fiske Papers, MHI.

258   **armies to wage war in places like Manchuria** GCM to Acheson, 28 August 1946, Marshall Mission Records 2, NARA.

258   **Marshall saw the ambush** GCM-Zhou meeting notes, 15 August 1946, Marshall Mission Records 4, NARA; **"it would be a victory"** FRUS 1946 Vol. 10, 874.

258   **"there is no reason"** Chang to GCM, 10 August 1946, GCM Papers 122/13, GCMRL; **a force capable of balancing** FRUS 1946 Vol. 10, 830.

258   **"advocate discussion groups"** JM to Hellman, 16 November 1945, JM
       Papers 36, HSTL; **"stand between the two primitive giants"** Melby, *Mandate*, 200; **"They are learning"** JM to Hellman, 6 August 1946, JM Papers
       36, HSTL.

259   **walking with Katherine in the moonlight** JM to Hellman, 29 September
       1946, JM Papers 36, HSTL.

259   **"formal invitation to Russia"** Papers Vol. 5, 663; **"false power"** *FRUS*
       1946 Vol. 10, 170.

259   **"pressure does not work"** Qin, *Chronicles*, Vol. 6.1, 2990; **Chiang simply
       refused** CKS diary, 19 August 1946, Hoover; **major push in Rehe** Military intelligence review, 5 September 1946, Naval Aide Files 18/4, HST
       Papers, HSTL; **evaded conversation** CKS diary, 25 August 1946, Hoover;
       "He can use the sale of goods" CKS diary, 2 September 1946, Hoover;
       "to install a totalitarian" *FRUS* 1946 Vol. 10, 92; **Truman promptly
       wrote back** *FRUS* 1946 Vol. 10, 147; **"We can get along"** Beal, *Marshall*,
       181.

260   **"I am not"** GCM-Zhou meeting notes, 5 September 1946, Marshall Mission Records 4, NARA; **sincerely** *FRUS* 1946 Vol. 10, 89; **his last trump
       card** GCM to HST, 6 September 1946, Secretary's Files 160/10, HST
       Papers, HSTL; **National Assembly on his terms** CKS diary, 9 September
       1946, Hoover; **Only military defeat** GCM to HST, 13 September 1946,
       Secretary's Files 160/10, HST Papers, HSTL.

260   **by October** GCM-Zhou meeting notes, 4 September 1946, Marshall Mission Records 4, NARA; **"a somewhat Chinese view"** GCM to HST, 30
       August 1946, Secretary's Files 160/10, HST Papers, HSTL; **he conceded
       to Truman** GCM to HST, 13 September 1946, Secretary's Files 160/10,
       HST Papers, HSTL.

260   **sat Katherine down, "Only he"** Bland, *George C. Marshall's*, 587; **"Disregard all press"** GCM to Chamberlin, 3 September 1946, GCM Papers
       17/22, GCMRL.

260   **"messenger boy"** Beal, *Marshall*, 156; **She reported to a friend** Papers Vol.
       5, 669.

260–61 **"a problem like China"** JM to Hellman, 16 September 1946, JM Papers
       36, HSTL; **"the General was presented with a problem"** JHC to Betty
       Caughey, 29 June 1946, JHC Papers 2/9, GCMRL.

261   **"walk on water"** Chern, *Dilemma*, 201.

261   **three more games** CKS diary, 17 September 1946, Hoover.

261   **he would not return** GCM-CKS meeting notes, 15 and 17 September
       1946, Marshall Mission Records 20, NARA.

261   **"on behalf of"** Papers Vol. 5, 686; **"War has engulfed"** GCM to Byrnes,
       18 September 1946, Marshall Mission Records 2, NARA; **radio broadcasts from Yenan** *FRUS* 1946 Vol. 10, 195.

261   **"It is clear"** CKS diary, 17 September 1946, Hoover; **"dreams of mediating"** CKS diary, 16 September 1946, Hoover.

13. The Rock and the Whirlpool

265   **"Giving the best I had"** Papers Vol. 1, 78.

265   **signs of fall** GCM to Chamberlin, 3 September 1946, GCM Papers 17/22, GCMRL; **"I suspect I have been wrong"** Beal, *Marshall*, 201.

265–66 **"playing against futility and despair"** JM to Hellman, 24 September 1946, JM Papers 36, HSTL; **"Here is a great man"** JHC to Timberman, 22 September 1946, JHC Papers 1/13, GCMRL; **"He subjugates himself"** JHC to Betty Caughey, 8 September 1946, JHC Papers 2/10, GCMRL.

266   **"450 million Chinese"** JHC to Betty Caughey, 8 September 1946, JHC Papers 2/10, GCMRL.

266   **"order out of chaos"** Cotter to GCM, 6 September 1946, GCM Papers 122/26, GCMRL; **"my money on Marshall"** FRUS 1946 Vol. 10, 205; **paraphrased lines from Kipling** Ridgway to GCM, 28 October 1946, GCM Papers 123/34, GCMRL.

266   **"Confused and maddening"** GCM to HST, 23 September 1946, Secretary's Files 160/10, HST Papers, HSTL.

266   **"I know you can"** Papers Vol. 5, 690; **"Looks like Marshall will fail"** Robert H. Ferrell, *Dear Bess*, 538.

266   **"George will not give up"** Papers Vol. 5, 669.

267   **summer in Kuling** Bland, *George C. Marshall's*, 589; **Chiang reasoned** CKS diary, 24 September 1946, Hoover.

267   **"final rupture"** GCM to Acheson, 2 October 1946, Secretary's Files 151/9, HST Papers, HSTL; **"in line with my intentions"** CKS diary, 27 September 1946, Hoover.

267   **"attitude of tolerance"** FRUS 1946 Vol. 10, 241.

267   **"Communist nerve center"** Military intelligence review, 3 October 1946, Naval Aide Files 19/1, HST Papers, HSTL; **proposed site** Gillem journal notes, 25–28 February 1946, Alvan Gillem Papers, MHI; **Chiang would follow** CKS diary, 29 September 1946, Hoover.

267   **"fat's in the fire"** Beal, *Marshall*, 195; **Chiang had agreed** GCM to Acheson, 2 October 1946, Marshall Mission Records 4, NARA.

268   **He fumed afterward** CKS diary, 30 September 1946, Hoover.

268   **time for a showdown** FRUS 1946 Vol. 10, 270; **"I wish merely"** GCM to CKS, 2 October 1946, Marshall Mission Records 2, NARA.

268   **"This old man"** Qin, *Chronicles*, Vol. 6.1, 3016.

268   **He informed Marshall he would call off** Final report, 282.

268   **"violent temper"** Stuart diary, 4 October 1946, John Leighton Stuart Papers, Hoover; **"irritable"** CKS diary, 5 October 1946, Hoover; **once again hot** JM to Hellman, 1 October 1946, JM Papers 36, HSTL; **"valley of the shadow"** JM to O'Sullivan, 3 October 1946, JM Papers 1, HSTL.

268   **Chiang avoided Marshall** CKS diary, 5 October 1946, Hoover; **Stuart**

persuaded Chiang CKS diary, 5 October 1946, Hoover; **not blamed if Marshall left** CKS diary, 3 October 1946, Hoover.

268   **Chiang laid out** GCM-CKS meeting notes, 4 October 1946, Marshall Mission Records 20, NARA; **duty to his state** CKS diary, 4 October 1946, Hoover.

269   **Chiang thought he had gotten his point across** CKS diary, 5 October 1946, Hoover.

269   **"stooge"** *FRUS* 1946 Vol. 10, 261.

269   **message to the president** GCM to HST, 22 May 1946, Secretary's Files 160/10, HST Papers, HSTL.

270   **"heroic behavior"** Shaw, *American*, 105; **he worried now** *FRUS* 1946 Vol. 9, 1390 and 1466.

270   **he panicked** Stuart diary, 5 October 1946, John Leighton Stuart Papers, Hoover.

270   **Marshall-Chiang meeting** *FRUS* 1946 Vol. 10, 309.

270   **dictated the details** *FRUS* 1946 Vol. 10, 349.

270   **Zhou refused to return** *FRUS* 1946 Vol. 10, 311.

270   **"completely baffled"** Papers Vol. 5, 712; **"I very much fear"** *FRUS* 1946 Vol. 10, 317–318.

271   **"seemed so pathetic"** Bland, *George C. Marshall's*, 589; **Marshall seemed repentant** CKS diary, 8 October 1946, Hoover.

271   **At 9 o'clock** Stuart diary, 9 October 1946, John Leighton Stuart Papers, Hoover; **Gillem had invited** Alvan Gillem Oral History, GCMRL; **put Zhou on the spot** Beal, *Marshall*, 230.

271   **"most accomplished actor"** Stoler, *George C. Marshall*, 78.

271   **"damn near died"** Alvan Gillem Oral History, GCMRL.

271–72 **"avoiding Marshall"** Han, *Eldest*, 194; **rooting for World War III** *Washington Post* 20 September 1946; **"camouflage the true"** *FRUS* 1946 Vol. 10, 211–212; **Marshall pointedly reminded** *FRUS* 1946 Vol. 10, 247; **"stupid piece of business"** *FRUS* 1946 Vol. 10, 245.

272   **Marshall wanted to try** GCM to HST, 10 October 1946, Secretary's Files 160/10, HST Papers, HSTL.

272   **Marshall-Zhou discussion** GCM-Zhou meeting notes, 9 October 1946, Marshall Mission Records 5, NARA; **he did not disclose** GCM to HST, 10 October 1946, Secretary's Files 160/10, HST Papers, HSTL.

273   **"psychoneurotic," half an hour quibbling** GCM to HST, 10 October 1946, Secretary's Files 160/10, HST Papers, HSTL.

273   **Stuart gushed privately** *FRUS* 1946 Vol. 10, 331.

273   **marched into Zhangjiakou** Westad, *Decisive*, 48.

273   **unflyable for weeks** Caughey to Eisenhower, 16 October 1946, GCM Papers 122/32, GCMRL; **appeared unfazed** JHC to Betty Caughey, 13 October 1946, JHC Papers 2/10, GCMRL; **"just another blow"** Bland, *George C. Mar-*

shall's, 589; **a telegram arrived** Carter to GCM, 13 October 1946, GCM Papers 123/42, GCMRL; **Marshall had gotten word** Carter to GCM, 4 October 1946, GCM Papers 123/42, GCMRL; **memorial service** GCM to Mrs. Stilwell, 20 October 1946, GCM Papers 86/14, GCMRL.

273 **Stilwell had been on Chiang's mind** CKS diary, 20 November 1946 and 8 January 1947, Hoover.

274 **conquest of Zhangjiakou** Westad, *Decisive,* 48.

274 **Chiang restarted national conscription** Final report, 313; **He announced** *FRUS* 1946 Vol. 10, 358; **a separate assembly** JHC to Betty Caughey, 13 October 1946, JHC Papers 2/10, GCMRL **radio address** *FRUS* 1946 Vol. 10, 359; **total Nationalist victory within five months** Taylor, *Generalissimo,* 361.

274 **recognizing the risk** Tanner, *Battle,* 191; **Chiang had refrained** Tanner, *Where Chiang Kai-shek,* 45; **he had decided to wipe out** Tanner, *Where Chiang Kai-shek,* 46; **"straining at the leash"** *FRUS* 1946 Vol. 10, 235.

274 **Even the Kremlin** Westad, *Decisive,* 57; **Stalin himself was surprised** Westad, *Decisive,* 49.

274–75 **more successful than he had anticipated** *FRUS* 1946 Vol. 10, 199; **"almost unlimited room"** *FRUS* 1946 Vol. 10, 235; **Nationalist lines were stretching** Papers Vol. 5, 730.

275 **American intelligence assessed** Military intelligence review, 17 October 1946, Naval Aide Files 19/1, HST Papers, HSTL.

275 **"How exhausting"** CKS diary, 12 October 1946, Hoover; **"cold shoulder"** CKS diary, 10 October 1946, Hoover; **"Marshall's attitude"** CKS diary, 12 October 1946, Hoover.

275–76 **constrain him** Tang Tsou, *America's Failure in China,* 428; **"My state and I"** CKS diary, 31 October 1946, Hoover; **well supplied** Westad, *Decisive,* 49; **"FDR party"** Westad, *Decisive,* 58; **"by Marshall's mood"** CKS diary, 25 October 1946, Hoover.

276 **Marshall was aware that his mood** GCM-CCP delegation meeting notes, 4 October 1946, Marshall Mission Records 22, NARA; **"My endurance"** *FRUS* 1946 Vol. 10, 264; **"unhappy duty"** *FRUS* 1946 Vol. 10, 215; **private comments** GCM to Chang, 5 October 1946, GCM Papers 122/13, GCMRL; **Aides joked** JM to Hellman, 8 October 1946, JM Papers 36, HSTL; **"Chickens come home"** *FRUS* 1946 Vol. 10, 285.

276 **massage every morning** GCM letter, 7 January 1947, GCM Papers 123/39, GCMRL; **Katherine thought he looked** Bland, *George C. Marshall's,* 589; **"My ambitions"** GCM to Somervell, 22 September 1946, GCM Papers 123/40, GCMRL; **He had heard little** Papers Vol. 7, 859.

276 **"general objective of all concerned"** JM to Hellman, 16 October 1946, JM Papers 36, HSTL.

277 **"The struggle has"** Sheng, *Battling,* 143; **"educate the masses"** He in Bland, *George C. Marshall's,* 197; *Emancipation Daily* **published** *FRUS* 1946 Vol. 10, 365.

277 "Marshall's attitude" Beal, *Marshall*, 297; **John Beal had been trying to drive home** Beal to Soong, 1 October 1946, T. V. Soong Papers, Hoover.

277 "a very short-sighted one" *FRUS* 1946 Vol. 10, 285; "It is impossible" *FRUS* 1946 Vol. 10, 231.

278 "I am not interested" *FRUS* 1946 Vol. 10, 252.

278 **swing vote** *FRUS* 1946 Vol. 10, 422; "great hope" *FRUS* 1946 Vol. 10, 415.

278 "a democratic republic" Chang to Marshall, 10 August 1946, GCM Papers 122/13, GCMRL; "as long as there is poverty" Qing, *From Allies*, 75; **revive negotiations** *FRUS* 1946 Vol. 10, 410.

278 "spirit of revenge" *FRUS* 1946 Vol. 10, 364.

278 "jumbled in thought" *FRUS* 1946 Vol. 10, 375; "heart sick," "so much depends" JHC to Betty Caughey, 13 October 1946, JHC Papers 2/10, GCMRL.

279 **hot and dry** JM to Hellman, 26 October 1946, JM Papers 36, HSTL; **Zhou appeared unannounced** GCM to HST, 26 October 1946, Secretary's Files 160/10, HST Papers, HSTL.

279 "as ready to save the country" *FRUS* 1946 Vol. 10, 398.

279 "skeleton size" Melby, *Mandate*, 197; **At the Executive Headquarters** Final report 333; "There is an increasing" *New York Times* 2 November 1946.

279 **Zhou-Marshall discussion** *FRUS* 1946 Vol. 10, 432.

280 **island's possibilities** Taylor, *Generalissimo* 362; **He had assured Marshall** *FRUS* 1946 Vol. 10, 416; **Marshall did not conceal** CKS to GCM, 27 October 1946, Marshall Mission Records 20, NARA, and Melby, *Mandate*, 200.

280 "I can make no predictions" GCM to HST, 26 October 1946, Secretary's Files 160/10, HST Papers, HSTL.

280 **auspicious moment for a last great act** Papers Vol. 5, 751.

280 **had come on Chiang's invitation** Carter to GCM, 20 October 1946, Marshall Mission Records 31, NARA.

280 "What Should America Do in the Far East" Luce to GCM, 27 September 1946, GCM Papers 123/15, GCMRL; **Marshall declined** GCM to Luce, 10 October 1946, GCM Papers 123/15, GCMRL; **Luce's publications** Herzstein, *Luce*, 55, and *Time* 25 March 1946.

280–81 **dinner, Luce explained** Beal, *Marshall*, 256; **secret reports** Herzstein, *Luce*, 72; **the Communist problem** JM to Hellman, 2 November 1946, JM Papers 36, HSTL; **the Republicans were poised** Beal, *Marshall*, 257.

281 **surprise excursion** Jeans, *Marshall Mission*, 170; **firecrackers, planes** *Time* 11 November 1946; **Tai Lake visit** JHC to Betty Caughey, 1 November 1946, JHC Papers 2/11, GCMRL; **locals greeted the party** JHC to Betty Caughey, 1 November 1946, JHC Papers 2/11, GCMRL; **happiest day in a decade** *Time* 11 November 1946.

281 **Marshall changed the subject** Herzstein, *Luce*, 72; "taken for a ride" Beal, *Marshall*, 313; **accepting with little question** Marshall interviews,

575; **"Luce has warm friendship"** GCM to McCloy, 6 December 1946, Marshall Mission Records 2, NARA.

281   **"If the Generalissimo"** *Time* 11 November 1946.

14. At the Point of a Gun

282   **approval rating** Gallup, *Gallup*, 604.

282   **promising to cut taxes** Christensen, *Useful*, 40; **"appeasing Russia"** Donovan, *Conflict*, 231; **"a fight between Americanism and Communism"** *Chicago Tribune* 1 November 1946.

283   *GOP TRIUMPH* *Chicago Tribune* 8 November 1946.

283   **"even at the expense"** *Chicago Tribune* 18 September 1946; **"get tough with Russia"** *Chicago Tribune* 23 September 1946.

283   **Gromyko stood and denounced** *FRUS* 1946 Vol. 10, 875.

284   **"to contain [the Soviets] both militarily and politically"** Kennan, *Memoirs*, 304.

284   **appoint a commission** Donovan, *Conflict*, 292; **"What should be done about the Communists"** Christensen, *Useful*, 52.

284   **"War will come again"** *Los Angeles Times* 26 September 1946.

284   **he asked Ambassador Stuart** *FRUS* 1946 Vol. 10, 473; **requested vote tallies, Luce had told Chiang** Beal, *Marshall*, 277; **Zhou also wondered** *FRUS* 1946 Vol. 10, 537.

284–85 **saw the analyses** Butterworth to GCM, 16 September 1946, W. Walton Butterworth Papers, GCMRL; **skimmed daily digests** Beal, *Marshall*, 29; **"I am at war"** Papers Vol. 5, 762; **aides had been sending it back** Carter to Acheson, 28 October 1946, GCM Papers 124/25, GCMRL.

285   **White House sent a message of reassurance** HST to GCM, 7 November 1946, GCM Papers 124/25, GCMRL.

285   **Kohlberg in China** Beal, *Marshall*, 277.

285   **a piercing chill** JM to Hellman, 14 November 1946, JM Papers 36, HSTL; **dusk came early** Beal, *Marshall* 214; **"beauty of fall"** Melby, *Mandate*, 198.

285   **He had resolved** CKS diary, 31 October 1946, Hoover.

285–86 **"irritating language"** *FRUS* 1946 Vol. 10, 481; **missed opportunity** *FRUS* 1946 Vol. 10, 491; **"point of a gun"** GCM to HST, 5 October 1946, Secretary's Files 160/10, HST Papers, HSTL.

286   **"total war"** *FRUS* 1946 Vol. 10, 440; **Marshall-Zhou discussion** *FRUS* 1946 Vol. 10, 509.

286   **Committee of Three** Committee of Three minutes, 11 November 1946, Marshall Mission Records 4, NARA.

286   **"mock gesture," "Chinese affairs"** GCM-Zhou meeting notes, 12 November 1946, Marshall Mission Records 22, NARA.

287   **Delegates arrived, the most important event** Beal, *Marshall*, 279; **"one**

party proposition" GCM to HST, 8 November 1946, Marshall Mission Records 2, NARA.

287 **"a feeling that nothing"** JM diary, 14 November 1946, JM Papers 1, HSTL.

287 **uncharacteristically haggard** FRUS 1946 Vol. 10, 458.

287 **"intoxicated with the idea"** GCM-Zhou meeting notes, 16 November 1946, Marshall Mission Records 5, NARA.

288 **considered it his obligation** GCM to HST, 16 November 1946, Marshall Mission Records 2, NARA.

288 **"I felt very grateful"** GCM-Zhou meeting notes, 16 November 1946, Marshall Mission Records 5, NARA; **"wise man"** Zhang in Bland, *George C. Marshall's*, 224.

288 **smarter people** Zhang in Bland, *George C. Marshall's*, 219; **skillful negotiator** Transcript of GCM comments, Conference on Problems of United States Policy in China, Secretary's Files 152/4, HST Papers, HSTL; **champion of reconciliation** Papers Vol. 5, 650; **"liberal-minded man"** FRUS 1946 Vol. 9, 1506; **Zhou never hesitated** Transcript of GCM comments, Conference on Problems of United States Policy in China, Secretary's Files 152/4, HST Papers, HSTL.

289 **"Every time Zhou"** Beal, *Marshall*, 292.

289 **American cryptographers had labored** Dana to Bland, 27 January 1984, A. Fairfield Dana Papers, GCMRL; **"one-time pads"** Taylor, *Generalissimo*, 342; **When Chiang or a general** John F. Melby Oral History, James Shepley Oral History, GCMRL.

289 **as Marshall could tell** Beal, *Marshall*, 50; **a spy on the personal staff** Westad, *Decisive*, 142; **Sol Adler** In 1950, after being forced out of the Treasury Department under a cloud of suspicion, Adler left the United States and eventually went to work for Mao's government, never returning home; **had passed information** John Earl Haynes, *Venona*, 90, 139; **Adler was warning** FRUS 1946 Vol. 10, 1007; **"indispensable"** Papers Vol. 5, 451.

289-90 **Marshall posed one last question** GCM-Zhou meeting notes, 16 November 1946, Marshall Mission Records 5, NARA; **he would have a definitive reason** Beal, *Marshall*, 293.

290 **Zhou dropped by** GCM to HST, 23 November 1946, Marshall Mission Records 2, NARA; **trench coat and fedora** Photograph, JHC Papers 5/7, GCMRL.

290 **Mao grasped his hand** Rittenberg, *The Man*, 83; **a warm coat** Wilson, *Zhou*, 173; **still in favor** Han, *Eldest*, 194.

290 **Zhou apologized** Zhang in Bland, *George C. Marshall's*, 231; **"There was uncertainty"** Westad, *Decisive*, 60.

290 **Victory might take** Heinzig, *Soviet Union*, 118; **Even if the Nationalists** Short, *Mao*, 407; **The reactionaries** Kennedy, "Can the weak," 897.

291   **already playing out in Manchuria** Levine, *Anvil*, 156; **Join the revolu-
        tion** Levine, *Anvil*, 153.

291   **"The postwar world"** Sheng, *Battling*, 145.

291   **the Kremlin had concluded** Goncharov, *Uncertain*, 230; **secret military
        training** Westad, *Decisive*, 52.

291   **report on the Anping incident** Anping investigation report, 8 October
        1946, Marshall Mission Records 3, NARA; **"General feeling"** Gillem jour-
        nal notes, 30 November 1946, Alvan Gillem Papers, MHI.

291-92 **"Very few people know"** JM to Hellman, 29 September 1946, JM Papers
        36, HSTL; **"He has taken from them"** JM to Hellman, 17 August 1946,
        JM Papers 36, HSTL.

292   **"swindlers"** He in Bland, *George C. Marshall's*, 109; **"smoke-screen"** Tsou,
        America's, 433.

292   **"digest them"** Papers Vol. 6, 40.

292-93 **Marshall found much unchanged** Marshall letter, 30 November 1946,
        GCM Papers 122/12, GCMRL; **little of the post's late-imperial glamor**
        Aplington, "Sunset," 174.

293   **one-third of the teams** Final report 377; **abandoned post** Gillem journal
        notes, 14 November 1946, Alvan Gillem Papers, MHI; **"We had tried"** Gil-
        lem journal notes, 16 November 1946, Alvan Gillem Papers, MHI.

293   **A poll asked** National Opinion Research Center Foreign Affairs Survey,
        University of Chicago, October 1946; **MILLION AMERICAN MEN** Tele-
        gram to Truman, 28 September 1946, White House Central Files, 757/13
        HST Papers, HSTL.

293-94 **Acheson pledged** Acheson to GCM, 19 November 1946, Marshall Mis-
        sion Records 27, NARA; **Marshall recognized that further withdraw-
        als** Papers Vol. 5, 743; **an "irritant"** Spector, *In the Ruins*, 267; **"could not
        be liquidated"** Shepley to HST, 26 February 1946, GCM Papers 124/28,
        GCMRL; **"Half a million"** Tuchman, *Stilwell*, 103.

294   **Marines had been consolidating** Shaw, *United States Marines*, 18; **Fewer
        than 20,000** FRUS 1946 Vol. 10, 386; **troops' initial charge** Executive
        Headquarters memo on transfer of repatriation mission, 7 February 1947,
        Alvan Gillem Papers 8, MHI; **Marshall drew up plans** Carter to Acheson,
        22 November 1946, GCM Papers 124/26, GCMRL; **A drawdown would
        "purify"** Papers Vol. 5, 744; **"before some new incident"** GCM to Carter,
        26 November 1946, Marshall Mission Records 27, NARA.

294   **ongoing American intelligence capability** Yu, *OSS*, 161.

295   **Chiang wanted American officers** McClure to AW, 7 April 1946, AW
        Papers 82/18, Hoover; **military planners called for supporting** Schna-
        bel, *Joint Chiefs*, 203; **"cause silent rejoicing"** Papers Vol. 5, 735.

295   **Marshall could see that the collapse** Final report 380; **"international
        bickerings"** FRUS 1946 Vol. 10, 253; **"principal problem"** FRUS 1946 Vol.
        10, 559.

296   **useful pressure on Moscow** Transcript of GCM comments, Conference on Problems of United States Policy in China, Secretary's Files 152/4, HST Papers, HSTL; **Harriman** Wehrle in Bland, *George C. Marshall's*, 88.

296   **"Soviet intent"** *FRUS* 1946 Vol. 10, 28; **"colonization"** *FRUS* 1946 Vol. 10, 1185; **"iron curtain"** *FRUS* 1946 Vol. 10, 1146.

296–97   **"same tune"** Papers Vol. 6, 38; **recalled the portraits** Transcript of GCM comments, Conference on Problems of United States Policy in China, Secretary's Files 152/4, HST Papers, HSTL; **secret radio communication** Stuart to GCM, 30 November 1946, Marshall Mission Records 27, NARA; **evidence of some** SSU report, 4 October 1946, Marshall Mission Records 27, NARA; **less than the Nationalists** Papers Vol. 6, 38; **"negative action"** Transcript of GCM comments, Conference on Problems of United States Policy in China, Secretary's Files 152/4, HST Papers, HSTL; **He figured Stalin** Beal, *Marshall*, 178; **finalizing a commercial agreement** Tanner, *Where China*, 138; **Stalin remained cautious** Tanner, *Where China*, 142.

297   **Kennan had also speculated** *FRUS* 1946 Vol. 9, 118–119.

297   **"compartmented"** AW to Hutchin, 1 September 1946, Paul W. Caraway Papers, MHI.

297   **"lesser of two evils"** Beal to Soong, 17 September 1946, T. V. Soong Papers, Hoover.

298   **disabuse hard-liners** *FRUS* 1946 Vol. 10, 444; **push through some assistance** *FRUS* 1946 Vol. 10, 587; **humanitarian efforts** *FRUS* 1946 Vol. 10, 1032; **Total aid** Westad, *Decisive*, 87; **instructing congressional leaders** Papers Vol. 5, 733; **With Nationalist officials** Papers Vol. 5, 744; **stinginess of the new Congress** *FRUS* 1946 Vol. 10, 1023.

298   **"If you let this bunch"** Beal, *Marshall*, 246.

298   **one Nationalist official** *FRUS* 1946 Vol. 10, 765; **drive out "the FDR party"** Westad, *Decisive*, 58.

299   **half of China's imports** Harry Harding, *Sino-American Relations*, 143; **"new national humiliation"** Sheng, *Battling*, 151; **"new unequal treaty"** Qing, *From Allies*, 52.

299   **He worried that Nationalist** *FRUS* 1946 Vol. 10, 558.

299   **Luce** Herzstein, *Luce*, 53; **Judd** Franz Schurmann, *Republican China*, 328; **Chennault** Davies, *Dragon*, 370; **anti-Communist officers** Memorandum for the commanding general, 25 January 1946, GCM Papers 124/28, GCMRL.

299   **"wanted to cry"** JM to Hellman, 29 October 1946, JM Papers 36, HSTL; **"great experiment," "Marshall feels"** JM to Hellman, 19 November 1946, JM Papers 36, HSTL.

300   **it snowed** Beal, *Marshall*, 304; **New England town** JHC to Betty Caughey, 30 November 1946, JHC Papers 1/21, GCMRL.

300   **evening with the Chiangs** GCM appointment list, 28 November 1946, Marshall Mission Records 7, NARA; **bridge, Chinese checkers** JHC to

Betty Caughey, 30 November 1946, JHC Papers 1/21, GCMRL; **bits of English** Beal, *Marshall*, 269; **"great shine"** Beal, *Marshall*, 177.

300　**Chiang learned** CKS diary, 30 November 1946, Hoover; **winter in Honolulu** GCM to Ayres, 12 December 1946, GCM Papers 122/4, GCMRL; **the news fed** *FRUS* 1946 Vol. 10, 572.

300　**"still daydreaming"** CKS diary, 30 November 1946, Hoover; **Chiang raged to his diary** CKS diary, 20 November 1946, Hoover.

301　**"at the point of a gun"** Stuart journal, 29 November 1946, John Leighton Stuart Papers, Hoover.

301　**Marshall resolved to wait** *FRUS* 1946 Vol. 10, 572.

15. All of Chiang's Horses and All of Chiang's Men

302　**Marshall warned Madame Chiang** Marshall interviews, 607.

302　**"calculated to put the Communists"** Papers Vol. 6, 40; **corruption kept so much tax revenue** Westad, *Decisive*, 73; **only in sowing chaos** *FRUS* 1946 Vol. 10, 577.

302-3　**To Marshall's mind** Papers Vol. 5, 750; **made collapse more likely** *FRUS* 1946 Vol. 10, 603; **"if China collapses"** Beal, *Marshall*, 342; **"spread like wildfire"** *FRUS* 1946 Vol. 10, 620.

303　**Nationalists had squandered** Papers Vol. 5, 755; **"rottenness and corruption"** GCM to HST, 6 September 1946, Secretary's Files 160/10, HST Papers, HST; **"hard-boiled element"** *FRUS* 1946 Vol. 10, 542; **"coolly calculated"** Papers Vol. 5, 754.

303　**Chiang's own advisers** Eastman, *Seeds*, 123; **Wedemeyer had recently written Chiang** AW to CKS, 2 August 1946, AW Papers 81/2, Hoover.

303-4　**more brutally frank** Beal, *Marshall*, 313; **modern-day George Washington** Marshall interviews, 607.

304　**foot tracing circles** Beal, *Marshall*, 313; **over an hour** GCM to HST, 2 December 1946, Marshall Mission Records 2, NARA.

304　**Chiang brushed aside, assured Marshall** GCM to HST, 2 December 1946, Marshall Mission Records 2, NARA; **Communist guerrilla methods** *FRUS* 1946 Vol. 10, 581.

304　**military force was the only way** GCM to HST, 2 December 1946, Marshall Mission Records 2, NARA; **demanded a complete reconsideration** Papers Vol. 5, 752; **There was still time** CKS diary, 7 December 1946, Hoover.

304-5　**reflected on Marshall's selection** CKS diary, 1 December 1945, Hoover; **"Communist Party's scheme"** CKS diary, 31 December 1945, Hoover; **"If I were to give up"** CKS diary, 8 November 1946, Hoover.

305　**only to be thwarted** Spence, *To Change*, 269; **"customary willingness"** Papers Vol. 6, 482; **the real purpose of Chiang's offer** GCM to HST, 28 December 1946, Secretary's Files 160/10, HST Papers, HSTL.

305   **"There are few harder stunts of statesmanship"** Feis, *China*, 272; **"crack the whip"** Papers Vol. 6, 42; **"if he gives us the opportunity"** Papers Vol. 6, 41.

305-6   **Chiang had bet** Beal, *Marshall*, 114; **"serious error"** FRUS 1946 Vol. 10, 604; **"army is draining"** Beal, *Marshall*, 293.

306   **consequential errors** Westad, *Decisive*, 9.

306   **he was fond of the Generalissimo** Papers Vol. 6, 381, Marshall interviews, 607, and Wilson, *General Marshall*, 377; **aides were struck by their mutual graciousness** John Hart Caughey Oral History, GCMRL; **"personal integrity"** Papers Vol. 6, 381; **"always too late"** Beal, *Marshall*, 339, and Stuart, *Fifty Years*, 278.

306   **"God never uses"** Taylor, *Generalissimo*, 260; **speak of democracy** Tanner, *Where*, 166; **"return to the people"** CKS Constitution Presentation speech, 29 November 1946, JM Papers 1, HSTL; **Confucian terms** Tanner, *Where*, 47; **two percent success** Beal, *Marshall*, 247.

307   **this final act** GCM to HST, 2 December 1946, Marshall Mission Records 2, NARA.

307   **three hours** GCM to HST, 2 December 1946, Marshall Mission Records 2, NARA; **Chiang reflected** CKS diary, 1 December 1946, Hoover; **Marshall reflected** Final report, 405.

307   **Marshall had come to see stubbornness** Papers Vol. 6, 31.

307   **"Along with the great problem"** Stoler, *George C. Marshall*, 144.

307   **inflation surging** Pantsov, *Mao*, 352; **Shanghai cost-of-living** *China Weekly Review*, 30 November 1946, GCM Papers 123/33, GCMRL; **hoarded rice** Peck, *Two Kinds*, 107; **workers went on strike** Westad, *Decisive*, 76; **"We are begging food"** Westad, *Decisive*, 100.

308   **unsupportable expectations** Westad, *Decisive*, 65.

308   **American financial adviser** Arthur Young Oral History, HSTL; **"ancient evils"** Stuart, *Fifty Years*, 277; **Mandate of Heaven** *New York Times* 7 February 1947, and Melby, *Mandate*, 241.

308   **former aide sent Marshall** Kinkead to Chamberlin, 19 April 1946, GCM Papers 123/8, GCMRL; **"all of Chiang's horses"** *New Yorker* 4 May 1946.

308   **"yours and yours alone"** FRUS 1946 Vol. 10, 583.

309   **statements to journalists** Summary of telegrams, 20 November 1946, Naval Aide Files 22/3, HST Papers, HSTL; **Planeload after planeload of Communists** JM diary, 14 November 1946, JM Papers 1, HSTL.

309   **Zhou's demands** FRUS 1946 Vol. 10, 591.

309   **"beyond our reach"** FRUS 1946 Vol. 10, 594; **hope that his presence** GCM to HST, 28 December 1946, Secretary's Files 160/10, HST Papers, HSTL; **wet, windy, and cold** Papers, Vol. 5, 759.

309   **She did not know how long** Papers Vol. 5, 759.

309-10   **Marshall pestered aides** JHC to KTM, 20 September 1946, JHC Papers 1/8, GCMRL; **he joined Madame Chiang for a long walk** GCM to Madame

CKS, 5 February 1947, GCM Papers 60/55, GCMRL; **strenuous enough** JHC to Betty Caughey, 10 December 1946, JHC Papers 2/11, GCMRL; **"lost without her"** JM diary, 8 November 1946, JM Papers 1, HSTL.

310   **another flurry of rumors** *New York Times* 9 December 1946; **barrage of phone calls** Chamberlin to JHC, 10 December 1946, JHC Papers 1/7, GCMRL; **Chinese newspapers, Caughey instructed** Connors to Betty Caughey, 21 December 1946, JHC Papers 1/14, GCMRL.

310   **"The General came out here"** JM to Hellman, 10 December 1946, JM Papers 36, HSTL.

310   **"It appears now very likely that I should return"** *FRUS* 1946 Vol. 10, 624.

310   **a long message by hand** Papers Vol. 5, 776; **"see the handwriting"** *FRUS* 1946 Vol. 10, 622.

311   **Luce** Carter to GCM, 3 December 1946, Marshall Mission Records 2, NARA; **negotiation unnecessary** Papers Vol. 5, 757; **"If the U.S. does not openly"** *Time* 16 September 1946; **"shallow, if not completely biased"** *FRUS* 1946 Vol. 10, 600.

311   **"If George Marshall remains in China"** Bayne to Soong, 21 December 1946, W. Walton Butterworth Papers 1/7, GCMRL; **Marshall sensed** Beal, *Marshall*, 329; **"seriously weaken my hand"** Papers Vol. 5, 756.

311   **"Chiang Kai-shek's brand of democracy"** Fairbank, *Chinabound*, 320.

311–12 **when it arrived in Nanjing** JM to Hellman, 9 November 1946, JM Papers 36, HSTL; **"We are left as the patrons"** White, *Thunder*, 317–318.

312   **White on Marshall** *New Republic* 16 December 1946.

312   **Acheson wrote Marshall** *FRUS* 1946 Vol. 10, 609; **"impartial observers"** Papers Vol. 5, 760; **"vest pocket of George Marshall"** *New Republic* 16 December 1946.

312   **Truman policy statement** White Paper 694.

312   **Wits in the American embassy had taken to standing** JM to Hellman, 6 December 1946, JM Papers 36, HSTL.

313   **little of the hope or good feeling** JM to Hellman, 25 December 1946, JM Papers 36, HSTL; **Katherine's absence** JHC to KTM, 19 December 1946, JHC Papers 1/8, GCMRL; **coming down with a cold** Beal, *Marshall*, 326; **fruit and candy** Madame CKS to GCM, December 1946, GCM Papers 122/20, GCMRL.

313   **"If America wants"** *New York Times* 20 December 1946; **"working hand in glove"** Press clipping, 14 December 1946, JHC Papers 1/3, GCMRL; **Fliers scattered** *FRUS* 1946 Vol. 10, 586; **Communist outlets compared Americans** *FRUS* 1946 Vol. 10, 641.

313   **Chiang repeated his request** *FRUS* 1946 Vol. 10, 621; **Marshall's advice** *FRUS* 1946 Vol. 10, 624; **"What is important"** CKS diary, 19 December 1946, Hoover.

313   **"Their publicity campaign"** Papers Vol. 5, 755.

314   **"destroy the foundation"** *FRUS* 1946 Vol. 10, 555; **"useless to expect"**

GCM to HST, 23 November 1946, Marshall Mission Records 2, NARA; **speculate offhandedly** *FRUS* 1946 Vol. 10, 619.

314   **"I have been using"** Papers Vol. 5, 756; **"genuine democratic document"** *FRUS* 1946 Vol. 10, 539.

314   **biggest gathering of its kind** Dikötter, *Age*, 22; **draft constitution** Draft constitution, JM Papers 1, HSTL.

315   **"what happens when"** Papers Vol. 6, 37; **"constructive opposition"** Papers Vol. 5, 744; **"I did not expect the Kuomintang"** Papers Vol. 5, 745; **"cannot reform itself"** *FRUS* 1946 Vol. 10, 542.

315   **Nationalist repression** Papers Vol. 5, 744.

315   **"It is an ugly sight"** JM to Hellman, 17 December 1946, JM Papers 36, HSTL.

315–16   **he had canceled plans** JHC to Sims, 24 December 1946, GCM Papers 122, GCMRL; **Christmas party** JHC to KTM, 27 December 1946, JHC Papers 1/8, GCMRL, and JHC to Betty Caughey, 24 December 1946, JHC Papers 2/11, GCMRL; **party broke up** Beal, *Marshall*, 333.

316   **Marshall declined an invitation to attend** Invitation to attend National Assembly, 25 December 1946, GCM Papers 123/24, GCMRL; **"fake constitution"** *FRUS* 1946 Vol. 10, 678; **Chiang had stood firm** *FRUS* 1946 Vol. 10, 666; **"collection of words"** GCM to HST, 28 December 1946, Secretary's Files 160/10, HST Papers, HSTL; **feeling of accomplishment** Beal, *Marshall*, 335.

316–17   **"Yanks, go home"** Xixiao Guo, "The Anticlimax of an Ill-Starred Sino-American Encounter," 230; **"Get out you beasts"** Military intelligence review, 9 January 1947, Naval Aide Files 19/4, HST Papers, HSTL; **Nationalist authorities ordered police protection** Westad, *Decisive*, 101; **"Every major turning"** White, *Thunder*, 58.

317   **"the Commies don't have a chance"** Belden, *China Shakes*, 9; **spears, sickles, pig knives** Belden, *China Shakes*, 351; **Communist units were in retreat** Westad, *Decisive*, 47; **Chiang's forces had claimed** Lew, *Third*, 55; **80 percent, 15 percent** Westad, *Decisive*, 69; **"fight like babies"** Belden, *China Shakes*, 351.

317   **irritations of Marshall's mission** Tanner, *Where*, 82; **Chiang's plan** Lew, *Third*, 56.

317   **no longer placed** Beal, *Marshall*, 293; **extending his writ** Christopher P. C. Chung, "Drawing the U-Shaped Line."

318   **"You can sometimes win"** Marshall interviews, 387.

318   **"faulty and optimistic"** Papers, Vol. 5, 768.

318   **In his assessment, Chiang's army** Papers Vol. 5, 761; **"The military position"** Military intelligence review, 7 November 1946, Naval Aide Files 19/2, HST Papers, HSTL.

318   **"China is simply too vast"** AW to Soong, 10 August 1946, AW Papers 83/7, Hoover.

319   **American vehicles, Antitank guns, snow boots** Victor Shiu Chiang Cheng, "Modern War on an Ancient Battlefield," 45–46; **"We do not know**

how much the Government" Papers Vol. 6, 41; his sources suggested
Papers Vol. 6, 372; Communist troops sang Barrett, *Dixie*, 91.

319   Nationalist general estimated Taylor, *Generalissimo*, 359; Chiang continued to send Papers Vol. 6, 483.

319   "worst advised military commander" Papers Vol. 6, 130; misleading
assessments Transcript of GCM comments, Conference on Problems of
United States Policy in China, Secretary's Files 152/4, HST Papers, HSTL;
embassy analysis Assessment of U.S. Military Aid Program Toward
China, 5 July 1947, W. Walton Butterworth Papers 1/7, GCMRL.

320   thwarted coordination and hoarded resources Westad, *Decisive*, 149;
"corruption and degeneracy" Lloyd E. Eastman, "Who Lost China?,"
663; "Jeeps had a habit" Papers Vol. 6, 483; better treatment Intelligence
summary, 1 June 1946, AW Papers 86/3, Hoover; In Manchuria, residents
started to complain Jonathan D. Spence, *The Search for Modern China*, 471.

320   Marshall had pointed out FRUS 1946 Vol. 10, 447; Chiang's own experience Mitter, *Forgotten*, 148; "luring the enemy in deep" Pantsov, *Mao*,
268; "gallant peasant army" Qing, *From Allies*, 90; "knew precisely"
White, *Thunder* 229.

320–21 "dark ages of warlordism" FRUS 1946 Vol. 10, 635; total Communist
victory Steven I. Levine, "A New Look at American Mediation in the Chinese Civil War," 374; collapse was a real possibility Papers Vol. 5, 768;
"General Marshall concluded" Shepley to HST, 26 February 1946, GCM
Papers 124/28, GCMRL.

321   "father of the country" GCM to HST, 28 December 1946, Secretary's
Files 160/10, HST Papers, HSTL.

321   Marshall message to Truman GCM to HST, 28 December 1946, Secretary's Files 160/10, HST Papers, HSTL.

16. Into the Fire

322   Caughey was awakened JHC to Betty Caughey, 4 January 1947, JHC Papers
2/11, GCMRL; "so depressed" JHC to Betty Caughey, 24 December 1946,
JHC Papers 2/11, GCMRL; still did not know Jeans, *Marshall Mission*, 189.

322   Marshall birthday party Beal, *Marshall*, 344, and GCMRL photographs;
a relapse of his lingering cold JHC to Betty Caughey, 4 January 1947, JHC
Papers 2/11, GCMRL.

323   "anti-U.S.-brutality" Jeffrey N. Wasserstrom, *Student Protests in Twentieth-
Century China*, 239; worried about what might happen JHC to Betty
Caughey, 4 January 1947, JHC Papers 2/11, GCMRL.

323   building had previously belonged Melby, *Mandate*, 214; "Bloody GI"
New York Times 4 January 1947; circuitous routes JHC to Betty Caughey, 4
January 1947, JHC Papers 2/11, GCMRL; Crowds screamed Robert Shaf-
fer, "A Rape in Beijing," 38; Stuart met *New York Times* 4 January 1947;

blown out of proportion *South China Morning Post* 7 January 1947; **"Drey-fus case"** Shaffer, "A Rape," 59; **Communist setup** JHC to Betty Caughey, 4 January 1947, JHC Papers 2/11, GCMRL.

323   **In a radio broadcast** *New York Times* 1 January 1947.

323   **"struggle to the death"** *New York Times* 1 January 1947; **rape of Shen Chung** Jon W. Huebner, "Chinese Anti-Americanism," 121.

323–24 **The popular outrage** Military intelligence review, 9 January 1947, Naval Aide Files 19/4, HST Papers, HSTL; **just the kind of sentiment** Xixiao, "Anticlimax," 240; **long recognized that patriotic students** Westad, *Decisive*, 140; **"Confused, frustrated and faithless"** *New York Times* 5 January 1947.

324   **"America is the very best"** Taylor, *Generalissimo*, 8; **they were instead cursing the United States** Wasserstrom, *Student*, 254; **Shanghai newspaper** Huebner, "Chinese," 122; **Canadian shopkeepers** Xixiao, "Anticlimax," 242.

324   **"Widespread resentment"** *FRUS* 1947 Vol. 7, 15; **"successful in stirring"** Papers Vol. 5, 755; **"naïve"** *FRUS* 1946 Vol. 10, 664.

324   **endless stories** Gallicchio, *Scramble*, 134; **drunk sailor** Xixiao, "Anticlimax," 227; **"city tigers"** Joseph K. S. Yick in Bland, *George C. Marshall's*, 375; **residents hinted darkly** Spector, *In the Ruins*, 58; **negotiated a deal** Huebner, "Chinese," 118.

324–25 **"fund of Chinese good-will"** Final report, 8; **"tossed to the winds"** GCM to Milholland, 2 February 1946, GCM Papers 123/22, GCMRL.

325   **"lost an amount of goodwill"** JM to Hellman, 24 November 1946, JM Papers 36, HSTL.

325   **telegram from Secretary of State Byrnes** Byrnes to GCM, 3 January 1947, Marshall Mission Records 10, NARA.

325   **Truman wanted Marshall back** *FRUS* 1946 Vol. 10, 681.

325   **"Your country is fortunate"** Carter to GCM, 30 December 1946, GCM Papers 124/37, GCMRL; **"the Chinese have fallen"** *FRUS* 1946 Vol. 10, 549.

326   **"both so frequently"** Papers Vol. 5, 755.

326   **If Democrats and Republicans** *South China Morning Post* 9 April 1946; **arguing about their own civil war** *FRUS* 1946 Vol. 9, 582.

326   **"all should combine"** *FRUS* 1946 Vol. 9, 464.

327   **embassy reassessment** *FRUS* 1947 Vol. 7, 7–12.

327   **"I fully understand"** Papers Vol. 5, 769.

327   **time the public announcement** Draft White House press release, 6 January 1947, Secretary's Files 160/10, HST Papers, HSTL; **sink in for a few days** Papers Vol. 5, 769.

328   **accepted invitations** Burns to GCM, 3 January 1946, GCM Papers 122, GCMRL; **stop forwarding mail** GCM to Carter, 4 January 1947, GCM Papers 124/38, GCMRL; **delayed packing** JHC to Betty Caughey, 8 January 1947, JHC Papers 1/7, GCMRL; **games of darts** Connors to JHC, 8 January 1947, JHC Papers 1/15, GCMRL.

328   **dreary weekend** JM to Hellman, 5 January 1946, JM Papers 36, HSTL; **rainy and windy** Beal, *Marshall*, 346.

328   **past American slights** GCM-CKS meeting notes, 6 January 1947, Marshall Mission Records 5, NARA.

329   **"courage and patriotism"** *FRUS* 1946 Vol. 10, 687.

329   **"almost impossible to deal with the Communists"** Beal, *Marshall*, 340.

329   **saw T. V. Soong** GCM-Soong meeting notes, 7 January 1947, Marshall Mission Records 23, NARA.

329   **his driver** GCM commendation letter, 7 January 1947, GCM Papers 60/35, GCMRL; **a group of children** *Time* 20 January 1947; **gift from the embassy** Lee to GCM, 12 August 1946, GCM Papers 123/11, GCMRL.

329–30 **Marshall praised Chiang's** Taylor, *Generalissimo*, 365; **"really big man"** *FRUS* 1946 Vol. 10, 690; **thought he may have made his case, "He was grateful"** CKS diary, 7 January 1947, Hoover.

330   **"symbolic of the triumph"** JHC to Madame CKS, 8 January 1947, JHC Papers 1/5, GCMRL; **note signed by Chiang** *FRUS* 1946 Vol. 10, 687.

330   **almost a month** Papers Vol. 5, 776; **exact specifications** GCM to Carter, 5 January 1947, Marshall Mission Records 10, NARA; **vitriol would be clarifying** *FRUS* 1946 Vol. 10, 682; **sideline hard-liners** Final report 428.

330   **Final statement text** Papers Vol. 5, 772–776.

331   **"friendly and constructive"** Military intelligence review, 16 January 1947, Naval Aide Files 19/4, HST Papers, HSTL; **"accept good-naturedly"** *FRUS* 1946 Vol. 10, 703.

331   **Chen Li-fu** *New York Times* 14 January 1947.

331   **"unusually frank"** *FRUS* 1946 Vol. 10, 693; **"55 percent"** Beal, *Marshall*, 349.

331–32 **Zhou would condemn** Zhang in Bland, *George C. Marshall's*, 231; **"this rotten government"** Lutze, *China's*, 63; **Mao would proclaim** Lutze, *China's*, 70.

332   **censor key portions** Final report 434; **military-backed Nationalist outlet, "reactionary"** Embassy Nanjing to State Department, Marshall Mission Records 24, NARA.

332   **"That General Marshall has not accomplished"** *FRUS* 1946 Vol. 10, 695.

332   **judging the statement fair** Wellington Koo Oral History, Columbia; **"blow the whistle"** Herzstein in Bland, *George C. Marshall's*, 143.

332   **"ugly role of Chiang Kai-shek's herald"** Papers Vol. 5, 498; **"reactionary Republicans"** Westad, "Losses," 109.

332   **"plague on both"** Melby, *Mandate*, 218; **"American interest in China"** Melby, *Mandate*, 229.

332–33 **slick with snowmelt, limousine** *Time* 20 January 1947; **the Chiangs accompanied, "Come back"** *Time* 20 January 1947; **Chiang looked into Marshall's eyes** CKS diary, 8 January 1947, Hoover.

333   **Most of the gifts** Caughey to Chamberlin, 22 November 1946, GCM
       Papers 122/12, GCMRL; **Caughey, who was glad** JHC to Betty Caughey, 8
       January 1947, JHC Papers 2/11, GCMRL; **"Adequate words"** JHC to Betty
       Caughey, 8 January 1947, JHC Papers 1/7, GCMRL.

333   **"It was a gallant cause"** JM to Hellman, 24 March 1947, JM Papers 36,
       HSTL; **"really ugly part"** JM to Hellman, 6 December 1946, JM Papers 36,
       HSTL.

333   **tears, "man of sentiments"** CKS diary, 8 January 1947, Hoover; **Marshall
       would be on his side** CKS diary, 10 January 1947, Hoover; **final phase of
       operations** CKS diary, 9 January 1947, Hoover; **"He and I ending"** CKS
       diary, 8 January 1947, Hoover; **"It occurred to me"** CKS diary, 11 January
       1947, Hoover.

334   **over Okinawa** GCM Memorandum on China for HST, 18 May 1954, GCM
       Papers 241/5, GCMRL, and JHC to Betty Caughey, 8 January 1947, JHC
       Papers 2/11, GCMRL; **"Congratulations, Mr. Secretary"** JHC to Betty
       Caughey, 8 January 1947, JHC Papers 1/7, GCMRL.

334   **cockpit radio** JHC to Betty Caughey, 8 January 1947, JHC Papers 1/7,
       GCMRL; **A leak had forced** James F. Byrnes, *All in One Lifetime*, 388; **"into
       the fire"** GCM to AW, 21 January 1947, GCM Papers 124/10, GCMRL.

334   **bottle of scotch** Connors to JHC, 8 January 1947, JHC Papers 1/15,
       GCMRL; **"Poor Mrs. Marshall"** JHC to Betty Caughey, 8 January 1947,
       JHC Papers 1/7, GCMRL.

Epilogue: Losing China

335   **Two years before, war** Papers Vol. 5, 38; **one year before, the China** GCM
       to Conant, 20 April 1946, GCM Papers 122/25, GCMRL.

336   **Patrick Hurley** Carter to GCM, 13 January 1947, GCM Papers 71/31,
       GCMRL; **persistent rumor** *Chicago Tribune* 9 January 1947; **He reiterated
       to reporters** Papers Vol. 6, 8.

336   **"Peace has yet to be secured"** Papers Vol. 6, 48; **"We can act for our own
       good"** Papers Vol. 6, 255.

336   **"Certain things have to happen"** Papers Vol. 6, 34.

336–37 **Communist personnel to Yenan** Underwood to JHC, 9 March 1947,
       Marshall Mission Records 34, NARA; **remaining members of the Dixie
       Mission** *FRUS* 1946 Vol. 10, 719; **equipment for Marshall's** Minutes of
       Executive Headquarters meeting, 11 February 1947, Alvan Gillem Papers
       8, MHI; **Chiang had taken Marshall's exit** Westad, *Decisive*, 65; **accepted
       Marshall's apology** CKS diary, 10 January 1947, Hoover; **"All over and in
       all"** JM to Hellman, 1 June 1947, JM Papers 36, HSTL.

337   **"'I told you so'"** Papers Vol. 6, 35.

337   **Chiang's chief of staff said the Communists** Tsou, *America's*, 450.

337   **found its language too sweeping** John Lewis Gaddis, "Was the Truman Doctrine a Real Turning Point?," 390; **"No amount of assistance," "strikingly similar"** *Washington Post* 15 February 1947.

338   **"basic responsibility for European recovery"** Papers Vol. 6, 250.

338   **"avoid trivia"** Kennan, *Memoirs*, 326.

338   **Marshall Plan for China** *New York Times* 18 June 1947; **for Latin America** Cray, *General*, 651; **for the entire Far East** Intelligence staff study on the possibility of a Marshall Plan in the Far East, 4 August 1947, AW Papers 95/2, Hoover.

338   **"not big things"** Transcript of GCM comments, Conference on Problems of United States Policy in China, Secretary's Files 152/4, HST Papers, HSTL.

338-39 **"hungry table"** Pogue, *Ordeal*, 48; **Communists' aptitude for chaos** John Lewis Gaddis, *Strategies of Containment*, 58; **"There is a tendency to feel"** Papers Vol. 6, 368.

339   **"fight no battle"** Spence, *Mao*, 107.

339   **"strategic nightmare"** Mark A. Stoler, "George C. Marshall and the 'Europe-First' Strategy," 12; **"impose incalculable burdens"** Papers Vol. 6, 255; **quickly heartened** Marshall statement before House Foreign Affairs Committee, 12 January 1948, GCM Papers 157/80, GCMRL; **"greatest decision in our history"** Stoler, *George C. Marshall*, 166.

339   **"Only the Europeans," "the main part"** Marshall statement before House Foreign Affairs Committee, 12 January 1948, GCM Papers 157/80, GCMRL.

339-40 **"China does not itself"** Papers Vol. 6, 378; **industrial capacity** Leffler, *Preponderance*, 191; **crucial base in a war** Leffler, *Preponderance*, 125; **China was thirteenth** Dorothy Borg, *Uncertain Years*, 72; **Korea and Japan** Leffler, *Preponderance*, 148; **chagrin of Nationalist officials** Papers Vol. 5, 744.

340   **"twice the size of Europe"** Davies, *China Hand*, 302; **size of Greece** White Paper 351.

340   **economies working again** GCM to Patterson, 4 March 1947, Secretary's Files 151/10, HST Papers, HSTL; **neglecting training** Papers Vol. 6, 372; **overextending lines** Marshall statement before House Foreign Affairs Committee, 12 January 1948, GCM Papers 157/80, GCMRL; **alienating local populations** Papers Vol. 6, 375; **"They greeted me"** Papers Vol. 6, 370.

340-41 **Washington's supposed double standard** Westad, *Decisive*, 159-160; **"identical"** Daniel Yergin, *Shattered Peace*, 294; **"racist and naïve"** Papers Vol. 6, 257; **"yellow-skinned"** CKS diary, 19 March 1948, Hoover; **If the United States was set** Papers Vol. 7, 100; **"If I thought for a moment"** Gaddis, *Strategies*, 40.

341   **He rejected calls** Papers Vol. 6, 371; **"sand in a rathole"** Thomas G. Pat-

erson, "If Europe, Why Not China?," 32; **"coup de grace"** Papers Vol. 6, 631; **asked colleagues for ideas** Millis, *Forrestal Diaries*, 286; **solicited proposals** GCM Resume of the world situation, 7 November 1947, Naval Aide Files 16/10, HST Papers, HSTL; **"provide a breathing space"** Marshall statement before the House Foreign Affairs Committee, 12 January 1948, GCM Papers 157/80, GCMRL; **Nationalist armies had been well supplied** GCM to Patterson, 4 March 1947, Secretary's Files 151/10, HST Papers, HSTL; **Chiang's disregard** Tsou, *America's*, 428; **munitions dumps** Chinese Embassy analysis, 2 March 1948, AW Papers 99/11, Hoover; **scrapping the embargo** Gallicchio, *Scramble*, 180.

341   **"I have tortured my brain"** May, *Truman*, 20.

341–42   **"Marshall Plan for China"** *Washington Post* 29 July 1947; *years* **"apathy," "pathetic"** AW to GCM, 29 July 1947, AW Papers 95/8, Hoover; **police suppression** AW to GCM, 17 August 1947, AW Papers 95/8, Hoover; **"make rich men richer"** AW to MacArthur, 20 October 1947, AW Papers 93/44, Hoover; **Washington should try to save** Eiler in Bland, *George C. Marshall's*, 110; **he excoriated Nationalist officials** Stuart, *Fifty Years*, 186, and Melby, *Mandate*, 294; **"The insult imposed"** CKS diary, 30 August 1947, Hoover; **"excellent spirit," "spiritually insolvent"** AW to GCM, 29 July 1947, AW Papers 95/8, Hoover; **He recommended** Marshall refused to publicly release Wedemeyer's official report, because of an inflammatory recommendation for a United Nations trusteeship in Manchuria—inflammatory to Chiang above all. Later, this refusal became fodder for conspiracy theories, critics charging that Marshall had suppressed the report because he did not want to help Chiang.

342   **to head off opposition** Christensen, *Useful*, 65; **At 10 percent** Leffler, *Preponderance*, 249; **"buying time"** Army Secretary's report to the National Security Council, 26 July 1948, Secretary's Files 178/17, HST Papers, HSTL.

342   **"overlook no"** White Paper 280.

342–43   **"foretold"** Papers Vol. 6, 30; **American advisers urged** Paine, *Wars*, 256; **huge quantities of American arms** Westad, *Decisive*, 112; **"He is losing"** Westad, *Decisive*, 160; **Chang Chi-chung** Lionel Max Chassin, *The Communist Conquest of China*, 218; **Chiang retracted promises** Westad, *Decisive*, 164.

343   **world-war scale** Westad, *Decisive*, 199; **Stalin took another look** Pantsov, *Mao*, 353; **increased the flow** Westad, *Brothers*, 62; **CCP griping** Westad, *Decisive*, 165; **face-to-face meeting** Westad, *Decisive*, 217; **Central Intelligence Agency** CIA report on Soviet objectives in China, 15 September 1947, Secretary's Files 213/8, HST Papers, HSTL.

343   **"snowball rolling"** AW to Luce, 14 July 1947, AW Papers 93/42, Hoover; **baseball analogy** Paterson, "If Europe," 21.

343–44   **"head examined"** Taylor, *Generalissimo*, 396; **10,000 advisers** Gallic-

chio, *Scramble*, 182; **leeway to get more closely involved** AW to CKS/
Madame CKS, 15 December 1947, AW Papers 98/17, Hoover; **a plan to
revive the Flying Tigers** Papers Vol. 6, 631; **Senior army officers** May,
Truman, 14; **"stand and hold"** Edward J. Marolda in Bland, *George C.
Marshall's*, 417; **American advisers** Soong to Butterworth, 5 July 1947,
W. Walton Butterworth Papers 1/7, GCMRL; **American bases** Belden,
China Shakes, 445; **Bullitt *Life* essay** Schurmann, *Republican China*, 356–
357; **unseat Chiang** White Paper 285.

344   **intervening with Truman** Ernest R. May, "When Marshall Kept the U.S.
Out of War in China," 1009; **"direct responsibility"** Papers Vol. 6, 376;
"sucked in" Papers Vol. 6, 483; **"have to be prepared," "a continuing
commitment"** Papers Vol. 6, 377.

344–45 **"more vital regions"** Papers Vol. 6, 378–379; **"obligations and responsibilities"** Papers Vol. 6, 372–373; **"American intervention"** Shepley to
HST, 26 February 1946, GCM Papers 124/28, GCMRL; **several hundred
thousand** David Halberstam, *The Coldest Winter*, 229, and Averell Harriman Oral History, GCMRL; **loose talk of World War III** Papers Vol. 6,
377; **"The Chinese have long been intent"** Papers Vol. 6, 483.

345   **"Every time I see soldiers"** CKS diary, 24 January 1949, Hoover; **"Since
God loves me"** CKS diary, 8 June 1948, Hoover.

345   **Chiang had been hearing** Bullitt letter, 22 May 1948, JM Papers 3, HSTL,
and Shaw, *American*, 223; **"If Marshall does not change"** CKS diary, 30
November 1947, Hoover; **Thomas Dewey** Tsou, *America's*, 489; **messages
from Wedemeyer** AW to Stuart, 25 October 1948, AW Papers 98/76, Hoover;
Chen Li-fu Boorman, *Biographical Dictionary*, Vol. 1, 210; **seeing Marshall**
Papers Vol. 6, 501; **"almost mystical"** Cohen, *America's Response*, 161; **troops
withdrawing into cities** Belden, *China Shakes*, 415; **Dewey led in the polls**
Gallup, *Gallup*, 749 and 757.

345   **"The diplomatic situation"** Tanner, *Where*, 275.

346   **"hope to those who desperately"** Stoler, *George C. Marshall*, 167.

346   **Marshall had expected that American success** Papers Vol. 6, 243; **"long-
anticipated crisis," Pessimistic strategists** CIA Review of the world sit-
uation, 17 November 1948, Secretary's Files 178/27, HST Papers, HSTL;
"When the issue of subservience" Memorandum for the National
Security Council on Possible Developments in China, 3 November 1948,
National Security Council Files 8/6, HST Papers, HSTL.

346   **Chen Li-fu** Papers Vol. 6, 503; **"extension of the Marshall Plan"** Wang
to GCM, 27 December 1949, GCM Papers 164/8, GCMRL; **Another would
acknowledge** Li to GCM, 5 May 1949, GCM Papers 60/36, GCMRL; **$3
billion** Summary of U.S. aid to China, 2 March 1948, AW Papers 101/30,
Hoover; **more than half military** Paine, *Wars*, 246; **"dispersion of U.S.
resources"** Minutes of National Security Council, 23 November 1948,
Secretary's Files 178/27, HST Papers, HSTL.

347 **"all the American women," General Flicker** Madame CKS to KTM, 19 September 1948, KTM Papers, GCMRL; **just below Eleanor Roosevelt** Jespersen, *American Images*, 106; **pleaded for increased assistance** Director of Central Intelligence memo, 10 December 1948, Secretary's Files 152/1, HST Papers, HSTL; **see that her pleaded had failed** CKS diary, 5 December 1948, Hoover.

347 **"People want action"** Transcript of GCM comments, Conference on Problems of United States Policy in China, Secretary's Files 152/4, HST Papers, HSTL.

347 **"who lost us"** Taylor, *Generalissimo*, 388; **Chiang wished he had prevented** CKS diary, 16 June 1951, Hoover.

347 **scattered his forces** Taylor, *Generalissimo*, 393; **overcommitted** Eastman, "Who Lost," 664; **"muddle-headed," "degenerate"** Eastman, "Who Lost," 658–659; **"I increasingly realize"** CKS diary, 20 August 1949, Hoover.

348 **Acheson's takeaway** Isaacson, *Wise Men*, 476; **Chiang condemned it** Westad, *Decisive*, 307; **Mao held it up** Tsou, *America's*, 510; **Mao's paranoia** Westad, *Decisive*, 307; **"whitewash"** Isaacson, *Wise Men*, 476.

348–49 **"full-dress attack"** *New York Times* 25 June 1949; **"moral retreat"** Lewis McCarroll Purifoy, *Harry Truman's China Policy*, 116; **John F. Kennedy** Purifoy, *Harry Truman's*, 110, and Dallek, *Lost*, 226; **fight Communism in Vietnam** Yergin, *Shattered*, 406; **"plunged by political"** Papers Vol. 7, 9.

349 **"exploit . . . any rifts"** Gaddis, *Strategies*, 68; **"Even if the devil"** Gaddis, *Strategies*, 100.

349 **Mao went out of his way, responded to American feelers** Chen Jian, "The Myth of America's 'Lost Chance' in China," 81–82; **"It is not possible"** Hunt, *Genesis*, 180; **wary of CCP independence** Murray, "Stalin," 16; **"The Russians cannot dominate"** Harding, *Sino-American*, 165.

349 **Although Soviet aid to Mao** Tanner, *Where*, 277; **"They were Communists"** Transcript of GCM comments, Conference on Problems of United States Policy in China, Secretary's Files 152/4, HST Papers, HSTL.

350 **revolutionary euphoria** Geoffrey Roberts, *Stalin's Wars*, 367; **What had changed** John Lewis Gaddis, *We Now Know*, 290; **Mao could help Kim** Roberts, *Stalin's*, 368; **Mao in a quagmire** Gaddis, *We Now Know*, 76.

350 **He needed to drag Marshall** Papers Vol. 7, 130; **"When the President motors down"** Papers Vol. 7, 146; **"They are still charging me"** Cray, *General*, 685; **six months** Stoler, *George C. Marshall*, 182.

351 **"Jenner? Jenner?"** Cray, *General*, 686.

351 **He had told reporters that defeating** Papers Vol. 7, 478; **"unfinished China war"** Walter Judd Oral History, HSTL.

351 **"If we lose this war"** Papers Vol. 7, 478.

351–52 **"cold-blooded calculation"** Papers Vol. 7, 463; **Marshall was adamant** George F. Kennan, *The Kennan Diaries*, 258–259; **"a very small peninsula"**

Papers Vol. 7, 463; **"carefully laid Russian trap"** Papers Vol. 7, 260; **Countering demands** Papers Vol. 7, 504; **"the wrong war"** Cray, *General*, 720.

352 **praise of Marshall's efforts** Cotter to GCM, 6 September 1946, GCM Papers 122/26, GCMRL; **"greatest blunders"** Papers Vol. 7, 550.

352 **"empty triumph"** Papers Vol. 7, 903; **"dynamic force"** Papers Vol. 7, 95; **reinforced by both** Papers Vol. 7, 383.

352 **"benighted people"** Papers Vol. 7, 765.

353 **"You have earned your retirement"** Papers Vol. 7, 630; **"This does not seem as remarkable to me"** Papers Vol. 7, 811.

354 **Wedemeyer helped quietly** McCarthy to AW, 13 January 1953, AW Papers 49/7, Hoover; **"easy prey"** Albert C. Wedemeyer, *Wedemeyer Reports!*, 369; **"so disheartened and demoralized"** Wedemeyer, *Wedemeyer*, 403; **"not to be completely factual"** Caraway memoir, Paul Caraway Papers, MHI.

354 **"sobering lesson"** Pogue, *Statesman*, 497; **When he got in front of the crowd** Smith, *Eisenhower*, 544; **"sold him out"** McCullough, *Truman*, 912.

355 **"dirty business"** Papers Vol. 7, 852; **"I felt because of the vigorous attacks"** Smith, *Eisenhower*, 523; **"I pray especially"** GCM to Eisenhower, 7 November 1952, GCM Papers 228/10, GCMRL.

355 **Frank McCarthy** McCarthy to Eisenhower, 3 August 1954, Frank McCarthy Papers, GCMRL; **"I know how sensitive"** McCarthy to KTM, 5 August 1954, Frank McCarthy Papers, GCMRL.

355 **"If I have to explain at this point"** Cray, *General*, 723; **Vouching for former aides** Papers Vol. 7, 80; **issued a warning** Papers Vol. 7, 83.

355–56 **"desperation on our side"** Russell F. Sizemore, "The Prudent Cold Warrior," 203; **"difficult to sit by"** Sizemore, "Prudent," 206.

356 **help refugees** GCM to Judd, 26 April 1952, GCM Papers 222/6, GCMRL; **pushed for asylum** Papers Vol. 7, 704; **signed a petition** Madame CKS to GCM, 21 December 1953, GCM Papers 225/37, GCMRL; **Cold War delirium** Westad, *Brothers*, 20.

357 **"wasteland"** Kahn, *China Hands*, 275; **"God almighty"** Robert A. Caro, *The Years of Lyndon Johnson: The Passage of Power*, 534.

357 **Truman called Marshall** *New York Times* 17 October 1959; **Eisenhower** *New York Times* 17 October 1959; **Kennan** *New York Times* 18 October 1959.

357 **When Chiang heard** CKS diary, 17 October 1959, Hoover.

Postscript: Substitutes for Victory?

359 **"trying to keep to the things"** Marshall interviews, 556.

359 **"You are dealing all the time"** Marshall interviews, 407.

359–60 **"Monday-quarterback business"** Marshall interviews, 416; **"later states of mind"** Marshall interviews, 406.

361 **"had lost their effectiveness"** Richard E. Neustadt, *Thinking in Time*, 86;

calling Vietnam an opportunity; Walter Judd Oral History, HSTL; **Even into the 1980s** See, for example, Jeane Kirkpatrick's "Dictatorships and Double Standards," *Commentary Magazine*, November 1979; **"the whole course of the subsequent Cold War"** May, "When Marshall," 1003–1004.

361   **Odd Arne Westad** Westad, "Losses," 105.

362   **"It continually introduces the factor of one's own reputation"** Papers Vol. 3, 208.

363   **he read thick volumes** Pogue, *Organizer*, 306; **asked newspaper publishers** Papers Vol. 3, 530; **"By looking back"** Neustadt, *Thinking*, 248.

363   **"too many conflicting and disturbing factors"** Papers Vol. 7, 688; **"impressions retained"** Papers Vol. 1, 220; **"great value in broadening"** Papers Vol. 3, 530.

SOURCES

ARCHIVAL MATERIALS

Dean Acheson Papers, Harry S. Truman Library, Independence, Missouri

David D. Barrett Papers, Hoover Institution Archives, Palo Alto, California

W. Walton Butterworth Papers, George C. Marshall Research Library, Lexington, Virginia

Paul Caraway Papers, Military History Institute, Carlisle Barracks, Pennsylvania

Marshall Carter Papers, George C. Marshall Research Library, Lexington, Virginia

John Hart Caughey Papers, George C. Marshall Research Library, Lexington, Virginia

Chiang Kai-Shek Diaries, Hoover Institution Archives, Palo Alto, California

Clark Clifford Papers, Harry S. Truman Library, Independence, Missouri

O. Edmund Clubb Papers, Hoover Institution Archives, Palo Alto, California

A. Fairfield Dana Papers, George C. Marshall Research Library, Lexington, Virginia

John Paton Davies Papers, Harry S. Truman Library, Independence, Missouri

Tillman Durdin Papers, University of California, San Diego, Library, San Diego, California

George Elsey Papers, Harry S. Truman Library, Independence, Missouri

John M. Ferguson Papers, George C. Marshall Research Library, Lexington, Virginia

Alvan Gillem Papers, Military History Institute, Carlisle Barracks, Pennsylvania

Frederick Harris Papers, George C. Marshall Research Library, Lexington, Virginia

John E. Hull Papers, Military History Institute, Carlisle Barracks, Pennsylvania

Wellington Koo Papers, Columbia University Library, New York, New York

William D. Leahy Papers, Library of Congress, Washington, DC

Virginia Lee Papers, George C. Marshall Research Library, Lexington, Virginia

Li Zongren Papers, Columbia University Library, New York, New York

Lawrence Lincoln Papers, Military History Institute, Carlisle Barracks, Pennsylvania

L. J. Lincoln Papers, George C. Marshall Research Library, Lexington, Virginia

John Lucas Papers, Military History Institute, Carlisle Barracks, Pennsylvania

Marshall Mission Records, National Archives, College Park, Maryland

George C. Marshall Papers, George C. Marshall Research Library, Lexington, Virginia

Katherine Tupper Marshall Papers, George C. Marshall Research Library, Lexington, Virginia

Frank McCarthy Papers, George C. Marshall Research Library, Lexington, Virginia

John F. Melby Papers, Harry S. Truman Library, Independence, Missouri

Edwin Pauley Papers, Harry S. Truman Library, Independence, Missouri

Peiping Headquarters Group Papers, George C. Marshall Research Library, Lexington, Virginia

Wilbur Peterkin Papers, Hoover Institution Archives, Palo Alto, California

P. Frank Price Papers, George C. Marshall Research Library, Lexington, Virginia

Marie Singer Sargent Papers, George C. Marshall Research Library, Lexington, Virginia

T. V. Soong Papers, Hoover Institution Archives, Palo Alto, California

Joseph W. Stilwell Papers, Hoover Institution Archives, Palo Alto, California

John Leighton Stuart Papers, Hoover Institution Archives, Palo Alto, California

John D. Sumner Papers, Harry S. Truman Library, Independence, Missouri

Timberman-Fiske Papers, Military History Institute, Carlisle Barracks, Pennsylvania

Harry S. Truman Papers, Harry S. Truman Library, Independence, Missouri

John Watson Papers, George C. Marshall Research Library, Lexington, Virginia

Albert Wedemeyer Papers, Hoover Institution Archives, Palo Alto, California

Richard C. Wing Papers, George C. Marshall Research Library, Lexington, Virginia

Ivan D. Yeaton Papers, Hoover Institution Archives, Palo Alto, California

ORAL HISTORIES

Columbia University Library, New York, New York:
Chen Kuang-fu, Chen Li-fu, Wellington Koo
Foreign Service Oral History Collection, Library of Congress, Washington, DC:
Henry Byroade, Ralph Clough, Everett Drumright, John F. Melby, John S. Service
George C. Marshall Research Library, Lexington, Virginia:
Dean Acheson, David D. Barrett, W. Walton Butterworth, James F. Byrnes, Henry A. Byroade, Marshall S. Carter, John Hart Caughey, A. Fairfield Dana, Dwight D. Eisenhower, William M. Farr, Alvan C. Gillem, Averell Harriman, Richard Hickey, John E. Hull, C. E. Hutchin, Philip Jessup, George F. Kennan, George C. Marshall, Katherine Marshall, Frank McCarthy, John Melby, Luther D. Miller, William D. Pawley, Walter Robertson, Eleanor Roosevelt, James R. Shepley, Harry S. Truman, George V. Underwood, Wang Shih-Chieh, Albert Wedemeyer, Richard C. Wing, Yu Ta-wei
Harry S. Truman Library, Independence, Missouri:
W. Walton Butterworth, Henry Byroade, John M. Cabot, O. Edmund Clubb,

Matthew Connelly, George M. Elsey, R. Allen Griffin, Hubert F. Havlik, Walter H. Judd, Edwin Locke, Robert Lovett, John F. Melby, Paul H. Nitze, Arthur Ringwalt, John S. Service, Philip D. Sprouse, Philip Tresize, Arthur N. Young

PUBLISHED MATERIALS

Acheson, Dean. *Present at the Creation: My Years in the State Department*. New York: W. W. Norton, 1969.

———. *Sketches From Life: Of Men I Have Known*. New York: Harper & Brothers, 1959.

Aplington, Henry, II. "Sunset in the East: A Memoir of North China, 1945–47." *Journal of American–East Asian Relations* 3 (Summer 1994): 155–175.

Apter, David E., and Tony Saich. *Revolutionary Discourse in Mao's Republic*. Cambridge, MA: Harvard University Press, 1998.

Auden, W. H. "In Time of War." *The Collected Poetry of W. H. Auden*. New York: Random House, 1945.

Auden, W. H., and Christopher Isherwood. *Journey to a War*. London: Faber & Faber, 1939.

Barrett, David D. *Dixie Mission: The United States Army Observer Group in Yenan, 1944*. Berkeley: University of California, Berkeley, Center for Chinese Studies, 1970.

Beal, John Robinson. *Marshall in China*. New York: Doubleday, 1970.

Belden, Jack. *China Shakes the World*. New York: Monthly Review Press, 1949.

Bernstein, Richard. *China 1945: Mao's Revolution and America's Fateful Choice*. New York: Alfred A. Knopf, 2014.

Bianco, Lucien. *Origins of the Chinese Revolution, 1915–1949*. Stanford, CA: Stanford University Press, 1971.

Bird, Kai. *The Color of Truth: McGeorge Bundy and William Bundy: Brothers in Arms*. New York: Simon & Schuster, 1998.

Bland, Larry I., ed. *George C. Marshall Interview and Reminiscences for Forrest C. Pogue*. Lexington, VA: George C. Marshall Foundation, 1986.

———, ed. *George C. Marshall's Mediation Mission to China*. Lexington, VA: George C. Marshall Foundation, 1998.

Bland, Larry I., and Sharon R. Ritenour, eds. *The Papers of George Catlett Marshall: Volume 1: "The Soldierly Spirit," December 1880–June 1939*. Baltimore: Johns Hopkins University Press, 1981.

Bland, Larry I., Sharon R. Ritenour, and Clarence E. Wunderlin Jr., eds. *The Papers of George Catlett Marshall: Volume 2: "We Cannot Delay," July 1, 1939–December 6, 1941*. Baltimore: Johns Hopkins University Press, 1981.

Bland, Larry I., and Sharon Ritenour Stevens, eds. *The Papers of George Catlett Marshall: Volume 3: "The Right Man for the Job," December 7, 1941–May 31, 1943*. Baltimore: Johns Hopkins University Press, 1991.

———, eds. *The Papers of George Catlett Marshall: Volume 4: "Aggressive and Determined*

Leadership," June 1, 1943–December 31, 1944. Baltimore: Johns Hopkins University Press, 1996.

——, eds. *The Papers of George Catlett Marshall: Volume 5: "The Finest Soldier," January 1, 1945–January 7, 1947.* Baltimore: Johns Hopkins University Press, 2003.

Bland, Larry I., and Mark A. Stoler, editors. *The Papers of George Catlett Marshall: Volume 6: "The Whole World Hangs in the Balance," January 8, 1947–September 30, 1949.* Baltimore: Johns Hopkins University Press, 2013.

Boorman, Howard L., ed. *Biographical Dictionary of Republican China,* Vols. 1–4. New York: Columbia University Press, 1967.

Borg, Dorothy, and Waldo Heinrichs, eds. *Uncertain Years: Chinese-American Relations, 1947–1950.* New York: Columbia University Press, 1980.

Brower, Charles F., ed. *George C. Marshall: Servant of the American Nation.* New York: Palgrave Macmillan, 2011.

Buhite, Russell D. *Patrick J. Hurley and American Foreign Policy.* Ithaca, NY: Cornell University Press, 1973.

——. *Soviet-American Relations in Asia, 1945–1954.* Norman: University of Oklahoma Press, 1981.

Buruma, Ian. *Year Zero: A History of 1945.* New York: Penguin Press, 2013.

Byrnes, James F. *All in One Lifetime.* New York: Harper & Brothers, 1958.

——. *Speaking Frankly.* New York: Harper & Brothers, 1947.

Caro, Robert A. *The Years of Lyndon Johnson: The Passage of Power.* New York: Alfred A. Knopf, 2012.

Carter, Carolle J. *Mission to Yenan: American Liaison with the Chinese Communists 1944–1947.* Lexington: University Press of Kentucky, 1997.

Chang, Iris. *The Rape of Nanking: The Forgotten Holocaust of World War II.* New York: Basic Books, 1997.

Chang, Jung, and Jon Halliday. *Mao: The Unknown Story.* London: Jonathan Cape, 2005.

Chassin, Lionel Max. *The Communist Conquest of China: A History of the Civil War 1945–49.* Cambridge: Harvard University Press, 1965.

Chen Jian. *China's Road to the Korean War: The Making of the Sino-American Confrontation.* New York: Columbia University Press, 1994.

——. *Mao's China and the Cold War.* Chapel Hill: University of North Carolina Press, 2001.

——. "The Myth of America's 'Lost Chance' in China: A Chinese Perspective in Light of New Evidence." *Diplomatic History* 21 (Winter 1997): 77–86.

Ch'en Li-fu. *The Storm Clouds Clear Over China: The Memoir of Ch'en Li-fu, 1900–1993.* Edited by Sidney H. Chang and Ramon H. Myers. Palo Alto, CA: Hoover Institution Press, 1994.

Cheng, Victor Shiu Chiang. "Imagining China's Madrid in Manchuria: The Communist Military Strategy at the Onset of the Chinese Civil War, 1945–1946." *Modern China* 31 (January 2005): 72–114.

——. "Modern War on an Ancient Battlefield: The Diffusion of American Military

Technology and Ideas in the Chinese Civil War, 1946–1949." *Modern China* 35 (January 2009): 38–64.

Chern, Kenneth S. *Dilemma in China: America's Policy Debate, 1945.* Hamden, CT: Archon Books, 1980.

Christensen, Thomas J. "A 'Lost Chance' for What? Rethinking the Origins of U.S.-PRC Confrontation." *Journal of American–East Asian Relations* 4 (Fall 1995): 249–278.

——. *Useful Adversaries: Grand Strategy, Domestic Mobilization, and Sino-American Conflict, 1947–1958.* Princeton, NJ: Princeton University Press, 1996.

Chung, Christopher P. C. "Drawing the U-Shaped Line: China's Claim in the South China Sea, 1946–1974." *Modern China* 42 (January 2016): 38–72.

Coffman, Edward M. "The American 15th Infantry Regiment in China, 1912–1938: A Vignette in Social History." *Journal of Military History* 58 (January 1994): 57–74.

Cohen, Warren I. *America's Response to China: A History of Sino-American Relations.* 4th edition. New York: Columbia University Press, 2000.

——. "Cold Wars and Shell Games: The Truman Administration and East Asia." *Reviews in American History* 11 (September 1983): 430–436.

——. "Conversations with Chinese Friends: Zhou Enlai's Associates Reflect on Chinese-American Relations in the 1940s and the Korean War." *Diplomatic History* 11 (Summer 1987): 283–289.

——. "Was There a Lost Chance in China?" *Diplomatic History* 21 (Winter 1997): 71–75.

Cray, Ed. *General of the Army: George C. Marshall, Soldier and Statesman.* New York: W. W. Norton, 1990.

Dallek, Robert. *The Lost Peace: Leadership in a Time of Horror and Hope, 1945–1953.* New York: Harper, 2010.

Davies, John Paton. *China Hand: An Autobiography.* Philadelphia: University of Pennsylvania Press, 2012.

——. *Dragon by the Tail: American, British, Japanese, and Russian Encounters with China and One Another.* New York: W. W. Norton, 1972.

D'Este, Carlo. *Eisenhower: A Soldier's Life.* New York: Henry Holt, 2002.

Destler, I. M., Leslie H. Gelb, and Anthony Lake. *Our Own Worst Enemy: The Unmaking of American Foreign Policy.* New York: Simon & Schuster, 1984.

Dikötter, Frank. *The Age of Openness: China Before Mao.* Berkeley: University of California Press, 2008.

——. *The Tragedy of Liberation: A History of the Chinese Revolution 1945–1957.* New York: Bloomsbury Press, 2013.

Dobbs, Michael. *Six Months in 1945: From World War to Cold War.* New York: Alfred A. Knopf, 2012.

Donovan, Robert J. *Conflict and Crisis: The Presidency of Harry S. Truman, 1945–1948.* New York: W. W. Norton, 1977.

Eastman, Lloyd E. *Abortive Revolution: China Under Nationalist Rule, 1927–1937.* Cambridge: Harvard University Press, 1990.

——. *Seeds of Destruction: Nationalist China in War and Revolution 1937–1949*. Stanford, CA: Stanford University Press, 1984.

——. "Who Lost China? Chiang Kai-shek Testifies." *China Quarterly* 88 (December 1981): 658–668.

Eastman, Lloyd E., Jerome Ch'en, Suzanne Pepper, and Lyman P. Van Slyke. *The Nationalist Era in China 1927–1949*. New York: Cambridge University Press, 1991.

Elleman, Bruce A., and S. C. M. Paine, eds. *Naval Coalition Warfare: From the Napoleonic War to Operation Iraqi Freedom*. New York: Routledge, 2007.

Esherick, Joseph W. "Ten Theses on the Chinese Revolution." *Modern China* 21 (January. 1995): 45–76.

Fairbank, John King. *Chinabound: A Fifty-Year Memoir*. New York: Harper & Row, 1982.

——. *The Great Chinese Revolution 1800–1985*. New York: Harper & Row, 1986.

——. *The United States and China*. 4th edition (enlarged). Cambridge, MA: Harvard University Press, 1983.

Feaver, John H. "The China Aid Bill of 1948: Limited Assistance as a Cold War Strategy." *Diplomatic History* 5 (Spring 1981): 107–120.

Feis, Herbert. *The China Tangle: The American Effort in China from Pearl Harbor to the Marshall Mission*. Princeton, NJ: Princeton University Press, 1953.

Fenby, Jonathan. *Chiang Kai-shek: China's Generalissimo and the Nation He Lost*. New York: Carroll and Graf, 2004.

Ferrell, Robert H., ed. *Dear Bess: The Letters from Harry to Bess Truman, 1910–1959*. New York: W. W. Norton, 1983.

——, ed. *The Eisenhower Diaries*. New York: W. W. Norton, 1981.

Finch, John D. *Marshall Blinks: Operational Art and Strategic Vision*. Fort Leavenworth, KS: School of Advanced Military Studies, 2014.

Gaddis, John Lewis. *Strategies of Containment: A Critical Appraisal of American National Security Policy during the Cold War*. Revised and expanded edition. New York: Oxford University Press, 2005.

——. "Was the Truman Doctrine a Real Turning Point?" *Foreign Affairs* 52 (January 1974): 386–402.

——. *We Now Know: Rethinking Cold War History*. New York: Oxford University Press, 1997.

Gallicchio, Marc S. *The Cold War Begins in Asia: American East Asian Policy and the Fall of the Japanese Empire*. New York: Columbia University Press, 1988.

——. *The Scramble for Asia: U.S. Military Power in the Aftermath of the Pacific War*. Lanham, MD: Rowman & Littlefield, 2008.

Gallup, George H. *The Gallup Poll: Public Opinion 1935–1971*. New York: Random House, 1972.

Gao Wenqian. *Zhou Enlai: The Last Perfect Revolutionary*. New York: PublicAffairs, 2007.

Garver, John W. *Chinese-Soviet Relations 1937–1945: The Diplomacy of Chinese Nationalism*. New York: Oxford University Press, 1988.

——. "Mao, the Comintern, and the Second United Front." *China Quarterly* 129 (March 1992): 171–179.

——. "The Opportunity Costs of Mao's Foreign Policy Choices." *China Journal* 49 (January 2003): 127–136.

Goncharov, Serge N., John W. Lewis, and Xue Litai. *Uncertain Partners: Stalin, Mao, and the Korean War.* Stanford, CA: Stanford University Press, 1993.

Halberstam, David. *The Coldest Winter: America and the Korean War.* New York: Hyperion, 2007.

Han Suyin. *Eldest Son: Zhou Enlai and the Making of Modern China, 1898–1976.* New York: Hill and Wang, 1994.

——. *Morning Deluge: Mao Tsetung and the Chinese Revolution 1893–1954.* Boston: Little, Brown, 1972.

Harding, Harry, and Yuan Ming, eds. *Sino-American Relations, 1945–1955: A Joint Reassessment of a Critical Decade.* Wilmington, DE: SR Books, 1989.

Harriman, W. Averell, and Elie Abel. *Special Envoy to Churchill and Stalin 1941–1946.* New York: Random House, 1975.

Haynes, John Earl, and Harvey Klehr. *Venona: Decoding Soviet Espionage in America.* New Haven, CT: Yale University Press, 1999.

He Di. "The Most Respected Enemy: Mao Zedong's Perception of the United States." *China Quarterly* 137 (March 1994): 144–158.

Heinzig, Dieter. *The Soviet Union and Communist China 1945–1950: The Arduous Road to the Alliance.* Armonk, NY: M. E. Sharpe, 2004.

Herzstein, Robert E. *Henry R. Luce, Time, and the American Crusade in Asia.* New York: Cambridge University Press, 2005.

Homeyard, Illoyna. "Another Look at the Marshall Mission to China." *Journal of American–East Asian Relations* 1 (Summer 1992): 191–217.

Hoopes, Townsend, and Douglas Brinkley. *Driven Patriot: The Life and Times of James Forrestal.* New York: Knopf, 1992.

Hsu, Kai-yu. *Chou En-Lai: China's Gray Eminence.* Garden City, NY: Doubleday, 1968.

Huebner, Jon W. "Chinese Anti-Americanism, 1946–1948." *Australian Journal of Chinese Affairs* 17 (January 1987): 115–125.

Hunt, Michael H. *The Genesis of Chinese Communist Foreign Policy.* New York: Columbia University Press, 1996.

Hunt, Michael H., and Odd Arne Westad. "The Chinese Communist Party and International Affairs: A Field Report on New Historical Sources and Old Research Problems." *China Quarterly* 122 (June 1990): 258–272.

Iriye, Akira, and Warren Cohen, eds. *American, Chinese, and Japanese Perspectives on Wartime Asia 1931–1949.* Wilmington, DE: SR Books, 1990.

Isaacson, Walter, and Evan Thomas. *The Wise Men: Six Friends and the World They Made.* New York: Touchstone, 1986.

Jeans, Roger B., ed. *The Marshall Mission to China, 1945–1947: The Letters and Diary of Colonel John Hart Caughey.* Lanham, MD: Rowman & Littlefield, 2011.

Jespersen, T. Christopher. *American Images of China 1931–1949*. Stanford, CA: Stanford University Press, 1996.

Kahn, E. J., Jr. *The China Hands: America's Foreign Service Officers and What Befell Them.* New York: Viking Press, 1975.

Keith, Ronald. *The Diplomacy of Zhou Enlai*. New York: St. Martin's Press, 1989.

Kennan, George F. *The Kennan Diaries*. Edited by Frank Castigliola. New York: W. W. Norton, 2014.

———. *Memoirs 1925–1950*. Boston: Little, Brown, 1967.

Kennedy, Andrew Bingham. "Can the Weak Defeat the Strong? Mao's Evolving Approach to Asymmetric Warfare in Yan'an." *China Quarterly* 196 (December 2008): 884–899.

Kirby, William C. "The Internationalization of China: Foreign Relations at Home and Abroad in the Republican Era." *China Quarterly* 150 (June 1997): 433–458.

Kissinger, Henry. *On China*. New York: Penguin Press, 2012.

Leahy, William D. *I Was There*. New York: McGraw-Hill, 1950.

Leffler, Melvyn P. *A Preponderance of Power: National Security, the Truman Administration, and the Cold War*. Palo Alto, CA: Stanford University Press, 1992.

Leung, Edwin Pak-wah. *Historical Dictionary of the Chinese Civil War*. Lanham, MD: Scarecrow Press, 2002.

Levine, Steven I. "A New Look at American Mediation in the Chinese Civil War: The Marshall Mission and Manchuria." *Diplomatic History* 3 (October 1979): 349–376.

———. *Anvil of Victory: The Communist Revolution in Manchuria, 1945–1948*. New York: Columbia University Press, 1987.

Lew, Christopher R. *The Third Chinese Revolutionary Civil War, 1945–49: An Analysis of Communist Strategy and Leadership*. New York: Routledge, 2009.

Li Tien-Min. *Chou En-Lai*. Taipei: Institute of International Relations, 1970.

Lin Hsiao-ting and Wu Su-feng. "America's China Policy Revisited: Regionalism, Regional Leaders, and Regionalized Aid." *Chinese Historical Review* 19 (December 2012): 107–127.

Liu, Xiaoyuan. *A Partnership for Disorder: China, the United States, and Their Policies for the Postwar Disposition of the Japanese Empire, 1941–1945*. New York: Cambridge University Press, 1996.

Louis, Wm. Roger. *Imperialism at Bay: The United States and the Decolonization of the British Empire, 1941–1945*. New York: Oxford University Press, 1978.

Lutze, Thomas D. *China's Inevitable Revolution: Rethinking America's Loss to the Communists*. New York: Palgrave Macmillan, 2007.

MacKinnon, Stephen R., and Oris Friesen. *China Reporting: An Oral History of American Journalism in the 1930s and 1940s*. Berkeley: University of California Press, 1987.

Mao, Joyce. *Asia First: China and the Making of Modern American Conservatism*. Chicago: University of Chicago Press, 2015.

Marshall, George C. *Memoirs of My Services in the World War.* Boston: Houghton Mifflin, 1976.

——. *Marshall's Mission to China, December 1945–January 1947: The Report and Appended Documents.* Edited by Lyman P. Van Slyke. Arlington, VA: University Publications of America, 1976.

Marshall, Katherine Tupper. *Together.* 1946. Reprint, Chicago: Peoples Book Club, 1947.

May, Ernest R. "1947–1948: When Marshall Kept the U.S. out of War in China." *Journal of Military History* 66 (October 2002): 1001–1010.

——. *The Truman Administration and China, 1945–1949.* Philadelphia: J. B. Lippincott, 1975.

McCarthy, Joseph R. *America's Retreat from Victory: The Story of George Catlett Marshall.* New York: Devin-Adair, 1951.

McCullough, David. *Truman.* New York: Simon & Schuster, 1992.

Melby, John F. *The Mandate of Heaven: Record of a Civil War, China 1945–49.* New York: Anchor Books, 1971.

Millis, Walter, ed. *The Forrestal Diaries.* New York: Viking Press, 1951.

Mitter, Rana. *Forgotten Ally: China's World War II, 1937–1945.* Boston: Houghton Mifflin Harcourt, 2013.

Moreira, Peter. *Hemingway on the China Front: His WWII Spy Mission With Martha Gellhorn.* Washington: Potomac Books, 2006.

Murray, Brian. "Stalin, the Cold War, and the Division of China: A Multi-Archival Mystery." Cold War International History Project, Working Paper No. 12 (June 1995).

Nagai, Yonosuke, and Akira Iriye. *The Origins of the Cold War in Asia.* Tokyo: University of Tokyo Press, 1977.

Neustadt, Richard E., and Ernest R. May. *Thinking in Time: The Uses of History for Decision-Makers.* New York: Free Press, 1986.

Newman, Robert P. "Clandestine Chinese Nationalist Efforts to Punish Their American Detractors." *Diplomatic History* 7 (Summer 1983): 205–222.

——. *The Cold War Romance of Lillian Hellman and John Melby.* Chapel Hill: University of North Carolina Press, 1989.

——. "The Self-Inflicted Wound: The China White Paper of 1949." *Prologue* 14 (Fall 1982): 139–156.

Niu Jun. *From Yan'an to the World: The Origin and Development of Chinese Communist Foreign Policy.* Norwalk, CT: EastBridge, 2005.

Paine, S. C. M. *The Wars for Asia, 1911–1949.* New York: Cambridge University Press, 2012.

Pakula, Hannah. *The Last Empress: Madame Chiang Kai-shek and the Birth of Modern China.* New York: Simon & Schuster, 2009.

Pantsov, Alexander V., with Steven I. Levine. *Mao: The Real Story.* New York: Simon & Schuster, 2012.

Paterson, Thomas G. "If Europe, Why Not China? The Containment Doctrine, 1947–1949." *Prologue* 13 (Fall 1981): 18–38.

———. "Presidential Foreign Policy, Public Opinion, and Congress: The Truman Years." *Diplomatic History* 3 (January 1979): 1–18.

Peck, Graham. *Two Kinds of Time*. Boston: Houghton Mifflin, 1950.

Pepper, Suzanne. *Civil War in China: The Political Struggle, 1945–1949*. Berkeley: University of California Press, 1978.

Perry, Mark. *Partners in Command: George Marshall and Dwight Eisenhower in War and Peace*. New York: Penguin Press, 2007.

Pogue, Forrest C. *George C. Marshall: Education of a General 1880–1939*. New York: Viking Press, 1963.

———. *George C. Marshall: Ordeal and Hope 1939–1942*. New York: Viking Press, 1965.

———. *George C. Marshall: Organizer of Victory 1943–1945*. New York: Viking Press, 1973.

———. *George C. Marshall: Statesman 1945–1959*. New York: Penguin, 1987.

Purifoy, Lewis McCarroll. *Harry Truman's China Policy: McCarthyism and the Diplomacy of Hysteria, 1947–1951*. New York: New Viewpoints, 1976.

Qin Xiaoyi. Zongtong jianggong dashi changbian chugao (The Chronicles of President Chiang, First Edition). Taipei: Zhongzheng wenjiao jijinhui, 1978. 總統蔣公大事長編初稿, 卷五, 下冊

Qing, Simei. *From Allies to Enemies: Visions of Modernity, Identity, and U.S.-China Diplomacy, 1945–1960*. Cambridge, MA: Harvard University Press, 2007.

Reardon-Anderson, James. *Yenan and the Great Powers: The Origins of Chinese Communist Foreign Policy 1944–1946*. New York: Columbia University Press, 1980.

Reist, Katherine K. "The American Military Advisory Missions to China, 1945–1949." *Journal of Military History* 77 (October 2013): 1377–1398.

Ricks, Thomas E. *The Generals: American Military Command from World War II to Today*. New York: Penguin Press, 2012.

Rittenberg, Sidney, and Amanda Bennett. *The Man Who Stayed Behind*. New York: Simon & Schuster, 1993.

Roberts, Geoffrey. *Stalin's Wars: From World War to Cold War, 1939–1953*. New Haven, CT: Yale University Press, 2006.

Rusk, Dean. *As I Saw It*. As told to Richard Rusk. New York: W. W. Norton, 1990.

Saich, Tony, ed. *The Rise to Power of the Chinese Communist Party: Documents and Analysis*. Armonk: M. E. Sharpe, 1996.

Schaller, Michael. *The U.S. Crusade in China, 1938–1945*. New York: Columbia University Press, 1979.

Schell, Orville, and John Delury. *Wealth and Power: China's Long March to the Twenty-First Century*. New York: Random House, 2013.

Schnabel, James F. *The Joint Chiefs of Staff and National Policy 1945–1947*. Washington: Office of the Chairman of the Joint Chiefs of Staff, 1996.

Schurmann, Franz, and Orville Schell. *Republican China: Nationalism, War, and the Rise of Communism 1911–1949*. New York: Vintage Books, 1967.

Selden, Mark. *The Yenan Way in Revolutionary China*. Cambridge, MA: Harvard University Press, 1971.

Service, John S. *Lost Chance in China: The World War II Despatches of John S. Service*. Edited by Joseph W. Esherick. New York: Random House, 1974.

Shaffer, Robert. "A Rape in Beijing, December 1946: GIs, National Protests, and U.S. Foreign Policy." *Pacific Historical Review* 69 (February 2000): 31–64.

Shaw, Henry I. *The United States Marines in North China 1945–1949*. Washington, DC: Historical Branch, G-3 Division, U.S. Marine Corps, 1968.

Shaw, Yu-Ming. *An American Missionary in China: John Leighton Stuart and Chinese-American Relations*. Cambridge, MA: Harvard University Press, 1992.

Sheng, Michael M. "America's Lost Chance in China? A Reappraisal of Chinese Communist Policy Toward the United States Before 1945." *Australian Journal of Chinese Affairs* 29 (January 1993): 135–157.

———. *Battling Western Imperialism: Mao, Stalin, and the United States*. Princeton, NJ: Princeton University Press, 1997.

———. "Chinese Communist Policy Toward the United States and the Myth of the 'Lost Chance' 1948–1950." *Modern Asian Studies* 28 (July 1994): 475–502.

———. "Mao and Stalin: Adversaries or Comrades?" *China Quarterly* 129 (March 1992): 180–183.

———. "The Triumph of Internationalism: CCP-Moscow Relations Before 1949." *Diplomatic History* 21 (Winter 1997): 95–104.

———. "The United States, the Chinese Communist Party, and the Soviet Union, 1948–1950: A Reappraisal." *Pacific Historical Review* 63 (November 1994): 521–536.

Short, Philip. *Mao: A Life*. New York: Henry Holt, 1999.

Sizemore, Russell F. "The Prudent Cold Warrior." *Ethics and International Affairs* 2 (1988): 199–217.

Smith, Jean Edward. *Eisenhower in War and Peace*. New York: Random House, 2012.

Snow, Edgar. *Red Star Over China*. New York: Random House, 1938.

Spector, Ronald H. *In the Ruins of Empire: The Japanese Surrender and the Battle for Asia*. New York: Random House, 2007.

Spence, Jonathan D. *The Gate of Heavenly Peace: The Chinese and Their Revolution*. New York: Penguin Books, 1981.

———. *Mao Zedong: A Life*. New York: Penguin Press, 1999.

———. *The Search for Modern China*. 2nd edition. New York: W. W. Norton, 1999.

———. *To Change China: Western Advisers in China, 1620–1960*. New York: Little, Brown, 1969.

Stimson, Henry L., and McGeorge Bundy. *On Active Service in Peace and War*. New York: Harper & Row, 1948.

Stoler, Mark A. "George C. Marshall and the 'Europe-First' Strategy, 1939–1951: A Study in Diplomatic as Well as Military History." *Journal of Military History* 79 (April 2015): 333–342.

——. *George C. Marshall: Soldier-Statesman of the American Century.* Boston: Twayne, 1989.

——., ed. *The Papers of George Catlett Marshall: Volume 7: "The Man of the Age," October 1, 1949–October 15, 1959.* Baltimore: Johns Hopkins University Press, 2016.

Stuart, John Leighton. *Fifty Years in China: The Memoirs of John Leighton Stuart, Missionary and Ambassador.* New York: Random House, 1954.

Sun Tzu. *The Art of War.* Translated by John Minford. New York: Penguin, 2002.

Tanner, Harold M. *The Battle for Manchuria and the Fate of China: Siping, 1946.* Bloomington: Indiana University Press, 2013.

——. "Guerrilla, Mobile, and Base Warfare in Communist Military Operations in Manchuria, 1945–1947." *Journal of Military History* 67 (October 2003): 1177–1222.

——. *Where Chiang Kai-shek Lost China: The Liao-Shen Campaign, 1948.* Bloomington: Indiana University Press, 2015.

Taylor, Jay. *The Generalissimo: Chiang Kai-shek and the Struggle for Modern China.* Cambridge, MA: Harvard University Press, 2009.

Terrill, Ross. *Mao: A Biography.* Stanford, CA: Stanford University Press, 1999.

Topping, Seymour. *Journey Between Two Chinas.* New York: Harper & Row, 1972.

Tsou, Tang. *America's Failure in China, 1941–1950.* Chicago: University of Chicago Press, 1963.

Tuchman, Barbara W. "If Mao Had Come to Washington: An Essay in Alternatives." *Foreign Affairs* 71 (October 1972): 44–64.

——. *Stilwell and the American Experience in China, 1911–45.* New York: Macmillan, 1970.

Tucker, Nancy Bernkopf, ed. *China Confidential: American Diplomats and Sino-American Relations, 1945–1996.* New York: Columbia University Press, 2001.

Unger, Debi, and Irwin Unger, with Stanley Hirshson. *George Marshall: A Biography.* New York: Harper, 2014.

United States Department of State. *The China White Paper, August 1949.* Stanford, CA: Stanford University Press, 1967.

——. *Foreign Relations of the United States, 1945.* Vol. 7: *The Far East, China.* Washington: Government Printing Office, 1969.

——. *Foreign Relations of the United States, 1946.* Vol. 9: *The Far East, China.* Washington: Government Printing Office, 1972.

——. *Foreign Relations of the United States, 1946.* Vol. 10: *The Far East, China.* Washington: Government Printing Office, 1972.

——. *Foreign Relations of the United States, 1947.* Vol. 7: *The Far East, China.* Washington: Government Printing Office, 1972.

Van Slyke, Lyman P., ed. *The Chinese Communist Movement: A Report of the U.S. War Department, July 1945.* Stanford, CA: Stanford University Press, 1968.

———. *Enemies and Friends: The United Front in Chinese Communist History.* Stanford, CA: Stanford University Press, 1967.

Wakeman, Frederic, Jr. *Spymaster: Dai Li and the Chinese Secret Service.* Berkeley: University of California Press, 2003.

Wakeman, Frederic, Jr., and Richard Louis Edmonds, eds. *Reappraising Republican China.* New York: Oxford University Press, 2000.

Waldron, Arthur. "China Without Tears." In *What If?: The World's Foremost Military Historians Imagine What Might Have Been.* Edited by Robert Cowley. New York: G. P. Putnam's Sons, 1999.

———. "War and the Rise of Nationalism in Twentieth-Century China." *Journal of Military History* 57 (October 1993): 87–104.

Wallace, Henry A. *The Price of Vision: The Diary of Henry A. Wallace.* Boston: Houghton Mifflin, 1973.

Wang Chen-Main, ed. *Maxie'er shihua tiaochu rizhi (1945 nian 11–yue-1947 nian 1 yue)* (A Daily Record of Marshall's Mediation in China (November 1945–January 1947)). Taipei: Guoshiguan, 1992. 马歇尔使华调解日志 (1945 年11月 - 1947 年1月)

Wang, Peter Chen-Main. "Revisiting U.S.-China Wartime Relations: A Study of Wedemeyer's China Mission." *Journal of Contemporary China* 18 (March 2009): 233–247.

Wasserstrom, Jeffrey N. *Student Protests in Twentieth-Century China: The View from Shanghai.* Stanford, CA: Stanford University Press, 1991.

Wedemeyer, Albert C. *Wedemeyer Reports!* New York: Henry Holt, 1958.

Westad, Odd Arne, ed. *Brothers in Arms: The Rise and Fall of the Sino-Soviet Alliance, 1945–1963.* Washington: Woodrow Wilson Center Press, 1998.

———. *Cold War and Revolution: Soviet-American Rivalry and the Origins of the Chinese Civil War.* New York: Columbia University Press, 1993.

———. *Decisive Encounters: The Chinese Civil War, 1946–1950.* Stanford, CA: Stanford University Press, 2003.

———. "Losses, Chances, and Myths: The United States and the Creation of the Sino-Soviet Alliance, 1945–1950." *Diplomatic History* 21 (Winter 1997): 105–115.

———. *Restless Empire: China and the World Since 1750.* New York: Basic Books, 2013.

White, Theodore H. *In Search of History: A Personal Adventure.* New York: Harper & Row, 1978.

White, Theodore H., and Annalee Jacoby. *Thunder Out of China.* New York: William Sloane, 1946.

Wilson, Dick. *Zhou Enlai: A Biography.* New York: Viking Press, 1984.

Wilson, Rose Page. *General Marshall Remembered.* Englewood Cliffs, NJ: Prentice-Hall, 1968.

Xiao Zhencai. *Dazhi dayong zhou'enlai zai 1946* (Tremendous Courage and Wisdom—Zhou Enlai in 1946). Beijing: Zhōngyāng wénxiàn chūbǎn shè, 2006. 大智大勇: 周恩来在 1946.

Xixiao Guo. "The Anticlimax of an Ill-starred Sino-American Encounter." *Modern Asian Studies* 35 (2001): 217–244.

Yang Kuisong. *1946 Nian Guo Gong Liang Dang Dou Zheng Yu Ma Xie Er Tiao Chu* (1946 Conflicts of the Two Parties and General Marshall's Mediation). Li Shi Yan Jiu, 1990. Vol. 5. 1946 年国共两党斗争与马歇尔调处

——. "The Soviet Factor and the CCP's Policy Toward the United States in the 1940s." *Chinese Historians* 5 (Spring 1992): 17–34.

Yergin, Daniel. *Shattered Peace: The Origins of the Cold War and the National Security State.* Boston: Houghton Mifflin, 1977.

Yu, Maochun. *OSS in China: Prelude to Cold War.* Annapolis, MD: Naval Institute Press, 1996.

Zhang Baijia. Zhou enlai yu maxie'er shiming (Zhou Enlai and the Marshall Mission). Beijing: Jin dai shi yan jiu, 1997. 周恩来与马歇尔使命

Zubok, Vladislav, and Constantine Pleshov. *Inside the Kremlin's Cold War: From Stalin to Khrushchev.* Cambridge, MA: Harvard University Press, 1996.

INDEX